TACITUS REVIEWED

Tacitus Reviewed

A. J. WOODMAN

CLARENDON PRESS · OXFORD
1998

Oxford University Press, Great Clarendon Street, Oxford OX2 6DP

Oxford New York

Athens Auckland Bangkok Bogotá Buenos Aires Calcutta
Cape Town Chennai Dar es Salaam Delhi Florence Hong Kong Istanbul
Karachi Kuala Lumpur Madrid Melbourne Mexico City Mumbai
Nairobi Paris São Paulo Singapore Taipei Tokyo Toronto Warsaw

and associated companies in
Berlin Ibadan

Oxford is a registered trade mark of Oxford University Press

Published in the United States
by Oxford University Press Inc., New York

British Library Cataloguing in Publication Data
Data available

Library of Congress Cataloging in Publication Data
Woodman, A. J. (Anthony John), 1945–
Tacitus reviewed/A. J. Woodman.
p.   cm.
Includes bibliographical references.
1. Tacitus, Cornelius.   Annales.   2. Rome—History—The five Julii,
30 B.C.–68 A.D.   3. Rome—Historiography.   I. Title.
DG281.W66   1998   937'.07—dc21   98–27415
ISBN 0–19–815258–2 (hb)

1 3 5 7 9 10 8 6 4 2

Typeset by J&L Composition Ltd, Filey, North Yorkshire
Printed in Great Britain on acid-free paper by
Bookcraft (Bath) Ltd, Midsomer Norton

PREFACE

The papers collected in this volume represent twenty-five years' unsystematic writing on Tacitus. Some of them result from my trying to understand the text of the *Annals* in order to be in a position to translate it; the majority result from teaching which I have chosen or been required to undertake. As far as is possible, their arrangement in the volume follows the sequence of the passages which are discussed.

One paper (Ch. 4) is entirely new; another (Ch. 7) has been redrafted and, to avoid some duplication of material, in part extensively rewritten; the remainder have been reprinted more or less unchanged, except that I have corrected any mistakes of which I am conscious, have revised footnotes to achieve some consistency of presentation, and occasionally, as indicated by square brackets, have added new references or other matter. Though the papers vary considerably in tone, density, and age, I venture to hope that collectively they will be thought sufficiently distinctive to justify their appearance in a single volume; and, though there is no single or common theme, in an Epilogue I have tried to draw together some of the threads.

This seems an appropriate place to pay tribute to the three eminent Taciteans whose friendship I have had the privilege of enjoying over the past thirty-five years. As a new postgraduate student I was captivated by the latent humour and unsurpassed Latinity displayed by G. B. A. Fletcher in his *Annotations on Tacitus* (1964). The better I became acquainted with him both in print and in person, the more I revered him as a scholar and cherished him as a friend. Not the least of his virtues was his unexpected receptiveness to new ideas. F. R. D. Goodyear initiated me into the mysteries of classical scholarship and for twelve chastening months supervised my research on Velleius. His commentary on the first two books of the *Annals* is, as has been said, 'the cornerstone of his monument', of which every inspection is a tragic reminder of his premature loss. When I showed him a draft of what became my first publication on Tacitus, his characteristic response was that he did not believe it but that I might find Ronald Martin more sympathetic. So it proved; and, if Ronald has become increasingly sceptical as my hypotheses have become increasingly wild, my unceasing demands upon his kindness and patience testify to the store I set by his learning and judgement, for the benefit of which I am more grateful than I can ever adequately express.

Finally I am most grateful to Oxford University Press for their willingness to publish this book, and to Hilary O'Shea for her support and encouragement.

A.J.W.

University of Durham
September 1997

ACKNOWLEDGEMENTS

For their permission to reprint material I am most grateful to the following (numerals in square brackets refer to chapter numbers):

Francis Cairns (Publications) Ltd.: 'A Death in the First Act: Tacitus, *Annals* 1. 6', *Papers of the Leeds International Latin Seminar*, 8 (1995), 257–74 [3].

Cambridge University Press: 'Self-Imitation and the Substance of History: Tacitus, *Annals* 1. 61–5 and *Histories* 2. 70, 5. 14–15', in David West and Tony Woodman (eds.), *Creative Imitation and Latin Literature* (1979), 143–55, 231–5 [5]; 'Nero's Alien Capital: Tacitus as Paradoxographer (*Annals* 15. 36–7)', in Tony Woodman and Jonathan Powell (eds.), *Author and Audience in Latin Literature* (1992), 173–88, 251–5 [10].

University of Leeds: 'From Hannibal to Hitler: The Literature of War', *University of Leeds Review*, 26 (1983), 107–24 [1].

Museum Helveticum: '*praecipuum munus annalium*: The Construction, Convention and Context of Tacitus, *Annals* 3. 65. 1', *Mus. Helv.* 52 (1995), 111–26 [6].

Oxford University Press: 'Remarks on the Structure and Content of Tacitus, *Annals* 4. 57–67', *CQ* 22 (1972), 150–8 [8]; 'Tacitus' Obituary of Tiberius', *CQ* 39 (1989), 197–205 [9]; 'The Preface to Tacitus' *Annals*: More Sallust?', *CQ* 42 (1992), 567–8 [2].

Princeton University Press: 'Amateur Dramatics at the Court of Nero: *Annals* 15. 48–74', in T. J. Luce and A. J. Woodman (eds.), *Tacitus and the Tacitean Tradition* (1993), 104–28 [11].

Routledge: 'History and Alternative Histories: Tacitus', *Rhetoric in Classical Historiography* (1988), 160–96 [7].

CONTENTS

ABBREVIATIONS

Tacitus' works are generally abbreviated as *A.* (*Annals*), *H.* (*Histories*), *Agr.* (*Agricola*), *G.* (*Germania*), and *D.* (*Dialogus*). When referring to passages of the *Annals*, however, I often omit *A.* altogether if the reference is clear from the context; likewise I omit the book number when repeated reference is made to the same book of the *Annals*.

Periodical abbreviations are generally as in *L'Année philologique*; abbreviated references to other secondary works may be traced via the following list and the Bibliography.

ANRW W. Haase and H. Temporini (eds.), *Aufstieg und Niedergang der römischen Welt* (Berlin and New York, 1972–).

BGU *Berliner griechische Urkunden* (Berlin, 1895–).

CAH² A. K. Bowman, E. Champlin and A. Lintott (eds.), *Cambridge Ancient History*, vol. x (2nd. edn.; Cambridge, 1996).

CE *Carmina Latina Epigraphica*, ed. F. Buecheler and E. Lommatsch, 3 vols. [= *Anthologia Latina* II] (Leipzig, 1895–1926).

CHCL P. E. Easterling and E. J. Kenney (eds.), *Cambridge History of Classical Literature*, 2 vols. (Cambridge, 1982–5).

CIG *Corpus Inscriptionum Graecarum.*

CIL *Corpus Inscriptionum Latinarum.*

EJ V. Ehrenberg and A. H. M. Jones, *Documents Illustrating the Reigns of Augustus and Tiberius* (2nd edn.; repr. Oxford, 1976).

FGrH *Die Fragmente der griechischen Historiker*, ed. F. Jacoby (Berlin and Leiden, 1923–58).

K–S R. Kühner and C. Stegmann, *Ausführliche Grammatik der lateinischen Sprache*, ii. *Satzlehre*, Parts 1 and 2 (4th edn.; repr. Hanover, 1971).

LH C. S. Kraus and A. J. Woodman, *Latin Historians* (*Greece & Rome* New Surveys in the Classics, 27) (Oxford, 1997).

L–H–S	M. Leumann, J. B. Hofmann, and A. Szantyr, *Lateinische Grammatik*, ii. *Syntax und Stilistik* (revised edn., Munich, 1972).
OCD	*Oxford Classical Dictionary.*
OLD	*Oxford Latin Dictionary.*
RAC	*Reallexikon für Antike und Christentum.*
RE	*Paulys Real-Encyclopädie der classischen Altertumswissenschaft.*
RICH	A. J. Woodman, *Rhetoric in Classical Historiography* (London, Sydney, and Portland, Or., 1988).
SCPP	*Senatus Consultum de Cn. Pisone Patre.*
SEG	*Supplementum Epigraphicum Graecum* (Leiden, 1923–).
TLL	*Thesaurus Linguae Latinae.*

I

Introduction: The Literature of War

To the memory of Lord Boyle

It was on the last Monday in January exactly fifty years ago that Adolf Hitler became Chancellor of Germany. The event has been described by Alan Bullock in his celebrated book:[1]

During the morning a silent crowd filled the street between the Kaiserhof and the Chancellery. . . . At a window of the Kaiserhof, Röhm was keeping an anxious watch on the door from which Hitler must emerge. Shortly after noon a roar went up from the crowd: the Leader was coming. He ran down the steps to his car and in a couple of minutes was back in the Kaiserhof. As he entered the room his lieutenants crowded to greet him. The improbable had happened: Adolf Hitler, the petty official's son from Austria, the down-and-out of the Home for Men, the despatch-runner of the List regiment, had become Chancellor of the German Reich.

This account is not without its drama. There is a brief reference to the waiting crowd and its reaction to Hitler's appearance; and there is a poignant contrast, which Bullock underlines by the word 'improbable', drawn between Hitler's sudden eminence and three of the insignificant positions he had occupied earlier in his life. But these are the only emotional flashes which Bullock has permitted to obtrude into his account of that momentous day. The keynotes are stylistic reserve and brevity. The whole account amounts to only one paragraph of ten lines in the Pelican edition.

The events of that same day have also been described by William Shirer in his equally celebrated book on the Third Reich:[2]

This is the text (slightly changed in places) of an inaugural lecture originally entitled 'From Hannibal to Hitler: The Literature of War' and delivered at the University of Leeds on Monday 31 January 1983.
    [1] *Hitler: A Study in Tyranny* (1975 edn.), 250.
    [2] *The Rise and Fall of the Third Reich* (1964 edn.), 16–17.

Shortly before noon on Monday, January 30, 1933, Hitler drove over to the Chancellery for an interview with Hindenburg that was to prove fateful *for himself, for Germany, and for the rest of the world*. From a window in the Kaiserhof, Goebbels, Roehm and other Nazi chiefs kept an anxious watch on the door of the Chancellery, where the Fuehrer would shortly be coming out. 'We would see from his face whether he had succeeded or not', Goebbels noted. For even then they were not quite sure. 'Our hearts are torn back and forth between doubt, hope, joy and discouragement', Goebbels jotted down in his diary. 'We have been disappointed too often for us to believe wholeheartedly in the great miracle.' ||

A few moments later they witnessed the miracle. The man with the Charlie Chaplin moustache, who had been a down-and-out tramp in Vienna in his youth, an unknown soldier of World War I, a derelict in Munich in the first grim postwar days, the somewhat comical leader of the Beer Hall Putsch, this spell-binder who was not even German but Austrian, and who was only forty-three years old, had just been administered the oath as Chancellor of the German Reich.

He drove the hundred yards to the Kaiserhof and was soon with his old cronies, Goebbels, Goering, Roehm and the other Brownshirts who had helped him along the rocky, brawling path to power. 'He says nothing, and all of us say nothing', Goebbels recorded, 'but his eyes are full of tears.'

That evening from dusk until far past midnight the delirious Nazi stormtroopers marched in a massive torchlight parade to celebrate the victory. By the tens of thousands, they emerged in disciplined columns from the depths of the Tiergarten, passed under the triumphal arch of the Brandenburg Gate and down the Wilhelmstrasse, their bands blaring the old martial airs to the thunderous beating of the drums, their voices bawling the new Horst Wessel song and other tunes that were as old as Germany, their jackboots beating a mighty rhythm on the pavement, their torches held high and forming a ribbon of flame that illuminated the night and kindled the hurrahs of the onlookers massed on the sidewalks. From a window in the palace Hindenburg looked down upon the marching throng, beating time to the military marches with his cane, apparently pleased that at last he had picked a Chancellor who could arouse the people in a traditionally German way. Whether || the old man, in his dotage, had any inkling of what he had unleashed that day is doubtful. . . .

A stone's throw down the Wilhelmstrasse Adolf Hitler stood at an open window of the Chancellery, beside himself with excitement and joy, *dancing up and down, jerking his arm up continually in the Nazi salute, smiling and laughing until his eyes were again full of tears.*

Shirer's account, which takes up a full page in the paperback edition, is completely given over to the dramatic nature of the event. Like Bullock, he mentions the crowd; but he adds to it a description of the Nazi stormtroopers which itself takes up one full paragraph and which is packed with details of their movements and activities. Again like Bullock, Shirer draws a contrast (which he calls a 'miracle', as opposed to Bullock's more judicious 'improbable') between Hitler's present position and his former life. But again his description of this one item takes up a whole paragraph, he lists four of Hitler's lowly roles as opposed to the three mentioned by Bullock, and he adds in three further contrasts (dealing with Hitler's age and appearance) for good measure.

So much for where Shirer covers the same ground as Bullock. But Shirer adds three quite new ingredients as well. First, he comments on the fateful nature of that day and in a three-part climax (italicized) looks forward briefly to the terrible consequences that were to stem from it. Second, he describes the reaction of Hitler's immediate entourage and quotes from Goebbels' own account of the event. And finally, in yet another three-part climax (also italicized), he focuses upon the mood of Hitler himself, dancing about at the open window and giving Nazi salutes. Shirer's recipe, so much more elaborate than the basic Bullock, produces a narrative which satisfies the reader's need for the authentic and the dramatic, and whets his appetite for more of the same in other episodes.

Now which of these two accounts would have appealed most to the reader in ancient Rome? Cicero has left us a record of what he expected from history, and it goes like this. 'The narrative should be built up in both subject-matter and style. . . . A mere chronicle of events holds very little interest for us, no more than the entries in the official almanac. But the uncertain and varied fortunes of a man who rises to prominence provoke admiration, suspense, joy, sorrow, hope, or fear; and if they end in a striking dénouement, the mind enjoys one of the greatest pleasures that reading can give. . . . For nothing is more calculated to please the reader than the changes and chances of fortune.'[3] Cicero, it is clear, is looking for an expanded and dramatic narrative; and it is Shirer who provides this, rather than Bullock.

[3] Cic. *De Or.* 2. 63, *Fam.* 5. 12. 5 and 4.

At this point it is interesting to reflect why Shirer's account is so different from that of Bullock. Bullock is a professional historian, concerned with || analysis and interpretation. This is clear as early as his title-page, where we read: *Hitler: A Study in Tyranny.* There can be few less dramatic words in English than the word 'study'; and the success which Bullock's book has enjoyed is perhaps due to the fact that its distinguished author has risen above the limitations of his professional genre. For it has been argued that many modern historians are losing touch with the art of communication. Peter Gay, himself a well-known academic historian, discusses the whole problem in his book *Style in History,* and what he says is this:[4]

Much historical work is innocent of even a nodding acquaintance with the writer's art. We have all encountered those dreary, dutiful chronicles piling up mounds of facts that everyone knows or nobody wants to know; those narrow, earnest monographs choking in their garlands of ibids and parched in their deserts of charts. We have wondered at those mountainous and learned theses that do strive for distinction but founder in literary incoherence, with their style borrowed from the ungainly informativeness of the railway timetable. Whatever else it may be, history is not an art all of the time.

As a general rule, a modern historian has only a very limited readership. Provided he can persuade someone to publish his work, he is thereafter concerned only with the relatively few other professionals who will be competent to understand the issues he discusses. (The same is of course even more true of classicists. . . .)

By contrast, Shirer is a professional news reporter, and reporters have to satisfy a vast, non-specialist audience whose demands are twofold. On the one hand readers of newspapers demand consistent subject-matter and content; on the other, they demand that newspapers justify their name by presenting their repetitious material in new or different ways. The reader's appetite for news is particularly obvious during wartime, something with which the ancient Romans were obsessed: 'the vicissitudes of battles', writes Tacitus, 'take over and stimulate the readers' imagination'.[5] So too during the American Civil War a New York newspaper sold five times its normal circulation when it ran details of a big battle;[6]

[4] *Style in History* (1975), 186–7.   [5] Tac. *A.* 4. 33. 3.   [6] Knightley (1975), 23.

and during the First World War one of Lord Northcliffe's editors
wrote that 'war not only creates a supply of news, but a demand
for it. So deeprooted is the fascination in war and all things
pertaining to it . . . that a paper has only to be able to put up
on its placard, A GREAT BATTLE for sales to mount up.'[7] It is appropriate to reflect that the fascination of war is still very much with
us, as the opinion polls indicated during the Falklands campaign.
Hardly a season goes by without there being at least one war-
serial on television; and feature-length war films are still being
produced. *A Bridge Too Far,* which cost twice as much as the
actual operation it depicts,[8] is only one of the more recent
examples. Reviewing that film in *The Times*, a critic wrote
that 'audiences flock to war films to exult in scenes of battle,
to || identify with acts of courage, and vicariously share in
military glory'.[9] This is the kind of demand which Shirer, as
an American reporter in Europe before and during the last war,
was obliged to satisfy almost daily. And it is clear from the
extract I quoted that his instincts as a reporter did not desert
him when he came to write his book on Hitler's Germany. As
with Bullock, this is clear as early as Shirer's title-page. When
we read the words *The Rise and Fall of the Third Reich* we infer
that the book will be concerned with the violent fluctuations of
fortune which are beloved by the drama-hungry readers of
newspapers and which were equally beloved, as we have seen,
by Cicero and Tacitus.

   It is, however, interesting to observe that Shirer's book has not
found favour with professional historians. Reviewing the book
some years after its publication, an American historian wrote as
follows:

William Shirer's history of the Third Reich is woefully inadequate. . . .
The inadequacies . . . could be dismissed out of hand if his book had not
found an enormous audience. . . . The book is a literary tour de force.
Much that is trivial has been elaborated because it is entertaining; much
that is important has been omitted because it might be dull. . . . [The
reading] is neither painful nor dull. . . . The lesson steadily mounts in
interest to become increasingly exciting. The narrative, poor though it

---

[7] Knightley (1975), 85.
[8] According to *The Sunday Times*, 23 October 1977, p. 12.
[9] Philip French, *The Times*, 24 June 1977, p. 9.

may be as history, has a sustained dramatic tension. Each episode moves to a climax, and the successive episodes achieve a grand climax—the Wehrmacht's defeat and Hitler's suicide.[10]

In this review we see neatly encapsulated the antithesis which has grown up between literature-and-entertainment on the one hand, and 'real' history on the other.

This antithesis can be illustrated again and again in books which deal with history or historiography. The well-known American reporter Theodore H. White begins his autobiography *In Search of History* by contrasting good reporters, who organize facts in 'stories', with good historians, who organize lives and episodes in 'arguments'.[11] But the contrast need not be between history and a literary genre. Discussing the relationship between history and film, Donald Watt, professor of international history at the London School of Economics, alludes to the two common propositions that 'the historian's main concern is accuracy; the producer of film and television is concerned with entertainment. The unspoken premise of the first proposition is that to be accurate is to be dull. The unspoken premise of the opposed proposition is that to be entertaining it is necessary to distort or misrepresent.'[12] Yet entertaining the reader was precisely the aim of the ancient historian, who was writing for a non-professional audience whose only other narrative genre, apart from historical prose, was epic poetry. Ancient historians, in fact, were expected to entertain their readers in exactly the same way as modern reporters, and statements || of this expectation are found in ancient authors from the fourth century BC to the fifth century AD, including such distinguished authors as Cicero and Tacitus. For example, the Hellenistic historian Duris in a famous fragment criticized two of his predecessors on the grounds that they did not provide entertainment in their works. When Cicero describes his own reading of the Greek historians, he says he usually reads them only for entertainment; and in his well-known letter to Lucceius, advising his friend how to write history, Cicero emphasizes its entertainment potential no less than nine times. The architect Vitruvius declared that the essence of history

[10] W. O. Shanahan, *American Historical Review,* 68 (1962–3), 126–7.
[11] *In Search of History* (1979), 2.
[12] D. Watt, 'History on the Public Screen I', in P. Smith (ed.), *The Historian and Film* (1976), 169.

was to retain the reader's interest, and Pliny in his letters said that history provides entertainment no matter how it is written. We have already noticed that this was also the view of Tacitus.[13]

Now anyone who has read Phillip Knightley's brilliant book *The First Casualty* will know that some modern war reporters will stop at nothing, including fabrication, to entertain their readers. One example which Knightley happens not to mention concerns Hermann Goering, who, destined to be hanged on 20 October 1946, cheated the executioner by taking poison the previous day. This event greatly embarrassed certain reporters, who, never dreaming that Goering would commit suicide, had already despatched to their editors vivid accounts of his death by hanging.[14]

To see whether Roman historians, similarly dedicated to entertaining their readers, adopted similarly fallacious techniques, I should like to examine three passages:

The season was winter, and snow was falling in the area which lies between the Alps and the Apennines; there were marshes and rivers in the locality, intensifying the bitter cold. Moreover, men and horses had been turned out too quickly: there was no time to eat or snatch up coverings as protection against the cold. Warmth had drained from their bodies, and as they approached the vicinity of the river, the full force of the cold struck them more keenly.

As the campaigning season approached, Gaul still lay beneath its snow. The snow stretched . . . all across the hills as the army marched east from Cularo, a white blanket across the slopes of the Alps, embroidered by the black and leafless trees; the snow covered the gray ice of the frozen lakes, just beginning to show the seams and cracks of coming thaw. . . . Under the snow it is impossible to tell poor farm from rich farm, for snow forces farmers to shelter livestock and equipment indoors.

There were no tree trunks or roots by which a man could hoist himself up, only smooth ice and thawing snow, over which they were always rolling. . . . Four days were spent at the cliff, and the animals nearly perished of starvation; for the mountain tops are all practically bare, and such grass as does grow is buried beneath the snow. Lower down one comes to valleys, and slopes bathed in sunlight, || and streams, and near to them are woods, and places more suitable for human habitation.

---

[13] Duris fr. 1 Jacoby; Cic. *De Or.* 2. 59, *Fam.* 5. 12. 4–5; Vitr. 5 *praef.* 1; Plin. *Ep.* 5. 8. 4; Tac. *A.* 4. 33. 3.   [14] Airey Neave, *Nuremberg* (1978), 316.

Which of these three passages was written by Livy? Unless you happen to know your Livy almost off by heart, the problem is not easy. Each passage deals with winter travel, each contains specific detail of an eyewitness nature, and each passage has a dramatic or romantic flavour about it. In fact the second of these passages was written by the American reporter Theodore H. White to whom I have already referred. It is taken from his book of Kennedy's presidential campaign in 1960 and I altered some geographical and other items in order to make my point. The original is:[15]

As the primary approached, Wisconsin still lay beneath its snow. The snow stretched . . . all across the hills as the plane flew west from New York, a white blanket across the slopes of the Appalachians, embroidered by the black and leafless trees; the snow covered the gray ice of the frozen lakes, just beginning to show the seams and cracks of coming thaw. . . . Under the snow it is impossible to tell poor farm from rich farm, for snow forces farmers to shelter automobiles and equipment indoors.

Now the radical journalist Paul Foot has written a highly critical review of White's book; and commenting on the passage I have just quoted, Foot says this:[16]

No detail is too irrelevant to include in this exhilarating chronicle; for, however banal, each detail proved that the historian himself was actually *there*. He too moved with the gods, and he could bring any literate American right into the Kennedy compound at Hyannisport or the cabin of the Kennedy campaign plane as it travelled from cheering crowd to cheering crowd, over the white snow, the blue sea, the green valleys, or whatever.

Theodore White is obsessed with descriptive detail: Foot interprets this obsession as White's proof that he actually took part in the events which he relates. No doubt Foot is quite correct; but we must also remember that descriptive detail is the hallmark of the fabricator of history. A classic case is that of Sir Edmund Backhouse, who spent most of his life in China and there forged the sources for the history of China on which he collaborated with an unsuspecting colleague and which for many years was accepted as the standard history of its period. As Trevor-Roper writes in his life of Backhouse, one element in the man's plausi-

[15] *The Making of the President 1960* (1961), 82–3.
[16] *The Politics of Harold Wilson* (1968), 12.

bility was his extraordinary circumstantiality and his minute and scrupulous detail. 'Backhouse's language was never loose or vague. He impressed everyone by his remarkable "memory", which in turn seemed a guarantee of truth.'[17]

Livy is the author of the two other passages: they are taken from his account of Hannibal's march across the Alps in Book 21.[18] Livy's descriptions here are just as detailed as Theodore White's, yet Livy was || writing two full centuries after the event itself had taken place. How did he come by such authentic description? It might have come from his sources, like the Greek historian Polybius, who wrote:[19]

The summits of the Alps, and the parts near the tops of the passes, are all quite treeless and bare, owing to the snow lying there continuously both winter and summer. But the parts half-way up on both sides are wooded and generally inhabitable.

This extract is indeed very similar to the second passage of Livy which I quoted. Polybius in his turn will have got such information from Silenus, who actually did accompany Hannibal across the Alps in 218 BC. It is possible, in other words, to argue that Livy's description is ultimately based on an eyewitness account. But you will have noticed that Polybius mentioned only woods lower down. Livy mentioned woods too, but added valleys, streams, and slopes bathed in sunlight. His Latin for this last phrase is *apricos colles*: *apricus* is a favourite word of the poets, found in romantic and descriptive passages of Virgil and Horace,[20] but only here in the whole of Livy that has survived. I think that in places like this Livy is relying on no source at all but is adding purely fictitious detail which he remembered from his days at school when he would have been taught the basic techniques of how to describe landscapes.

Higher education at Rome was in the hands of professional rhetoricians whose main aim was the entertainment of their audience. 'I say many things', admitted one of them, 'not because they please me but because they please my audience.'[21] And we happen to know that one of the most enjoyable things for an

---

[17] H. Trevor-Roper, *A Hidden Life: The Enigma of Sir Edmund Backhouse* (1976), 277.
[18] Respectively 21. 54. 7–8 and 36. 7, 37. 4–5.   [19] Polyb. 3. 55. 9.
[20] Virg. *Ecl.* 9. 49, *G.* 2. 522, *Aen.* 5. 128, 6. 312; Hor. *S.* 1. 8. 15, *C.* 1. 8. 3, 26. 7, 3. 18. 2, *Epist.* 1. 14. 30, *AP* 162.   [21] Cestius Pius *ap.* Sen. *Contr.* 9. 6. 12.

audience to hear was the description of natural scenery or landscape. There is of course nothing unusual in this. John Buchan
once observed that only two ingredients are essential to the
successful thriller writer: an ability to create likeable characters,
and a feel for landscape by which to satisfy the armchair traveller's
hunger for a sense of place.[22] And so we learn from numerous
Roman authors that rhetoricians were expected to have a stock of
ready-mixed, easy-to-use landscapes which they could insert into
any composition in order to entertain their audience.[23]

Now we have seen that Cicero believed that history should
entertain its readers; but when in the 50s BC he looked back on
the writings of the early Roman historians, he was extremely
disappointed: they had, he complained, paid no attention to the
description of landscape, giving only the barest indications of
natural scenery.[24] Now history is of course a most appropriate
genre in which to include the description of landscape; and
since such descriptions were, as we have seen, extremely popular
with audiences and readers in general, Cicero suggested that
historians should || make far more use of landscape description
than hitherto. 'The nature of historical writing', he said,
'demands chronological sequence and landscape description.'
In fact he even went so far as to define history as the genre
'in which the narrative is elaborate and landscape descriptions
are given'.[25]

It seems clear from the extract I quoted above that Livy took
Cicero at his word. But Roman historians were hardly great
travellers, doing on-the-spot research into the distant places
they described in their works. They were notoriously armchair
writers, whose only course of action, if they took Cicero's advice
(and they did), was to follow the standard but ever-popular
methods of describing landscapes that were already being practised by rhetoricians. This is exactly what Livy has done in the

---

[22] According to R. W. Winks, *The Historian as Detective: Essays on Evidence* (1968), 3.
[23] See Sen. *Contr.* 2 *praef.* 3, 2. 1. 13; Quint. 4. 3. 12; Brink on Hor. *AP* 16–18,
Woodman on Vell. 96. 3. On the transferability of such topoi (conventional motifs) from
one composition to another see e.g. Cic. *Inu.* 2. 48 and Sen. *Contr.* 1 *praef.* 23.
[24] Cic. *De Or.* 2. 53 'sine ullis ornamentis monumenta solum . . . locorum . . .
reliquerunt'.
[25] Respectively *De Or.* 2. 63 'rerum ratio ordinem temporum desiderat, regionum
descriptionem' and *Or.* 66 '(historia) in qua et narratur ornate et regio saepe . . . describitur'.

modest passage which I quoted. Feeling that the information he had inherited from Polybius was a little dull, he filled it out with some descriptive detail. The detail sounds authentic enough, otherwise I would not have been able to compare it with the extract from Theodore White's book; but we have no guarantee at all that the detail is true. On the contrary, its utterly conventional nature and its similarity to descriptive passages elsewhere indicate that it is highly suspect.

Now it may be felt that this conclusion is relatively unimportant. Why should it matter if Livy's description on this occasion was invented rather than true? I think there are two reasons why it matters. First, there is evidence that the procedure recommended by Cicero and put into practice by Livy gained increasing popularity during the first century AD, reaching its climax when Tacitus began to write. It is, I believe, significant that writers at the end of the first century AD refer to landscape description as a primarily historical device and not the rhetorical device which it had been for Cicero a century and a half earlier.[26] An excellent example is to be found in Curtius Rufus' *History of Alexander the Great*, written in the middle of the first century AD. He is describing Persia:[27]

At the foot of the mountains a spacious plain slopes down, a fertile land, abounding in many villages and cities. Through these fields the River Araxes rolls the waters of many torrents into the Medus . . . a river which is more favourable to the growth of vegetation than any other, and it clothes with flowers whatever it flows near. Plane trees and poplars cover its bank, so that to those who view them from far off, the groves along the banks seem to be a continuation of those on the mountains. For the shaded stream flows in a channel sunk deep in the soil, and over it hang hills which themselves are rich in foliage.

Another most effective and detailed piece of description. But Curtius was surely relying on the ignorance of his readers— much as did the makers of an early newsreel film which purported to show gallant British medical staff at work during the Boer War but which was actually shot on || Hampstead Heath.[28] For the two alleged rivers are one and the same (there seems never

---

[26] Cf. Plin. *Ep.* 2. 5. 5 'descriptiones locorum . . . non historice tantum sed prope poetice prosequi fas est'; Quint. 10. 1. 33 'licet tamen nobis in digressionibus uti uel historico nonnumquam nitore'.   [27] Curt. 5. 4. 6–8.   [28] See Knightley (1975), 75.

to have been a river Medus) and the mountains in the area are barren and, to judge from present-day evidence, never supported extensive vegetation at all.[29] Curtius' description is simply a collection of various landscape motifs which he knew would paint a pretty picture for the pleasure of his readers. Cicero and Livy between them encouraged a fashion from which no later historian was immune.[30]

There is a second reason why I think that the procedure adopted by Livy matters. If Livy could resort to invention on the occasion we have been discussing, there is nothing to stop him doing exactly the same thing on other, much more important, occasions. Livy is our main source for many of the great battles of Roman history: have we any guarantee at all that his descriptions of the scenes and sites of these battles are correct? How would we feel if a modern historian, having given a vivid account of the Battle of the Ardennes, later admitted that he knew little about the area except that it was covered with forest? In fact, if the procedure of the Roman historians is as I have described, it is perhaps creative writers, not historians, that rather come to mind. When setting out as a young man for America, W. H. Davies wrote a full description of the country before his ship left Liverpool dock; and what he had done was discovered only because he posted his account from the ship's first port of call in Ireland, in a letter bearing a British stamp. Similarly Anthony Burgess advised that 'it's best to imagine your own foreign country. I wrote a very good account of Paris before I ever went there. Better than the real thing.'[31] But whereas such practices cause no concern in the cases of Davies and Burgess, we would be scandalized if they were adopted by modern historians and we should be equally alarmed when we find that they are adopted on a large scale by their ancient counterparts.

Of course many people do not think much of Livy as a historian; and Curtius Rufus is generally acknowledged to be a

---

[29] For the Araxes and the non-existent Medus see *RE* ii. 404 s.v. Araxes 4; the *Medum flumen* at Hor. *C.* 2. 9. 21 is the Euphrates (see Nisbet–Hubbard ad loc.), which flows away from the Araxes at right angles. The lack of vegetation in the area is observed by J. C. Rolfe in his edition (Loeb, 1946) ad loc. (I acknowledge the help of Prof. O. A. W. Dilke with some of the points in this note.) [A more positive view of Curtius' passage, however, is now taken by J. E. Atkinson in his recent commentary (1994) ad loc.]

[30] See also Sall. *J.* 17–19, *H.* 3. 61–80; R. Syme, *Sallust* (1964), 194–5; Thomas (1982), 2–5.   [31] For these two examples see P. Fussell, *Abroad* (1980), 174–5.

second-rate writer of whom nothing better could be expected.
Tacitus, the greatest of the Roman historians, is the yardstick
against which to judge. So let us turn to the third book of Tacitus'
Histories, where he describes an incident which allegedly took
place in the civil wars of AD 68–9:[32]

> I find that some widely read historians vouch for the truth of the
> following story. The victors displayed such disregard for right and
> wrong that a trooper, claiming to have killed his brother in the recent
> battle, demanded a reward from his leaders. Common morality
> deterred them from honouring the murder, and the very nature of
> civil war from punishing it. In the end, it seems, they decided to put
> the man off by saying that the reward he deserved was too great to be
> paid on the spot. There is no further information. However, according
> to Sisenna, an equally ghastly act had occurred in a previous civil war,
> for in the battle against || Cinna on the Janiculum, a soldier of
> Pompeius Strabo killed his brother, and then, when he realised what
> he had done, committed suicide. Thus in earlier generations merit
> evoked keener appreciation, and wicked actions keener remorse. Any-
> how, it will not be inappropriate for me to cite these and similar
> anecdotes from ancient history when the context calls for lessons in
> right conduct or consolation for evil.

The extract is typically Tacitean. It deals with a subject, namely
fratricide, which was nearly as popular as landscape with Roman
audiences,[33] and you can almost hear Tacitus' disappointment
when he says that he has no further information about it. But
this admission turns out to be a device whereby he can introduce
a corresponding example from a previous civil war in order to
contrast earlier nobility with present decadence. Now the example from the previous civil war is attested not only by Sisenna, as
Tacitus says, but also by Livy;[34] but what of the incident which
Tacitus himself describes? Though he claims rather defensively to
rely on 'some widely read historians', did the incident ever take
place? There are two reasons why I am sceptical.

Several chapters earlier in the same book of the *Histories*,
Tacitus had described another incident with remarkable similarities to the present one:[35]

---

[32] Tac. *H.* 3. 51 (trans. K. Wellesley, slightly changed).

[33] See Winterbottom (1974), index III s.v. 'parricide' (there loosely defined as 'killing of
father or other near relative').   [34] Liv. *per.* 79.

[35] Tac. *H.* 3. 25. 2–3 (trans. K. Wellesley, slightly changed).

The slaughter was even more noteworthy because of an instance of parricide. I record the incident and the names on the authority of Vipstanus Messalla. A recruit to the Hurricane Legion, one Julius Mansuetus from Spain, had left a young lad at home. Soon after, the boy came of age, and having been called up by Galba for service in the Seventh, chanced to encounter his father in this battle and wounded him seriously. As he was searching the prostrate and semiconscious figure, father and son recognised each other. Embracing the dying man, the son prayed in words choked by tears that his father's spirit would be appeased and not bear him ill-will as a parricide: the act was not a personal one; and what was one soldier but an infinitesimal fraction of the forces engaged in the civil war? With these words, he took up the body, dug a grave, and discharged the last duty to his father. Some nearby troops noticed this, then more and more; and so throughout the lines ran a current of wonder and complaint, and men cursed this cruellest of all wars. Yet this did not stop them killing and robbing relatives, kinsmen and brothers; they told each other that a crime had been done, and in the same breath did it themselves.

Parricide was another subject which the Romans enjoyed,[36] and Tacitus' enthusiasm for this incident is clear both from his opening words that the slaughter was 'even more noteworthy' because of it, and also from the number of emotional words he uses in the course of the passage (e.g. *oblatum forte, semianimem ~ exsanguem,* agn*itus* agn*oscensque, uoce flebili, miraculum, questus, saeuissimi belli execratio*). Now the details of this episode are solemnly repeated as true by the author of a recent book on this period,[37] but as long ago as 1918 the French scholar Courbaud || realized that something was amiss: 'Tacitus, who hardly ever cites any source, has taken care (wisely, in the circumstances) to name the authority on whom he is based. But did things take place exactly as he describes? Did the son bury his father there and then in the middle of the battle? Are his complaints not stereotyped . . . ? We recognize the technique: Tacitus has worked up the details with which he was furnished, and developed them so that they appeal more to our sense of drama and pathos.'[38]

Courbaud is on the right lines, and the very fact that this incident so closely resembles the previous one suggests to me that one or other of them is unlikely to be genuine. But my

---

[36] See n. 34.   [37] K. Wellesley, *The Long Year* A.D. 69 (1975), 148.
[38] E. Courbaud, *Les Procédés d'art de Tacite dans les 'Histoires'* (1918), 153–4.

second piece of evidence will, I think, cast doubt on the genuineness of *both* of the episodes which Tacitus describes. Among the
small collection of poems which are attributed to the younger
Seneca, but which are in fact anonymous and of unknown date,
there are two pieces of verse which purport to describe an
incident in the famous civil war between Octavian and Mark
Antony which took place after the civil war which Sisenna and
Livy described but before that which Tacitus describes in the
Histories. The first of these poems begins as follows:[39]

A soldier from Octavian's side called Maevius dared to jump on an
enemy boat and overturn it; but his happiness depended upon a personal
loss: he was fated to be a sacrilegious victor since he was unwittingly
exultant over the murder of his brother. While he was tearing away his
enemy's armour in the hunt for battle trophies, he recognised his
brother's sad face. His noble act had been a crime.

After almost a dozen lines of platitudinous soliloquy, in the course
of which Maevius decides to commit suicide, the poem concludes
as follows:

He was still uncertain whose sword to use for the deed. 'Shall I die by
my own sword, stained as it is by an unspeakable murder? The person for
whom I am dying will supply the sword for my death.' With these words
he took up his brother's sword and fell on top of his brother, one and the
same hand putting an end to both victor and victim.

The second poem is shorter and less complicated, but otherwise
very similar. It begins thus:[40]

Maevius was delighted to think he had killed one of the enemy, but his
happiness turned to sadness since it was his brother he had killed. He
could not escape finding out: while he savagely stripped the body of his
victim, he came upon trophies that belonged to his own family. Simultaneously he recognized his brother and his crime.

This poem too concludes with a soliloquy in which Maevius
decides to redeem himself by committing suicide. ||
  Both these poems are desperately impoverished, as my translations make only too clear, but they nevertheless provide valuable
evidence that what we are dealing with is a stock motif. Fratricide,

---

[39] [Sen.] *Epig.* 69 Prato, lines 13–36. For help with the interpretation of this and the
following epigram I am much indebted to Prof. R. H. Martin and to my wife Dorothy.
  [40] [Sen.] *Epig.* 70 Prato, lines 3–18.

as I have said, was a conventional and popular theme; and Maevius is a stock name.[41] What the authors of these poems have done is take the incident. in the first civil war, to which Tacitus referred at the end of the first extract I quoted, and applied it to the civil war between Octavian and Mark Antony. And in my opinion Tacitus himself has adopted a very similar procedure, except that, being an infinitely superior writer, he has accomplished his task more effectively. In the second passage of his which I quoted, he has in effect told the Maevius story and applied it to the civil wars of AD 68–9; he has used an almost identical recognition scene, but changed the crime from fratricide to parricide and substituted a noble burial for the more melodramatic suicide. In the first passage of his which I quoted, Tacitus has rung further changes: he has retained the crime of fratricide but made the murderer claim credit for his deed, and to emphasize still further the twist he has introduced, he then retells the original story of fratricide and suicide on which, in my opinion, all the other versions are based.

You may of course object that history does tend to repeat itself, often in the most curious details. From Robert Graves's *Goodbye to All That* we learn that in 1914 a place called Festubert became a nightmare when the inmates of the local lunatic asylum, caught in cross-fire between the German and British lines, broke out from their enclosure and ran all over the countryside.[42] And during Operation Market Garden thirty years later, as we learn from Cornelius Ryan, German ammunition caches exploded in woods near a place called Wolfheze, and a mental institute received direct hits—whereupon sixty terrified inmates, mostly women, started to wander about the woods.[43] A more bizarre example, reputedly

[41] Or so I inferred, perhaps over-optimistically, from Hor. *Epod.* 10; yet Fraenkel (1957), 26 n. 3, notes that Mevius, used as a symbolic name (like Titius, etc.), occurs frequently in legal texts. [And see now Mankin on Hor. *Epod.* 10. 2.] Prof. W. Liebeschuetz has pointed out to me that the parricide-motif recurs in Sil. 9. 66–177, a passage discussed by K.-H. Niemann, *Die Darstellung der röm. Niederlagen in den Punica des Silius Italicus* (1975), 174–7 (a reference I owe to Dr W. R. Barnes). Niemann observes that an earlier scholar (R. Rebischke, *De Silii Italici Orationibus* (1913), 103–4) had suggested that 'unwitting parricide in civil war' was perhaps a suasorial theme in the rhetorical schools. [See also Spaltenstein on Sil. 9. 66.]   [42] *Goodbye to All That* (1966 edn.), 146.

[43] *A Bridge Too Far* (1977 edn.), 185. Another very similar incident had taken place in northern France slightly earlier (see J. Keegan, *Six Armies in Normandy* (1982), 185), and, amazingly, Dr G. A. Loud has pointed out yet another example from near Lille in 1940 (see A. Bryant, *The Turn of the Tide 1939–1943* (1957), 127).

the greatest series of coincidences in history, is associated with the Menai Straits. On three occasions (in 1664, 1785, and 1860) a ship has sunk there with all passengers except one. On each occasion the date of the disaster was 5 December, and on each occasion the name of the sole survivor was Hugh Williams.[44] Certainly in the first of these examples, and perhaps in the second, no one would wish to deny the genuineness of the incidents on the grounds that something very similar was recorded elsewhere. But of course the repetition of motif from one author to another is commonly used nowadays to deny the authenticity of incidents described in ancient poetry. Horace, we are told, cannot really have thrown away his shield at the battle of Philippi, as he alleges, because several of the Greek lyric poets had already told similar stories of themselves.[45] This argument has recently been subjected to sarcastic criticism by an American scholar, who points out that in their respective || autobiographies Mortimer Wheeler, A. J. Ayer, and E. R. Dodds each describe an encounter with a prostitute (a different one in each case, of course!) whose charms each of them rejected.[46] Are we to accuse these distinguished scholars of plagiarism and fabrication? Presumably not. But that is merely to underline the difference between ancient and modern. The kind of operation which I have been conducting on isolated passages of Livy and Tacitus can be repeated time and again on the texts of these and other ancient historians. Recently I was able to demonstrate that one of the most celebrated episodes in the whole of Tacitus' *Annals* is largely fabrication by the historian,[47] a conclusion which the latest commentator on the *Annals* has accepted, rightly adding that it has troublesome implications.[48]

There are two obvious conclusions which can, I think, be drawn from my argument. The first is simply that ancient and modern historiography are two quite different things. Because we use the same word 'history' to describe what is now written by

---

[44] See D. Wallenchinsky and I. and A. Wallace, *The Book of Lists* (1977 edn.), 463. On the idea of history repeating itself see G. W. Trompf, *The Idea of Historical Recurrence in Western Thought* (1979).

[45] Hor. *C.* 2. 7, with Nisbet–Hubbard ad loc. for the evidence from Greek lyric. Add B. Seidensticker, 'Archilochus and Odysseus', *GRBS* 19 (1978), 5–22.

[46] W. M. Calder III, 'The Spurned Doxy: An Unnoticed Topos in English Academic Autobiography', *CW* 73 (1980), 305–7.

[47] *A.* 1. 61–5 is 'borrowed' from *H.* 2. 70 and 5. 14–15: see Woodman (1979) [= Ch. 5 below].   [48] See Goodyear (1981), 108.

A. J. P. Taylor and what was once written by Tacitus, for example, we tend to imagine a continuous tradition of historiography in which the difference between these two authors is merely one of chronology. We tend, in other words, to approach both authors, ancient and modern, with the same assumptions. Yet nothing could be more dangerous. What we ought to be doing is approaching ancient historians as the writers of literature which they are. They should be compared with Latin poets, as I have suggested in the case of Tacitus, or with modern reporters or creative writers, as I have suggested in the cases of Livy and Curtius respectively. Now if the ancient historians were indeed writers of the kind I have described, it follows that their works cannot simply be used as historical evidence by modern historians in the traditional way. Although epigraphy, archaeology, and numismatics naturally contribute to our knowledge of ancient history, it is upon the texts of the ancient historians themselves that most of our information about the detailed events of the ancient world traditionally depends. But if I am right to suggest that these texts are different in kind from what they are generally assumed to be, then the study of ancient history itself requires modification. Our primary response to the texts of the ancient historians should be literary rather than historical since the nature of the texts themselves is literary. Only when literary analysis has been carried out can we begin to use these texts as evidence for history; and by that time, as I hope I have indicated, such analysis will have revealed that there is precious little historical evidence left. The implications of this are indeed troublesome.

The second conclusion to be drawn from my argument follows on from the first, and it is this. One cannot conduct the kind of scholarly activity || which I am describing without an appropriate knowledge of Greek and Latin. To think that one can carry out literary analysis on the basis of a Penguin translation and achieve the potentially significant results which I have mentioned is simply to live in a fool's paradise. Now it is no secret that in the early 1970s the number of candidates for A-level Latin suddenly and sharply declined, with the result that there have been many fewer students applying to university to study Latin. This situation has not, however, been caused by any unpopularity of Latin at school level, nor is it due to some endemic deficiency in the language and literature of Rome which it has taken 2,000 years to detect. Latin has been the victim of circumstances. The early 1970s saw the realization of an educational system which, as I understand it, was intended among other things to provide more pupils with a wider choice of subject than previously. As far as Latin and some other subjects are concerned, the theory has gone badly wrong. Either because it was regarded as an 'élitist' subject and so out of step with the allegedly egalitarian atmosphere of the times, or simply because the timetable difficulties of the new schools excluded minority subjects from the curriculum, Latin has been almost squeezed out. Schoolchildren are being deprived of the opportunity of knowing the language and literature of a civilization which has greatly influenced Western European society. [. . .]

'War is the father of all things', said the Greek philosopher Heraclitus,[49] and war is the subject to which most historians in the ancient world devoted their attention. In this lecture I have suggested that these writers are different in kind from their modern counterparts and are more appropriately compared with writers in other genres, both ancient and modern. By way of a final illustration of my thesis, I should like to leave || you with the following quotation. It is the opening paragraph to a longer piece:

This is an episode rich in disasters. . . . Four successive rulers have died violent deaths . . . and the country fallen victim to catastrophes which are either without precedent or have not occurred for centuries: whole towns burned down . . . and the capital severely damaged by fires which destroyed its most venerable buildings. . . . There has been adultery in high places. The whole Mediterranean swarmed with refugees, and the cliffs of its rocky islands ran with blood. . . . But the episode is not without its compensating features. . . . People's relatives stood resolute and loyal even under torture . . . and prominent men driven to suicide faced their last agony with unflinching courage.

Violence, bloodshed, death, torture, acts of individual heroism, and sex. These are the traditional elements of sensational war literature, and the paragraph might very well have introduced almost any Middle Eastern *coup d'état* as reported in a Sunday tabloid during the past decade or more. In fact, however, the

---

[49] Heraclitus 53 DK = 29 Markovich.

paragraph was written early in the second century AD by the most respected and allegedly most sober of all the Roman historians: Tacitus. It is the opening paragraph of the work we know as the *Histories*,[50] and it was written to whet the appetite of his readers. It seems to have had the desired effect, since Pliny on reading it wrote to his friend Tacitus predicting that the *Histories* would be immortal.[51] The prediction, as we have seen this evening, has turned out to be true—which is perhaps more than can be said for the *Histories* themselves.

[50] Tac. *H.* I. 2. I–3. I.

[51] Plin. *Ep.* 7. 33. I, presumably referring to the first parts of the *Histories* 'to be 'published'.

The Preface to the *Annals*: More Sallust?

Commentators on the *Annals* naturally observe that the famous first sentence of Tacitus' preface ('Urbem Romam a principio reges habuere') alludes to the preface of Sallust's *Bellum Catilinae* (6. 1 'Urbem Romam, sicuti ego accepi, condidere atque habuere initio Troiani'). But it seems that none of them has observed a further allusion to Sallust's preface in the *last* sentence of Tacitus', which is almost equally famous (1. 1. 3):

inde consilium mihi pauca de Augusto et extrema tradere, mox Tiberii principatum et cetera, sine ira et studio, quorum causas procul habeo.

The expression *procul habere* appears to occur ten times in authors earlier than Tacitus: Sall. *C.* 4. 1; Liv. 2. 52. 4, 4. 21. 8, 58. 12, 24. 45. 8, 37. 28. 1, 41. 5. 12; Ov. *Ex P.* 3. 2. 44; Plin. *NH* 5. 51; Curt. 4. 2. 15. In all but one of these cases the expression is used literally of geographical location (thus Liv. 37. 28. 1, 'haud procul inde Antiocho statiua habente'); the exception is Sallust, who uses it metaphorically of location in the course of the following long sentence (*C.* 4. 1–2):

ubi animus ex multis miseriis atque periculis requieuit et mihi relicuam aetatem a re publica *procul habendam* decreui, non fuit *consilium* socordia atque desidia bonum otium conterere, neque uero agrum colundo aut uenando, seruilibus officiis intentum aetatem agere; sed, a quo incepto studioque me ambitio mala detinuerat, eodem regressus statui res gestas populi Romani carptim, ut quaeque memoria digna uidebantur, perscribere, eo magis quod mihi a spe, metu, partibus rei publicae animus liber erat.

It will be seen that Sallust, after offering a disingenuous account of his ignominious retirement from politics ('ubi animus . . . decreui'), provides various justifications for his writing history:

I am grateful to Alyson Wright for a Pandora search and to Ronald Martin for improving an earlier draft.

the first of them is negative ('non fuit consilium . . . agere'); the last of them, appended to the rest of the sentence ('eo magis quod . . . animus liber erat'), || professes impartiality by returning to the theme of the beginning of the sentence, in which the expression *procul habere* occurred.

Since Tacitus' political career had been anything but ignominious, as readers are told in the preface to his *Histories* (1. 1. 3), his first justification for writing history pointedly uses the same word *consilium* in a quite different context ('inde consilium . . .'). And his last justification, also appended to his sentence ('sine ira et studio . . .'), similarly uses *procul habere* metaphorically to profess his own impartiality. Given Tacitus' general Sallustianism, the proximity of the two passages seems too close to be mere coincidence. Moreover, if the allusion is accepted, it can be argued that *causas procul habeo* is not equivalent to *nullas causas habeo*, as Goodyear and others have suggested (ad loc.), but means 'I keep at a distance', as does its counterpart in Sallust. We know from 4. 33. 4 that the incidents of Tiberius' principate could still be live issues amongst Tacitus' contemporaries.

3

A Death in the First Act
(*Annals* 1. 6)

For Ronald Martin at 80

I

Tacitus begins his *Annals* with a brief preface, the last sentence of which sets out his programme for the rest of the work (1. 1. 3):

inde consilium mihi pauca de Augusto et extrema tradere, mox Tiberii principatum et cetera, sine ira et studio, quorum causas procul habeo.

The words *pauca de Augusto* refer to the first section of narrative from 1. 2. 1 ('Postquam Bruto . . .') to 1. 4. 1 ('. . . dum Augustus' *aetate ualidus* seque et domum et pacem sustentauit'); *extrema* (sc. *de Augusto*) refers to the second section from 1. 4. 2 ('Postquam *prouecta iam senectus* aegro et corpore fatigabatur *aderatque finis* . . .') to 1. 5. 4 ('simul *excessisse Augustum* et rerum potiri Neronem fama eadem tulit'); *Tiberii principatum* refers to the Tiberian narrative as a whole, which thus begins at 1. 6. 1 ('Primum facinus *noui principatus* fuit . . .') and ends with Tiberius' obituary at 6. 51. 3; *cetera* refers to the remainder of the work, i.e. Book 7 (which is no longer extant) to the end (which is also no longer extant). Although some scholars still seem not to have realized that Tacitus first announces such a programme in his preface and then proceeds to carry it out in his main narrative,[1] the articulation seems perfectly clear; and

Ronald Martin will, I trust, relish the appositeness of my dedicating to him this particular paper, of which he has read and commented on more drafts than he will care to remember. References, unless otherwise stated, will be to Tacitus' *Annals*.

[1] Thus Goodyear has no relevant note on 1. 1. 3 and, like many other scholars, misleadingly treats 1. 5–6 as a unit (1972: 125). Sage (1990), 970, says 'It is best to take the first three chapters as a preface': that would mean that the main narrative begins at 1. 4. 1 ('Igitur uerso ciuitatis statu . . .'), which seems unlikely. The correct scheme may be found in Leeman (1973), 188–9. See also below, n. 46.

from it one can see at a glance that Tacitus begins his Tiberian narrative with the death of Agrippa Postumus.

Now the death of Agrippa Postumus has been the subject of numerous discussions over the past seventy years or more, most of them directed at such questions as 'Who ordered the killing of Agrippa Postumus?'[2] I shall not be concerned at all with 'what really happened'. My more restricted aim is to discuss Tacitus' narrative of the man's death, which several scholars betray evidence of not having understood. ||

II

I shall begin with a text and translation of Tacitus' narrative (1. 6):[3]

Primum facinus noui principatus fuit Postumi Agrippae caedes, [a] 1 quem ignarum inermumque quamuis firmatus animo *centurio* aegre con*fecit*. [e] nihil de ea re Tiberius **apud senatum** disseruit: [f] **patris** iussa simulabat, quibus praescripsisset tribuno custodiae adposito ne cunctaretur Agrippam morte adficere quandoque ipse supremum diem expleuisset. multa sine dubio saeuaque Augustus de moribus 2 adulescentis questus, ut exilium eius senatus consulto sanciretur perfecerat; ceterum in nullius umquam suorum necem durauit, neque mortem nepoti pro securitate priuigni inlatam credibile erat: propius uero Tiberium ac Liuiam, illum metu, hanc nouercalibus odiis, suspecti et inuisi iuuenis caedem festinauisse. [b] nuntianti *centurioni* (ut mos militiae) 3 *factum* esse quod IMPERASSET, neque IMPERASSE sese et RATIONEM facti REDDENDAM **apud senatum** respondit. [c] quod postquam Sallustius Crispus particeps secretorum (is ad tribunum miserat codicillos) comperit, metuens ne reus subderetur, iuxta periculoso ficta seu uera promeret, [d] monuit Liuiam ne arcana domus, ne consilia amicorum, ministeria militum uulgarentur, neue Tiberius uim principatus resolueret cuncta **ad senatum** uocando: eam condicionem esse IMPERANDI ut non aliter RATIO constet quam si uni REDDATUR.

The first act of the new principate was the slaughter of Postumus 1 Agrippa, unawares and unarmed, [a] whom a *centurion*, despite bracing himself in spirit, despatched only with difficulty. [e] Tiberius did not

---

[2] See e.g. Levick (1976), 245 n. 66 and W. Suerbaum, 'Zweiundvierzig Jahre Tacitus-Forschung: Systematische Gesamtbibliographie zu Tacitus' Annalen 1939–1980', *ANRW* 2. 33. 2 (1990), 1180. A summary of earlier views, going back to 1903, may be found in Detweiler (1970), 292–4.

[3] The letters in square brackets will be explained in due course.

speak about the matter **in the senate**: [*f*] he was pretending there were orders from **his father**, in which he had written in advance to the tribune in charge of the guard that he should not hesitate in putting Agrippa to death whenever he himself breathed his last. Now there is no doubt that Augustus had often complained savagely about the young man's behaviour and had ensured that his exile was sanctioned by decree of the senate; but he never hardened himself to execute any of his own relatives, nor was it credible that he had done his grandson to death for the sake of his stepson's unconcern: more likely, Tiberius and Livia had speeded the slaughter of a suspected and resented young man, the former through fear, the latter through stepmotherly hatred. [*b*] When the *centurion* announced, in a soldier's fashion, that the action which he had COMMANDED had been taken, he replied that he had issued no COMMAND and that an ACCOUNT of the action would have to be RENDERED **in the senate**. [*c*] When this was discovered by that accessory to secrets Sallustius Crispus (it was he who had sent the note to the tribune), he was afraid that a defendant might be supplied (it being equally dangerous whether he produced a fabricated or a true statement) and [*d*] he warned Livia that the mysteries of the household, the advice of friends and the services of soldiers should not be made public and that Tiberius should not discharge the power of the principate by calling everything to the || attention of **the senate**: it was a condition of issuing COMMANDS that the ACCOUNT would balance only if it were RENDERED to a single individual.

The death is ironically placed and ironically described. It is doubly pointed to open a book's main narrative with the death of a man called Postumus, especially when Tacitus' is the only account of his death which uses that name.[4] Agrippa was given the name Postumus because he was born after the death of his natural father, Vipsanius Agrippa: here Tacitus' reversal of his two *cognomina* emphasizes the name Postumus[5] and underlines the fact that he died after the death of his adoptive father, Augustus, to which reference was made in the immediately preceding sentence (1. 5. 4).[6] Each father missed

---

[4] The other accounts of the death are Suet. *Tib.* 22 and Dio 57. 3. 5–6. For the pointedness of starting with Postumus (*Primum* ~ *Postumi*) cf. Cic. *Mur.* 57 'respondebo igitur Postumo primum': I owe this reference (not to be found in H. Holst, *Die Wortspiele in Ciceros Reden* (1925)) to Dr C. S. Kraus. There is a comparable double point in the preface of Tacitus' *Histories*, where he begins a new section with Nero's death, which he calls an 'end': *H.* 1. 4. 2 'Finis Neronis . . .' [see *LH* 88–90].

[5] For a similar case see 3. 33. 1 *Seuerus Caecina*, where a transposed *cognomen* alludes to Cato the Elder: see Woodman–Martin ad loc. and note Goodyear on 1. 38. 2.

[6] This point is made also by J. Henderson, 'Tacitus/The World in Pieces', in A. J. Boyle (ed.), *The Imperial Muse: Flavian Epicist to Claudian* (1990), 202–3 n. 72.

a terminal point of the man's existence; and, just as his natural father predeceased the birth for which he was partly responsible, so there is perhaps already a pre-emptive innuendo that his adoptive father was partly responsible for the death which he predeceased. The transposition of *cognomina* also has the effect of juxtaposing *Agrippae* with *caedes*, a juxtaposition which, since the name Agrippa was thought to be derived from *aegre* and *partus* (Plin. *NH* 7. 45),[7] is picked up at the end of the sentence with the words *aegre confecit*: the man whose name suggests a difficult birth for his mother was killed with difficulty by his executioner. All these nuances are typical of Tacitus[8] and serve to confirm that he, if anyone, must have intended some significance to be inferred from his opening a new narrative with the episode of Agrippa's death. But what is the significance?

Many scholars have seen significance in the first four words of the episode: *Primum facinus noui principatus*. 'These words', says Goodyear in his commentary, 'are calculated to set the tone of the later treatment of Tiberius' principate.'[9] R. H. Martin, in a paper published forty years ago, wrote more specifically that 'the phrase *primum facinus* . . . implies . . . that Agrippa Postumus' death . . . was only the first of many such crimes'.[10] Moreover, scholars further assume that Tiberius himself is being blamed by Tacitus for the murder. Martin again, writing in 1981 and comparing the similar language with which Tacitus will introduce the reign of Nero at the start of Book 13 (1. 1 'Prima nouo principatu mors'), added this comment: 'The parallelism in language is designed to focus the reader's attention. But the differences between the two situations are no less important than their similarity. In the case of Tiberius the act is the first act *of* the principate; responsibility firmly attaches to the *princeps* himself. In the || case of Nero Tacitus speaks of the first death *in* the new reign.'[11] Detweiler agrees that Tacitus makes Tiberius responsible for the murder,[12] while Barbara Levick in her biography of the emperor maintains

---

[7] See further Maltby (1991), 20; M. Bettini, *Anthropology and Roman Culture* (1991), 293–4.
[8] For other plays on names in Tacitus see Woodman–Martin on 3. 75. 1 [and also below, Ch. 12, Sect. I].   [9] Goodyear ad loc.   [10] Martin (1955), 127.
[11] Martin (1981), 162.
[12] Detweiler (1970), 291 and 294–5, adding that Tacitus makes Livia jointly responsible.

that 'Tacitus . . . put[s] the blame squarely on the shoulders of
Tiberius'.[13] These scholars are by no means alone in their opinion, as we shall see in due course;[14] but are they right?

Having said that Postumus was murdered by a centurion,
Tacitus next says (i) that Tiberius did not speak about the matter
in the senate and (ii) that he pretended Augustus had ordered the
murder. The relationship between statements (i) and (ii) poses a
problem. If Tiberius remained silent in the senate, his pretence of
orders from his father cannot have been voiced in the senate. Yet,
if the pretence was not voiced in the senate, how does Tacitus
know about it? Was this a non-senatorial statement which Tiberius was famous for having uttered? Or did Tiberius in fact say
nothing at all, merely letting Augustus' responsibility be generally
assumed by people (perhaps by declining to deny his father's
involvement)?[15] Or is Tiberius' pretence of orders from his father
nothing more than an inference or even an invention on Tacitus'
part?

Robin Seager, who in his biography of Tiberius often follows
Tacitus' narrative very closely, suggests a scenario in which 'Tiberius announced to a disbelieving senate . . . that Augustus had left
orders for Agrippa to be executed as soon as the news of his own
death reached Planasia'.[16] But no evidence for such an announcement is provided by Tacitus at least, since he explicitly states that
Tiberius 'did not speak about the matter in the senate'. On the
other hand Levick, though acknowledging that 'Tiberius did not
speak on the subject in the House', says that the emperor 'merely
issued a statement that his father had given orders that Agrippa
was not to survive him'.[17] This may possibly be what Tacitus
means; but he does not say so, and the possibility seems remote.[18]
The most we can say is that the verb *simulabat* indicates that in
Tacitus' opinion it was not Augustus who had ordered his grand-
son's murder; and, when the verb is coupled with Tiberius' silence
in the senate, the impression is given that it was indeed Tiberius
himself who was responsible for Postumus' death.

The impression that Augustus had no part in the murder seems
to be supported by Tacitus' next sentence, in which he says that,

---

[13] Levick (1976), 65.   [14] See below and n. 21.   [15] So Dio 57. 3. 6.
[16] Seager (1972), 50.   [17] Levick (1976), 65 with n. 69.
[18] It seems far more likely that 'No official statement was ever published' (Syme (1958), 399).

although Augustus had disliked Postumus, 'he never hardened himself to execute any of his own relatives, nor was it credible that he had done his grandson to death for the sake of his stepson's || unconcern'. The first of these sentences ('ceterum . . . dur-auit') is Tacitus' own comment, the second a statement of what was felt at the time of the murder ('neque . . . credibile erat'); and both sentences, taken together, seem to acquit Augustus of all guilt.[19] This conclusion in its turn seems to be supported by what follows: 'propius uero Tiberium ac Liuiam, illum metu, hanc nouercalibus odiis, suspecti et inuisi iuuenis caedem festinauisse'. But it will be observed that the phrase *propius uero* lacks a verb, which we as readers are obliged to supply. What should this verb be?

   No comment at all is made by such older commentators as Walther, Ruperti, Ritter, Orelli, Pfitzner, Furneaux, and Nipperdey–Andresen.[20] That the missing verb is *est* is implied by numerous more recent scholars such as Hohl, Shotter, Lewis, Martin, and Baar.[21] Goodyear too implies that the missing verb should be *est*, but he then adds a footnote, saying that 'alternatively we might (with Koestermann) . . . understand' *erat*.[22] Kehoe also appeals to Koestermann for the notion that we should understand *erat*,[23] although Koestermann in his commentary makes it quite clear that he understands the missing verb to be *est*.[24] Kehoe for his part implicitly prefers *est* at the start of his paper but argues explicitly for *erat* at the end.[25]

   Evidently there is disagreement and confusion on a grand scale—and on a point whose crucial significance seems not always to have been appreciated by those who have discussed the passage. If the missing verb is *est*, the sentence will convey Tacitus' own opinion of what was the case. But, if the missing verb is *erat*, the

   [19] Seager (1972), 48 says that Tacitus 'is chiefly concerned to exculpate Augustus' (though I disagree with 'chiefly'). See also below, n. 35.
   [20] For the dates of their commentaries see the Bibliography.
   [21] Hohl (1935), 351; Shotter (1965), 360; J. D. Lewis, 'Primum Facinus Novi Principatus?', in B. F. Harris (ed.), *Auckland Classical Essays Presented to E. M. Blaiklock* (1970), 166–7, 180; Martin (1981), 162; M. Baar, *Das Bild des Kaisers Tiberius bei Tacitus, Sueton und Dio* (1990), 93.   [22] Goodyear ad loc. (with n. 1).
   [23] Kehoe (1984/5), 253, explaining (n. 19) that his reference is to Koestermann's 1960 Teubner text, to which Goodyear (above) must also have been referring.
   [24] Koestermann (1963) ad loc. Earlier Koestermann (1961), 335 was not altogether clear on this point, although he there states that in Tacitus' opinion both Sallustius and Livia were responsible.   [25] Kehoe (1984/5), 248 and 253.

implication will be that Tacitus is reporting opinion contemporary with Postumus' death. There is obviously a very great difference between these two alternatives, and it seems extraordinary of Goodyear to imply that it makes little difference which we choose and that our choice will not affect, or will not be affected by, the argument of the passage as a whole.

Goodyear himself, as we have just seen, preferred to understand *est*, a preference based partly on the argument that understanding *erat* is 'more difficult than to accept the slightly abrupt transition which the other view entails'.[26] The 'transition' in question is that from expressed *erat* to unexpressed *est*, which does indeed seem 'slightly abrupt': if the choice is between understanding *est* and *erat*, the latter seems far easier. Yet Goodyear also suggested that the missing verb might be 'zeugmatically *credebatur* or *uidebatur*', suggestions which highlight a hidden difficulty in understanding *erat*, namely that we should be obliged also to understand a reference || to the persons to whom the matter was *propius uero*: that is, we must understand an expression such as *iis qui eo tempore uiuebant* or, more simply, *eo tempore aestimantibus*. And there may be a further difficulty with *erat*:[27] all other examples of the phrase exhibit a verb in the present tense.[28] On the other hand, this phenomenon may simply be due to coincidence, since it is hard to envisage a reason why *propius uero* should not be accompanied by a past-tense verb.

So what is the missing verb? The fact is that, at this point in the narrative, we have no means of deciding. The most we can say is that the clause which depends on *propius uero* does nothing to remove suspicion from Tiberius ('Tiberium . . . caedem festinauisse').

This uncertainty is not immediately resolved by the sequel, since the following sentence, which returns us to the centurion who actually committed the murder, is asyndetic: 'nuntianti centurioni (ut mos militiae) factum esse quod imperasset, neque imperasse sese et rationem facti reddendam apud senatum

---

[26] Goodyear, 135 n. 1.   [27] I owe this point to Ronald Martin.
[28] Cf. Liv. 4. 37. 1 'quod propius uero est', 8. 37. 5 'fortuna Samnitium . . . propius ut sit uero facit non Apulis ab Samnitibus arma inlata', 9. 36. 4 'sed propius est uero praecipuum aliquid fuisse in eo qui se tam audaci simulatione hostibus inmiscuerit', 40. 50. 7 'propius uero est serius in prouinciam peruenisse', Ov. *F.* 4. 801–2 'num tamen est uero propius, cum condita Roma est, | transferri iussos in noua tecta Lares . . . ?'

respondit'. Once again we as readers are obliged to supply the missing connection for ourselves. But what should the connection be? Since the contents of the centurion's announcement tend to support the suspicion insinuated by *propius uero* (namely that Tiberius was responsible for the murder), we might assume initially that the missing connective is *et* or *nam*; but the main verb (*respondit*) introduces Tiberius' reply, the first part of which is a flat denial of his responsibility. It therefore becomes clear that the asyndeton is adversative and that the missing connective is *sed*. Of course, given the slant of the preceding narrative, we might dismiss Tiberius' denial as a bare-faced lie;[29] but he adds to his denial a requirement that an account of the matter should be rendered in front of the senate. This requirement is less easy to dismiss, and numerous scholars have agreed with Seager's view that 'there is no reason to suppose' that Tiberius' reply as a whole was not genuine.[30] But in fact we may go further, since in Tacitus' version of events we are given every reason to suppose that Tiberius' reply was indeed genuine.

The exchange between Tiberius and the centurion is described in almost identical language by both Tacitus and Suetonius,[31] but, whereas Suetonius concludes his account of Postumus' death with the exchange and thereby declines to remove the suspicion of guilt from Tiberius, Tacitus is unique in proceeding to introduce into the story the figure of Sallustius Crispus:[32] he it was, Tacitus says, who had actually sent the message which the centurion had eventually received. Now Sallustius could have been acting on Tiberius' || instructions: after all, the centurion clearly believed that his instructions had come directly from the emperor. But Tiberius' denial of his own involvement seems confirmed by the reaction which Tacitus attributes to Sallustius when the latter hears that Tiberius has ordered the matter to be brought to public attention. Sallustius both goes into a panic and approaches Livia. Had Sallustius been acting on Tiberius' instructions, we might have expected Tacitus to tell us either that Sallustius sheltered

---

[29] Some examples of false denials are given by Kehoe (1984/5), 250 n. 12.

[30] Seager (1972), 49–50, referring to Hohl (1935); see also Detweiler (1970), 292–3.

[31] Cf. Suet. *Tib.* 22 'Tiberius renuntianti tribuno factum esse quod imperasset, neque imperasse se et redditurum eum senatui rationem respondit, inuidiam scilicet in praesentia uitans: nam mox silentio rem obliterauit.'

[32] Sallustius' role is rightly stressed, but for different reasons, by Kehoe.

behind the *princeps'* authority or that he appealed to the *princeps* for aid or both. That we are told none of these things suggests very strongly that Tacitus has introduced Sallustius in order to indicate that Tiberius' reply to the centurion was genuine. How, then, did the centurion come to assume that his message was written by the emperor?

Some scholars have believed that Sallustius himself forged Tiberius' signature, but it seems to me unlikely that a man in Sallustius' position would impersonate the *princeps*. We should rather infer from Sallustius' decision to approach Livia that it was she who had authorized the message, an inference which may be confirmed by the very wording of Sallustius' approach to her. Sallustius begins with a tricolon, diplomatically arranged in descending order of importance (1. 6. 3): 'ne arcana domus, ne consilia amicorum, ministeria militum uulgarentur'. The last element of the tricolon, *ministeria militum*, clearly refers to the roles played by the centurion and tribune at the start of the story (1. 6. 1). The central element, *consilia amicorum*, evidently refers to Sallustius himself: we know from his later obituary that he was an official *amicus* (3. 30. 3). The first element, almost by a process of elimination, must refer to Livia herself: *arcana domus* suggests an involvement which was close to, but distinct from, the *princeps* himself.[33]

Tacitus' deployment of Sallustius and Livia finally absolves Tiberius from the guilt which his earlier narrative seemed designed to imply. We may therefore now return to the issue which we were obliged previously to leave in uncertainty. If Tacitus has ended his story by indicating that Tiberius was innocent, *propius uero* cannot constitute an authorial comment, since upon it depends a clause which alleges Tiberius' guilt (*caedem festinauisse*). Thus the verb to be understood cannot be *est*. Yet *erat*, the most frequently canvassed alternative, requires, as we have seen, the awkward assumption of a further ellipse. The missing verb is surely neither of these but *esse*, with a colon placed after *credibile erat* to indicate that the *oratio obliqua* continues after it: 'nor

[33] Contrast e.g. 2. 59. 3 *dominationis arcana*. Livia's propensity to authorize action is a key element in the tradition about her: cf. 3. 64. 2; Dio 57. 12. 2; Purcell (1986), 88, 90–1 [and also below, Ch. 12, Sect. III]. Note esp. 2. 43. 4, her advice to Plancina about Agrippina (and perhaps Germanicus too), an intervention which, given the outcome, our passage may foreshadow.

was it credible that . . .: < people said it || was > more likely that Tiberius and Livia . . . had speeded the slaughter of a suspected and resented young man'. This is of course a quite regular construction,[34] but in the interests of innuendo Tacitus has delayed our realization that he has used it.[35]

Thus, since the allegation introduced by *propius uero* is immediately denied by Tiberius himself, and since his denial is subsequently demonstrated to have been genuine, it follows that the articulation of the passage is this: people at the time thought it more likely that Tiberius was guilty *but* [adversative asyndeton] in convincing circumstances he denied having ordered the murder. Though this articulation becomes clear only in retrospect and does not coincide with what the majority of scholars believe Tacitus to be saying, a much more interesting scenario results from Tiberius' innocence than from his guilt. We now have a moment of high farce, in which a lowly centurion not only takes it for granted that the first act of the new emperor has been to order the death of a threatening relative but also dutifully confronts the emperor with his supposed act. Yet not only has Tiberius not ordered the murder but, as is clear from his requiring a senatorial hearing, he has no idea whatsoever who did issue the order. Despite having just become the most powerful man in the world, he is shown to be pitifully ignorant.

III

Now we know from the start of the episode that Tiberius did not carry through his demand for a senatorial hearing. It therefore follows not only that Livia passed on Sallustius' warning to her son but also that Tiberius took the warning to heart and acted upon it. It also follows that Tiberius' silence in the senate, about which we were told at the very start of the episode, is chronologically subsequent to Sallustius' advice to Livia, which occurs in

---

[34] See e.g. K–S 2. 536 Anm. 1, where is noted the frequency with which an affirmative verb of saying or thinking is to be understood from a preceding negative(d) verb (cf. also 563).

[35] Tacitus' successive sentences are decreasingly authorial (see also above, p. 28): he moves from *durauit* to *neque . . . credibile erat* (contrast *credibile est* at *Agr.* 11. 3, *G.* 28. 1) to *propius uero* [sc. *esse*]. I am grateful to Prof. J. G. F. Powell for discussion of this and related points.

the narrative last of all. Yet this is exactly the opposite of the
scenario outlined by Shotter, who maintains that 'Tiberius' first
reaction after the murder was . . . to blame Augustus' and that 'his
second was . . . to have the blame publicly shifted to Sallustius'.[36]
Such remarks show the danger of assuming that a narrative,
especially a Tacitean narrative, should always be read sequentially.
The true chronological order of events, as presented by Tacitus,
is indicated by bracketed letters in the text above (Section II).[37]
Contrary to what Shotter says, Tiberius' first reaction after the
murder was to require a senatorial hearing; his second, after the
interventions of Sallustius and Livia, was to say || nothing in the
senate; only then did he let someone else take the blame, and
the victim was not Sallustius but Augustus. As will be seen from
the set of italicizations in the text, the first half of the narrative
illustrates ring-composition: *centurio . . . confecit* at the end of the
first sentence (6. 1) is picked up by *nuntianti centurioni . . . factum
esse* below (6. 3), the latter returning us to the point in the
narrative which we left at the end of the first sentence. What
intervenes between these two points is displaced material, which
seems to have been inserted solely to cast suspicion on Tiberius by
means of a detailed exoneration of Augustus. Tiberius is seemingly accused but in fact excused within the same passage, an early
and excellent example of Tacitus' classic technique of having his
cake and eating it.

It may be thought that this detailed and complicated analysis
has resulted merely in the straightforward conclusion that in
Tacitus' opinion Sallustius and Livia between them ordered the
murder of Postumus. This is, after all, a variant on the second of
the hypotheses advanced by Suetonius, and it is also what some
modern scholars believe actually to have happened 'in real life'.[38]
Yet Tacitus' narrative has been deliberately deceptive, and, as we
have seen, the majority of modern scholars has been duly
deceived by it: regardless of what they think *actually* happened,

[36] Shotter (1965), 360.

[37] Since working this out, I have discovered that a similar scheme, also designated by
letters, is presented by E. Löfstedt, *Roman Literary Portraits* (1958), 168–70. Löfstedt,
however, works inwards to Tacitus' narrative from 'what must have happened', uses his
scheme to make an entirely different point, and does not make it clear whether in his view
Tiberius is being represented by Tacitus as guilty or not.

[38] Suet. *Tib.* 22 'quos codicillos dubium fuit . . . an nomine Augusti Liuia et ea conscio
Tiberio an ignaro dictasset'. See the survey of scholarly views by Detweiler (1970), 292–4.

they have believed that *Tacitus* presents as guilty the emperor whom he in fact presents as innocent.[39]

IV

If the above conclusions are correct, it is worth asking whether they affect the significance of this opening episode, a matter on which there has hitherto been general agreement (above, Section II and nn. 9–14). If Tiberius is being presented as guilty, as most readers seem to have assumed, the emperor's imputation of murder to Augustus is simply a cynical and perhaps desperate attempt at self-exculpation which has the effect of compounding his own guilt. But, if Tiberius is being presented as innocent, the pretence of orders from his father takes on a different perspective.

When Tiberius discovered from Livia the truth about the murder, he was placed in an impossible position. He could hardly go ahead and admit that his mother was responsible, for that would be to accuse her of 'sacrilege of the highest order'.[40] Nor could Tiberius say that he was himself responsible, since the responsibility was not his. He was therefore compelled to give the impression that the responsibility lay with Augustus,[41] who, being now dead, was beyond || any indictment. That was the only available option; yet it involved Tiberius in being forced to begin his reign by slandering the memory of a man who will be deified a few chapters later (1. 8. 1, 11. 3) and whose good example Tiberius will invoke many times throughout his reign.[42] Indeed Tiberius' contemporaries may well have regarded his present behaviour as an early (if ruthless) demonstration of such filial devotion,[43] since the *princeps* appeared to have sanctioned orders which he had the power to countermand; but the reader of Tacitus knows that Tiberius had been compelled to pretend the existence of the orders in the first place, and by this pretence, which he steadfastly maintained (*simulabat* at 6. 1 is imperfect), he

---

[39] See above, pp. 26–7. Syme (1958), 485, believed that Tacitus' narrative offers 'no plain answer'.

[40] The phrase is that of S. Jameson, 'Augustus and Agrippa Postumus', *Historia*, 24 (1975), 314.

[41] But it will be remembered that we do not know how this impression was conveyed (above, n. 15).　　　　　　[42] For this familiar theme see e.g. Seager (1972), 174–7.

[43] As Dr C. S. Kraus has observed; see also Hohl (1935), 354.

effectively repudiated the virtue of *pietas* even before he had a chance to lay claim to it.[44] These ironies Tacitus delicately underlines by his choice of the word *patris* rather than *Augusti* at the start of the episode.[45]

It will therefore be clear that, so far from being presented as a guilty perpetrator, Tiberius is being presented as an innocent victim. The episode as a whole is indeed significant, as scholars have believed; yet the reason is not that it portrays the first of Tiberius' many murders but that it shows how crucial actions, including murder, are from the very start carried out by powers behind the throne and in spite of Tiberius himself. The opening of *Annals* 13 ('Prima nouo principatu mors . . . ignaro Nerone per dolum Agrippinae paratur'), which has been invoked in order to emphasize by contrast Tiberius' guilt here in Book 1 (above and n. 11), turns out instead to provide a parallel rather than a contrast. At the opening of Book 13 we are told specifically that the first death in the new principate was arranged by Nero's mother and without Nero's knowledge, an exact repetition of the events of Book 1; the difference is that, whereas Nero's ignorance and his mother's guilt are clearly stated at 13. 1. 1, *noui principatus* at 1. 6. 1 is an ambiguous genitive and is seen in retrospect to be the first of the successive deceptions which, as we have noted, Tacitus practises upon his readers throughout the paragraph. And his modern readers have been duly deceived by it (above, Section II).

Livia's role in our episode harmonizes perfectly with the narrative which precedes and which itself foreshadows the end of Book 12.[46] In the preceding section, the second of those announced by Tacitus in his preface (above, Section I), we have been given a comprehensive picture of Livia's methods of working. Before Augustus' death people dreaded her *impotentia* (1. 4. 5); she was rumoured to be responsible for Augustus' death

[44] Such 'double focalization' is typical of Tacitus: thus at 1. 8. 6 'prouisis etiam heredum in rem publicam opibus', where Goodyear has a long discussion of whether *in* = 'against' or 'for', the answer will depend upon the implied point of view. The same issue arises at 3. 24. 2, where see Woodman–Martin ad loc.

[45] Hohl (1935), 354 n. 3, suggested as part of his argument that with *patris* we should understand, not *Tiberii*, but *Postumi*. (In either case the reference is to Augustus, who adopted both men together on 26 July AD 4.)

[46] For this see e.g. Martin (1955), 123–4. Since 1. 5 foreshadows 12. 66–8, whereas 1. 6. 1 foreshadows 13. 1. 1, this is another argument in favour of the view (see Sect. I) that a new section starts at 1. 6. 1 in the same way as a new book starts at 13. 1. 1.

(1. 5. 1); and she was instrumental in || ensuring Tiberius' succession (1. 5. 3–4). The present episode shows that people's fears concerning her were amply borne out in the very first act of the new principate: she was pulling the strings, and Tiberius knew nothing about it. This is a theme which will resurface later in the narrative, when his mother's habitual interventions constitute one of the alleged reasons why Tiberius at last decides to retire to Capri (4. 57. 3 'traditur etiam matris impotentia extrusum, quam dominationis sociam aspernabatur neque depellere poterat').

Yet Livia did not act alone: Tiberius is also the victim of Sallustius Crispus. Shotter, starting out from the presumption that Tacitus makes Tiberius guilty, alleged that the emperor is 'trying to have the blame publicly shifted to Sallustius';[47] but nothing could be further from the text: it is Sallustius who, in a successful effort at saving his own skin, at the same time extricates Tiberius from the embarrassment of a senatorial hearing. Sallustius' role is underlined by the set of capitalized words in the text (above, Section II), which indicates the ironical relationship between Tiberius' exchange with the centurion and Sallustius' approach to Livia. In the former Tiberius insists that he has issued no command ('neque imperasse sese') and that an account of the murder must be rendered in the senate ('rationem facti reddendam apud senatum'); in the latter Sallustius in effect tells Livia that Tiberius knows neither how to behave as 'commander' or *imperator* ('eam condicionem esse imperandi . . .') nor to whom an account should really be rendered ('ut . . . ratio . . . uni reddatur').[48] The picture is that of an out-of-touch ruler, who is ignorant of the realities of power and compelled to rely on the advice of an influential adviser.[49]

---

[47] Shotter (1965), 360.

[48] See also Koestermann (1961), 339. There is a theoretical possibility that Sallustius' words *eam condicionem . . . imperandi* could, if taken by themselves, refer to a specific command of Tiberius (that Postumus be murdered) and hence that they confirm Tiberius' guilt; but this possibility seems precluded by the context. Indeed it might be argued that on such an interpretation the rest of Sallustius' advice ('. . . ut non aliter ratio constet quam si uni reddatur') would be redundant, since the centurion had indeed reported to Tiberius. (Note that Tacitus makes Sallustius use a metaphor appropriate to a man famous for his wealth.)

[49] Dr T. E. J. Wiedemann reminds me that the theme of the 'evil adviser' seems to be standard in descriptions of tyrants.

This picture too is in harmony with the rest of the Tiberian narrative. We next meet Sallustius in Book 2, where Tiberius is exercised by the sudden appearance of a false Agrippa Postumus (39–40). By now, of course, three years have passed and in the interval Tiberius has learned something about how to behave as *imperator*. The emperor handed the matter over to Sallustius Crispus (2. 40. 2 'dat negotium Sallustio Crispo'): Tacitus makes no further comment but surely relishes the irony of the situation and the cynicism with which Tiberius acted. Sallustius for his part arranged for the man to be arrested, and the impostor, like the real Postumus before him, was murdered. Yet, if the episode in Book 2 shows that Tiberius has learned the lessons of command, subsequent events were to show that his education had not proceeded far enough. The *princeps'* manipulation by Sallustius in the first episode of the || Tiberian narrative is exactly mirrored in his manipulation by Sejanus in Book 4. The only difference is that, whereas Sallustius' secret machinations result in nothing more dangerous for Tiberius than his farcical confrontation with the centurion, those of Sejanus would almost destroy him. Thus the significance of the episode of Postumus' death is that it portrays Tiberius as dependent on others and influenced by them, a portrait which re-emerges in his obituary at the end of Book 6 (51. 3), closing the frame of the Tiberian narrative.[50]

V

Although the significance of Postumus' death is enhanced by its being placed at the start of Tacitus' Tiberian narrative (above, Section II), this placement involves a final problem of interpretation. In his note on the words *At Romae*, with which the next episode begins (1. 7. 1), Goodyear quotes the following observations of Ronald Martin:[51]

At Romae is a common form of transition in Tacitus when he switches from events abroad (or outside Rome), but here there is an additional point. If its normal function is to make a switch from one locale to another, with what does it contrast here? Not with anything in ch. 6,

---

[50] For this interpretation of the obituary see Woodman (1989) [below, Ch. 9].
[51] Goodyear ad loc.

but with ch. 5 (events at Nola). Ch. 6 is thus structurally indicated as a
digression from the main narrative.

Sir Ronald Syme agrees: chapter 6 is 'a digression, as shown by
the phrase "At Romae" (7,1), which looks back to 5,4'.[52] Yet how
can chapter 6, which is proved by Tacitus' own preface to be the
start of the Tiberian narrative (above, Section I), be at the same
time 'a digression from the main narrative'?

The remarks of Martin and Syme seem to imply that the events
of chapter 6, like those of chapter 7, take place in Rome. But this
is not the case with the very first sentence of chapter 6: the
murder of Postumus presumably took place on the island of
Planasia, where, as we have already been told (1. 3. 4), he was
living in exile. Now it is precisely after this first sentence, as we
have seen (Section III), that the chronological disruption of the
narrative occurs. The next two sentences, designated [*e*] and [*f*] in
the text above (Section II), are the result of the actions described
in sentence [*d*], which occurs at the end of the chapter. In other
words, all but the first sentence of chapter 6 is framed by references to Tiberius' not discussing Postumus' murder in the senate
(1 'nihil de ea re Tiberius apud senatum disseruit' ~ 3 'neue ||
Tiberius . . . ad senatum uocando').

Now the earliest opportunity on which Tiberius could have
discussed the murder in the senate does not occur until 1. 8. 1
primo senatus die. But that meeting seems to be preceded in time by
many of the events of chapter 7, not least by the edict through
which Tiberius called the senators to that meeting (1. 7. 3). In
other words, the non-discussion of the murder in the senate is a
flash forwards across the events of chapter 7 to the first sentence of
chapter 8. And, since the topic of Tiberius' silence frames all except
the first sentence of chapter 6 (see above), it would seem to follow
from the presence of this frame that the greater part of chapter 6 is
a digression from the main chronological narrative of events.[53]
This chronology may be illustrated schematically as follows:

(1) 1. 6. 1 Primum facinus noui principatus fuit Postumi
              Agrippae caedes

---

[52] Syme (1984), 1024 n. 37.

[53] It has to be admitted, however, that the closing of the frame at sentence [*d*] is anterior
in time to its opening at sentence [*e*] and that [*d*] is subsequent in time to [*b*], which,

(2) 1. 7. 1   At Romae ruere in seruitium consules, patres, eques
(3) 1. 7. 3   edictum . . . quo patres in curiam uocabat
(4) 1. 8. 1   Nihil primo senatus die agi passus nisi de supremis
              Augusti
(5) 1. 6. 1   nihil de ea re [sc. Postumi caede] Tiberius apud
              senatum disseruit

The reaction of the consuls, senators and knights (1. 7. 1) is not
unnaturally introduced by the phrase *At Romae*, since it contrasts
with the murder of Postumus, which took place on Planasia. And
not only is the murder of Postumus 'the first act of the new
principate' but *Primum facinus noui principatus* is also where the
main narrative of Tiberius begins—which is exactly what we
should expect after the programme which Tacitus set out in the
very first chapter of his work.

though within the digressive frame, is the earliest event in the chapter apart from Postumus' murder ([*a*]) and is therefore of critical importance. From the very use of the phrase
At Romae at 1. 7. 1 it might be argued that [*b*]–[*d*] are to be envisaged as taking place
elsewhere than at Rome: if that is the case, the only alternative locale is the journey of
Augustus' cortège, accompanied by Tiberius and (presumably) Livia, from Nola to Rome.
But this hypothesis presupposes that the cortège had not yet reached Rome in the time it
took both news of Augustus' death to travel from Nola to Planasia and the centurion's
news of Postumus' death to travel back from Planasia to Tiberius. Such a scenario, though
perhaps possible (as emphasized to me by Mr J. M. Carter), nevertheless involves a tight
scheduling of events which are themselves uncertain and controversial (see Martin (1981),
254 n. 18), and on the whole I prefer to suppose that everything in ch. 6, apart from
Postumus' murder in the first sentence, is imagined as taking place at Rome.

4

Tacitus on Tiberius' Accession

I

In the autumn of AD 14, probably on 17 September, there took place in the senate the so-called 'accession debate', at which the formalities of Tiberius' succeeding Augustus were to be handled.[1] The debate has generated a very great deal of interest among modern scholars, many of whom have been preoccupied with the questions of precisely when Tiberius succeeded and what the constitutional implications of his succession were.[2] Three accounts of the debate have come down to us from antiquity, in Tacitus' *Annals* (1. 10. 8–13. 5), Suetonius' biography of Tiberius (24–5), and Dio (57. 2–3); but most scholars have tended to concentrate on Tacitus, whose account is agreed to be 'the fullest' and 'certainly the best we have'.[3]

It is universally accepted that Tacitus, with characteristic malice, has manipulated his narrative to portray Tiberius in an unpleasant light. That unpleasantness resides above all in the emperor's hypocrisy. In the latest book on Tacitus, published in 1995, Sinclair says that 'Tacitus uses this particular incident early in Tiberius's reign to make general observations about the deceit-

For their very valuable comments on successive drafts of this paper I am most grateful to several friends and colleagues, including C. S. Kraus, D. S. Levene, R. H. Martin, C. B. R. Pelling, J. G. F. Powell, R. J. Seager, and T. P. Wiseman. It should not be assumed that any of them believes a single word of it. References are to Tacitus' *Annals* unless stated otherwise; references to Book 1 usually omit the book number.

[1] The date is assumed by scholars to be the same as that of Augustus' deification, which is known from inscriptions: see Goodyear on 1. 10. 8.

[2] There is a bibliography in Goodyear, 171–2, who also has his own discussion (169–76); add Kampff (1963); Seager (1972), 50–7; D. Flach, 'Der Regierungsanfang des Tiberius', *Historia*, 22 (1973), 551–69; Levick (1976), 68–81; Sage (1982/3); J. H. W. G. Liebeschuetz, in C. Deroux (ed.), *Studies in Latin Literature and Roman History* (1986), iv. 354–7; P. Schrömbges, 'Zu den angeblichen Reichsteilungsplänen des Tiberius (Dio 57, 2, 4 F.)', *RhM* 135 (1992), 298–307; Griffin (1995), esp. 37–43. Significant earlier discussions are incorporated into the commentaries of Koestermann and Goodyear.

[3] Goodyear, 169 and 176; cf. e.g. Levick (1976), 78.

fulness of the ruler's character and his public pronouncements.'[4] In the same year Griffin, the most recent writer to discuss the accession debate, went even further. Saying that the debate 'presented Tacitus with a wonderful opening', she explains how 'The falsity of the Principate could become incarnate in the hypocrisy of the new Princeps'.[5]

In the following discussion my primary concern will be neither with chronological or constitutional matters nor with the questions of 'what really happened' or whether Tiberius was 'really' hypocritical, this last being an issue on which modern scholars are anyway divided.[6] I propose rather to examine Tacitus' account to see whether scholars are justified in the interpretation which they have placed upon it.

II

Tacitus describes a meeting of the senate which consisted of a series of exchanges between members and Tiberius and which is aptly summed up in the words *negare et rogari* at the very end of the account (13. 5): the senators kept asking and he kept declining. The first set of exchanges (10. 8–11. 3) establishes the terms of the debate, and its interpretation is crucial to everything that follows:

Ceterum sepultura more perfecta templum et caelestes religiones decer-   8
nuntur. uersae inde ad Tiberium preces. et ille uarie disserebat de   11
magnitudine imperii, sua modestia: solam diui Augusti mentem tantae
molis capacem; se in partem curarum ab illo uocatum experiendo
didicisse quam arduum, quam subiectum fortunae regendi cuncta
onus. proinde in ciuitate tot inlustribus uiris subnixa non ad unum
omnia deferrent: plures facilius munia rei publicae sociatis laboribus
exsecuturos. plus in oratione tali dignitatis quam fidei erat; Tiberioque   2
etiam in rebus quas non occuleret, seu natura siue adsuetudine, suspensa
semper et obscura uerba; tunc uero nitenti ut sensus suos penitus
abderet, in incertum et ambiguum magis implicabantur. at patres, quibus   3
unus metus si intellegere uiderentur, in questus, lacrimas, uota effundi;
ad deos, ad effigiem Augusti, ad genua ipsius manus tendere, cum
proferri libellum recitarique iussit.

[4] Sinclair (1995), 82.   [5] Griffin (1995), 36.
[6] See e.g. Seager (1972), 56–7, criticized by Syme (1984), 942.

Tacitus begins by saying that, after religious honours had been decreed for the dead Augustus (10. 8), the senators switched their prayers to the living Tiberius (11. 1). We are not told the contents of the prayers, but they no doubt related to the formal motion of the consuls which Tacitus mentions only towards the end of his account (13. 4 *relationi consulum*). Whatever the case,[7] the prayers are followed by Tiberius' response (11. 1), which is rendered by Tacitus in indirect speech and summarized thus by Levick: 'it is a rejection of the "*regendi cuncta onus*" and a request for help from the numerous distinguished men in the state. They should not refer everything to one man, but take responsibility themselves. That is the theme of the speech reported by Tacitus.'[8]

There next follows Tacitus' own comment on Tiberius' response (11. 2). The comment comes in two parts, of which the first is a typically apophthegmatic statement: 'in such a speech there was more *dignitas* than *fides*'. What does *fides* mean here? According to the Tacitean lexicon the word means 'sincerity', as if *bona fides*: indeed Church and Brodribb actually translate the word as 'good faith'.[9] Furneaux in his school edition opts for 'honesty'; the Budé editor, P. Wuilleumier, chooses *franchise* or 'frankness', 'candour'.[10] Ramsay prefers 'sincerity', while Martin's version ('noble but insincere') is followed closely by Sinclair ('nobility exceeded sincerity').[11] Whichever word is chosen, the general consensus seems clear.

The second part of Tacitus' comment is an extended observation on the emperor's obscurity. 'Here in a single sentence', says Ronald Martin, 'is what Tacitus regards as the clue to the understanding of Tiberius' character. Tacitus does not entertain the possibility that there could be any reason for Tiberius' hesitancy other than hypocrisy.'[12] Thus the two parts of Tacitus' comment are together designed to show that the emperor's speech was insincere and hypocritical. In other words, the *princeps* meant the opposite of what he said: as Griffin has recently expressed

---

[7] Syme (1958), 410 n. 7, believed that the prayers included the *relatio*, which I think unlikely (below, p. 61).

[8] Levick (1976), 76–7; see also e.g. Griffin (1995), 39–40 (but also below, n. 36).

[9] Gerber–Greef, 426b; Church and Brodribb, 7.

[10] H. Furneaux, *Cornelii Taciti Annalium Libri I–IV*[2] (1897), 222; Wuilleumier, 16.

[11] Ramsay, 24; Martin (1981), 113; Sinclair (1995), 82.

[12] Martin (1981), 113. See also below, n. 29.

it, 'Tacitus is concerned to show that Tiberius was insincere . . . by pretending that he did not want the power when he did.'[13]

This interpretation seems confirmed by the final section of the passage (11. 3), in which Tacitus gives us the senators' reaction to Tiberius' speech and which is rendered by Jackson in the Loeb edition as follows: 'But the fathers, whose one dread was that they might seem to understand him, melted in plaints, tears, and prayers'. Evidently the senators have seen through Tiberius' insincerity, but, frightened to reveal to him their perception, they decide to take his speech at its face value and to protest against it. As a result, the emperor emerges with the power which he wanted all along. The whole scene exemplifies collusive hypocrisy. It is called 'a ritual' by Sinclair, 'a charade' by Martin, and a 'solemn comedy' by Syme.[14] Such language goes all the way back to Suetonius, who famously described the accession debate as 'a quite shameless pantomime' (*Tib.* 24. 1).[15]

Thus the first set of exchanges comprises speech from Tiberius (11. 1) and reaction by the senators (11. 3), the two being separated by authorial comment (11. 2) which influences our reading of both. Once we have been told by Tacitus in the middle of the passage that Tiberius was being insincere, it becomes clear that speech and reaction are mutually supportive; and this relationship has appeared so convincing that no one seems to have questioned it.

III

There are nevertheless some disquieting features. The comparative formulation of Tacitus' first comment, 'plus . . . dignitatis quam fidei', has all the hallmarks of a typical example of Tacitean cynicism;[16] yet it is worth reflecting whether a speech can be described as simultaneously possessing *dignitas* but lacking *fides*. On the traditional view *fides* is given a moral dimension ('sincerity', 'good faith'), and the same is true of *dignitas*: Martin's version,

---

[13] Griffin (1995), 37.

[14] Sinclair (1995), 170; Martin (1981), 113; Syme (1958), 410. See also Goodyear, 173–4.

[15] *impudentissimo mimo* (Gronovius: *animo* MSS). The emendation is generally accepted, but H. Lindsay in his recent commentary seems unsure (*Suetonius: Tiberius* (1995), 108–9).

[16] See e.g. Pippidi (1944), 50 n. 1; Plass (1988), 50–4.

'noble but insincere', is echoed, as we have seen, by Sinclair. Yet
how can this be? The presence of nobility (*dignitas*) is incompa-
tible with the absence of sincerity (*fides*), as may be seen from the
frequency with which the two nouns in question are *coupled* by
other authors, most notably by Cicero.[17] It is of course true that
Tacitus will often twist or reverse standard expressions, perhaps
especially if they are found in Cicero; but the contrasting of these
two particular terms is extremely difficult. Tacitus might have said
that Tiberius' speech 'appeared' noble but 'was' insincere, but he
has not done so: *erat* clearly applies to the whole sentence. Later
in the same book of the *Annals* (52. 2–3) he will contrast what
Tiberius says about Germanicus ('*in speciem* uerbis adornata') with
what he says about Drusus ('*fida* oratione'); but in our passage
there is no such expression as *in speciem*. It seems to me that the
interpretation of *fides* as 'sincerity', if not an insuperable difficulty,
is at least a major obstacle.

The conventional view also takes scant account of Tacitus'
remarks on the emperor's obscurity (11. 2). The remarks themselves are famous and are often quoted out of context to illustrate
Tiberius' habits of speech;[18] but scholars have paid less attention
to their place in the passage in which they occur. Tacitus' remarks
are introduced by a 'foil', where he tells us that Tiberius' speech
was habitually obscure ('Tiberioque . . . obscura uerba'); and then
there follows the statement that on this particular occasion the
emperor was striving to be, and succeeded in being, especially
obscure ('tunc uero . . . implicabantur'). It seems self-evident that
this elaborate presentation is designed to emphasize the degree of
obscurity with which the emperor spoke in this debate; yet on the
traditional view of the passage the senators have no difficulty in
understanding him: their fear of appearing to understand ('quibus
. . . uiderentur') presupposes that they have understood perfectly
well. There thus seems to be an inconsistency between Tacitus'
authorial comment (11. 2) and the senators' reaction (11. 3).

---

[17] Cf. Cic. *Fam.* 13. 32. 2, 13. 53. 1, *Fin.* 2. 76; *Bell. Alex.* 26. 1; Liv. 36. 26. 3; Flor. 1. 6.
6. For the close relationship between the two terms cf. J. Hellegouarc'h, *Le Vocabulaire latin
des relations et des partis politiques sous la république* (1963), 388–97. It is true that Plato has the
concept of the 'noble lie' (see e.g. C. Gill in Gill and Wiseman (eds.), *Lies and Fiction in the
Ancient World* (1993), 52–3), but this is scarcely relevant to the position of those who
believe Tiberius to be hypocritical. See also below, n. 35.
[18] e.g. Pippidi (1944), 37; Mellor (1993), 92.

This inconsistency depends upon the usual translation of *quibus . . . uiderentur*: 'whose one dread was that they might seem to comprehend him'. But such an interpretation, which seems universal, founders upon a point of syntax. 'Die Verbindung *metus si* ist sehr selten', observes Koestermann, evidently understanding *metus si* as equivalent to *metus ne*.[19] He quotes three alleged parallels for this usage, all of them from Tacitus and all of them repeated by Goodyear.[20] Koestermann first compares *H.* 4. 72. 2 'Cerialis autem, metu infamiae si licentia saeuitiaque imbuere militem crederetur, pressit iras'. Though Goodyear rightly reserves this example for last, it is very surprising that he quotes it at all, since *si* clearly has nothing to do with *metus*: 'But Cerialis, in dread of disgrace if he were thought to be imbuing the soldiers with licence and savagery, suppressed his anger.' Goodyear's own first parallel comes from Book 16 of the *Annals* (5. 2): 'quippe grauior inerat metus, si spectaculo defuissent, multis palam et pluribus occultis ut nomina ac uultus, alacritatem tristitiamque coeuntium scrutarentur.' But here the meaning clearly is 'For, if they left the spectacle, they felt a greater dread': the *si*-clause once again does not depend upon *metus*. The final case also comes from the *Annals* (11. 28. 1): 'igitur domus principis inhorruerat, maximeque quos penes potentia et, si res uerterentur, formido, non iam secretis colloquiis sed aperte fremere.' But in this passage not only does *metus* not occur but the word-order seems to preclude the taking of *si* with *formido*: 'and especially those at whose door lay power and, if things should change, fear'. In short, there is no parallel for *metus si* in the sense of *metus ne*, and it is quite proper that none of the alleged examples, including that in the accession debate, is listed in the *Thesaurus Linguae Latinae*.[21] In our passage *metus si* must have a different meaning; but, as soon as we deny the conventional meaning to the clause *quibus . . . uiderentur*, we remove the very relationship between the senators' reaction and Tiberius' allegedly insincere speech on which the conventional interpretation of the whole passage depends (Section II above). A different reading of the passage is therefore required.

---

[19] Koestermann ad loc.; '*si* pro *ne*', as Ruperti bluntly remarks.
[20] Goodyear ad loc.   [21] *TLL* 8. 909. 38–910. 11.

IV

It seems to me that there are two difficulties with which scholars have failed to come to terms in their reading of this passage. The first is one of preconception. Because Tiberius is elsewhere presented as hypocritical, it is assumed that he is always so presented and that he is being presented as hypocritical here: 'The dissimulation of Tiberius is an integral part of the tradition'.[22] Indeed we have seen that his alleged hypocrisy in this passage is taken as programmatic for the portrait which is to follow (above, pp. 40–1). The second difficulty is that scholars have tended to regard the passage as some sort of defective blueprint for Tiberius' constitutional position rather than as the narrative of a developing drama. If we are to read the passage correctly, we must try to understand Tacitus' words without preconceptions and with due regard for the sequential nature of the exchanges between emperor and senators.

Let us look again at Tiberius' speech (11. 1). It comprises two pairs of sentences. In the first sentence the *princeps* says that only Augustus' mind was capable of administering the *moles* of the empire without help (*solam*);[23] in the next he says that he himself had helped Augustus and had thereby learned the nature of his burden (*onus*). The burden is described as steep (*arduum*) and exposed to fortune (*subiectum fortunae*), as though a great weight had to be borne uphill, always to be cast down again by fortune in a never-ending cycle of *longus labor*.[24] The metaphorical flight is typical of Tiberius' speeches,[25] but in this case the bizarre assimilation of the *princeps* to Sisyphus no doubt contributed to the general obscurity.

In the first of the second pair of sentences Tiberius says that the senators should not devolve everything (*omnia ~ cuncta*) upon one man (*unum ~ solam*); in the next he says that several men (*plures ~ unum*) would more easily (*facilius ~ arduum*) share (*sociatis ~ partem*) the burden (*laboribus ~ onus ~ molis*). Now it is vital to realize that the meaning of this latter pair of sentences is unclear. Tiberius may be suggesting the adoption of an arrangement similar to that

---

[22] Syme (1958), 422–3, quoting Suet. *Tib.* 24–5 on the accession debate.
[23] For this interpretation of *solam* see Woodman (1989), 199 and n. 12 [below, Ch. 9, n. 12]; note also *OLD* s.v. 4.   [24] Cf. Hor. *C.* 2. 14. 19–20.
[25] See Woodman–Martin on 3. 12. 4.

which obtained under Augustus (and which he has just described in his first pair of sentences), except that he, in Augustus' place, would require the involvement of several helpers (*plures*). This is precisely the meaning inferred by Levick from the sentences (above, p. 42). Yet, although the series of clearly articulated verbal links no doubt leads one to think that this is indeed the emperor's suggestion, his words are nevertheless not inconsistent with a much more drastic proposal: that he wished to withdraw entirely from public affairs and to let the senators get on with the job by themselves. Later it will emerge which of these two alternatives is correct; but the speech itself crucially leaves the matter uncertain.

Tacitus' own first comment on the speech, as we have seen, is that in it there was more *dignitas* than *fides* (11. 2). Since we have had reason to doubt that *fides* here means 'sincerity', we must ask what it really means; and, since the author is attributing *fides* to a speech (*in oratione tali*), it is surely relevant to note that *fides* is a standard quality for a speech to possess: in the Ciceronian works on rhetoric *fides* is regularly combined with the word *oratio*.[26] The precise meaning of the term will vary between 'credibility' and 'credence' depending on viewpoint, and in the present passage it is most natural to assume that the former is correct.[27] Moreover, we should also note that *dignitas* too is almost technical in oratorical contexts, where it is rendered as 'impressiveness'.[28] Tacitus is saying that, in the case of a speech such as Tiberius had just delivered, there was more impressiveness than credibility. This is a factual statement, not a moral judgement. He is not saying that Tiberius himself was insincere but that his speech lacked credibility: it was the kind of speech destined scarcely to be believed by its audience. But it will turn out later that the senators *do* believe it—which is one reason why their reaction is introduced by an adversative conjunction (11. 3 *at patres* . . .).

If the senators are to believe the *princeps'* speech, they must first understand what he has said; and the rest of this section of authorial comment is designed, as we have seen, to emphasize Tiberius' particular obscurity on this occasion. Tacitus nowhere

---

[26] Cf. *Rhet. Herenn.* 1. 17, Cic. *Inu.* 1. 25, 34, *De Or.* 2. 156, 3. 104, *Part. Or.* 27; *TLL* 6. 1. 683. 16–28. In general see Quint. 5. 10. 8 ff.

[27] Jackson in the Loeb edition renders 'was more dignified than convincing', but, since the latter adjective is ambiguous, it is not clear what exactly is meant.

[28] See *TLL* 5. 1. 1136. 15–37 ('oratoria'), *OLD* 2c.

says that the emperor did not mean what he said (that is, that he was insincere);[29] what Tacitus does say is that the emperor was striving to hide his meaning ('nitenti ut . . . abderet') and that the result was uncertainty and ambiguity ('in incertum et ambiguum'). This statement corresponds exactly with the above analysis of Tiberius' speech. Tiberius had expressed himself in such a way that his words were capable of two different interpretations (*ambiguum*) and it was uncertain (*incertum*) which was correct. The articulation of the speech perhaps implied that he was proposing a variation on the arrangement which obtained under Augustus; but, if the senators cast their minds back two decades and remembered the moment in 6 BC when Tiberius, after just receiving the tribunician power, had suddenly retired to Rhodes for six years, they might well have concluded that the much more drastic interpretation of his words was the correct one. They could not know for certain which was correct, but his tribunician power had just been renewed in the previous year, a month had now passed since his father's death, and he had refused to discuss his position at the first meeting of the senate (1. 8. 1). Was history about to repeat itself? It was better to err on the side of caution, so the senators protested effusively (11. 3 *at patres* . . .). But Tacitus pointedly omits to say what the precise burden of their protests was: after all, they cannot be absolutely sure what it is that they are protesting against.

The effusion of the senators' reaction ('in questus . . . effundi') is preceded by the relative clause in which Tacitus describes their feeling of dread: 'quibus unus metus si intellegere uiderentur'. What does this troublesome clause mean? The form of words *unus metus si* illustrates a regular Latin idiom whereby a noun, qualified by *unus* or *solus* or a demonstrative and the like, is explained by a clause introduced by *quod, cum, ut* or *si.*[30] In such circumstances *si* intro-

---

[29] Pippidi (1944: 37) resembles other scholars (e.g. n. 12 above) in his slide from passages illustrating 'la dissimulation' to our passage, on which he comments: 'Et il nous paraît également naturel qu'il ait cherché à cacher ses véritables sentiments sous un langage sibyllin.' Tacitus' text provides no justification for this.

[30] See L–H–S 666 (§366 (c)). Although they distinguish this kind of clause from those where a si-clause is 'in Abhängigkeit von Subst.', they regard our passage as an example of the latter; Koestermann's note, which seems to depend on L–H–S without mentioning them, is not really clear or straightforward. Carmody (1926: 133–4) rightly says that '*Si* clauses also occur in Tacitus . . . as explanatory of *metus, in eo*, etc.', quoting our passage amongst others and adding that 'The subjunctive in all the above passages is oblique, due either to informal or formal *oratio obliqua*'. See also Woodman–Martin on 3. 6. 1,

duces 'a substantival clause expressing a fact or assumed fact',[31] and I think that in the present example the meaning is: 'whose one dread was that they seemed to understand'. On this interpretation *uideri* is elliptical for *sibi uideri*,[32] and, by supplying a reference to what the senators *thought* was the case, it does justice to the emphasis which Tacitus has laid on the emperor's obscurity. Tiberius had been particularly obscure, but the senators, though uncertain, nevertheless thought that they understood—which is a second reason why their reaction is introduced by the adversative conjunction (11. 3 *at*).

On this new interpretation of the passage as a whole, the episode is designed to underline, not the collusive hypocrisy of the senate, but its abject subservience to, and complete dependence on, the *princeps*. After forty-five years of Augustus' domination, the members could not envisage any other way of life, a point which Tacitus has already made earlier (1. 3. 7–4. 1):

Younger men had been born after the Actian victory, and the majority even of the elderly in the course of the citizens' wars: what size was the remaining proportion, who had seen the republic? As a result, along with the changed state of the community, nowhere was there a trace of pristine and unadulterated behaviour: with equality cast aside, all fixed their gaze on the orders of the *princeps*, with no alarm for the present, while Augustus had the strength and years to support both himself and his household and the peace.

But Augustus was now dead, and Tiberius might be about to retire even before taking up office. No wonder the senators were filled with dread and protested!

V

Such an interpretation, based on the emperor's sincerity on the one hand and on the senators' dread on the other, makes perfect

---

Martin–Woodman on 4. 33. 2, Durry on Plin. *Pan.* 11. 4, and for the subjunctive cf. e.g. Liv. 5. 8. 9 'una spes erat si ex maioribus castris subueniretur'.

[31] *OLD si* 12 (cf. c).

[32] See *OLD uideo* 21, where many of the examples are followed, as here, by an infinitival verb of perceiving or knowing *vel sim.* It is true that many of the examples are first-person, but I think that *uiderentur* is mimetic, imitating what the senators themselves said (cf. e.g. 15. 2. 1 *uidebar*): see e.g. Cic. *Rep.* 1. 14. 2 and 18. 4 with Zetzel ad locc. It seems reasonable to assume that, had Tacitus wanted to say 'they were afraid lest they should appear to understand', he would have used *metus ne*, as he does regularly elsewhere (Gerber–Greef, 830a). Conversely one cannot use *metus ne* to express in Latin the idea 'fear that they thought they understood'.

sense of the effusive reaction which follows and which in its turn
prompts Tiberius to resort to an alternative method of persuasion:
he calls dramatically for a *libellus* and orders it to be read out (11. 3).
This was a booklet which Augustus had written in his own hand
and in which he had itemized in full the assets and extent of the
empire (11. 4). Scholars have naturally realized that Tiberius'
purpose in resorting to this intervention was to support the message of his opening speech;[33] but the effect is to set off a further
series of exchanges between senators and *princeps* (12. 1–3):

Inter quae senatu ad infimas obtestationes procumbente dixit forte
Tiberius se, ut non toti rei publicae parem, ita quaecumque pars sibi
mandaretur eius tutelam suscepturum. tum Asinius Gallus 'interrogo',   2
inquit, 'Caesar, quam partem rei publicae mandari tibi uelis.' perculsus
inprouisa interrogatione paulum reticuit; dein collecto animo respondit
nequaquam decorum pudori suo legere aliquid aut euitare ex eo cui in
uniuersum excusari mallet. rursum Gallus (etenim uultu offensionem   3
coniectauerat) non idcirco interrogatum ait ut diuideret quae separari
nequirent, sed ut sua confessione argueretur unum esse rei publicae
corpus atque unius animo regendum.

The recitation of the booklet's contents reduced the senate to
even baser—but still indeterminate—appeals (12. 1), during
which Tiberius remarked by chance (*dixit forte*) that, although
he was unequal to the *res publica* as a whole, he would undertake
to protect whichever part was entrusted to him. This is a crucial
remark which requires careful analysis.

   The first part of Tiberius' remark, in which he expresses his lack
of competence, repeats in different words what he had said already
in his first speech: namely, that only Augustus had been capable of
managing the empire single-handed (11. 1). Now it seems usually to
be thought that the second part of the remark, in which he offers to
undertake part of the empire, is also a repetition of his first speech,
when he had said that a plurality of men would more easily carry out
the responsibilities. But the reference to 'chance' (*forte*) precludes
the possibility that the emperor is now repeating something
which he had uttered quite deliberately in his earlier speech.[34]

----

[33] See e.g. Levick (1976), 77; denied by Kampff (1963), 33–4.

[34] This is confirmed by the intervention of Asinius Gallus (see below). If repetition
were itself the point (if, that is, Tiberius were reminding members, firmly but politely, that
he intended to play some role), we should have expected Tacitus to say e.g. *iterum dixit*.

We are therefore obliged to infer that he is saying something different from his earlier speech; and, since he is now stating plainly that he is prepared to shoulder part of the burden, we are also obliged to infer that his earlier speech, though ambiguously expressed, was intended to prepare his audience for his complete withdrawal.[35] Indeed that was the reason for his carefully weighed and obscure language (cf. 11. 2 'suspensa . . . et obscura uerba'): knowing the likely effect of his withdrawal on the senate, he had been attempting to break it to them gently. Thus Tiberius' remark at 12. 1 demonstrates that the senators, though they had only 'thought' they understood his meaning (11.3 *uiderentur*), had in fact been right; and, since Tiberius is now saying something different from what he said before, it follows that their protests, based on what they thought was the case, have had some effect.

This interpretation is confirmed by the fact that it is only at this point, when Tiberius has stated plainly that he is prepared to play some part, that Asinius Gallus asks him what part it is that he is willing to play (12. 2). Gallus' question reduces the emperor to momentary silence; but then, collecting himself, he replies that it is not at all consistent with his reserve to choose or to avoid any element of that from which he would prefer to be excused totally. Tiberius' stunned reaction to Gallus' question would be highly implausible if he had intended all along to administer part of the empire; and that his original intention had been complete withdrawal is confirmed when he himself admits that his own preference would be to be excused entirely (*in uniuersum*). But Tiberius' chance remark and Gallus' pointed question are destined to have unfortunate consequences, as Tacitus proceeds to describe.

Gallus, realizing that Tiberius resented thus being put on the spot, tried to smooth things over by saying that his purpose in asking his question had been, not that Tiberius should divide what could not be divided, but that Tiberius should himself acknowledge that the body of the State was a unity which needed to be ruled by one man's mind (12. 3). Yet Tiberius' anger was not

[35] *forte* also precludes the view that the Tacitean Tiberius had really wanted a partnership of himself and others all along and that his opening speech was some sort of 'noble lie' designed to alarm the senate so much that they would accept what appeared to be a compromise. Had Tacitus intended that, he would have been obliged to write e.g. *quasi forte*, which seems indeed to be what Furneaux ad loc. thinks he has written ('as if unguardedly').

assuaged (12. 4), which is hardly surprising: for, though Gallus' first *ut*-clause was designed to assure Tiberius that no trick question had been intended, that clause is identical with the second *ut*-clause in its insistence that the empire could not be divided up. It is therefore no surprise again when L. Arruntius, making a point similar to Gallus', likewise offends Tiberius (13. 1). Yet, just as the senators' protests at 11. 4 provoked Tiberius into his offer of partial responsibility (12. 1), so the interventions of Gallus and Arruntius seem to have caused him to withdraw his offer, of which nothing further is heard. Either Tiberius has been persuaded by Gallus and Arruntius that his offer is indeed impracticable, or he has been so angered by their interventions that, in a fit of pique, he has returned to his original and much more drastic intention. Whichever of these is the case, the later interventions of Q. Haterius and Mamercus Scaurus appear to be based on the premiss of his complete withdrawal (13. 4). And this seems not to be contradicted by the sentence with which Tacitus brings the accession debate to its ambiguous conclusion (13. 5): 'And, exhausted by everyone's shouting and the protests of individuals, he gradually changed tack—not to the point of admitting that he was assuming command [*suscipi a se imperium*], but to that of ceasing to refuse and be asked'.[36]

Thus, on this new interpretation of Tacitus' account, the accession debate appears almost to have come full circle. At the beginning Tiberius was intending complete withdrawal; and, although the protests of the frightened senators extracted from him a compromise suggestion, that suggestion in its turn seems to be abandoned in the light of further senatorial reaction. Tiberius at the end seems no further forward than he was at the start.

VI

Before Tacitus proceeds to the other subjects which were debated by the senate on this same occasion (14–15), he uses the conven-

---

[36] Griffin (1995) quotes 13. 5 as evidence that Tacitus has obscured the idea of partnership (above, n. 8) and has treated the matter 'as a straight offer and denial of power' (41); but this takes no account of the dramatic and developmental nature of Tacitus' narrative. It is interesting to note that Dio distinguishes between a total rejection of the empire and a request for partners or helpers (57. 2. 4 καὶ τὸ μὲν πρῶτον καὶ πᾶσαν αὐτὴν [sc. τὴν ἀρχὴν] . . . ἐξίστασθαι ἔλεγεν· ἔπειτα δὲ κοινωνούς τέ τινας καὶ συνάρχοντας . . . ᾔτει).

tional device of a digressive passage (13. 6) to indicate that he has now concluded the subject of Tiberius' accession.[37] Yet it is agreed by commentators on Tacitus and by historians of Tiberius alike that, before proceeding to those other subjects, he ought to have inserted the explanatory material which now appears several chapters earlier at 7. 6–7. To put the matter another way, Tacitus has transposed to 7. 6–7 explanations of Tiberius' reluctance which in his source were appended to, or integrated with, an account of the accession debate. Three considerations seem to have led to this scholarly consensus: the explanatory material is said to be implausible and awkward in its present context; very similar material accompanies Suetonius' and Dio's accounts of the accession debate; and, finally, Tacitus has allegedly desired to highlight, at the earliest possible moment in his Tiberian narrative, characteristics of the *princeps* which will become prominent later.[38] Yet this widespread and influential thesis fails to take proper account of the context in which the explanatory material occurs and which itself raises far more problems than scholars have realized.

VII

The material at 7. 6–7 is preceded by the following passage (7. 3–5):

ne edictum quidem quo patres in curiam uocabat nisi tribuniciae potestatis praescriptione posuit sub Augusto acceptae. uerba edicti fuere   4
pauca et sensu permodesto: de honoribus parentis consulturum, neque
abscedere a corpore, idque unum ex publicis muneribus usurpare. sed   5
defuncto Augusto signum praetoriis cohortibus ut imperator dederat;
excubiae, arma, cetera aulae; miles in forum, miles in curiam comitabatur. litteras ad exercitus tamquam adepto principatu misit, nusquam
cunctabundus nisi cum in senatu loqueretur.

Tacitus is discussing the edict whereby Tiberius summoned members to the previous meeting of the senate, the first of the reign, which is assumed to have taken place in early September.[39]

---

[37] See Woodman–Martin, 500 (index: 'digressions, separating or closural function of'). That the subjects of 14–15 were debated on 17 September is an assumption; as far as I know, we cannot be certain.

[38] See e.g. Koestermann, 89; Goodyear, 141 and 176; Martin (1990), 1510.

[39] For a possible date (4 September) see e.g. Sage (1982/3), 306.

Tacitus explains that the edict was issued only by virtue of Tiberius' tribunician authority (7. 3) and that its words were few and of
limited purport (7. 4): Tiberius would consult only about honours
for Augustus and was not leaving the body, and that was the only
public responsibility to which he was asserting his right.[40] Yet on
Augustus' death the watchword had been given to the praetorian
guard by Tiberius *ut imperator*,[41] and various other manifestations
of imperial behaviour were in evidence, the last of which (7. 5
'litteras . . . misit') ends with a characteristically Tacitean 'appendix' ('nusquam . . . loqueretur');[42] and this appendix is extremely
problematical.

Grammarians, commentators, and critics alike are agreed that
the *cum*-clause is frequentative and means 'whenever';[43] but it is
instructive to observe the conclusions, if any, to which this agreement leads. Furneaux and Goodyear draw no conclusions at all.
Martin says that Tacitus' is a 'generalising statement' and that it
refers to a habit which Tiberius 'retained throughout his reign'.[44]
Koestermann, though his comment is not without its ambiguities,
both seems to agree with Martin ('das endlose Zögern des Tiberius') and suggests that Tacitus is referring to Tiberius' behaviour
in the accession debate described later (at 10. 8–13. 5).[45] Yet
Martin's suggestion is contradicted immediately by the first of
the *causae* which Tacitus proceeds to provide for Tiberius' *cunctatio*
(7. 5): Tacitus says that the *causa praecipua* was fear of Germanicus
('ex formidine ne Germanicus . . .'), which is so localized an
allusion that it clearly cannot refer to something which endured
'throughout his reign'. Koestermann's view, if my earlier analysis
of the accession debate is correct (Sections IV–V above), is also
unacceptable. The burden of Tiberius' complaint in the accession
debate is that the principate is too onerous (11. 1 'magnitudine
imperii', 'tantae molis', 'onus', 'laboribus', 12. 1 'toti rei publicae'), and this is a recurring theme (e.g. 3. 54. 5 'laborum

---

[40] Scholars have debated whether *id . . . unum* refers to Tiberius' accompanying the
body or (perhaps oddly) to his summoning of the senate: see e.g. Furneaux ad loc. By
mentioning the body, Tacitus implies that the edict was issued *en route* from Nola.

[41] *ut*, as elsewhere in Tacitus (e.g. 3. 60. 1, 4. 39. 2), is ambiguous ('as' or 'as if'): only
when we reach *tamquam* do we know that it means the latter.

[42] See Kohl (1959), though this example is not discussed.

[43] See Carmody (1926), 110; Furneaux and Koestermann ad loc.; Martin (1990), 1509
and n. 34. Goodyear makes no comment.   [44] Martin (1990), 1509–10.

[45] Koestermann ad loc.

meorum', 56. 4 'noti laboris', 69. 4 'satis onerum principibus'): it is nothing less than astonishing both that no reference to this onerousness features in the list of *causae* for Tiberius' *cunctatio* and (in particular) that it does not constitute the *causa praecipua*. An alternative explanation of Tacitus' sentence is required.[46]

In my opinion scholars have been misled by a failure to realize that the appendix to Tacitus' sentence is elliptical and that with *nusquam cunctabundus* we are to supply *de adipiscendo principatu* from *tamquam adepto principatu* in the main clause: 'he sent a letter to the armies as though the principate were acquired, in no area reluctant <concerning the acquisition of the principate> except when he spoke in the senate'. Once the implication of the sentence is spelled out in full in this way, Tacitus' point becomes immediately clear: namely, that Tiberius did not speak at all in the senate about 'acquiring the principate'. In other words, the reference is to Tiberius' refusal to speak about the principate in the first senatorial debate: the sentence repeats, from a different perspective, the *uerba edicti* as presented earlier in the passage (7. 4 'de honoribus parentis consulturum', 'he would consult only about honours for his father'). Because scholars have believed the *cum*-clause to be frequentative, which on this interpretation it is not, they have failed to see that Tacitus is drawing a contrast between Tiberius' numerous examples of *princeps*-like behaviour outside the senate in the aftermath of Augustus' death (7. 5 *defuncto Augusto*) and his reluctance to speak, *during this very same period*, about the formalization of his position as *princeps*.[47] When the time came to speak, at the second meeting of the senate, he would do so. This radically different interpretation may be proved by examining the *causae* which Tacitus in the very next passage at 7. 6–7 proceeds to offer for Tiberius' *cunctatio*,[48] a proof which at

---

[46] Tiberius' *cunctatio* does not refer to his hesitancy of speech. Though the *princeps'* speech in the senate would sometimes be hesitant (e.g. 4. 31. 2), he shows no sign of it in the two debates which follow (8. 1, 8. 4, 8. 5; 11. 1–2, 13. 4). (I am assuming that speech is implied at 8. 1 *passus*, but it need not be; and I agree with Martin (1981), 113 and n. 16 that *suspensa* at 11. 2 means 'carefully weighed'. Tiberius is of course stunned into silence at 12. 2, but that is rather different.)

[47] Scholars may perhaps have been led to their interpretation of *cum* by a subconscious desire to contrast it with *nusquam* in the sense of 'never' (*OLD* 4).

[48] Although Sage (1982/3), alone of the scholars whose work I have checked, seems to have arrived at a similar interpretation of *nusquam . . . loqueretur* (by a different and almost intuitive route), he has not drawn the inevitable conclusions regarding 7. 6–7 (cf. 307 and e.g. 314).

the same time will demonstrate that the material in 7. 6–7 cannot refer, as scholars have believed, to the accession debate.

VIII

Tacitus offers three *causae* for Tiberius' *cunctatio*, the second and third of them being linked to the first by *et* and *etiam* respectively (7. 6–7):

causa praecipua ex formidine ne Germanicus, in cuius manu tot legiones, immensa sociorum auxilia, mirus apud populum fauor, habere imperium quam exspectare mallet. dabat et famae ut uocatus electusque   7
potius a re publica uideretur quam per uxorium ambitum et senili adoptione inrepsisse. postea cognitum est ad introspiciendas etiam procerum uoluntates inductam dubitationem: nam uerba, uultus in crimen detorquens recondebat.

Martin simply reflects the scholarly consensus when he says that these three reasons 'have little or no plausibility' and that 'they fit somewhat awkwardly into the context'.[49] But this consensus has come about only because scholars have misinterpreted both what it is that the *causae* are explaining, as we have just seen (Section VII), and what one *causa* in particular (the second) actually means. If we accept that the *causae* refer to Tiberius' *cunctatio* before the accession debate ('nusquam cunctabundus nisi . . .'), and if we interpret each *causa* correctly, we shall find that the *causae* are highly plausible and fit perfectly into their context.

Tacitus offers fear of Germanicus as the *causa praecipua* for Tiberius' refusal to speak about 'acquiring the principate' at the first meeting of the senate. It is important to remember that during this period, if Tiberius withdrew or died, Germanicus 'would succeed as head of the *domus Caesaris*'.[50] If Tiberius consented to 'acquire the principate' with all due form and ceremony, he risked provoking his adopted son, whose proximity to the throne is precisely the focus of Tacitus' words: 'habere imperium quam exspectare mallet'. It is clear from the same sentence as a whole that in Tacitus' view Tiberius was ignorant of Germanicus' intentions; nor could his ignorance be quickly rectified, since, as we learn later, at the time of Augustus' death Germanicus was

---

[49] Martin (1981), 110; (1990), 1510.   [50] T. E. J. Wiedemann, *CAH*[2] x. 206.

in distant Gaul (1. 31. 2, 33. 1). Given such ignorance, and given the numerous advantages which lay with Germanicus and which are duly noted by Tacitus ('tot legiones, immensa sociorum auxilia, mirus apud populum fauor'), Tiberius might well have feared that his own immediate and formal 'acquisition of the principate' would tip Germanicus towards civil war. Of course his fear proved unfounded (1. 34. 1); but Tiberius was not to know that at the time, and Tacitus describes the German legions as desirous of civil war (1. 31. 1).[51] By waiting till a later date to discuss his 'acquiring the principate', Tiberius was able to perform the appropriate familial and diplomatic courtesies and to assure himself of Germanicus' position.[52] According to Sage, fear of Germanicus 'bears no relationship to the course of the debate in the later narrative':[53] this is certainly true;[54] but, as the *causa praecipua* for the delay between mid-August and mid-September, fear of Germanicus is utterly convincing.

The second *causa* has been widely misrepresented. Levick, believing (like others) that Tacitus is explaining Tiberius' behaviour at the *second* meeting of the senate, says: 'The ancient writers were not backward in offering their own explanations [sc. for Tiberius' behaviour in the accession debate]. For Tacitus, caution and cunning were behind the Princeps' hesitation: Tiberius wanted to force the Senate into committing itself to him, and to appear as their freely chosen candidate.'[55] Likewise Syme says that Tiberius 'wished to rule at the call and summons of the "res publica", not as one ensconced in the power through a woman's intrigue and an old man's act of adoption.'[56] And Goodyear in his introductory note to the accession debate, referring back to the present passage, says: 'What he still wanted was to seem to have been put in that position by the *consensus* of the Senate, *ut uocatus electusque potius a re publica uideretur quam per uxorium ambitum et senili adoptione inrepsisse*.'[57] The common thread linking these

---

[51] Tacitus in fact uses civil-war language throughout his account of the mutinies (1. 16. 1, 36. 2, 49. 1); the contemporary Velleius talks in terms of a disaster waiting to happen (124. 1).

[52] Tacitus' point, which concerns Germanicus in person (above, n. 50), is obscured by those (e.g. Levick (1976), 72–5) who discuss the mutinies in the context of 7. 6.

[53] Sage (1982/3), 314 and n. 115.

[54] Goodyear nevertheless allows some plausibility to the *causa praecipua* (140–1), even though he believes it is misplaced in the narrative.   [55] Levick (1976), 71.

[56] Syme (1958), 481.   [57] Goodyear, 175.

interpretations, which appear also in Koestermann, Brunt, Martin, and Sage,[58] is the assumption that the *ut*-clause represents something which Tiberius 'wanted' or 'wished'. There is no evidence in Tacitus' text for this assumption. On the contrary, each of these scholars has omitted consideration of the words *dabat . . . famae*, which Goodyear himself elsewhere translates, quite correctly, as 'He conceded to public opinion'.[59] If anything, the implication of these words is that the *ut*-clause represents something which Tiberius did *not* wish. The *princeps* is making a concession; what was it?

If *fama* refers to public opinion, it follows that according to Tacitus there was a substantial body of contemporaries who wanted the proper formalization of Tiberius' position as *princeps* ('ut . . . uideretur'). As long as such formalization was lacking, Tiberius' position was arguably out of keeping with the dignity of the Roman State and its people ('per uxorium ambitum et senili adoptione'). Yet at the first meeting of the senate Tiberius had expressly prevented any such formalization from even being discussed (7. 4, 7. 5, cf. 8. 1): the concession, therefore, consists in the fact that he *was* permitting such a discussion at the *second* meeting of the senate. The logical relationship between *nusquam cunctabundus nisi cum in senatu loqueretur* (7. 5) and this second of the *causae* may be illustrated by the following paraphrase: 'Why was Tiberius reluctant, at the first meeting of the senate, to talk about his acquiring the principate? One reason was that, as a concession to public opinion, there was going to be a second meeting *ut uocatus electusque . . . a re publica uideretur.*' The logic is flawless.[60]

---

[58] Koestermann (1961), 342; P. A. Brunt, 'Lex de imperio Vespasiani', *JRS* 67 (1977), 97; Martin (1990), 1510; Sage (1982/3), 307.

[59] Goodyear ad loc.; so too Furneaux ad loc., who rightly explains that the accusative has been omitted and that 'the object here is supplied from *ut . . . uideretur*', quoting 2. 58. 1 'daturumque honori Germanici ut ripam Euphratis accederet', to which Goodyear adds 3. 69. 5 'darent Iuniae familiae . . . ut Cythnum potius concederet'. In her commentary (1959) N. P. Miller ad loc. makes explicit the 'slide' which other scholars have assumed: '"he conceded to public opinion that he should . . ." i.e. "in deference to public opinion he wished . . . "'. Such a note simply reveals the lack of evidence for the scholarly consensus.

[60] Those who believe in the conventional view of the Tacitean Tiberius may be tempted to infer from the second *causa* that Tiberius was initially determined to rule *without* any formalization of his position and despite the slur against him (7. 7 'per uxorium . . . inrepsisse') and that it was only as a concession to public opinion that he would submit to the process of formalization. But such an inference is contradicted by an essential

The difficulty of the third *causa* centres on the word *inductam*, which most scholars have taken as a metaphor of 'putting on' or 'assuming' a mask, cloak, or disguise.[61] Goodyear rightly expressed grave doubts about this interpretation on grounds of Latinity,[62] but a more decisive objection, certainly on the present interpretation of *nusquam . . . loqueretur* (Section VII above), is one of logic. Tiberius' reluctance to speak at the first meeting of the senate was a fact: he did not speak on the subject of his position (7. 5, 8. 1). If *dubitationem* refers to that reluctance, as it seems reasonable to accept, then *inductam* cannot mean 'put on' or 'assumed', which would result in a logical incompatibility.[63] It is therefore more likely, as suggested in the *Thesaurus Linguae Latinae*, that the meaning is 'introduced': 'that his hesitancy had been introduced so that he could scrutinise also the dispositions of the leaders'.[64]

Yet again the *causa* makes excellent sense in the context of the period from mid-August to mid-September. Tacitus has already told us that the most illustrious individuals were also the most hypocritical (7. 1): nothing was more natural in the circumstances than that Tiberius should wish to know where he stood with them. This third *causa* is the obverse of the more general feeling expressed by the word *famae* in the second *causa*, and Tacitus duly gives us an example of Tiberius' putting into practice, at the first meeting of the senate, his policy of 'scrutinising the dispositions of the leaders' (8. 4: the case of Valerius Messalla).

IX

Now that we have examined the three individual *causae* in turn, we might ask why Tacitus should have bothered to explain, in such

element in the same conventional view, namely that Tiberius' speech in the accession debate (11. 1) was insincere and designed precisely to extract from the senators their explicit support. Besides, if Tiberius were so ruthlessly determined to rule that he preferred to eschew the formalization of his position, it is scarcely likely that he would care what the *proceres* thought of him (7. 7).

[61] So e.g. Furneaux and Koestermann ad loc.; *OLD* s.v. 15a.   [62] Goodyear ad loc.
[63] The 'distancing' effect of the acc. + infin. is negligible, since the qualifying verb (*cognitum est*) appears to give authorial assent to the indirect speech.
[64] *TLL* 7. 1. 1238. 1–2 (with *ab eo* to be understood). Professor Powell has suggested that the meaning is 'doubt was induced/encouraged [sc. in other people (primarily the senators) by Tiberius]': see *OLD induco* 6a. There is a similarly awkward occurrence of the same verb at Suet. *Tib.* 30 (see P. A. Brunt, 'The Role of the Senate in the Augustan Regime', *CQ* 34 (1984), 424).

elaborate and itemized detail, a circumstance of whose presence in his text almost no modern reader has even been aware. The answer is that, from every perspective, Tiberius' reluctance to speak about his position at the first meeting of the senate was remarkable. In the century preceding Tacitus' composition of the *Annals* there had been numerous transfers of imperial power, involving at one period a descent into the ultimate competition of civil war; yet here was a man who, though marked out for the succession (cf. 3. 3), refused to discuss the formalization of his position. Contemporaries, as we may infer from Tacitus, will have been even more perplexed. They knew that Tiberius had been chosen by Augustus as his successor (10.7 *successorem*), and, as soon as word was received that Augustus had died, they were told also that Tiberius was 'in charge of affairs' (5. 4). Their immediate response was a spontaneous rush to take the formal oath of loyalty to the new ruler (7. 1–2), while he for his part immediately acted as if he were *princeps* (7. 5). In such circumstances it is not surprising that Tacitus mentions Tiberius' refusal on three separate occasions (7. 4 'de honoribus parentis consulturum', 7. 5, 8. 1) and then by implication shows him putting it into practice (8. 3 'tum consultatum de honoribus'). It was indeed remarkable that the new *princeps* refused to discuss his position at the earliest possible moment in the one body which had the power to formalize that position; and, since Tiberius' concession of a second debate is described as a response to public opinion (7. 7 'dabat . . . famae'), that description presupposes a refusal so noteworthy that public opinion required it to be rectified.

Tiberius' concession to public opinion implies a public pronouncement of a second debate; but it is to be inferred from the sequence of *causae* that Tiberius' contemporaries did not know when his *cunctatio* would end, or, putting it another way, when his concession of a debate ('dabat . . . ut . . .') would be honoured. Whether we regard the concession as focalized from Tiberius' or the author's point of view,[65] the second *causa* implies merely that a

---

[65] The matter can be argued either way. If it is Tiberius who focalizes *dabat*, we must infer that Tacitus is alluding to, or imagining, an edict in which Tiberius said that he was bowing to public pressure. If *dabat* is straightforwardly authorial, Tacitus is perhaps retrojecting from the accession debate some slight degree of initial reluctance here. (Clearly the words *per uxorium ambitum et senili adoptione inrepsisse* cannot be focalized from Tiberius' point of view, although it is possible to regard them as focalized by his contemporaries: such an interpretation is not inconsistent with the popular desire (*famae*) that Tiberius' position as *princeps* should be formalized, as may be seen from p. 58 above.)

subsequent debate will take place; there is no implication of a date. It is true that the first and third *causae* between them imply some kind of time-scale (the debate would take place when Tiberius had received assurances from Germanicus and when he had satisfied himself as to the *procerum uoluntates*); but neither of these two *causae* represents information which was publicly available to Tiberius' contemporaries in the aftermath of Augustus' death. The third *causa* is explicitly stated to have become public knowledge only at a later date (7. 7 'postea cognitum est'), while the first *causa*, of its very nature (7. 6 'ex formidine ne Germanicus . . .'), is scarcely likely to have been public at the time but constitutes an authorial interpretation of events.

Tiberius' contemporaries were thus left in a state of ignorance and suspense,[66] and it is this which provides the contextual background for the moment when Tacitus resumes the theme of Tiberius' accession at 10. 8–11. 1:

Ceterum sepultura more perfecta templum et caelestes religiones decernuntur. uersae inde ad Tiberium preces.

The attention of modern readers tends to be caught by the typically Tacitean cynicism whereby the religious connotations of the deferred noun *preces* are activated by its juxtaposition with *templum et caelestes religiones*: the senators turn, as it were, from a dead god to a living. But such cynicism should not obscure the fact that *preces* also denotes the relief with which the senators begged Tiberius to end the suspense in which he had kept them for so long.

Now, apart from the *cunctatio* itself, the senators have been given no evidence that Tiberius would not 'acquire the principate' when it was formally offered to him. But the *cunctatio* was now ended, and the very fact that the second debate had been convened meant that any refusal to 'acquire the principate' was unthinkable.[67]

---

[66] The suspense is expressed in narrative terms by the section on opinions about Augustus (9–10), which is marked as digressive (8. 6 *sepultura* ~ 10. 8 *sepultura . . . perfecta*).

[67] On this matter Tacitus' readers are better informed than Tiberius' contemporaries, who, as we have just seen, had no access to the first and third *causae*. Each of these *causae* implies that Tiberius will formalize his position as *princeps* in due course: there would be little point in his waiting upon Germanicus or the *proceres* if he were not intending to accept the summons when he was ready to receive it. Hence, from the readers' point of view, Tiberius has changed his mind during the time which has passed between 7. 3–7 and 10. 8–11. 1. Tacitus provides no explicit reason for this development, no doubt because

Thus, when Tiberius began to respond to the senators' *preces* (11. 1), his speech was destined to be regarded as scarcely credible (11. 2 'plus in oratione tali dignitatis quam fidei erat': above, pp. 46–7); but, as the senators put two and two together (that is, when they considered both Tiberius' recent reluctance to speak and his previous history), the awful, if ambiguous, truth dawned on them: Tiberius appeared to be refusing to be *princeps*. So they reacted by pouring out protests, tears, and vows (11. 3).

The above analysis relies on the supposition, which seems to me incontrovertible, that the *causae* of 7. 6–7 relate specifically and exclusively to the *cunctatio* of 7. 5. In other words, Tacitus has distinguished a *cunctatio loquendi* (7. 5) from the *recusatio imperii* (11. 1). Since no other source has done this, it is easy to understand how scholars have been misled into thinking that the *cunctatio* and the *recusatio* are one and the same and that the *causae* for this allegedly single phenomenon have simply been inserted at an earlier point where they are both implausible and awkward.[68]

he wishes his narrative to imitate the unpreparedness of the audience of Tiberius' speech at the accession debate; but, since Tiberius begins that speech by alluding to the capability of Augustus, the juxtaposition with the popular talk at 10. 7, in which Tiberius' alleged denigration by Augustus is reported ('ne Tiberium quidem . . . quaesiuisse'), is highly suggestive and quite in line with Tacitus' general portrayal of Tiberius (see further below, pp. 241–2): the man was disheartened before he even started. Moreover, Tacitus' very voicing of the first and third *causae* has already raised for readers the question of what Tiberius would have done if he had failed to assure himself about Germanicus and the *proceres* (see also n. 65 above on *dabat*); and, in any case, Tiberius' change of mind was not such as would prevent him from making a compromise proposal during the debate in response to senatorial pressure (12. 1) or from continuing to rule despite the ambiguous manner in which the debate ends (13. 5).

[68] The contemporary Velleius, who mentions none of the three *causae* (but refers to a *uotum*), makes no distinction between a *cunctatio loquendi* and the *recusatio imperii* (124–125. 1): if we assume that Tacitus accurately records 'what really happened', we should therefore be obliged to infer that Tiberius' coevals not unnaturally interpreted his *recusatio imperii* on 17 September in terms of his earlier refusal to discuss the formalization of his position (i.e. in retrospect there was no distinction to be made). If, on the other hand, it is Velleius who records accurately, we must assume that Tacitus has represented in an individual and more plausible manner the similar material which appears in Suetonius and Dio.

Velleius also makes the interesting statement: 'solique huic [sc. Tiberio] contigit paene diutius recusare principatum quam, ut occuparent eum, alii armis pugnauerant' (124. 2). In my commentary ad loc. I suggested that Velleius had in mind the period from mid-August to mid-September (i.e. from Augustus' death to the accession debate) and that his parallel (*alii*) was perhaps Marius. At the time I did not express much confidence in the suggestion, although it was endorsed by Sage (1982/3), 295 n. 10; but my analysis of Tacitus has indicated how significant Tiberius' silence at the first debate was, a silence which was not rectified until mid-September: hence the period after Augustus' death was indeed crucial. All this evidence suggests that the theory of K. Wellesley, that the accession debate took

X

In the preceding discussion I have presented a radically new interpretation of almost every aspect of the passages in which Tacitus deals with Tiberius' accession. One striking conclusion in particular has emerged: there has been no evidence for Tacitus' portrayal of Tiberius as a dissembling and hypocritical *princeps* who pretended, in Griffin's words (above, p. 43), 'that he did not want the power when he did'.[69] Whether this unsettling conclusion can be sustained, however, depends upon the interpretation of a single, short sentence in the one passage which remains to be discussed and which again is far more problematical than most scholars have realized.

Tacitus begins his Tiberian narrative with the murder of Agrippa Postumus (6. 1–3), after which he continues as follows in chapter 7 (1–3):

At Romae ruere in seruitium consules, patres, eques. quanto quis inlustrior, tanto magis falsi ac festinantes uultuque composito, ne laeti excessu principis neu tristiores primordio, lacrimas, gaudium, questus, adulationem miscebant. Sex. Pompeius et Sex. Appuleius consules primi in uerba Tiberii Caesaris iurauere apudque eos Seius Strabo et C. Turranius, ille praetoriarum cohortium praefectus, hic annonae; mox senatus milesque et populus. nam Tiberius cuncta per consules incipiebat, tamquam uetere re publica et ambiguus imperandi. ne edictum

2

3

place very early in September, is mistaken ('The *dies imperii* of Tiberius', *JRS* 57 (1967), 23–30).

[69] On the contrary, if my analysis in n. 67 is correct, readers of Tacitus are being told that Tiberius had been prepared to accept power but changed his mind. Since scholars very often assume that the Tacitean Tiberius is in some sense the 'real' Tiberius, it is worth indulging in some further speculation. Contemporaries of Tiberius, less well disposed than Velleius but (like him) seeing the *recusatio imperii* in terms of the *cunctatio loquendi* (n. 68), will have assumed from Tiberius' speech in the senate (11. 1) that he had been deceiving them for the past several weeks: i.e. he had not changed his mind but had been pretending that he wanted the power when he did not! This is not only the exact opposite of what modern scholars suppose but may help to explain (and may even be the origin of) Tiberius' reputation for *dissimulatio*, which, as we know from *Tab. Siar.* IIb. 16, was already current early in the reign. That this is not Tacitus' own view, however, is clear from 7. 6–7 (n. 67): ironically it is Tacitus who provides the evidence for a non-dissembling Tiberius.

Even if we accept the usual view (which has been disputed by D. Timpe, *Untersuchungen zur Kontinuität des frühen Prinzipats* (1962), 51–5) that *cunctatione ficta* at 1. 46. 1 refers to Tiberius' reluctance at 'acquiring the principate' rather than to his hesitancy at 1. 47. 3, the phrase occurs within indirect speech and so does not contradict my interpretation of the accession episode.

quidem quo patres in curiam uocabat nisi tribuniciae potestatis praescriptione posuit sub Augusto acceptae.

At Rome there was a rush to servitude by consuls, senators, and
knights,[70] the degree of their hypocrisy and haste being propor-
tionate to their individual distinction (7. 1). The consuls were the
first to swear loyalty to Tiberius (7. 2 *consules primi*), followed by
two *praefecti*, the senate, soldiery, and people. There next follows a
sentence which, since it begins with *nam* (7. 3), appears to have a
causal or explanatory relationship with the preceding sentence;
and indeed there seems to be a verbal link between *per consules
incipiebat* here and *consules primi* above. But any such relationship
would require us to infer (from *incipiebat*) that it was Tiberius who
both instigated the oath and got the consuls to swear to it before
anyone else did. This, as Koestermann saw, is impossible.[71] Tacitus
has already told us that the general reaction was spontaneous (7.
1): it makes no sense at all now to imply that the oath-taking was
initiated by Tiberius himself.[72] And who but the consuls could
possibly have taken the lead in swearing the oath?

There are other problems also. This sentence too ends with an
appendix, introduced by *tamquam* and evidently comprising a
familiar *uariatio* of ablative phrase ∼ nominative adjective: 'as if
the old republic were in existence and he were undecided about
commanding', the implication of which is understood to be that
Tiberius was not at all undecided about commanding but positively wanted power.[73] How does this appendix relate either to
the problematical main clause or to the wider context? Goodyear,
as before, has no note. Koestermann explains the sentence as a
whole by describing it as an 'anticipation' of Tiberius' pretended

---

[70] The juxtaposition of the words *Romae* and *ruere* is perhaps intended to recall Hor.
Epod. 16. 2 *Roma . . . ruit*, which involves a complicated etymological word-play (C.
Macleod, *Collected Essays* (1983), 218–19). I also wonder whether *consules primi* just below
(7. 2) is an ironical allusion to Liv. 2. 1. 8 *primi consules* (though the phrase or a variation
thereon recurs elsewhere in Livy and in other authors): the passage is followed almost
immediately (9) by the words *auidum nouae libertatis populum . . . iure iurando adegit* [sc.
Brutus] *neminem Romae passuros regnare*.

[71] Koestermann ad loc., though differing in details.

[72] It was in fact a defining feature of this particular oath that it should be spontaneous
(Weinstock (1971), 225, quoting *Res Gestae* 25. 2 'iurauit in mea uerba tota Italia sponte
sua'); Kampff, however, uses our passage as evidence for Tiberius 'demanding the oath of
allegiance' (1963: 27).

[73] See e.g. Gerber–Greef 1623b (under the rubric 'falsam speciem indicat'). This
appendix too is not discussed by Kohl (1959).

republicanism: that is, he understands the verb in a generalizing sense ('Tiberius was in the habit of beginning . . .'). Yet, even if we make repeated allowances for rhetorical exaggeration in the word *cuncta*, this interpretation is variously unsatisfactory. First, it is unfortunate that Koestermann seems contradicted immediately by the very first meeting of the senate, at which, as Tacitus himself tells us, it was Tiberius, not the consuls, who dictated the terms of the debate (8. 1 'nihil primo senatus die agi passus nisi . . .'). Second, the whole point of an episode such as 3. 60–3 (note especially 3. 60. 1 and 3, 63. 1–2) would be lost if Tacitus had already informed us that Tiberius would assume republican features in 'everything' (*cuncta*). Finally, and conversely, when Tacitus at 4. 6. 2 comes to sum up the years AD 14–22, to which he devotes half of his Tiberian narrative, he gives no hint at all of the pretence which on Koestermann's interpretation is presented with such programmatic prominence here. This inconsistency serves to underline the fact that it is logically quite difficult to reconcile a generalizing main clause with the counterfactual allegation of the appendix: if Tiberius 'was in the habit of beginning *everything* with the consuls', how can that square with someone acting '*as if* undecided about commanding'? There surely comes a point at which pretence stops being pretence and becomes reality. In short, these objections suggest that Tacitus' sentence cannot have the generalizing sense which Koestermann wishes to give it.[74]

Furneaux suggested that Tacitus refers to the *interregnum* between Augustus' death and (presumably) the formalization of Tiberius' position at the second meeting of the senate: during this period Tiberius began everything through the consuls 'as if he had not made up his mind to rule'.[75] Although this suggestion does not produce an illogical relationship between main clause and appendix, it is disproved by a later section of this very same chapter (7. 5), where there is no trace of consular agency in the

---

[74] Though it is a commonplace that Tiberius showed respect for, or even deference to, the *senate*, the conventional interpretation of 7. 3 perforce attributes to him a quite unusual relationship with the consuls in particular. Tacitus will later say *sua consulibus . . . species*, but he says the same about praetors and mentions also the lesser magistrates and the senate in general (4. 6. 2); Velleius likewise refers to magistrates and senate (126. 2). Only Suetonius seems to single out the consuls (*Tib.* 31. 2), and his one instance seems at best double-edged. [75] Furneaux ad loc. and on p. 98.

initiatives which Tacitus ascribes to Tiberius during precisely this period. How, then, is this problematical sentence to be interpreted?

It is clear from later in this same chapter that in Tacitus' view Tiberius had not yet 'acquired the principate' (7. 5 'tamquam adepto principatu'): the formalization of the *princeps'* position lay in the future, at the second meeting of the senate. That formalization in its turn depended on the now notorious motion of the consuls (13. 4 'relationi consulum'); and I suggest that that is what Tacitus is referring to when he says that Tiberius 'began everything through the consuls'. On this interpretation the sentence may be rendered: 'And in fact Tiberius began his whole reign with the consuls.' In other words, *cuncta* is not a rhetorically exaggerated reference to a series of individual initiatives but is being used collectively and in an allusive sense which is characteristically Tacitean (cf. 1. 1. 1 'qui [sc. Augustus] cuncta . . . accepit', 1. 3. 3 'illuc [sc. ad Tiberium] cuncta uergere', 1. 11. 1 'regendi cuncta onus'). *incipere*, in a twist which is also typical of Tacitus, is simply a transitive example of a verb which came to be used almost technically of the start of a *princeps'* reign and which is so used again a few chapters later (1. 19. 2 'incipientis principis'), where Goodyear quotes Koestermann's parallels.[76] And, finally, the relationship between the primacy of the consuls' action here and their primacy in the preceding sentence (7. 2 *consules primi*) is expressed by a regular usage of *nam* 'which both confirms a previous statement and asserts a following one'.[77] It was a sharp irony that the beneficiary of Rome's first imperial succession should depend for his position on a motion which was put by quintessentially republican magistrates in a quintessentially republican way.[78]

This interpretation not only avoids the objections to which

---

[76] For a similar expression cf. Liv. 30. 27. 11 'ut placatis dis omnia inciperent agerentque', 30. 30. 12 'omnia audacissime incipientem'. Tacitus' imperfect tense belongs to a general usage which is classified by grammarians as expressing intended, expected or proposed actions in past time. Cf. e.g. *A*. 13. 15. 1 'propinquo die quo quartum decimum aetatis annum Britannicus explebat' ('on which Britannicus would complete the fourteenth year of his life'), 14. 45. 2 'omne iter quo damnati ad poenam ducebantur militaribus praesidiis saepsit' ('along which the condemned would be led').

[77] G. H. Poyser, 'A Usage of *nam*', *CR* 2 (1952), 8–10 (at 9).

[78] If readers are disappointed at being deprived of an overtly cynical reading, it is open to them to supply the thought 'but things would change', if they wish.

Koestermann and Furneaux are open but provides an explanation for the relationship between this sentence and the preceding (above, p. 64). Moreover, the words *tamquam uetere re publica* underline very neatly the irony inherent in the motion of 17 September. However, if it is correct to refer the main clause of this sentence to the accession debate, that reference serves merely to intensify the problem of the words (*tamquam*) *ambiguus imperandi* in the appendix: for, in so far as those words imply that Tiberius positively wanted power,[79] they seem to offer belated, if solitary, support for the conventional view that Tiberius was insincere in his speech at the accession debate (11. 1). Yet, since Tiberius' alleged insincerity in that debate depends upon an untenable interpretation of two key passages (11. 2–3), as I believe I have shown (Section III above), the foreshadowing of any such insincerity here is anomalous. This anomaly may be removed by the simple expedient of punctuating after *re publica* rather than after *ambiguus imperandi*:[80]

nam Tiberius cuncta per consules incipiebat, tamquam uetere re publica; et, ambiguus imperandi, ne edictum quidem quo patres in curiam uocabat nisi tribuniciae potestatis praescriptione posuit sub Augusto acceptae.

There is, as everyone knows, nothing sacred about the punctuation of classical texts, and this minimal alteration makes it clear that the two resulting sentences refer to two different occasions.

On this repunctuation of the passage Tacitus, as in the previous episode (6. 3), is capitalizing on the fact that in the immediate context *imperare* means 'to issue commands'. Having just mentioned the primacy of the consuls in taking the oath of loyalty (7. 2), he slides to Tiberius' beginning his whole reign with the consuls, an ironical echo of republican practice (7. 3 'tamquam uetere re publica'). This republican practice in turn leads him to Tiberius' deployment of a republican power, the *tribunicia potestas*, with the mention of which the narrative reverts to the period

---

[79] See above, n. 73. In fact the words need not necessarily have this implication, but I do not propose to discuss the matter further here.

[80] For a similar beginning to a sentence elsewhere in Tacitus see 14. 33. 1 'ibi ambiguus an . . .'; in the manuscript of Tacitus our passage has semicolons both before *tamquam* and after *imperandi*, for what that is worth. For a recent repunctuation of an even more famous passage (3. 65. 1) see *MH* 52 (1995), 111–26 [= below, Ch. 6].

before the first meeting of the senate ('edictum . . . quo patres in curiam uocabat'). And, since the deployment of *tribunicia potestas* represents a minimalist use of power ('ne . . . quidem . . . nisi'),[81] Tacitus' statement of that use is very aptly preceded by the phrase *ambiguus imperandi*, which it illustrates.[82] The articulation of the repunctuated passage seems unexceptionable in itself and admirably suited to the immediate context; later, when in the accession debate Tiberius does his best to avoid formalizing his position, we may conclude that his reluctance was already foreshadowed here, in which case *ambiguus imperandi* will acquire an extra and pointed dimension of meaning ('undecided about being *princeps*').[83]

XI

Tacitus is well recognized as a difficult and deceptive writer. At the same time the *Annals* is an extremely familiar, even canonical, text. Tacitus' cynical view of the Julio-Claudians has influenced generations of students and scholars; his view of the early principate is also our view. A paradox results: it is his very familiarity which prevents scholars from realizing quite how difficult and deceptive his text can be.

[81] In this connection we might note that commentators either miss (so Koestermann and Goodyear) or misinterpret (so Furneaux) the significance of Scaurus' remark at 13. 4 'dixerat spem esse ex eo non inritas fore senatus preces quod relationi consulum iure tribuniciae potestatis non intercessisset'. Scaurus' point is not that Tiberius had not vetoed the motion but that he had not used his tribunician power to do so, a sarcastic allusion to the fact that Tiberius had earlier used 'only' his tribunician power to summon the fathers to the first meeting of the reign (7. 3 *ne . . . quidem . . . nisi*).

[82] It is worth emphasizing that *praescriptione* is technical (cf. *OLD* 1) and refers to the edict's heading or preamble, which presumably read 'Ti. Caesar Aug. f. tr. pot. xv', as on the coin of AD 13/14 (EJ 81) mentioned by Levick (1976), 63. On my punctuation, *ambiguus imperandi* is Tacitus' inference from, or gloss on, such a *praescriptio*. Further, in so far as the word *ambiguus* implies a duality, Tiberius' minimalist use of power at 7. 3 sets up a contrast with 7. 5 below (*sed . . .*), where he acts with more power than (according to Tacitus) he yet possessed (*ut . . . tamquam . . .*) and where *imperator* looks back to *imperandi*.

[83] Likewise the second *causa* at 7. 7 takes on a retrospective resonance, since, if read out of its immediate context, it could be taken to imply that Tiberius preferred to avoid altogether a process of formalization which would only make the management of an eventual withdrawal more difficult, and that it was only as a concession to public opinion that he would submit to that process. Such a reading in fact seems precluded by the first and third *causae* (see above, n. 67), unless we assume that Tiberius had indeed been in two minds (*ambiguus imperandi*): see above, n. 65. It is worth noting that according to Tacitus (13. 5) the debate ended without Tiberius' position being formalized (see pp. 51–2) and that according to Suetonius, 'recepit imperium, nec tamen aliter quam ut depositurum se quandoque spem faceret' (*Tib.* 24. 2).

On the death of Augustus, Tiberius found himself in control of affairs (5. 4) but he declined the immediate formalizing of his position (7. 5); in issuing commands he relied both on minimal power (7. 3) and on power which he had not yet formally accepted (7. 5); although he had intended to formalize his position at the later debate (7. 6–7), he began that debate by trying to withdraw entirely from his affairs (11. 1); that attempt at withdrawal was superseded by a compromise proposal that he should be given helpers (12. 1); when that compromise seemed abandoned, he reverted to the constitutional limbo in which he had been since Augustus' death (13. 5); although he did not confess that he was assuming command (13. 5), he proceeded to rule for more than twenty years; and, although his compromise proposal had seemed abandoned (12. 3–13. 5), he immediately adopted it in practice by taking on his sons Germanicus and Drusus as his helpers.[84] This is not the conventional picture, nor is it that of a dissembling and hypocritical tyrant; it is the subtle and plausible portrait of a man whose sense of responsibility was in perpetual conflict with his desire for withdrawal, of a man who was truly *ambiguus imperandi*. It is a perfect—and perfectly Tacitean—irony that Tiberius would eventually find himself at the mercy of the last of his helpers, Sejanus, one of whose successes had been to persuade him to undertake the complete withdrawal for which he had expressed such desire, albeit in obscure language, during the accession debate in the autumn of AD 14.

[84] On this see below, Ch. 12, Sect. III.

5

Self-Imitation and the Substance of History
(*Annals* 1. 61–5 and *Histories* 2. 70, 5. 14–15)

⌜In the year AD 15 Germanicus, nephew and adopted son of the emperor Tiberius, led a Roman army into the heart of Germany. Finding himself near the Teutoburg Forest, where Quintilius Varus and three legions had been massacred by the native chieftain Arminius six years before, Germanicus decided to visit the site of the disaster and pay his last respects to his dead countrymen. We owe our knowledge of this episode to two main sources: Suetonius, who mentions it in one brief sentence,[1] and Tacitus, whose account is, by contrast, extremely long (*Annals* 1. 61–2):

Igitur cupido Caesarem inuadit soluendi suprema militibus ducique, permoto ad miserationem omni qui aderat exercitu ob propinquos, amicos, denique ob casus bellorum et sortem hominum. praemisso Caecina ut occulta saltuum scrutaretur pontesque et aggeres umido paludum et fallacibus campis imponeret, incedunt maestos locos uisuque ac memoria deformis. primo[2] Vari castra lato ambitu et dimensis principiis trium legionum manus ostentabant; dein semiruto uallo, humili

2

This essay was begun at Vandœuvres, Geneva: I am most grateful to the Fondation Hardt for the opportunity of working in that *locus amoenus*. I must express my gratitude also to Ian DuQuesnay, Frank Goodyear and David West, to whose comments and criticisms the present version of this essay owes a great deal.

[1] *Gai.* 3. 2 '*caesorum clade Variana* ueteres ac dispersas reliquias uno tumulo *humaturus* [sc. Germanicus], *colligere* sua manu et comportare primus adgressus est'. In fact, the episode is briefly mentioned also by Dio, as excerpted by Xiphilinus (57. 18. 1 'Germanicus . . . collected and buried the bones of *those who had fallen with Varus*'); but in view of the great similarity of wording, I believe that Dio is here (as elsewhere) deriving his information from Suetonius.

[2] Scholars have rightly seen that Tacitus is aiming at a cinematographical view of the site, moving his eye from Varus' camp to the rampart, then to the middle of the plain, and finally to the adjacent woods (see Koestermann (1963), 211). I thus prefer Koehler's *primo* as the first signpost in the sequence 'dein . . . medio campi . . . *adi*acebant . . . lucis propinquis' rather than *prima*, the reading of the MS.

fossa accisae iam reliquiae consedisse intellegebantur. medio campi
albentia ossa, ut fugerant, ut restiterant, disiecta uel aggerata. adiacebant   3
fragmina telorum equorumque artus, simul truncis arborum antefixa
ora. lucis propinquis barbarae arae, apud quas tribunos ac primorum
ordinum centuriones mactauerant. et cladis eius superstites, pugnam aut   4
uincula elapsi, referebant hic cecidisse legatos, illic raptas aquilas; primum ubi uulnus Varo adactum, ubi infelici dextera et suo ictu mortem
inuenerit; quo tribunali contionatus Arminius, quot patibula captiuis,
quae scrobes, utque signis et aquilis per superbiam inluserit. ||

igitur Romanus qui aderat exercitus sextum post cladis annum trium·   62
legionum ossa, nullo noscente alienas reliquias an suorum humo tegeret,
omnes ut coniunctos, ut consanguineos aucta in hostem ira maesti simul
et infensi condebant. primum exstruendo tumulo caespitem Caesar
posuit, gratissimo munere in defunctos et praesentibus doloris socius.
quod Tiberio haud probatum, seu cuncta Germanici in deterius tra-   2
henti, siue exercitum imagine caesorum insepultorumque tardatum ad
proelia et formidolosiorem hostium credebat; neque imperatorem
auguratu et uetustissimis caerimoniis praeditum adtrectare feralia
debuisse.

Germanicus was therefore overwhelmed by a desire to pay his last
respects to the soldiers and their commander; and the army there present
was moved to pity for their relatives and friends, for the fortunes of war
and the fate of men. Caecina had been sent ahead to reconnoitre the
unknown forests, to bridge the flooded marshes and to shore up any
ground likely to prove treacherous. Then they entered the melancholy
site, which was gruesome to set eyes upon and in the memories which it
evoked. First there was Varus' camp, a wide area with its headquarters   2
marked out, testifying to the strength of the three legions; next there
was the rampart, half-destroyed, and the low ditch where the mortally
wounded had evidently huddled together. In the middle of a plain there
were whitening bones, lying scattered where soldiers had fled, and piled
up where they had made their last stand. Broken pieces of weapons lay   3
nearby, and horses' limbs, and skulls fixed to the trunks of trees. In the
surrounding woods there were altars at which the barbarians had
engaged in the ritual slaughter of tribunes and first-rank centurions.
And survivors of the disaster, who had escaped from the battle or from   4
captivity, recalled where the legates had fallen and where the standards
had been captured, where Varus had received his first wound and where
he had died by his own doomed hand. They pointed to the mound
where Arminius had held his victory rally and arrogantly mocked the
military standards, to the number of gibbets for the prisoners of war, and
to the pits.

And so the Roman army there present, six years after the disaster,   62 started to bury the bones of the three legions: since no one knew whether they were covering over the remains of relatives or || not, they treated everyone as if they were kith and kin, while their anger against the enemy mounted with their grief. It was Germanicus who, in sympathy with his men and as a welcome gesture towards the dead, laid the first turf for the burial mound. But Tiberius did not approve—either   2 because he criticized everything Germanicus did, or because he believed that the sight of the unburied dead had deterred the army from fighting and increased their fear of the enemy; besides, a general empowered as an augur to celebrate the sacred rites ought not in his opinion to have come into contact with relics of the dead.

It will be seen that Tacitus has taken great care over the structure of this account. The first sentence introduces two themes: (*a*) Germanicus' desire to bury the dead soldiers ('igitur cupido Caesarem inuadit . . . militibus ducique'), (*b*) the reaction of the present army ('permoto ad miserationem omni *qui aderat exercitu* ob propinquos . . . et sortem hominum'). There then follows a long central 'panel' (*c*) where Tacitus describes the scene of devastation which had brought about (*a*) and (*b*): 'praemisso Caecina . . . per superbiam inluserit'. Finally Tacitus returns to the two themes with which he began, although in reverse order: (*b*) 'igitur Romanus *qui aderat exercitus* . . . infensi condebant', (*a*) 'primum exstruendo tumulo caespitem Caesar posuit . . . feralia debuisse'. The whole episode is thus an example of ring-composition (*abcba*),[3] which on one occasion is made explicit by the repetition of a key phrase (italicized, just above).[4] While it is clear that Tacitus regarded (*a*) as historically the most important element in the episode, as we shall see below (pp. 75–6), there can be no doubt that his literary imagination was roused more by the remainder of the episode. My evidence for this last statement may be gathered by way of an enquiry into Tacitus' source for the event.

From where did Tacitus derive the information for his account? After all, the detailed nature of his description is remarkable,

---

[3] Ring-composition in Tacitus has in general not been investigated, but for one elaborate example in *Annals* 4 see Woodman (1972), 150–5 [below, Ch. 8, Sect. II]. For a rather different view of the structure of the present passage see Soubiran (1964), 62.

[4] *qui aderat exercitus* is a key phrase because it illustrates 'the contrast of the living with the dead, the victorious with the slaughtered army, (which) is evidently prominent in the mind of the writer' (Furneaux).

considering that the event took place a full century before he came to describe it. Since it is known that *Bella Germaniae* had been written by the earlier historians Aufidius Bassus and the elder Pliny, scholars have suggested one or other of these works (both of which have conveniently failed to survive) as a possible source.[5] But I would rather point to a quite different possibility. In AD 69 Vitellius had visited the site of the first Battle of Cremona; and Tacitus, a few years before he came to describe Germanicus' visit to the Teutoburg Forest in the *Annals*, had already described this more recent visit of Vitellius in *Histories* 2. 70: ||

Inde *Vitellius* Cremonam flexit et spectato munere Caecinae insistere Bedriacensibus campis ac uestigia recentis uictoriae lustrare oculis *concupiuit*. foedum atque atrox spectaculum: intra quadragensimum pugnae diem lacera corpora, *trunci artus*, putres uirorum *equorumque* formae, infecta tabo humus, protritis arboribus ac frugibus dira uastitas. nec   2 minus inhumana facies uiae, quam Cremonenses lauru rosaque constrauerant, *exstructis altaribus caesisque uictimis* regium in morem; quae laeta in praesens mox perniciem ipsis fecere. *aderant* Valens et Caecina   3 *monstrabantque* pugnae *locos*: *hinc* inrupisse legionum agmen, *hinc* equites coortos, *inde* circumfusas auxiliorum manus; iam tribuni praefectique, sua quisque facta extollentes, falsa uera aut maiora uero miscebant. uolgus quoque militum clamore et gaudio deflectere uia, spatia certaminum recognoscere, *aggerem* armorum, *strues corporum* intueri mirari; *et erant quos uaria sors rerum lacrimaeque et misericordia subiret*. at non Vitellius   4 flexit oculos nec tot milia insepultorum ciuium exhorruit: laetus ultro et tam propinquae sortis ignarus instaurabat sacrum dis loci.

From there Vitellius deviated to Cremona, and having seen Caecina's gladiatorial exhibition, he desired to set foot on the plain at Bedriacum and see with his own eyes the traces of the recent victory. It was a macabre and horrifying sight: less than forty days had elapsed since the battle, and there were mutilated corpses, trunks, limbs, and the shapes of decomposed men and horses; the ground was stained with gore, and the flattened trees and crops presented a scene of terrible devastation. Equally barbaric was the view of the road, where the people of Cre-   2 mona had strewn laurel and roses, and built altars for the victims whom they slaughtered: such tyrannical behaviour, however satisfying at the time, was soon to be the cause of their own destruction. Valens and   3 Caecina were present, and they pointed out the various important areas

---

[5] Pliny's work is in fact mentioned by name at *A.* 1. 69. 2.

of the battle-site: where the legionary column had burst out, where the horsemen had massed, and where the auxiliaries had completed their encirclement. Already the tribunes and prefects were each boasting of their own achievements, adding fabrications and exaggerating the truth; and the ordinary soldiers too, shouting happily as they left the road, retraced the battlefield and proudly examined the || pile of weapons and heaps of corpses. Some were affected by the variability of fate, by tears and by pity; but not Vitellius, who gazed impassively on the many thousands of unburied citizens. Unable to restrain his delight, and unaware of the fate that was so soon to befall him, he sacrificed to the gods of the place.

As may be seen from the italicized words and phrases, there are numerous and noteworthy similarities between this passage and that from *Annals* 1 already quoted. How are they to be explained?[6] A *first* suggestion might be that the similarities are inevitable, given the comparable subject-matter of each passage. One would expect to find corpses in any description of a battlefield, and the reflections on fate and pity are hardly unusual in such a context. Again, Tacitus' phrase *ut fugerant, ut restiterant, disiecta uel aggerata* (*ossa*) in *Annals* is paralleled quite closely by a passage of Livy in which Hannibal revisits the site of the Battle of Cannae (22. 51. 6 'iacebant tot Romanorum milia, pedites *passim* equitesque *ut quem cuique fors aut pugna iunxerat* aut *fuga*');[7] and both *hic . . . illic . . . ubi* etc. in *Annals* and *hinc . . . hinc . . . inde* in *Histories* are paralleled by a passage of Virgil in which the Trojans wander over the deserted battlefield of the Troad (*Aeneid* 2. 29–30 '*hic* Dolopum manus, *hic* saeuus tendebat Achilles; | classibus *hic* locus, *hic* acie certare solebant'). Alternatively, one might use these same correspondences with Livy and Virgil to put forward a *second* suggestion: perhaps there existed a literary prototype (for example, in a now lost passage of Ennius) which has exerted a common influence over Livy and Virgil on the one hand and the two Tacitean passages on the other?

Yet I do not think that either of these suggestions constitutes

---

[6] Since the two passages concern events which are more than fifty years apart and which take place in different areas of the Roman world, I do not think the similarities are to be explained by postulating a common historical source (except in the sense mentioned below, n. 26).

[7] Cf. also *A*. 6. 19. 2 'iacuit immensa strages . . . dispersi aut aggerati', but the context is different.

the true explanation of the similarity between the two passages of Tacitus. The most remarkable parallel between the two passages is the way in which, half-way through each, Tacitus introduces the men who had survived their respective disasters and who conveniently happened to be on hand to point out various important areas. This detail seems to me so unusual, and unparalleled elsewhere,[8] that it places the many other correspondences in a different light. In view of this detail I would contend that Tacitus in *Annals* 1. 61–2 has imitated his earlier account in the *Histories*,[9] and that this contention is corroborated both by the number and variety of the other correspondences and also by the fact that he repeats the process in *Annals* 1. 64–5, a few chapters later. I shall return to this last point in the next section (pp. 77–80); but || first I should like to note how Tacitus in the present case has varied his earlier account in *Histories* 2. 70.

When in the ancient world a writer imitated another writer, he would take care to weld the imitated material into its new context, to vary it, and if possible, to improve upon it. That this practice also held good for self-imitation is shown by Tacitus here. In *Histories* Tacitus refers to the vicissitudes of fortune at the end of his description ('et erant quos uaria sors rerum . . . '), whereas in *Annals* the corresponding sentiment ('permoto ad miserationem . . . ob casus bellorum et sortem hominum') is placed at the beginning of the episode: in *H.* the statement is thus emphatically and climactically placed because Tacitus wishes to draw from the episode the moral that Vitellius will himself be soon overtaken by the vagaries of fate ('laetus ultro et tam propinquae sortis ignarus');[10] whereas in *A.* he wishes nothing to conflict in

---

[8] It does not occur in Lucan, 9. 789 ff. (the aftermath of Pharsalus), a reference which I owe to Prof. P. G. Walsh and which is the only comparable passage that I know. The very paucity of such 'visits to battle-fields' in Latin literature is another reason why I do not believe there can have been a common literary prototype from which Livy, Virgil, Lucan, and Tacitus all derive: if such a prototype had existed, it would surely have been used more frequently than this.

[9] Self-imitation is the term used also by C. Brakman, 'Tacitea', *Mnem.* 53 (1925), 195, whose brief comparison of the two passages (which I had not seen until my essay was completed) goes no further than noting some of the parallels: he was in no way concerned to place the passages in any wider context. The only comment of Koestermann is 'vgl. das Gegenstück Hist. II 70', while Heubner makes no comparison at all between the two passages.

[10] The irony has been prepared for by *recentis uictoriae* at the beginning and *quae laeta in praesens* in the middle of the episode.

importance or significance with the moral of chapters 61–2 as a whole, namely Tiberius' characteristically critical reaction to Germanicus' act of piety. Again, in *H.* Tacitus continually stresses the appearance presented by the battlefield of Cremona (cf. *lustrare oculis, spectaculum, monstrabant, non . . . flexit oculos*),[11] whereas in *A.* he dispenses with such mediating vocabulary and tells his story in a more immediate and vivid manner (cf. only *uisu . . . deformis*). On another occasion, however, the same word is used both times but its meaning has changed: *trunci* in *H.* is either an adjective = 'mutilated' (agreeing with *artus*, 'limbs') or a noun = 'trunks of bodies', whereas in *A.* it means 'trunks of trees'.

Instead of the prosaic *Vitellius . . . concupiuit* in the *Histories* we now have *cupido Caesarem inuadit* in the *Annals*, an echo of Sallust's phrase *potiundi Marium maxuma cupido inuaserat* (*J.* 89. 6).[12] Instead of *exstructis altaribus* we now have *barărae ārae*, which Soubiran well describes as 'cacophanie évidente . . . elle suggère concrètement la barbarie des rites d'immolation et la répulsion du narrateur romain'.[13] And while there is one clear echo of Virgil in *Histories* (*infecta tabo humus* ~ *Georgics* 3. 481 *infecit pabula tabo*), there are several in *Annals*: *medio campi albentia ossa* ~ *Aeneid* 12. 36 *campique ingentes ossibus albent*;[14] *truncis arborum antefixa ora* ~ *Aeneid* 8. 196–7 *foribusque adfixa superbis | ora*;[15] and *uulnus . . . adactum* ~ *Aeneid* 10. 850.[16]

It is interesting to note that none of these three Virgilian reminiscences belongs to the same category of imitation. The first is an example of what I shall later call 'substantive imitation' (for a definition see below, p. 81): it is highly unlikely that Tacitus had any historical evidence for whitening bones in the middle of

---

[11] This point emerges from the analysis of the episode by U. Rademacher, *Die Bildkunst des Tacitus* (1975), 136–9: it provides additional support for E. Wolff's emendation *facies uiae* (for the MSS' *pars uiae*) in sect. 2.

[12] I am not of course suggesting that *H.* 2. 70 is devoid of Sallustian phraseology, which is demonstrably not the case (see Heubner ad loc.).

[13] Soubiran (1964), 60. For other examples of word-play (paronomasia) on adjacent words see Austin on *Aeneid* 2. 27; for other types of word-play involving changes of vowel-quantity, as here, see Woodman on Vell. 108. 2. [See also below, Ch. 12, Section I.]

[14] Baxter (1972), 255 states that commentators have missed this parallel; but it is in F. Kuntz, *Die Sprache des Tacitus* (1962), 137.

[15] *ora* = 'skulls' seems not to be found before Tacitus except here in Virgil and in a line of Ovid which is also an echo of Virgil (*Heroides* 9. 89 'adfixa penatibus ora').

[16] Baxter (1972), 256 claims to be the first to spot this parallel; but it is in Koestermann ad loc. and Soubiran (1964), 62.

the plain; more probably || he has added an apparently factual detail which in reality is simply borrowed from Virgil. The second is a 'significant imitation': since the doorposts on which the skulls hang belong to Cacus, whom Virgil describes as *semihomo* (8. 194), this monster thus serves as a prototype for the semi-human barbarians who fastened Roman skulls to tree-trunks.[17] The third is merely a 'verbal echo', but even from this lowest form of imitation conclusions can be drawn: the very fact that Tacitus' phraseology may be traced back to Rome's most illustrious epic poet indicates the elevated style of the passage—an observation which remains true whether or not the echo was intentional and whether or not Tacitus' readers recognized it.

ANNALS I. 64–5

After Germanicus' visit to the site of the Varian disaster, his legate Caecina is compelled by harrying natives to pitch an uncomfortable camp amidst constant defensive fighting. On this occasion our knowledge of the incident derives from Tacitus alone (*A.* 1. 64. 1–3, 65. 1):

Barbari, perfringere stationes seque inferre munitoribus nisi, lacessunt circumgrediuntur occursant: miscetur operantium bellantiumque clamor. et cuncta pariter Romanis aduersa: locus uligine profunda, idem   2 ad gradum instabilis, procedentibus lubricus; corpora grauia loricis; neque librare pila inter undas poterant. contra Cheruscis sueta apud paludes proelia, procera membra, hastae ingentes ad uulnera facienda quamuis procul. nox demum inclinantis iam legiones aduersae pugnae   3 exemit. Germani ob prospera indefessi . . .

  nox per diuersa inquies, cum barbari festis epulis, laeto cantu aut truci   65 sonore subiecta uallium ac resultantis saltus complerent, apud Romanos inualidi ignes interruptae uoces, atque ipsi passim adiacerent uallo, oberrarent tentoriis, insomnes magis quam peruigiles.

In their efforts to break through the guardposts and attack the workers, the barbarians engaged in harassment, encircling manoeuvres and charges. The shouts of the workers and fighters were confused, and   2 everything was equally unfavourable to the Romans: the place, with its deep mud, provided unreliable footholds and was too slippery to allow any progress; their bodies || were weighed down by armour, and in the waves they were unable to throw their javelins. On the other hand, the

---

[17] For Germans as hardly human see Woodman on Vell. 117. 3.

Cherusci were long accustomed to fighting in marshland: they had long limbs, and their huge spears were effective at long-range wounding. Nightfall finally rescued the now sagging legions from their losing 3 battle; but the Germans, tireless in success . . .

It was a disturbed night, though for different reasons. The barbarians 65 at their celebration feasts filled the valleys and echoing forests with their victory or war songs. On the Roman side the fires were fitful, and voices hesitant: they lay against the rampart, or wandered among the tents, unable either to sleep or keep watch.

Again we must ask how Tacitus could possibly have acquired so many details of a routine frontier engagement which had taken place a century before he came to describe it. And again I would point to another such battle between Romans and Germans which took place in AD 70 and which Tacitus had already described in his *Histories* (5. 14. 2–15. 2):

Ea loci forma, incertis uadis subdola et *nobis aduersa*: quippe miles Romanus *armis grauis* et nandi pauidus, Germanos *fluminibus suetos* leuitas armorum et *proceritas corporum* attollit. igitur *lacessentibus* Batauis 15 ferocissimo cuique nostrorum coeptum certamen; deinde orta trepidatio, cum *praealtis paludibus* arma equi haurirentur. Germani notis uadibus persultabant, omissa plerumque fronte latera ac terga *circumuenientes*. neque ut in pedestri acie comminus certabatur, sed tamquam nauali pugna uagi *inter undas* aut, si quid *stabile* occurrebat, totis illuc corporibus *nitentes* . . . *eius proeli euentus utrumque ducem diuersis animi motibus* ad 2 maturandum summae rei discrimen erexit: Ciuilis instare fortunae, Cerialis abolere ignominiam; *Germani prosperis feroces*, Romanos pudor excitauerat. *nox apud barbaros cantu aut clamore, nostris* per iram et minas acta.

Such was the appearance of the place, treacherous with hidden swamps and unfavourable to us: for the Roman soldiers were weighed down by weapons and terrified of swimming, whereas the Germans, long accustomed to the rivers, took advantage of their light armour and tall bodies. While the Batavi therefore engaged in harassment, our most intrepid 15 men all began to fight; but || panic struck when weapons and horses started to be swallowed up in the unusually deep marshes. But the Germans fairly ran through their native swamps, and disregarding the opposing front-line they encircled the flanks and rear. Contrary to what you would expect in an infantry battle, there was no close fighting, but the men wandered in the waves as if during a naval encounter; or else, if a reliable patch of ground showed up, they strove towards it with all their might . . . The result of that particular battle encouraged each 2 commander to bring the whole operation to a decision, although for different reasons: Civilis wished to press home his good fortune, Cerialis to redeem his disgrace. Thus the Germans were fierce on account of their success, while the Romans were spurred on by shame: night on the barbarian side was spent in singing or shouting, on ours in anger and threats.

As on the previous occasion, some of these correspondences are not unexpected in such a context: harassing and encircling (*lacessunt* and *circumgrediuntur* in *Annals* ~ *lacessentibus* and *circumuenientes* in *Histories*) take place in most battles, while the size of barbarians and the uncongeniality of their haunts (*procera membra* ~ *proceritas corporum*; *uligine profunda* ~ *praealtis paludibus*) were always remarked upon by Romans and belong to the conventions of ethnographical writing.[18] But there are also more specific and telling details (*Germani ob prospera indefessi* ~ *Germani prosperis feroces*); and most remarkable of all are the strikingly close accounts of the night scenes ('diuersis animi motibus . . . nox apud barbaros cantu aut clamore, nostris ~ nox per diuersa . . . barbari . . . laeto cantu aut truci sonore . . . apud Romanos')[19] and the coincidence in each passage of the phrase *inter undas*, a highly idiosyncratic description of fighting in swamps.[20]

These last two details seem to me to belong to the same category as the survivors in the previous pair of passages (see above, p. 75), and they persuade me that in *Annals* 1. 64–5 Tacitus is imitating his own earlier description in *Histories* 5. 14–15. On this occasion, however, Tacitus does not seem to have been much concerned to vary his earlier account. *nisi* in *Annals* is used of the successful efforts of the Germans, whereas *nitentes* in *Histories* is used of the desperate efforts of the Romans; and whereas in *H.*

[18] For such conventions in general see Syme (1958), 126 with refs. in n. 2; for size in particular see Woodman on Vell. 106. 1.

[19] The similarity of the night scenes was noted by Wolff (1888) on *Histories* 5. 15. 1.

[20] This striking correspondence was not noted by E. Norden, *Die germanische Urgeschichte in Tacitus' Germania* (1923), 214 n. 1, when he pointed to the general similarity of the two passages. But he was arguing a different case, namely that both passages derive from a common source (the *Bella Germaniae* of the elder Pliny). In fact, the phrase *inter undas* at *A.* 1. 64. 2 has seemed so strange to some scholars that they have emended it (*inter umida* Schütz: *inter uda* Polster), while K. Wellesley (*JRS* 54 (1964), 256) simply declares it to be 'impossible'. (I owe this textual information to Prof. Goodyear.)

the phrase *apud barbaros* is used merely for the sake of variation with *nostris*, in *A*. the phrase *apud Romanos* is used to show that 'the Romans are passive and helpless in contrast to the active and trimphant Germans' (cf. *Germani . . . complerent*).[21] ||

SUBSTANTIVE IMITATION

If this general hypothesis for *Annals* 1. 61–2 and 64–5 is accepted, it is natural to enquire to what extent, if at all, Tacitus' accounts in these chapters are true.[22] Did Germanicus visit the Teutoburg Forest at all, for example, or has Tacitus simply invented the whole episode on the basis of *Histories* 2. 70? It has already been noted that we also have Suetonius' statement attesting Germanicus' visit (above, p. 70), but this corroborates *Annals* 1. 61–2 only if it can be demonstrated that Suetonius has not derived his information from Tacitus. Unfortunately, Suetonius' relationship to Tacitus is in general obscure;[23] but some clarification is perhaps possible in the present case. Most scholars would agree that Tiberius' criticism of Germanicus' burying the soldiers, which Tacitus reports at 1. 62. 2, derives from the *acta senatus*;[24] and we should note that it is the act of burial, without any hint of criticism, which Suetonius singles out in his brief reference. It thus seems likely that both Suetonius (who as a top civil servant had access to the imperial archives) and Tacitus are independently indebted to the official records on this matter, in which case we may be fairly certain, at the very least, that Germanicus' visit actually did take place. For Caecina's battle with the Germans at 1. 64–5, on the other hand, we have no other evidence apart

[21] Miller (1959), 189. It is an interesting question why Tacitus varied *H*. 2. 70 when he repeated it as *A*. 1. 61 but did not do the same here. I suspect that in the former case his imagination responded to the challenge of describing a scene which, as we have noted (above, n. 8), was relatively novel, whereas in the present case such a stimulus was absent (battle-scenes were commonplace: see below, n. 39).

[22] At this point it is interesting to recall that Bacha (1906) suggested that numerous parts of the *Annals* could be seen as imitations of other parts of the same work and could thus be impugned as unhistorical. It should be clear from my discussion here that Bacha's thesis is by no means as silly as has generally been supposed, and that, if his book is to be dismissed, it is rather because of the unconvincing nature of his examples. (He mentions neither of the cases discussed here.)   [23] See Goodyear (1972), 135–6.

[24] See Kroll (1924), 382. For three other cases where Tacitus echoes Tiberius' own official words see Woodman on Vell. 129. 3; cf. also N. P. Miller, 'Tiberius Speaks', *AJP* 89 (1968), 1–19.

from Tacitus; but since he tells us a few chapters later that 'decreta eo anno [AD 15] triumphalia insignia A. Caecinae' (I. 72. I), we may assume that Caecina would hardly have received this honour from Tiberius if his activities in Germany had not warranted it.

I would therefore conclude that the plain fact of Germanicus' visit or of Caecina's battle is undeniable, but that the details of Tacitus' elaborate descriptions of each event are entirely derived from the passages of the *Histories* which I have quoted.[25] The passages from the *Annals* are thus examples of 'substantive imitation', by which I mean the technique of giving substance to a poorly documented incident by the imitating of one which is much better documented.[26] On this view, the question of Tacitus' sources for *Annals* I. 61–2 and 64–5, which I raised earlier (p. 72), must now be allowed to lapse: for the bulk of the narrative in these chapters Tacitus needed no source (in the generally accepted sense of that term) at all—whether Aufidius, Pliny or anyone else.

Tacitus' technique, as I have described it, may sound scandalous to the majority of his modern readers, who evidently still regard him as a faithful historian;[27] but that is because they fail to take account of the way in which ancient writers wrote history. In the first place, ancient historians were regularly far more concerned with probability than || reality,[28] and very often the relative antiquity and geographical distance of an event are guides as to how an ancient historian might have treated it: century-old episodes in the heart of Germany, such as Tacitus relates in *Annals* I. 61–5, were presumably more susceptible of falsification or elaboration than contemporary events close to home (though even these were

[25] This interpretation of Tacitus' *narrative* technique closely resembles Thucydides' account of his own *speech* technique at I. 22. I (as expounded by de Ste Croix (1972), 7–11), namely that there is a core of truth in every Thucydidean speech (ἡ ξυμπᾶσα γνώμη) but that the bulk of each speech is Thucydides' own invention (τὰ δέοντα). The main difficulty for modern scholars, as de Ste Croix remarks (p. 11), is that 'we can seldom be sure that we know how extensive the ξυμπᾶσα γνώμη is, and therefore we may often not be able to decide how much of a speech . . . is Thucydides' own formulation'. The same applies, *mutatis mutandis*, to Tacitus' narrative.

[26] Syme (1958), 176–7 mentions that among the sources available to Tacitus when he composed the *Histories* there were eye-witnesses and monographs on individual battles. If Tacitus used such a source at *H.* 2. 70, then there is a sense in which both that passage and *A.* 1. 61 derive from a 'common historical source' (see above, n. 6).

[27] The details of Tacitus' description of Germanicus' visit are still being repeated, without qualification, in modern textbooks of ancient history.

[28] See Wiseman (1979), ch. 3.

by no means immune). In the second place, ancient historians resorted to 'substantive imitation' far more regularly than is sometimes supposed. A few examples will illustrate this.[29]

Elsewhere in Book 1 of the *Annals* there is substantive imitation by Tacitus of Livy 1. 41 at chapters 5–6,[30] of Livy 3. 13 at chapter 23. 2, and of Livy 8. 32. 12–13 at chapter 35. 5.[31] Livy himself is recognized to have imitated Homer, Herodotus, and Thucydides.[32] Thucydides was in fact a favourite source for imitative historians. The second-century AD literary critic Lucian, in his book *How to Write History* (15), tells us of a contemporary historian who was so captivated by Thucydides that he inserted into his own history of the Parthian Wars a fictitious plague modelled entirely on the Athenian plague described so vividly by his eminent predecessor. 'He lifted it completely from Thucydides, except for the Pelasgicon and the Long Walls where those who had caught Thucydides' plague had settled; but as for the rest, it *began in Ethiopia* (as in Thucydides), then *descended into Egypt*.' We may at first sight find this hard to believe, but Procopius' description of the plague which is said to have hit Byzantium in AD 540 manifests exactly the same characteristics (2. 22–3).

I doubt whether it ever occurred to ancient historians to question their use of this technique, but if a philosopher of history

---

[29] I restrict my examples to 'substantive imitation', but we should remember how commonly ancient historians resorted to other types of imitation. One such type is mentioned above (p. 77), but imitation could be used to signal the tradition to which a historian belonged (so Tacitus begins his *Annals* with the same two words as Sallust had begun the historical section (6. 1) of his *Catiline*), or it could be a symptom of literary hero-worship (as in the case of Arruntius and his Sallustomania, cf. Sen. *Ep.* 114. 17–19), or it was a method whereby an historian demonstrated his superiority to a predecessor (*aemulatio*, cf. Liv. *praef.* 2 'scribendi arte rudem uetustatem superaturos'; Tac. *Agr.* 10. 1 'Britanniae situm populosque multis scriptoribus memoratos non [!] in comparationem curae ingeniiue referam'). Besides, all Roman historians will have been taught to imitate passages from the historical classics during their schooldays (cf. e.g. Quintilian, 10. 1. 31–4, 73–5). Since in the ancient world the writing of history was regarded as a literary pursuit little different from the writing of poetry, we should not be surprised that ancient historians resorted to the same literary techniques (such as *imitatio*) as poets.

[30] See Charlesworth (1927).

[31] See Goodyear (1972), 217–18 and 263 respectively.

[32] See Wiseman (1979), ch. 2. On other occasions Livy repeats under a slightly different guise a story he has already told elsewhere: thus Manlius' encounter with a giant Gaul at 7. 9. 6–10. 14 recurs at 7. 26. 1–9 where Corvinus meets another giant Gaul; and the rape of Lucretia at 1. 57–9 recurs, with judicious and appropriate variation, at 3. 44–9 (where the lady is called Verginia), 4. 9. 4 (the Maid of Ardea) and 38. 24. 3 ff. (the wife of one Ortiagon). On these rapes see Ogilvie (1965), 219–20, 477–8.

had pressed them to defend it, I suspect their answer would have been along the following lines. Thucydides believed that historical events will, at some point in the future and in more or less the same ways, recur, and that there are cycles of history.[33] This belief was taken up by numerous ancient writers,[34] among whom Tacitus himself is prominent (*A*. 3. 55. 5 'nisi forte rebus cunctis inest quidam uelut orbis, ut, quemadmodum temporum uices, ita morum uertantur'), and can easily be applied to the two cases we have been discussing. For example, given that Vitellius in AD 69 was visiting a battle-site and that such a visit was doubtless not much different from Germanicus' to the Teutoburg Forest in AD 15, Tacitus would not, I believe, have regarded it as in any way unusual that he should describe the latter in terms of the former: this was an illustration of history repeating itself, with the qualification that Vitellius had been victorious whereas Germanicus' predecessor Varus had not. ||

DELECTATIO LECTORIS

We can only speculate why Tacitus in *Annals* 1. 61–2 and 64–5 chose to spend so much time on episodes for which, on the present hypothesis, he had little or no source material. Sometimes, it is true, a writer will produce correspondences from which he wishes some particular significance to emerge: we have already noticed an occasion where Tacitus imitates *Aeneid* 8 for precisely this reason (above, p. 77), and some other examples of this phenomenon might be helpful. It has been shown that Tacitus has described Livia's role in the accession of Tiberius at *Annals* 1. 5–6 in very similar terms to his account of Agrippina's role in the accession of Nero at *Annals* 12. 66–13. 1:[35] by means of close linguistic correspondences Tacitus wishes 'to invest the accession of Tiberius with the same air of questionable legitimacy that attended Nero's accession and to stress how Tiberius, in just the same way as Nero, owed his position to the machinations of the emperor's widow'.[36] Again, when Tacitus begins the fourth book of the *Annals* with a character sketch of Sejanus which is

---

[33] Thucydides, 1. 22. 4, 2. 48. 3, 3. 82. 2. For the correct interpretation of these passages see de Ste Croix (1972), 29–33.

[34] e.g. Plato, *Laws* 688c–d; Diod. 1. 1. 3; Plut. *Sertorius* 1.

[35] See Charlesworth (1927) and Martin (1955).   [36] Martin (1955), 124.

closely modelled on Sallust's description of Catiline, he wishes his readers to see in Sejanus a reincarnation of the same criminal qualities which Catiline had displayed. I find it very hard to believe, however, that this happens in either of our two present cases: to see Germanicus as a forerunner of Vitellius, for example, would be absurd; and I do not see any evidence that Tacitus has presented Germanicus' behaviour as an ideal from which Vitellius has flagrantly departed.[37]

I think the reasons for Tacitus' 'substantive self-imitation' in *Annals* 1. 61–2 and 64–5 are more straightforward and lie elsewhere—in entertainment. However foreign it may be to us today, historians in the ancient world were expected to provide their readers with entertainment, *delectatio lectoris*,[38] a responsibility of which Tacitus expresses himself only too well aware (cf. *A*. 4. 32. 1, 33. 2–3). Battle-scenes such as that at *Histories* 5. 14–15 were a particularly common method of supplying this *delectatio*,[39] as Tacitus knew full well (*A*. 4. 33. 3 'uarietates proeliorum . . . retinent ac redintegrant legentium animos', cf. *H*. 1. 2. 1 'opus adgredior . . . atrox proeliis'); and if by some remote chance a writer of his calibre failed to realize the potential effect of an episode like *Histories* 2. 70, there was always his friend the younger Pliny to supply him with 'feedback' (see *Ep*. 7. 33). Naturally this suggestion cannot be proved; but I think it is significant that, as is generally recognized,[40] Tacitus' account of

---

[37] I make this latter point because S. Borzsák (*RE* Suppl. xi. 486–7) has suggested that Germanicus is an idealized counterpart to the Domitian-like Vitellius ('Durch einen Vergleich der beiden Inspektionen wird der Unterschied zwischen einem entmenschten Usurpator und einem wirklichen römischen imperator, der zusammen mit seinem Heere die *virtus, humanitas, pietas, disciplina* verkörpert, gehörig veranschaulicht'). While there is of course a general contrast between the motives and behaviour of the two commanders, Tacitus does not seem to me to have taken any measures that would bring the contrast to the attention of his readers. Besides, Tacitus portrays Germanicus in far more ambiguous terms than Borzsák has allowed (see Goodyear (1972), 239–41). Borzsák's is the longest comparison of *A*. 1. 61–2 with *H*. 2. 70 that I have seen, but he mentions none of the verbal parallels and his discussion came to my attention only after my ideas on *A*. 1. 61–5 as a whole had been formulated.

[38] Cf. Duris fr. 1 Jacoby; Cic. *De Or*. 2. 59 'delectationis causa . . . legere soleo', *Fam*. 5. 12. 4 'multam etiam casus nostri uarietatem . . . suppeditabunt plenam cuiusdam uoluptatis, quae uehementer animos hominum . . . tenere possit. nihil est enim aptius ad delectationem lectoris quam temporum uarietates fortunaeque uicissitudines . . . [5] expletur animus iucundissima uoluptate'; Vitr. 5 *praef*. 1; Plin. *Ep*. 5. 8. 4.

[39] Cf. Cic. *Or*. 66 '(historia) in qua . . . pugna describitur'; Hor. *C*. 2. 1. 17–24; Lucian, *Hist. Conscr*. 45.   [40] See Goodyear (1972), 30–1.

events in Germany in *Annals* 1 is quite out of proportion to their historical importance: he seems to have 'written up' these sections because he enjoyed them || and because he knew from experience that they would entertain his readers.

In 1935 the foreign correspondent of a certain English newspaper, finding himself without much material to report, despatched to England stories which supposedly dealt with the build-up to the Abyssinian War but which were in fact derived from an old colonel's military reminiscences, published several years previously in a book entitled *In the Country of the Blue Nile*. The correspondent's newspaper was delighted with the reception given to these stories by its readers, and accordingly sent him a series of congratulatory telegrams—whereupon a colleague remarked to him: 'Well, now we know, it's entertainment they want!'[41] The colleague had only then come to realize what had been known long ago to Tacitus, to whom the foreign correspondent's technique would have seemed very familiar.

---

[41] For a full account of this amazing and instructive story see Knightley (1975), 176–7 (whose book should be recommended reading for those who wish to understand how ancient historians worked). The reporter who deceived his newspaper and the public on this occasion assumed (quite rightly) that no one could check his stories on account of the distance involved. The same is even more true of ancient historians (see above, p. 81), who lived in a world where communications were so much more difficult.

6

Praecipuum Munus Annalium
The Construction, Convention, and Context of *Annals* 3. 65. 1

I

E. Fraenkel in the preface to his *Horace* reflected that on many occasions, when he thought he had disentangled himself from 'the snares of traditional exegesis', he found that he was 'still interpreting not the words of Horace but the unwarranted opinion of some of his commentators'.[1] Often it is the most familiar passages which are most resistant to such reinterpretation. In 1989 I suggested that one of the most famous passages in Tacitus' *Annals*, his obituary of the emperor Tiberius (6. 51), had been misinterpreted by generations of readers.[2] In the present paper I shall discuss another passage of the *Annals*, which is equally famous and which occurs during the narrative of AD 22 (3. 65. 1):

Exsequi sententias haud institui nisi insignes per honestum aut notabili dedecore, quod praecipuum munus annalium reor, ne uirtutes sileantur utque prauis dictis factisque ex posteritate et infamia metus sit.

This sentence, or at least the latter part of it, has been considered appropriate for use as an epigraph to translated and edited texts of the *Annals* and it is quoted or mentioned by most scholars who have written generally on Tacitus.[3] The almost universal appeal of

---

For their comments on earlier drafts of this paper I am most grateful to R. H. Martin, C. B. R. Pelling, T. P. Wiseman and especially T. J. Luce, whose own article on the same subject helped me to develop some lurking suspicions. It should not be assumed that all of these scholars agree with the thesis of my paper, to which the pre-publication reaction was generally one of disbelief and rejection. References, unless stated otherwise, are to Tacitus' *Annals*.

[1] Fraenkel (1957), p. vii.   [2] Woodman (1989) [Ch. 9 below].
[3] Most recently by Mellor (1993), 2. The translator is A. Murphy (1832), the editor H. Fuchs (1946). For some other examples see Sect. II.

the sentence is explained by the fact that here Tacitus is assumed to be offering his definition of 'history's highest function',[4] || which, if the assumption is correct, is obviously a valuable disclosure from Rome's greatest historian. I wish to suggest, however, that this assumption involves difficulties of construction, convention, and context which have been largely unrecognized or underestimated, and that there is an alternative way of reading the sentence by which these difficulties may be avoided.

II

We shall see in this section that scholars are evidently unanimous in their assumption about the general meaning of Tacitus' sentence but that they do not agree on how it comes to have that meaning—or, putting things another way, they do not agree on the construction of the sentence.[5]

Furneaux comments that *quod*, which he does not define, is 'explained by the following clause'.[6] Nipperdey–Andresen define *quod* as 'Relativpronomen mit nachfolgender Epexegese', words which are repeated exactly by Koestermann.[7] Yet such comments are by no means clear, as is shown by the passage at 4. 4. 3, which is quoted as a parallel in each of these three commentaries:[8]

percensuitque [sc. Tiberius] cursim numerum legionum et quas prouincias tutarentur. quod mihi quoque exsequendum reor, quae tunc Romana copia in armis, qui socii reges, quanto sit angustius imperitatum.

This latter passage is capable of being understood in two different ways.[9] If *quod* is an adverbial accusative ('With regard to which I reckon I too should go through what Roman forces . . . '), the implication is that 3. 65. 1 should be translated as it is by J. Jackson in the Loeb edition:[10] 'It is not my intention to dwell upon any senatorial motions save those either remarkable for their nobility or of memorable turpitude; *in which case* they fall within my

---

[4] This is the translation offered by Church and Brodribb and adopted by Luce (1991), 2904–27, esp. 2907–14.

[5] Commentators such as Lipsius, J. F. and J. Gronovius, Walther, Ruperti, Ritter, Orelli, Pfitzner, and Draeger–Heraeus make no comment at all on the construction, perhaps because it seemed to them self-evident (see further below, n. 30).

[6] Furneaux ad loc. [7] Nipperdey–Andresen ad loc.; Koestermann ad loc.

[8] Gerber–Greef, 1309a, add 6. 7. 3, which seems to me not relevant.

[9] See Martin–Woodman ad loc. [10] ii. 625.

conception of the first duty of history—to ensure that merit shall not lack its record and to hold before the vicious word and deed the terrors of posterity and infamy.' || But this seems less than satisfactory, since Jackson has been obliged to supply the words 'they fall within', which are not in the Latin. If, on the other hand, *quod* at 4. 4. 3 is to be taken with *exsequendum* ('Which I reckon I too should go through, namely what Roman forces . . .'), the construction is facilitated by the fact that *exsequi* is similar in meaning to *percensere* in the preceding sentence. No such similarity obtains between main clause and alleged relative clause at 3. 65. 1, which translators seem reluctant to render along comparable lines. The version of Church and Brodribb, however, will serve to show where the difficulty lies: 'My purpose is not to relate at length every motion, but only such as were conspicuous for excellence or notorious for infamy. This I regard as history's highest function, to let no worthy action be uncommemorated, and to hold out the reprobation of posterity as a terror to evil words and deeds.' Initially the reader is likely to understand 'This' as referring back to the previous sentence; only when we reach 'to let no worthy action . . .' do we realize that 'This' in fact looks forward. Now it would be difficult, I think, to suppose that 'This' performs both these functions simultaneously, and it is almost equally difficult, though perhaps not impossible,[11] to ascribe a similarly double function to *quod*.

It is no doubt for these reasons that other scholars assume, rather more simply, that *quod* at 3. 65. 1 is a causal conjunction ('because') and that it is *munus* which is explained by *ne uirtutes . . . metus sit.*[12] Thus in the Budé edition of P. Wuilleumier:[13] 'Mon dessein n'est pas de rapporter toutes les opinions, mais seulement celles qui se distinguent par leur noblesse ou par un insigne avilissement, parce que la tâche principale de l'histoire me paraît être de préserver les vertus de l'oubli et d'attacher aux paroles et aux actions perverses la crainte de l'infamie dans la posterité.' Or in the translation of Ronald Martin:[14] 'I have made it my aim not to go through in detail every motion, but only those that are signalised by their integrity or a conspicuous shamefulness; for I regard it as the special task of history to see that virtues should not

---

[11] See K–S 2. 320–1.   [12] Cf. Cic. *Fin.* 4. 17, 38; Liv. 1. 43. 3; 37. 56. 7.
[13] p. 193.   [14] Martin (1981), 126. So too e.g. Plass (1988), 39, 56.

be passed by in silence, and that base words and deeds should fear the obloquy of posterity.'

Finally there is a third group of scholars—amongst them H. Hommel, B. Walker and R. Syme—for whom *quod* seems to present no difficulty at all: they simply omit both it and the preceding words from their quotation of the passage.[15] Representative of this group is F. R. D. Goodyear, who writes: 'For ‖ Tacitus, as for Sallust and Livy, history has a moral and exemplary purpose, as he affirms expressly at *Ann.* 3. 65. 1: *praecipuum munus annalium reor, ne uirtutes sileantur utque prauis dictis factisque ex posteritate et infamia metus sit*'.[16] Since these scholars deprive *quod* of any antecedent to which it can relate, we must infer that they too interpret the word as a conjunction rather than a relative pronoun.

On this evidence, therefore, *quod* seems more likely to be the conjunction than a relative pronoun; but the difficulty remains that those who agree on the general meaning of the sentence cannot agree on how the sentence actually works. This difficulty should perhaps prompt us to ask whether that general meaning is itself correct.

III

Hitherto scholars have not questioned the general meaning of Tacitus' sentence because, like Goodyear, they have made the prior assumption that Tacitus' statement is hardly different, if at all, from statements in the prefaces of his great predecessors Livy and Sallust.[17] In 1991, however, T. J. Luce published a detailed discussion of Tacitus' sentence in which he argued (convincingly, to my mind) that this prior assumption is mistaken.[18]

Livy, in a famous passage of his preface (10), says that historiography is particularly wholesome and fruitful because it has an

---

[15] H. Hommel, 'Die Bildkunst des Tacitus', in: *Studien zu Tacitus* (Würzburger Studien zur Altertumswissenschaft, 9, 1936), 139; Walker (1952), 1; Syme (1958), 520. So too e.g. M. L. W. Laistner, *The Greater Roman Historians* (1947), 113; Grant (1970), 279.

[16] (1970), 29, repeated in his commentary: (1972), 27.

[17] See e.g. Furneaux (1896), 28; Avenarius (1956), 25; Herkommer (1968), 130–2 (with 132 n. 2); Grant (1970), 279; Fornara (1983), 118; and, I regret to say, Woodman on Vell. 92. 1. To the references to Livy and Sallust one could add the famous statement of Sempronius Asellio, fr. 2 (= Gell. 5. 18. 9): 'nam neque alacriores ad rem publicam defendundam neque segniores ad rem perperam faciundam annales libri commouere quicquam possunt.'

[18] See above, n. 4.

exemplary function: men are encouraged to virtue and discouraged from vice by simply reading the examples of behaviour which the historian describes in his text:[19]

hoc illud est praecipue in cognitione rerum salubre ac frugiferum, omnis te exempli documenta in inlustri posita monumento intueri: inde tibi tuaeque rei publicae quod imitere capias, inde foedum inceptu foedum exitu quod uites. ||

Sallust takes a similar view of the encouragement to virtue,[20] while elsewhere in the *Annals* Tacitus himself repeats that historiography has an exemplary function (4. 33. 2): 'haec conquiri tradique in rem fuerit, quia pauci prudentia honesta ab deterioribus, utilia ab noxiis discernunt, plures aliorum euentis docentur'. Yet not only is there no hint in this latter passage that the exemplary function of history is its 'highest' function[21] but in the famous passage at 3. 65. 1, as Luce has underlined, the exemplary function of historiography is not in question at all. This last point deserves brief elaboration.

On either interpretation of *quod* at 3. 65. 1 (see Section II above), the *praecipuum munus annalium* comprises the two elements *ne uirtutes sileantur* and *utque prauis dictis factisque ex posteritate et infamia metus sit*. These elements in their turn attribute to historiography two aspects: on the one hand the plain commemoration of moral excellence and, on the other, the capacity to deter readers from crookedness by the thought that one day they too may be exposed to criticism in the pages of some future historian. As Luce has pointed out,[22] both the precise formulation of these two aspects and especially their precise combination here are quite different from the more conventional statements in Livy's preface and elsewhere. Indeed the nearest parallels to Tacitus' sentence as a whole, so far as Luce has been able to discover, are in Diodorus Siculus (1. 1. 5, 15. 1. 1).[23]

Yet there are two difficulties in this conclusion, of which the

---

[19] In general see now J. D. Chaplin, *Livy's Use of Exempla and the Lessons of the Past*, diss. (Princeton University, 1993).

[20] His view of the usefulness of history (*J*. 4. 1 'magno usui est memoria rerum gestarum') has to be inferred from his analogy (4. 5 *nam*) with *maiorum imagines* (4. 6 'memoria rerum gestarum eam flammam egregiis uiris in pectore crescere neque prius sedari quam uirtus eorum famam atque gloriam adaequauerit').

[21] So far from being assertive, the tone of the passage is apologetic throughout: see Martin–Woodman, 169–72.   [22] Luce (1991), 2907–14.   [23] Luce (1991), 2913.

first is that it is based on a different analysis of Tacitus' sentence
from that which Luce himself provides.[24] The second difficulty is
whether, if Luce's conclusion is || correct, it is likely that Rome's
greatest historian would have defined 'history's highest function'
in terms which are perceived by scholars to be emphatic but
which are so unconventional that they cannot be paralleled
except in a relatively minor Greek historian.[25]

IV

The various difficulties so far encountered can be removed if we
rethink the construction of the sentence once again. Let us
assume that *quod* is, after all, a relative pronoun rather than the
conjunction 'because' but that the resulting relative clause is
entirely *retro*spective rather than (as Furneaux, Nipperdey–
Andresen, and Koestermann say) partly prospective. On these
assumptions the meaning of the sentence will be as follows:

It has not been my practice to go through senatorial *sententiae* in detail
except those conspicuous for honour or of notable shame (which I

---

[24] Luce (1991) at the start of his discussion, though he makes no comment on the
troublesome *quod*, detects a 'double ellipse' in Tacitus' sentence (2906–7): 'The passage
. . . states first what history's role should be in respect to good behavior (*ne virtutes
sileantur*) and second what the purpose is in recording instances of bad behavior (*utque
pravis dictis factisque ex posteritate et infamia metus sit*). A curious double ellipsis results. We
must understand that the historian is obliged to record examples of bad behavior as well
as good (= *ne prava dicta factaque sileantur*; cf. *neque tamen silebimus* at Ann. 14. 64. 3), and
we are left to infer what the purpose of recording good behavior might be.' Then, after
discussing the hypothesized ellipse in the *ut*-clause, Luce remarks as follows about the *ne*-
clause: 'We might then infer that the recording of virtuous behavior will have the reverse
effect: i.e. it will serve as a stimulus or reward for good behavior (although Tacitus
nowhere says this).' Luce, in other words, sees Tacitus' sentence as illustrating 'antallage',
in which e.g. two clauses primarily fourfold in expression are set side by side and each of
them is shortened by the ellipse of an idea which is expressed in the other (A. J. Bell,
The Latin Dual and Poetic Diction (1923), 340 ff.). But the difficulty with this, as I mention
in the text, is that Luce, having raised the question of the double ellipse, proceeds to
discuss the clause *ne uirtutes sileantur* as if it were not elliptical at all: i.e. as if it denoted
simply the plain commemoration of moral excellence (see 2907–11). If the *ne*-clause
were to be regarded as elliptical, Tacitus' statement would in fact be closer to those of
Diodorus than Luce allows; but I have chosen to go along with Luce's notion of plain
'commemoration', rather than that of 'stimulus or reward', for reasons which will soon
become clear (below, n. 27).

[25] It should be acknowledged that Diodorus has often been thought to be a highly
derivative author, although this view has recently been challenged by K. S. Sacks, *Diodorus
and the First Century* (1990).

reckon to be a very great responsibility of annals), lest virtues be silenced and so that crooked words and deeds should, in the light of posterity and infamy, attract dread.

According to this interpretation the *quod*-clause is in effect parenthetic and the clauses *ne uirtutes . . . metus sit* become purposive,[26] following on direct || ly from the words *nisi . . . dedecore.*[27] Hence 'history's highest function' is no longer defined in terms of the commemoration of virtues and deterrence from vices. Indeed there is no longer any definition at all of 'history's highest function': for, if *quod* is retrospective, it would be absurd to say that

---

[26] For some other examples where a main clause is separated from a dependent *ne-* or *ut*-clause by a parenthesis see Tac. *A*. 12. 11. 2 'addidit praecepta (etenim aderat Meherdates), ut non . . . cogitaret'; possibly *D*. 17. 6 'colligi potest et Coruinum ab illis et Asinium audiri potuisse (nam Coruinus . . . Asinius . . . durauit), ne diuidatis saeculum et . . .'; Sall. *J*. 15. 5 'ueritus (quod in tali re solet) ne polluta licentia inuidiam accenderet'; Liv. 1. 60. 1 'flexit uiam Brutus (senserat enim aduentum), ne obuiam fieret'; 23. 35. 7 (possibly); 24. 25. 10; 26. 33. 4; 27. 28. 7; 29. 12. 10; 31. 46. 7 'eam classem in stationem ad Zelasium miserunt (Phthiotidis super Demetriadem promunturium est peropportune obiectum), ut, si quid inde mouerent Macedonum naues, in praesidio essent'. For examples of a parenthesis introduced by a relative pronoun see e.g. Tac. *A*. 15. 61. 2 'ubi haec a tribuno relata sunt Poppaea et Tigellino coram (quod erat saeuienti principi intimum consilium), interrogat an . . . ', *H*. 3. 71. 4 'hic ambigitur, ignem tectis oppugnatores iniecerint, an obsessi (quae crebrior fama) nitentes ac progressos depulerint'; Liv. 5. 46. 11; 7. 13. 6; 7. 28. 3; 26. 21. 4 'an quem tradere exercitum successori iussissent (quod nisi manente in prouincia bello non decerneretur) eum quasi debellato triumphare'; 27. 42. 3; 29. 25. 12 'inbelles (quod plerumque in uberi agro euenit) barbari sunt'; 42. 39. 5; Virg. *Aen*. 6. 96–7, 611 'nec partem posuere suis (quae maxima turba est)'; Sen. *Thy*. 176–8 'ignaue, iners, eneruis et (quod maximum | probrum tyranno rebus in summis reor) | inulte'; in general M. von Albrecht, *Die Parenthese in Ovids Metamorphosen und ihre dichterische Funktion* (1964), 76–8. Obviously there is a degree of subjectivity here, since readers will differ in their notions of what constitutes a parenthesis: on the subject in general see J. Lennard, *But I Digress: The Exploitation of Parentheses in English Printed Verse* (1991); also below, n. 50.

It can be argued whether, on my view of 3. 65. 1, the antecedent of *quod* is the whole of the preceding sentence *exsequi sententias . . . notabili dedecore* or merely the words *insignes per honestum aut notabili dedecore* [sc. *exsequi sententias*] or the noun *institutum*, inferred by synesis from *institui* in the main clause (for such *constructio ad sensum* see L–H–S 411); but there is little practical difference between these alternatives, and the sense seems at least as clear as that to be extracted from those scholars who offer neither an antecedent for relative *quod* nor a translation. Moreover, on the traditional interpretations, the singular *munus* is to be defined by the two separate clauses *ne . . . sileantur* and *utque . . . metus sit*, something which Furneaux simply sidesteps by referring to 'the following clause' (singular).

[27] For the idea (but not, admittedly, a clause) of purpose following *nisi* elsewhere cf. 1. 3. 6 'bellum ea tempestate nullum nisi aduersus Germanos supererat, abolendae magis infamiae . . .'. On my view of 3. 65. 1 the notion of 'recording' bad behaviour is explicit in the main clause (*exsequi*) and therefore does not require to be supplied in the *ut*-clause: there is thus no ellipse in the *ut*-clause which invites us to infer an earlier ellipse in the *ne*-clause. The latter therefore refers to the plain 'commemoration' of virtues (above, n. 24).

'going through senatorial *sententiae* only in significant cases of honour or shame' is '*the* highest function of history'. We must assume that Tacitus, using a language which did not distinguish between the definite and indefinite article, intended the latter ('*a* very great . . . ');[28] and, if we further assume that *munus* means 'responsibility' rather than 'function',[29] it becomes clear that Tacitus is saying, first, that he has gone through only those *sententiae* which are conspicuous for honour or of notable shame, and, second, that in so doing he has discharged one of the very great responsibilities of historiography.[30] ||

    Now it was of course a recognized convention of classical historiography to claim that one is dealing with only the most significant material. As is illustrated by G. Avenarius' collection of examples,[31] such claims occur in Greek and Roman historians of every period, they are deployed for a variety of purposes, and there are further examples in the *Annals* at 6. 7. 5, 13. 31. 1 ('res *inlustres annalibus* . . . mandare'), and 14. 64. 3 ('neque tamen *silebimus*, si quod senatus consultum adulatione nouum aut

[28] R. H. Martin has objected to me that at 2. 71. 3 ('non hoc praecipuum amicorum munus est prosequi defunctum ignauo questu', cf. Ulp. *Dig.* 21. 1. 14 'praecipuum munus feminarum est accipere ac tueri conceptum', quoted in *OLD munus* 1a) the same phrase 'must mean "the pre-eminent"'; but I think that the context determines the meaning, not the other way round. Thus at Plin. *Pan.* 85. 6 'praecipuum est principis opus amicos parare' the sense must be 'a principal task', unless we translate 'the principal task <in the context of *amicitia*>' (and of course a rendering such as the latter would suit my interpretation of 3. 65. 1 very well: 'the very great responsibility of annals <in the context of *sententiae*>'). Likewise R. G. Austin on Virg. *Aen.* 6. 611 (quoted in n. 26 above) felt obliged to comment that '*maxima* is "very great", rather than "greatest"'. Other scholars besides Martin (above, p. 88) have translated *praecipuum* at 3. 65. 1 as 'special' *vel sim.*, but in the *Annals* this adjective is used as an equivalent to the hackneyed *maximus* and almost never = 'special' (J. N. Adams, *CQ* 22 (1972), 361, not quoting our passage as one of the few exceptions). On *praecipuus* see further TLL 10. 2. 470. 35 ff.; at Liv. 43. 5. 8 *haec praecipua* [sc. *munera*] the meaning is 'gifts'.

[29] For *munus* see e.g. Cic. *De Or.* 3. 121 'non est paucorum libellorum hoc munus'; Quint. 2. 1. 8 'grammatices munus'; TLL 8. 1663. 34 ff.

[30] I had reached these conclusions about *ne* . . . *ut* and about *praecipuum* before I became aware that many older editors punctuate with either a colon (e.g. Lipsius, Walther) or a semicolon (e.g. Ritter, Orelli) after *dedecore*. Though typographical conventions have naturally changed from century to century, this punctuation may imply, as R. H. Martin has remarked to me, that those editors interpreted *quod* as a connecting relative, understood *praecipuum* as 'a principal' (*vel sim.*), and took *ne* and *ut* as purposive: '. . . of notable shame; and this [sc. the aforesaid] I reckon to be a principal *munus* of annals, lest virtues . . . and so that . . .'. This would certainly be close to my interpretation, which I nevertheless prefer because the verbal links *uirtutes* ~ *insignes per honestum* and *prauis dictis factisque* ~ *notabili dedecore* suggest to me that the purpose clauses depend upon the *institui*-sentence.

[31] See Avenarius (1956), 128–9, but making no reference to 3. 65. 1.

patientia postremum fuit').[32] If Tacitus at 3. 65. 1 is making an emphatic claim of this conventional type, as I am suggesting, we must ask why he does so.

V

It is striking not only that scholars are prepared to truncate their quotation of the famous sentence at 3. 65. 1, as we have seen (above, Sections I and II), but also that they give little or no consideration to even the immediate context in which the sentence occurs. The commentators either remain silent or make brief and widely diverging comments.

The famous sentence occurs in the course of the following passage (3. 64. 4–66. 1):

censuerat L. Apronius ut fetiales quoque iis ludis praesiderent. contra dixit Caesar, distincto sacerdotiorum iure et repetitis exemplis: neque enim umquam fetialibus hoc maiestatis fuisse; ideo Augustales adiectos quia proprium eius domus sacerdotium esset, pro qua uota persoluerentur.

Exsequi sententias haud institui nisi insignes per honestum aut not- 65 abili dedecore, quod praecipuum munus annalium reor, ne uirtutes sileantur utque prauis dictis factisque ex posteritate et infamia metus sit. ceterum tempora illa adeo infecta et adulatione sordida fuere ut non 2 modo primores ciuitatis, quibus claritudo sua obsequiis protegenda erat, sed omnes consulares, magna pars eorum qui praetura functi multique etiam pedarii senatores certatim exsurgerent foedaque et nimia censer- ent. memoriae proditur Tiberium, quotiens || curia egrederetur, 3 Graecis uerbis in hunc modum eloqui solitum: 'o homines ad seruitutem paratos!' scilicet etiam illum, qui libertatem publicam nollet, tam proiectae seruientium patientiae taedebat.

Paulatim dehinc ab indecoris ad infesta transgrediebantur. C. Silanum 66 pro consule Asiae, repetundarum a sociis postulatum, Mamercus Scaurus e consularibus, Iunius Otho praetor, Bruttedius Niger aedilis simul corripiunt obiectantque uiolatum Augusti numen, spretam Tiberii maiestatem.

Orelli, like Pfitzner and Draeger–Heraeus, says nothing about the context at all. Nipperdey–Andresen remark of chapter 65 as a whole that it 'hat keinen Bezug auf das nächstvorhergehende,

---

[32] Since I shall be arguing in Section VII that 3. 65. 1–3 must be interpreted as a whole, it is worth adding, apropos of 14. 64. 3, that *adulatio* also occurs at 3. 65. 3. For 4. 32–33. 4 see below, n. 41.

sondern ist vorbereitende Einleitung zum folgenden'. Furneaux expands on this by observing that chapter 65, 'though it does not appear to relate to those immediately preceding, leads from such motions as those mentioned in c. 57, to what follows in c. 66'.[33] As we shall see in Sections VI–VII below, such remarks about chapters 57 and 66 are correct; but it is clearly unsatisfactory to assume that chapters 58–64, which intervene, are simply irrelevant to the argument and structure of Tacitus' narrative.

Koestermann in his standard commentary first remarks, almost in passing, that Tacitus takes the proposal of Apronius at 64. 4 'zum Anlass für eine grundsätzliche Erklärung' at 65. 1; but then, after observing that 'Die alten römischen normativen Ideen der *virtus constantia fides* sind für Tacitus die Leitsätze, nach denen er das Auftreten einer Persönlichkeit bewertet', he continues with these remarks on chapter 65 as a whole:[34]

Wenn der Historiker seine programmatischen Betrachtungen gerade an dieser Stelle eingeschoben hat, so präludiert er damit der weiteren Entwicklung unter Tiberius, die nach seiner Überzeugung von nun an immer dunklere Züge aufwies: Das ganze Kapitel dient wesentlich dem Zweck, den scharfen Einschnitt, den er zwischen dem 3. und 4. Buch vorgenommen hat, dem Verständnis zu erschliessen.

These seem to be the most substantial comments by any commentator on chapter 65, and in them Koestermann looks forward eleven chapters to the end of the book (3. 76) in order to suggest what the effect of Tacitus' 'programmatic reflections' may be. But a brief allusion to Apronius' proposal scarcely explains why Tacitus 'has inserted his programmatic reflections precisely at this point' rather than at some other point, whether earlier or later. Luce, however, has elaborated on the passage at 64. 4 and has argued that the statement at 65. 1 is prompted by 'a proposal of the senator L. Apronius that the fetial priests should be added to other religious functionaries who were to preside at games voted for the recovery of the emperor's aged mother from a serious illness'.[35] || Apronius' proposal, continues

---

[33] Furneaux ad loc.

[34] Koestermann (1963), 545–6. Though he refers to F. Klingner for the ideals of *uirtus*, *constantia*, and *fides*, Furneaux (1896), 28 n. 1 had already traced them back to Ranke.

[35] Luce (1991), 2905.

Luce, was 'designed to flatter the imperial family'.[36] Yet, although such a hypothesis represents the converse (as it were) of that of Furneaux,[37] there are several objections which can be brought against it.

First, it seems implausible that Tacitus would have used the verb *exsequi* ('to go through in detail') to refer to his treatment of so brief an episode as that of Apronius. Second, it is not at all self-evident why Apronius' proposal should be thought flattering. The most natural explanation of the man's conduct is that he himself was a *fetialis* and, having no wish to see the *fetiales* excluded from the celebrations, risked Tiberius' displeasure in the same way as the *quindecimuir* Caninius Gallus some years later (6. 12. 1). (It must be admitted that there is no surviving evidence that Apronius was a *fetialis*, but it should also be noted that he was described as a 'priest' by Syme, who may therefore have interpreted the incident along the lines which I have suggested.[38]) Third, while Luce's hypothesis accommodates the notion of 'shame' (*dedecore*), which he sees as being illustrated by Apronius' proposal, it can scarcely be argued that the proposal illustrates '*notable* shame' (*notabili dedecore*); nor does his hypothesis take any account of this phrase's polar opposite, *insignes per honestum*, which Luce is required to illustrate by passages far removed from the present context.[39] It is true that these illustrations can be defended on Luce's own terms, since he, like most other scholars, regards 65. 1 as a generalized statement which is applicable to the *Annals* as a whole. But this in its turn brings us to the fourth and final objection, which is that the following sentence begins with the adversative conjunction

[36] Luce (1991), 2912, cf. 2913, 2918.

[37] In his note on 65. 1 Ritter had already mentioned both chapter 57 (like Furneaux) and chapter 64 (like Koestermann and Luce).

[38] R. Syme, *The Augustan Aristocracy* (1986), 293, cf. 349 n. 24 and 473 (index). It was Syme who drew the parallel with Caninius Gallus. Since L. Apronius' son was probably *septemuir* and possibly *flamen Quirinalis*, it is not unlikely that the father, one of Tiberius' trusted lieutenants, held a minor priesthood, despite its lack of attestation: in fact we know virtually nothing about the *fetiales* at this period (see M. W. Hoffman Lewis, *The Official Priests of Rome under the Julio-Claudians* (1955), 138–9; J. Scheid, 'Les Prêtres officiels sous les empereurs julio-claudiens', *ANRW* 2. 16. 1. 640). We do know that Augustus was a *fetialis* (*Res Gestae* 7. 3), so perhaps Tiberius was too; but this cannot have been the basis of Apronius' alleged flattery of Tiberius, who as *pontifex maximus* or *sodalis Augustalis* (for example) was amply qualified to preside at the games. See further the commentary of Woodman–Martin on this passage.   [39] Luce (1991), 2907–11.

ceterum. The implications of this are that the statement at 65. 1 is part of a larger argument which continues to unfold subsequently and that the following context too should therefore claim our attention.

If these objections have any validity, we should perhaps look elsewhere for the context of Tacitus' statement at 65. 1. ||

VI

It is, I believe, of crucial significance that the subject of 65. 1 is senatorial *sententiae.* For Tacitus' narrative of the present year, AD 22, contains an extremely high proportion of senatorial material (85 per cent). This figure is 20 per cent higher than any other Tiberian year except AD 32 (81 per cent); but, whereas the senatorial material of the latter year comprises a mere twelve chapters, with an interval between (6. 2. 1–10. 1, 12–14), that of the present year comprises a quite unparalleled total of twenty-one continuous chapters (52–72).[40] Thus the narrative of AD 22 is altogether exceptional, posing even more risk of the *rerum simili-tudo et satietas,* and of the corresponding lack of *uarietas,* to which Tacitus referred in his narrative of AD 24 (4. 33. 3). Moreover, the narrative of AD 22 is immediately preceded by a further five senatorial chapters at the end of the narrative of the previous year (47–51). What the reader might reasonably expect in these circumstances, as occurs in the narratives both of AD 24 (4. 32. 1–33. 4) and of 32 (6. 7. 5),[41] is some acknowledgement on Tacitus' part that his narrative is risking monotony.

Yet such an acknowledgement is precisely what we are given at 65. 1. Tacitus reassures his readers in conventional terms (*insignes, notabili*) that, despite any appearances to the contrary, he has gone through only the most significant material;[42] and he underlines his reassurance by saying that this is 'a very great responsibility' for the historian (above, p. 93). Tacitus in his statement refers to

---

[40] These figures are taken from Ginsburg (1981), 143.

[41] Each of these passages combines the 'monotony' motif with the 'significant material' motif, though at 4. 32. 1–33.4 the latter is presented in an unusual form (see Martin–Woodman ad loc.). For monotony see also 16. 16. 1–2.

[42] Though other scholars have invoked 3. 65. 1 to illustrate selectivity (e.g. Syme (1958), 281; Ginsburg (1981), 9, 81), they talk in terms of Tacitus' selecting from the *acta senatus,* not of his deploying a device to defend his present narrative.

senatorial *sententiae*, rather than to subject-matter in general, because they constitute the context which gives rise to the statement;[43] and the statement is cast negatively (*haud . . . nisi . . .*) because, given the sheer volume of senatorial material with which he is presently engaged, Tacitus is on the defensive.

The final defence in Tacitus' statement is provided by the clauses *ne uirtutes sileantur* and *utque prauis dictis factisque ex posteritate et infamia metus sit.* If these clauses are purposive rather than definitive of *munus*, as I have suggested (above, p. 92), it follows that they depend upon a verb in || the perfect tense (*institui*) rather than upon one in the present (*reor*). Tacitus is referring to a practice (*exsequi sententias*) which has already achieved its purposes rather than to an aspiration which can be defined only in generalized terms. And it can be shown that this twofold reference to achievement corresponds precisely and chiastically to the two immediately preceding senatorial debates to which the verb *exsequi* may reasonably be said to apply. These are: the debate on the proposed grant of *tribunicia potestas* to Tiberius' son Drusus (56–9) and the debate on provincial delegations concerning rights of asylum (60–3).

The two debates are presented as a contrasting pair. In the former the senators are collectively guilty of a whole range of *sententiae* which illustrate the vice of *adulatio* (57. 1 *quaesitior adulatio*). The individual motion of M. Silanus to honour Tiberius and Drusus (57. 1 '**honorem** principibus petiuit') and to record the event ('**ad memoriam** temporum . . . **praescriberentur**') involved contempt for consular tradition ('ex contumelia consulatus'), and he was duly criticized by Tiberius for *insolentiam sententiae* (59. 2);[44] Q. Haterius' proposal for commemorating the senatorial decrees of that day by fixing them in golden letters in the curia (57. 2 'cum **eius diei senatus consulta** aureis litteris **figenda** in curia censuisset') also drew criticism from Tiberius for being contrary to inherited practice (59. 2 'contra patrium

---

[43] As I have already observed, it is usual to see Tacitus' remarks at 65. 1 as generally applicable to the *Annals* as a whole: for a recent discussion see M. Vielberg, *Pflichten, Werte, Ideale: Eine Untersuchung zu den Wertvorstellungen des Tacitus* (1987), 105–8 'Ein Kompositionsprinzip der Annalen', with special reference to *adulatio*. It is of course obvious from Tacitus' other statements (e.g. above, n. 41) that he would wish the principle of selectivity to be seen as applicable ἐς πάντα λόγον (Hdt. 7. 152. 3).

[44] *insolentiam* here seems to mean both 'unaccustomedness' and 'insolence' (*OLD* 1–2 and 3–4 respectively). See below, p. 101.

morem'), as a result of which Haterius enjoyed only the infamy of his *adulatio* (57. 2 'foedissimae adulationis tantum *infamia* usurus'). It therefore seems clear both that this first debate is characterized by *sententiae notabili dedecore* and that the *praua dicta factaque* of individuals are intended to live in infamy in Tacitus' pages—exactly as he says at 65.1.

The latter debate is in every way the opposite of this. Once again the senate is responsible for a whole range of *sententiae* (60. 1 *disquisitionem patrum*), including the *senatus consulta* by which honour was to be conferred and asylum regulated and which were to be preserved on bronze and fixed in the temples (63. 4 'factaque **senatus consulta**, quis multo cum **honore** modus tamen **praescribebatur**, iussique ipsis in templis **figere** aera sacrandam **ad memoriam**'). But on this occasion it is Tacitus himself who praises the splendour 'of that day on which the senate investigated' (60. 3 'magnaque **eius diei** species fuit quo senatus . . . introspexit'): his reasons are that the senate did not (as before) act in contempt of old-fashioned practice but in conformity with it, and that in so doing the senate did not (as before) display *adulatio* but its opposite, *libertas* (60. 1 'imaginem antiquitatis', 3 'libero, ut quondam, quid firmaret mutaretue').[45] No individual senators are named, but among the provincial delegations the || Magnesians recall their *fidem atque uirtutem* (62. 1) and the Aphrodisians and Stratoniceans their *constantia* (62. 2).[46] It therefore seems clear both that this second debate is characterized by *sententiae insignes per honestum* and that Tacitus has ensured that the *uirtutes* by which it was distinguished are not silenced—again exactly as he says at 65. 1.[47]

Thus the sentence at 65. 1 is seen to refer directly to the narrative of the two senatorial debates which immediately precedes it, a reference which seems to have remained entirely obscure to scholars as long as it was assumed that the phrase *praecipuum munus annalium* offered a definition of 'history's highest

[45] Unlike e.g. Ginsburg (1981), 89–92, I think that ch. 60 is not ironic but is to be taken at face value and that the contrasts with 57–9 are evidence of this.

[46] It is an interesting coincidence that these are precisely the three ideals which, without any reference to the present context, scholars have mentioned apropos of 65. 1 (see above, p. 95 and n. 34).

[47] The conceit that free speech in particular should not be silenced is pleasingly Tacitean.

function'.[48] Yet, if 65. 1 refers back chiastically to chapters 56–63, what place has chapter 64, which intervenes?

It is regular for ancient historians to employ digressions or digressive passages in order to conclude a section of narrative or to make a transition between one section and the next.[49] Tacitus himself is particularly fond of this technique, of which an excellent example may be found in this same book of the *Annals* at 55. 1–5. The narrative of *luxus mensae*, which began at 52. 1, stops at 55. 1 ('luxusque mensae . . . paulatim exoleuere'); the narrative of Drusus' *tribunicia potestas* is about to start at 56. 1: Tacitus effects the transition between the two sections by means of the digression at 55. 1–5 ('causas eius mutationis quaerere libet . . . ex honesto maneant').[50] Another example from the same book is chapter 70, which effects a transition between the narrative of Silanus' trial (66–9) and the section on religious and other matters (71–2). And as a final example we may note the passage at 31. 5 ('idem Corbulo . . . saeuiebat'), which separates the 'main' Corbulo story (31. 2–4) from the African debate which follows (32–5). I suggest, therefore, that chapter 64 is another such digressive passage, separating the section on provincial asylum (60–3) from what follows. ||

Yet, if chapter 64 concludes a section, it seems to follow that chapter 65, despite the backward reference of its first sentence, must begin a new section. We are thereby returned to a point made earlier (pp. 95–6), that 65. 2 begins with *ceterum* and that the sentence at 65. 1 is thus part of a larger argument which unfolds subsequently.

---

[48] I have concentrated on the two debates at 56–9 and 60–3 because of their proximity to 65. 1 and because they illustrate so closely the points which Tacitus makes there. But it could also be argued that Tiberius' written *sententia* in the first debate of the year's narrative (53–4) illustrates the virtue of *moderatio* (cf. 56. 1 'Tiberius, fama moderationis parta'); and R. H. Martin has pointed out to me that, if it is legitimate to consider the senatorial material at the end of the previous year's narrative (see above, p. 97), there too there is an extended section (47 and 49–51) which illustrates the shame and crookedness of Dolabella and D. Haterius and the excellence of the virtuous M. Lepidus.

[49] See e.g. Woodman on Vell. 2. 110–16 (p. 154) [and Woodman–Martin, 500, index, s.v. 'digressions, separating or closural function of'].

[50] It is worth adding that the final sentence of this digression (55. 5 'nec omnia . . . maneant') is itself digressive: for some other digressive sentences at the end of Tacitean paragraphs see e.g. 1. 10. 7 'etenim . . . exprobraret'; 13. 3 'de prioribus . . . circumuenti sunt'; 13. 6 'constat . . . protegeretur'; 14. 3 'quo minus . . . erat'. Clearly there is again a degree of subjectivity here: readers will differ in their notions of what constitutes digressiveness and a paragraph. See above, n. 26.

VII

Although the statement at 65. 1 maintains a balance between virtues (*insignes per honestum* and *ne uirtutes sileantur*) and vices (*notabili dedecore* and *utque prauis . . . metus sit*), as is appropriate to the preceding narrative, it soon becomes clear that the statement also functions as a foil for the *ceterum*-sentence which follows at 65. 2 and in which vices alone are at issue. For the implication of the *ceterum*-sentence is obvious: even though the year AD 22 exhibited further *sententiae* whose detailed recording (*exsequi*) could be justified theoretically on the grounds of notoriety and deterrence, as Tacitus has just outlined (*notabili dedecore* and *utque prauis . . . metus sit*), such *sententiae* were in practice so common ('non modo primores ciuitatis . . . sed omnes consulares, magna pars eorum qui praetura functi multique etiam pedarii senatores') that they became, paradoxically, commonplace. As a result Tacitus cannot, or will not, go through them in detail (*exsequi*). Indeed Tacitus' refusal is all the more apposite, since, as is made clear by verbal correspondences, the undiscussed *sententiae* would have focused on *adulatio*, the vice that featured so prominently in the debate at 56–9 (above, p. 98): *adulatione* and *foedaque* at 65. 2 look back to *quaesitior adulatio* and *foedissimae adulationis* at 57. 1–2, while *nimia censerent* looks back to *insolentiam sententiae* at 59. 2.[51] The risk of monotony was thus doubled.

Yet, just as at 65. 1 Tacitus' justification of his preceding narrative turned out to be a foil for his subsequent refusal at 65. 2, so his refusal at 65. 2 turns out to be a foil for the anecdote which follows at 65. 3. This anecdote, which itself is introduced defensively (*memoriae proditur*), is designed to illustrate the universality of *adulatio* and hence to compensate for Tacitus' refusal at 65. 2 to speak about it in further detail. Thus the paragraph as a whole (65. 1–3), though beginning with a sentence (65. 1) which looks back over the narrative of 56–63, turns out to be an elaborate statement of the shamefulness of the age (*notabile dedecus*) as illustrated by *adulatio*.

In the light of this analysis it is surely significant that the next paragraph, the first in the lengthy narrative (66–9) of C. Silanus'

---

[51] See above, n. 44.

trial for *maiestas*,[52] is || introduced by the statement that men now passed 'from the shameful to the harmful' (66. 1 'Paulatim dehinc *ab indecoris ad infesta* transgrediebantur'). *indecoris* here looks back to *dedecore* at 65. 1,[53] just as the vocabulary of 65. 2 looked back to the manifestations of *adulatio* at 56–9. And, just as the *indecora* of *adulatio* were practised by everyone from consulars through praetors to the lowest senators (65. 2, quoted above), so the *infesta* of *maiestas*-accusations were espoused by the consular Mamercus Scaurus, the praetor Iunius Otho, and the aedile Bruttedius Niger (66. 1, quoted on p. 94), the itemization of rank demonstrating that the latter vice was as universal as the former. It thus becomes clear that the introductory sentence of Silanus' trial (66. 1) is to be seen in the light of statements in the previous paragraph (65). Tacitus' refusal to go into further details of *adulatio* (65. 1–2), which is nevertheless briefly illustrated by anecdote (65. 3), merely serves to emphasize the significance of the trial which he *will* describe in detail—a trial in which men transcended the boundaries of *indecora* and passed on to the even worse stage of *infesta*.

In other words the successive foils of 65. 1–3 together serve as a foil for 66–9; and, since there is a qualitative difference between *indecora* and *infesta*, it follows that Tacitus' detailed recording of the latter, as represented by Silanus' trial, avoids the monotonous repetition which would have resulted if he had re-embarked on a detailed recording of the former. Moreover, since Tacitus names Silanus' accusers at 66. 1 and then criticizes each of them (again by name) at 66. 2–3, just as he had named and criticized the *adulatores* at 57. 1–2 (above, p. 98), it also follows that his narrative of Silanus' trial expressly provides the kind of deterrence which, despite the implication of the purpose clause at 65. 1 (*utque . . . metus sit*), his generalized remarks at 65. 2–3 had failed to provide.

---

[52] The narrative of Silanus' trial ends at 69. 6 but the section as a whole does not end until 70. 3 (see p. 100). The fact that Silanus was condemned only for extortion and *saeuitia* (68. 1–2, as interpreted by Seager (1972), 160) is beside the point; it is the charges of *maiestas* with which Tacitus is primarily concerned (cf. 67. 3 'et ne quis necessariorum iuuaret periclitantem, maiestatis crimina subdebantur, uinclum et necessitas silendi').

[53] So too Martin (1990), 1539.

VIII

To conclude. In this paper I have suggested that the phrase *praecipuum munus annalium* does not define 'history's highest function' either in conventional terms (as most scholars have assumed) or unconventional (as Luce has argued). Rather the phrase forms part of an apologia, in which Tacitus defends his preceding narrative on conventional grounds of importance and selectivity and which at the same time constitutes the first in a series of foils whereby the significance of the following narrative is emphasized. That the narrative of Silanus' trial merits such emphasizing is confirmed, finally, by Tacitus' arrangement of the whole year's narative (52–76). That narrative, it seems to || me, is arranged in seven sections, as follows: (1) 52–5 *Luxus mensae*, (2) 56–9 *Tribunicia potestas* for Drusus, (3) 60–4 Asia and asyla, (4) 65–70 Silanus' trial, (5) 71–2 Religious and other matters, (6) 73–4 War in Africa, (7) 75–6 Obituary notices.[54] It will be seen that the trial occupies the central section of the seven, attracting to itself the importance conventionally associated with such a position.[55]

---

[54] This arrangement differs from those proposed by Ginsburg (1981), 132 and Wille (1983), 616–17.   [55] See e.g. Martin–Woodman, 17, 193.

7

History and Alternative Histories

Tacitus' reputation as the greatest Roman historian rests chiefly on the *Annals* and *Histories*, which together produced a total of thirty volumes and, when complete,[1] began with the death of Augustus in August AD 14 and ended eighty-two years later with the death of Domitian in September 96. The scale of treatment, which is ample, and the annalistic format, which is rigorously sustained throughout, alike served to remind his readers that Tacitus was writing history in the grand and time-honoured manner.

PREFACE TO THE *HISTORIES*

Although the *Histories* deal with the last third of Tacitus' chosen period, they were in fact written before the *Annals*.[2] There is sufficient evidence in the cases of Thucydides, Sallust, and Livy to show that historiographical prefaces were replete with 'signals' from which readers might infer what line a historian was intending to take.[3] The preface to the *Histories* falls into three clearly defined sections: (*a*) scope and impartiality (chapter 1), (*b*) content (2–4. 1), (*c*) retrospective survey of June–December AD 68 (4. 2–11. 3).[4] What would a contemporary reader have inferred from it? The text of the first two of these sections is as follows:

Initium mihi operis Seruius Galba iterum Titus Vinius consules erunt.   1
nam post conditam urbem octingentos et uiginti prioris aeui annos
multi auctores rettulerunt, dum res populi Romani memorabantur,

---

[1] We owe the figure thirty to Jerome. Since substantial portions of both works have been lost, the original number of volumes in each work is uncertain. It is often suggested that the *Histories* consisted of twelve books and the *Annals* of eighteen, but this is no more than speculation.

[2] The *Histories* were in progress in AD 106 (cf. Plin. *Ep.* 7. 33) and perhaps completed by 109 (so Syme). The dating of the *Annals* is disputed: 109–18, according to Goodyear (1981), 387–93; 114–20, according to Syme (1984), 1153–6. See also Martin–Woodman on *A.* 4. 5. 2.   [3] See *RICH* 6–7, 120–32.   [4] See further *LH* 88–90.

pari eloquentia ac libertate: postquam bellatum apud Actium atque omnem potentiam ad unum conferri pacis interfuit, magna illa ingenia cessere; simul ueritas pluribus modis infracta, primum inscitia rei pub- licae ut alienae, mox libidine adsentandi aut rursus odio aduersus dom- inantes: ita neutris cura posteritatis inter infensos uel obnoxios. sed   2 ambitionem scriptoris facile auerseris, obtrectatio et liuor pronis auribus accipiuntur; quippe adulationi foedum crimen seruitutis, malignitati falsa species libertatis inest. mihi Galba Otho Vitellius nec beneficio   3 nec iniuria cogniti. dignitatem nostram a Vespasiano inchoatam, a Tito auctam, a Domitiano longius prouectam non abnuerim: sed incorrup- tam fidem professis neque amore quisquam et sine odio dicendus est. quod si uita suppeditet, principatum diui Neruae et imperium Traiani,   4 uberiorem securioremque materiam, senectuti seposui, rara temporum felicitate, ubi sentire quae uelis et quae sentias dicere licet.

Opus adgredior opimum[5] casibus, atrox proeliis, discors seditionibus,   2 ipsa etiam pace saeuom. quattuor principes ferro interempti; trina bella ciuilia, plura externa ac plerumque permixta; prosperae in Oriente, aduersae in Occidente res: turbatum Illyricum, Galliae nutantes, perdo- mita Britannia et statim missa, coortae in nos Sarmatarum ac Sueborum gentes, nobilitatus cladibus mutuis Dacus, mota prope etiam Parthorum arma falsi Neronis ludibrio. iam uero Italia nouis cladibus uel post   2 longam saeculorum seriem repetitis adflicta: haustae aut obrutae urbes, fecundissima Campaniae ora; et urbs incendiis uastata, consumptis anti- quissimis delubris, ipso Capitolio ciuium manibus incenso. pollutae caerimoniae, magna adulteria; plenum exiliis mare, infecti caedibus scopuli. atrocius in urbe saeuitum: nobilitas, opes, omissi gestique hon-   3 ores pro crimine, et ob uirtutes certissimum exitium. nec minus praemia delatorum inuisa quam scelera, cum alii sacerdotia et consulatus ut spolia adepti, procurationes alii et interiorem potentiam, agerent uerterent cuncta odio et terrore. corrupti in dominos serui, in patronos liberti; et quibus deerat inimicus, per amicos oppressi.

Non tamen adeo uirtutum sterile saeculum ut non et bona exempla   3 prodiderit. comitatae profugos liberos matres, secutae maritos in exilia coniuges; propinqui audentes, constantes generi, contumax etiam aduersus tormenta seruorum fides; supremae clarorum uirorum neces- sitates, ipsa necessitas fortiter tolerata et laudatis antiquorum mortibus

---

[5] *opimum* has been questioned on the grounds (i) that it does not correspond to *casibus* as does *atrox* to *proeliis* and *discors* to *seditionibus*, (ii) that it is never used without special reference to richness of soil. (i) seems to me insubstantial since in the fourth element of the list *saeuom* too not only fails to correspond to *pace* but also produces a similar oxymoron. As for (ii), *opimum* seems defensible as contributing to a sustained agricultural metaphor which begins with 'uberiorem . . . materiam' at 1. 1. 4 and continues with 'non . . . uirtutum sterile' at 1. 3. 1. Tacitus will have in mind the relatively common image of the writer's or speaker's 'territory' (*terra, solum* etc.).

pares exitus. praeter multiplices rerum humanarum casus caelo terraque 2
prodigia et fulminum monitus et futurorum praesagia, laeta tristia,
ambigua manifesta; nec enim umquam atrocioribus populi Romani
cladibus magisue iustis indiciis adprobatum est non esse curae deis
securitatem nostram, esse ultionem.

Ceterum antequam destinata componam, repetendum uidetur, qualis 4
status urbis, quae mens exercituum, quis habitus prouinciarum, quid in
toto terrarum orbe ualidum, quid aegrum fuerit, ut non modo casus
euentusque rerum, qui plerumque fortuiti sunt, sed ratio etiam causae-
que noscantur.

My chosen starting point will be the consulships of Servius Galba (for 1
the second time) and Titus Vinius, since many historians have recorded
the preceding period of 820 years from the foundation of the city. For as
long as the achievements of the Roman people were their subject, their
record combined eloquence with free speech in equal proportions; but
after the Battle of Actium, when peace depended upon establishing an
autocracy, there were no more literary giants. Truth was shattered at
exactly the same time—first through blameless ignorance of a govern-
mental system which treated its subjects like aliens, later through a lust
for sycophancy or alternatively disgust towards the autocrats themselves.
In either case, opponents and victims abandoned all concern for posterity between them. Yet readers are automatically resistant to blatant 2
canvassing on the part of an historian, whereas they will readily lend
their ears to denigration and spite: adulation is open to the loathsome
accusation of servitude, but malice gives a false impression of free
speech. For myself I had no personal contact with Galba, Otho or 3
Vitellius for either good or ill. That my political career was started by
Vespasian, enhanced by Titus and carried further by Domitian, I have no
wish to deny; but no one should be treated with either affection or
disgust once a writer has stated that his reliability is beyond corruption.
If my life lasts, I have reserved the principate of Divine Nerva and the 4
command of Trajan, more productive and safer material, for my old age,
given the rare fertility of a climate in which it is allowed to think what
you want and say what you think.

The work on which I am now embarking is rich in crises, terrible 2
with battles, riven with rebellion, and savage even when at peace. Four
emperors perished by the sword. There were three civil wars, still more
against foreigners, and often conflicts which combined elements of
both. Success in the East was balanced by failure in the West. The
Balkans were in turmoil, the Gallic provinces wavered in their allegiance, and Britain was left to fend for itself no sooner than its conquest
had been completed. The Sarmatian and Suebian peoples rose upon us,
the Dacian distinguished himself in desperate battles won and lost, and

thanks to the activities of a charlatan masquerading as Nero, even Parthia
was on the brink of declaring war. Finally, Italy itself fell victim to   2
disasters which were quite unprecedented or had not occurred for many
centuries. Whole towns were burnt down or buried throughout the
richest part of the coast of Campania, and Rome suffered severely from
fires that destroyed its most venerable temples, the very Capitol being set
alight by Roman hands. Things holy were desecrated, there was adultery in high places. The Mediterranean swarmed with exiles and its
rocky islets ran with blood. The reign of terror was particularly ruthless   3
at Rome. Rank, wealth and office, whether surrendered or retained,
provided grounds for accusation, and the reward for virtue was inevitable death. The profits made by the prosecutors were no less odious
than their crimes. Some helped themselves to priesthoods and consulships as the prize of victory. Others acquired official posts and backstairs
influence, creating a universal pandemonium of hatred and terror. Slaves
were suborned to speak against their masters, freedmen against their
patrons, while those who had not an enemy in the world were ruined by
their friends.

However, the period was not so barren of merit that it failed to teach   3
some good lessons as well. Mothers accompanied their children in flight,
wives followed their husbands into exile. There were resolute kinsmen,
sons-in-law who showed steadfast fidelity, and slaves whose loyalty
scorned the rack. Distinguished men driven to suicide faced the last
agony with unflinching courage, and there were death-scenes not infer-
ior to those held up to our admiration in the history of early Rome. In   2
addition to manifold tragedy on the human plane, signs and wonders
occurred in heaven and earth, premonitory lightnings and tokens of
things to come, auspicious or ominous, doubtful or manifest. In short,
Rome's unparalleled sufferings supplied ample proof that the gods are
indifferent to our tranquillity, but eager for our punishment.

However, as a preliminary to my history proper, a retrospective survey   4
seems in order, covering the state of affairs in Rome, the intention of
the troops, the attitude of the provinces, and the areas of strength and
weakness across the world. In this way one can discover not only the
outcome and consequences of events, which are generally fortuitous,
but also their background and reasons.[6]

One of the curiosities of the preface, which has attracted scholarly
attention, is its very first sentence, where Tacitus announces that
his starting point is January AD 69 and not, as might perhaps have
been expected, the death of Nero in June 68. 'The decision

---

[6] The translation of 1. 1–2. 1 and 4. 1 is my own; that of 2. 1–3. 2 is by K. Wellesley.

Tacitus took', says the latest commentator, G. E. F. Chilver, 'was
surely influenced by his determination to open his work on the
lines laid down by his main model.'[7] The reference is to Sallust,
whose *Histories* had begun with the names of the consuls for 78
BC. 'It is as if Tacitus implicitly announces a work in the grand
manner of Sallust', says A. D. Leeman.[8] 'Like Sallust, too', adds
Chilver, 'he proceeds straight to a comparison between himself
and earlier historians, and then to an assertion of his own impartiality.'[9] Yet the matter is not quite as straightforward as these and
other scholars allow.

It is true that the first fragment of Sallust's *Histories*, in addition
to its annalistic rendering of consular names, contains the phrase
res populi Romani, which recurs in Tacitus' second sentence;[10] and
the phrase *magna . . . ingenia* in his third sentence, though found
in other authors too, is borrowed from Sallust's *Bellum Catilinae* (8.
3). But Tacitus' references to his predecessors and to his own
impartiality contain none of the striking verbal reminiscences
by which Livy, when referring to the same topics, makes his
debt to Sallust's *Histories* unmistakably clear.[11] It is also true that
Tacitus introduces his retrospective survey in 4. 2–11. 3 with
phraseology at 4. 1 which seems to echo that with which Sallust
had introduced his own retrospective surveys in the *Bellum Catilinae* (5. 9 'res ipsa hortari *uidetur* . . . supra *repetere* ac paucis . . .
quomodo rem publicam ha̲b̲u̲e̲r̲i̲n̲t̲ . . . disserere') and *Bellum
Iugurthinum* (5. 3 's̲e̲d̲ p̲r̲i̲u̲s̲q̲u̲a̲m̲ huiuscemodi rei initium expe-
dio, pauca supra *repetam*, quo ad co*gnoscendum* omnia illustria
magis magisque in aperto sint').[12] But though the echoes themselves seem clear enough, it has been argued by Syme that the
actual survey owes little to the technique of Sallust: 'The survey
. . . is not merely a marvellous device. It appears to lack precedent
or parallel in ancient historiography'.[13]

In fact many of Tacitus' allusions in the first section of his
preface are either to phrases which are found first in Cicero
(thus 2 *foedum crimen* ~ *Sull.* 90, 4 *uberiorem . . . materiam* ~ *Fin.*

---

[7] Chilver, 34.   [8] Leeman (1973), 176.
[9] Chilver, 33, referring to Sall. *H.* 1. 4 and 6.
[10] This point is not actually noted by Chilver, 35.   [11] See *RICH* 131.
[12] Only the latter is quoted by Chilver, 45. My italicizations indicate words which
Tacitus has taken over directly; dots indicate synonyms and the like.
[13] Syme (1958), 147.

4. 12)[14] or, more strikingly, to passages which seem exclusively Ciceronian. Thus the contrast between *amore* and *sine odio* in 3 recalls a famous passage of the *Pro Marcello*, 'sine amore . . . et rursus sine odio' (29), where Cicero's use of *rursus* seems also to be picked up by Tacitus earlier in 1: 'aut rursus odio'. Again, *uita suppeditet* in 4 occurs not only three times in the *Brutus* (105, 124, 245) but also in Cicero's third *Philippic* (15), a later section of which, dealing with freedom of thought and expression (36 'nimium diu teximus quid sentiremus; nunc iam apertum est: omnes patefaciunt in utramque partem quid sentiant, quid uelint'), seems also to be echoed by Tacitus in 4: 'ubi sentire quae uelis et quae sentias dicere licet'. Since Cicero's manner and style were the opposite of those of Sallust,[15] it would therefore appear that the signals presented at least by the first chapter of Tacitus' *Histories* are unclear. On the evidence so far considered, it certainly cannot be assumed without qualification that Sallust is, in Chilver's words, Tacitus' 'main model'.

If we now turn to the second section of the preface (2–4. 1), we shall find that Tacitus previews the content of his work in terms which are directly comparable with those laid down by Cicero, particularly in the *De Oratore* but also elsewhere.[16] Cicero had required that historiography should contain descriptions of geographical regions and battles:[17] Tacitus lists a large number of foreign countries and peoples which, by inference, he plans to describe;[18] he also promises that his work is 'terrible with battles', the transference of the adjective from *proeliis* to *opus* hinting that his work will reproduce the horror of the battles themselves and will thus engender in his readers the same kind of emotional response as was felt by the participants in the actual conflict.[19] This too was a Ciceronian requirement in the letter to Lucceius (*Fam.* 5. 12. 5). Cicero took it for granted that historiography would deal with important and memorable events ('in rebus magnis memoriaque dignis': *De*

---

[14] The former recurs in Val. Max. 4. 2. 5 and Mart. 2. 56. 2; the latter in Quint. 3. 1. 3.

[15] See *RICH* 117–26.   [16] For which see *RICH* 79–80.

[17] See *RICH* 79, 83–5, 88–9, 91, 95.

[18] Much of *H.* is of course now lost, but one of these full-scale descriptions (of Jerusalem and its inhabitants) survives at 5. 2–13.

[19] *atrox proelium* is a standard phrase.

Or. 2. 63), categories to which the episodes of Tacitus' promised narrative clearly belong; he also assumed that the spotlight would fall on great men ('qui fama ac nomine excellant': ibid.): Tacitus points out that four of his protagonists are emperors. Cicero emphasized that historians should deal with fluctuating and suspenseful events:[20] Tacitus isolates precisely this aspect of the foreign affairs with which he will be concerned (2. 1 *prosperae ~ aduersae, nutantes, perdomita ~ statim missa, cladibus mutuis*). In the letter to Lucceius and elsewhere Cicero shows a partiality for dramatic death-scenes, particularly if they involve great men:[21] Tacitus mentions that in his period four emperors perished by the sword, that distinguished men committed suicide, and that his death-scenes rival any of those in earlier history. Cicero referred to the emotional mileage to be gained from stories about exile (*Fam*. 5. 12. 5), a topic which Tacitus mentions twice (2. 2 *plenum exiliis mare*, 3. 1). Cicero had advocated that historians should acknowledge the role played by chance in human affairs (*De Or*. 2. 63), an element to which Tacitus alludes at 3. 2 ('praeter multiplices rerum humanarum casus caelo terraque prodigia et fulminum monitus'). Finally, Cicero said that the historian should reveal 'not only what was said or done but also in what manner, and in the case of consequences to explain all the reasons, whether they be of chance . . . ' (ibid.), which Tacitus seems to echo very closely at 4. 1: 'not only the outcome and consequences of events, which are generally fortuitous, but also their . . . reasons'.

Thus the second part of Tacitus' preface, so far from being the 'extensive and gloomy characterisation of the subject' described by Leeman,[22] reveals instead that the topics of his work, together with their detailed and emotional treatment, are in exact agreement with the recommendations for pleasurable historiography which were laid down by Cicero in the middle of the first century BC.[23] The implicit emphasis on pleasure is confirmed by a consideration of the other topics which Tacitus lists but which Cicero had happened not to mention. Sacrilege, adultery, and throwing victims from rocks (2. 2 'pollutae caerimoniae, magna adulteria

---

[20] See *RICH* 72, 85, 90–1, 97.   [21] See *RICH* 72, 100.

[22] Leeman (1973), 174, an extraordinary misreading—and instructive.

[23] This is not the impression given by Syme (1958), 146–7.

. . . infecti caedibus scopuli') are known to have been popular subjects with the auditors of declamation.[24] Claims that one's material is novel (2. 2 *nouis cladibus*) are standard in all branches of literature in the ancient world.[25] And the capturing and laying waste of cities were topics whose popularity stretches back through Thucydides to Homer.[26] Indeed the whole of the second section of Tacitus' preface clearly performs exactly the same function as the third part of Thucydides' own preface (especially 1. 23. 1–3) in that it heralds a 'disaster narrative' of the most vivid and dramatic type.[27]

But whereas Thucydides' work, like that of his imitator Sallust, is characterized by a pervasive pessimism which is well suited to the theme of decline and fall,[28] Tacitus goes out of his way at 1. 1. 4 to remark that the disasters of AD 69–96 were followed by *rara temporum felicitas*, which will constitute the subject of a later work. Such declarations of future intent become common under the empire and are not to be taken too seriously, since they often amount to little more than conventional formulae by which the present regime is praised.[29] Yet the mere act of referring to the happy present means that Tacitus denies in advance that any permanent damage was done to the Roman constitution by the disasters which he is about to catalogue. By thus depriving events of their potentially tragic significance, Tacitus introduces a note which is absent from Thucydides and entirely antithetical to the unrelieved disillusionment of Sallust. His reference to the reigns of Nerva and Trajan not only provides further confirmation that his interest in the disasters centres primarily on their capacity to furnish gripping narrative material, but also indicates the extent to which we must qualify any statement alleging that Sallust is his 'main model'.

[24] For sacrilege cf. Sen. *Contr.* 1. 2; for adultery, Sen. *Contr.* 2. 7 (where Winterbottom (1974) compares Sen. *Ben.* 1. 9. 4, 3. 16. 3; Juv. 6); for victims from rocks, Sen. *Contr.* 1. 3, Quint. 7. 8. 3, 5–6. Similarly, some of the topics which Cicero had mentioned were equally popular declamatory themes: e.g. torture at *Contr.* 2. 5, exile at 6.4.

[25] See Lausberg (1966), 1. 244–5 § 270, Herkommer (1968), 167 n. 4. For its particular application to historiography see esp. Vitr. 5 *praef.* 1 'habent enim [sc. historiae] nouarum rerum uarias exspectationes'; Heubner quotes Liv. 5. 51. 7 'urbis nostrae clades noua', and cf. also Sall. *C.* 4. 4 'periculi nouitate'.

[26] See *RICH* 29–30.   [27] See *RICH* 28–30. Cf. also Vell. 67. 2, App. *BC* 4. 12.

[28] See *RICH* 44 and 124–6.

[29] See A. J. Woodman, 'Questions of Date, Genre and Style in Velleius: Some Literary Answers', *CQ* 25 (1975), 287–8.

BOOK I OF THE *ANNALS*

Preface (Chapter 1)

The later work, when it came, did not in fact provide an encomiastic treatment of the contemporary world in the early second
century AD but instead was devoted to the Julio-Claudian period
which had begun a century earlier on the death of Augustus. Just
as a Horatian ode will sometimes start by alluding to lines of
whichever Greek poet was Horace's chief inspiration, so the
famous first sentence of Tacitus' *Annals* ('Urbem Romam a principio reges habuere') alludes simultaneously and unmistakably to
two of the prefaces of Sallust: *Bellum Catilinae* 6. 1 '*Urbem Romam
. . . habuere* initio Troiani' (the introduction to Sallust's account of
early republican history), and *Histories* 1. 8 '*a principio* urbis'. From
these allusions, the striking nature and prominence of which seem
to give them a significance denied to those in the preface of
Tacitus' *Histories*, a reader might well have inferred that Tacitus
was proposing to write history in the manner and style of
Sallust.[30] Such an inference would of course prove to be correct,
since Sallust's brevity, abruptness, *uariatio*, and phraseology are
successfully reproduced on almost every page of the *Annals*. Yet
since there had been no Sallustian historian of Rome for more
than a hundred years,[31] Tacitus' deviation from the style of his
immediate predecessors is remarkable. As Perret has well said, 'le
choix que Tacite fait de Salluste comme modèle est un fait
significatif, lourd d'intentions, expressif d'un goût personnel'.[32]
Yet it was only by rejecting the style of Cicero and Livy that
Tacitus could fully express his antagonism towards the encomiastic
historiography with which that style was associated; and it was
only by embracing the alternative style of Sallust that he could
portray himself fully as the historian of disenchantment. In the
same way Tacitus' own style was imitated by Gibbon more than
one and a half thousand years later.[33]

     The remainder of the preface to the *Annals* is enigmatic in its
brevity, and, in comparison with that to the *Histories*, notable for

---

[30] See also above, Ch. 2.   [31] See *RICH* 140–6.
[32] J. Perret, 'La Formation du style de Tacite', *REA* 56 (1954), 97. The study of A.
Michel, 'Le Style de Tacite et sa philosophie de l'histoire', *Eos*, 69 (1981), 283–92, is not
especially helpful, despite its promising title.
[33] See *RICH* 46 and *LH* 111–12 (with n. 121).

what it omits rather than for what it says. Gone is the promise of a future encomiastic work, and gone too is the detailed listing of representative topics of the narrative. Instead, after surveying republican history and early imperial historiography in roughly a dozen lines (1. 1–2), Tacitus merely says (1. 3): 'So my intention is to record Augustus briefly, and his final days, then the principate of Tiberius and its sequel, without animosity and partiality, the reasons for which I keep at a distance'.[34] From this laconic statement readers are left to draw what further conclusions they can about the narrative which begins with the very next sentence.

The German Campaign of AD 15

Tacitus' attraction to the theme of 'Germany' was already clear from the earlier publication of his geographical and ethnographical monograph *Germania*, which included within it a brief synopsis of the Germans' relations with Rome (G. 37). Previous writers who had treated the subject included Caesar in his *Gallic War* and Livy in Book 104, now lost (cf. *per.* 104 'prima pars libri situm Germaniae moresque continet'). It is eloquent testimony to the imaginative power of 'Germany' that Livy elsewhere breaches his narrative chronology in order to compare the Ciminian Wood in fourth-century BC Etruria with the *saltus* of Germany which had only recently been breached (9. 36. 1 'silua erat Ciminia magis tum inuia atque horrenda quam nuper fuere Germanici saltus'); and the defining impenetrability of the German landscape was confirmed by Tacitus' monograph, with its references to climate, gloom, woods, swamps, wetness, and wind (G. 2. 1 'informem terris, asperam caelo, tristem cultu aspectuque', 5. 1 'aut siluis horrida aut paludibus foeda, humidior qua Gallias, uentosior qua Noricum ac Pannoniam aspicit'). Such is the challenging and evocative theme which Tacitus resumes in Book 1 of the *Annals*.[35]

Book 1 of the *Annals* deals principally with the first seventeen months of Tiberius' reign, two-thirds of the book being devoted to foreign affairs: mutinies in Pannonia and Germany in AD 14

---

[34] This is effectively a list of (very unequal) contents: see above, Ch. 3, Sect. I.
[35] In general on this see the stimulating pages of Schama (1995), ch. 2 ('*Der Holzweg*: The Track Through the Woods'), esp. 81–91.

(16–30, 31–51) and a campaign against the Germans in AD 15 (55–71). In Tacitus' narrative of the latter year the events in Germany precede an account of domestic affairs (72–81), although scholars are agreed that in 'real life' all but one of the domestic items will have preceded the foreign.[36] By thus transposing domestic and foreign in defiance of their actual chronology,[37] Tacitus not only gives a local prominence to the German campaign but also effects a measure of continuity with the foreign events of the previous year, when, at the very last, the settlement of the mutiny in Germany is transformed into an offensive expedition against the Germans themselves (49. 3–51. 4).[38]

Faced with a choice of direction which resembled that of the Romans at the Caudine Forks centuries earlier (50. 2 'duobus itineribus', cf. Liv. 9. 2. 6 'duae . . . uiae'), Germanicus had correctly chosen the longer and safer (50. 2–3). The choice augurs well for the expedition as a whole. Crying out to his troops that now was the time to obliterate the past (51. 3 'hoc illud tempus obliterandae seditionis clamitabat'), he was met with an enthusiastic response from his men as they burst through the German line, drove the enemy into open country, and slaughtered them (51. 4). The victory allows the soldiers to settle into their winter quarters with the past forgotten (51. 4 'priorum oblitus miles in hibernis locatur'). This repeated emphasis upon forgetting the past acts as a foil for the narrative of the following year, in which a principal theme will be the reactivation of another, even more troubled, past.

Six years earlier, in AD 9, Quintilius Varus and three legions had been lured by the German chieftain Arminius into the Teutoburg Forest in the heart of Germany and massacred.[39] It was a disaster of the first magnitude, which remained mourned but unavenged.

---

[36] See Ginsburg (1981), 70–3. The one exception is the short first sentence of 72. 1 (the decree of triumphal insignia).

[37] There may be a further transposition, if those scholars are right who think that the first sentence of 55. 1 ('decernitur Germanico triumphus manente bello') should really follow the narrative of the campaign which Tacitus is about to relate: see Goodyear ad loc. for discussion and references. Though Goodyear himself is sceptical, this further transposition would mean that the foreign narrative of AD 15 would begin as well as end on a note of paradox (see below, pp. 125–6). For the paradox of a triumph being awarded for an unfinished war, see Woodman–Martin on 3. 74. 4.

[38] See also below, pp. 218f., 227f. Bacha (1906), 117–18 in fact regards 49–51 as being repeated at 55–6.   [39] For discussion see W. John in *RE* xxiv. 922–84.

Already mentioned by Tacitus at the very start of the *Annals* (1. 3. 6),[40] the reverse was said by the contemporary Velleius to be the gravest since that of Carrhae in 53 BC, which itself lived in the Romans' collective memory as one of the worst in their history.[41] For months afterwards Augustus is said to have shouted out repeatedly 'Quintilius Varus, return the legions!', and the date of the disaster was observed as a day of mourning each year thereafter (Suet. *Aug.* 23. 2). It is with the latest news of the victorious Arminius, and with a rehearsal of the events which led to his victory, that Tacitus in an introductory paragraph begins his account of the campaign of AD 15 (55).

This introductory paragraph is matched by a concluding paragraph at the very end of the year's campaigning (71), and within this outer frame it is perhaps possible broadly to discern inner frames which enclose the centre of the narrative (ring-composition). Thus Germanicus' entry into enemy territory (56) corresponds to the withdrawal therefrom (70), while the section on Arminius and Segestes, son-in-law and father-in-law (57–60), corresponds to that on Agrippina and Tiberius, daughter-in-law and father-in-law (69). The centre of the narrative comprises the two parallel episodes with which I shall be principally concerned: the site of Varus' disaster (61–2), which itself constitutes an example of ring-composition (see above, p. 72), and the battle with the Germans (63–8).[42]

Appropriately for someone so interested in and associated with the past,[43] Germanicus on his approach builds a fort on the same site as his father had constructed a redoubt many years before (56. 1 'positoque castello super uestigia paterni praesidii'); and L. Apronius was left to shore up roads and river-banks because conditions were unusually dry for Germany (56. 2 'rarum illi

[40] The context is assumed to be Tiberius' reprisals against the Germans in AD 10 (see e.g. Vell. 120. 1–2). Roman honour could not be said to be satisfied until the commemoration of the return of the standards which had been lost with Varus, and this did not take place until AD 16 (2. 41. 1).

[41] Vell. 119. 1. In general see A. T. Grafton and N. M. Swerdlow, 'Calendar Dates and Ominous Days in Ancient Historiography', *JWCI* 51 (1988), 14–42.

[42] Wille (1983), 372–5 and 604–5 proposes a different scheme. Only the episode at 63–8 is discussed by Everts (1926), 56–66; for a suggested relationship between 63–8 and 70 see Bacha (1906), 119–20 and 292. See also n. 43 below.

[43] For this see Pelling (1993), 72–4, whose whole discussion should be consulted for its insights and further references.

caelo') and flooding was feared on the way back—statements
designed to evoke thoughts of the grim reality of Germany as
described by Tacitus in his monograph (above, p. 113). Germanicus is met by legates from Segestes, who explain that their
leader is being besieged by his countrymen under the malign
influence of Arminius (57. 1). Once rescued from the siege by
Germanicus (57. 3), Segestes speaks in *oratio recta* (58. 1–4): he has
always preferred old-fashioned quiet to these new disturbances
(58. 3 'uetera nouis et quieta turbidis antehabeo'). Germanicus,
no doubt impressed by this sentiment, promises Segestes an abode
in the (suitably old) province of Germany (58. 5 'uetere in
prouincia'), while Segestes' daughter—Arminius' wife—was evidently despatched to Ravenna. Arminius himself reacts violently
at the news of these developments (59. 1);[44] he too delivers a
speech, this time to his countrymen and in *oratio obliqua* (59. 2–6):
if they prefer the old ways to new developments, they should
follow him rather than Segestes (59. 6 'si . . . antiqua mallent
quam dominos et colonias nouas'). The emphasis of both speakers
on the past, which of course means very different things to each
of them, provides a highly appropriate build-up to the centrepiece of the narrative, in which the past will be first revisited (61–
2) and then re-enacted (63–8). Like the *Variana clades* itself (cf. 55.
2, 57. 5, 58. 2, 59. 3), the concept of the past dominates the
opening scenes until the final sentence of the final paragraph is
reached.

Arminius' speech is so effective that even Inguiomerus joins
him against Rome (60. 1): since the latter had enjoyed influence
with the Romans from of old ('uetere apud Romanos auctor-
itate'), Germanicus' dread was all the greater ('maior Caesari
metus'). He deployed his forces in response to the Germans
(60. 3), while his subordinate L. Stertinius routed the Bructeri
and found in their possession 'the eagle of the nineteenth legion
lost with Varus' (60. 3). Tacitus' final sentence, chiastic and asson-
antal, concludes with a magnificently suspenseful 'appendix':

ductum inde agmen ad ultimos Bructerorum, quantumque Amisiam et
Lupiam amnes inter uastatum, | haud procul Teutoburgiensi saltu in quo
reliquiae Vari legionumque insepultae dicebantur.

---

[44] See also below, pp. 232–3.

ultimos in the first colon implies the extent of the Romans' penetration, *haud procul* in the appendix suggests the tantalizing proximity of the site. *saltus* conjures up the archetypal German terrain which so engaged Livy (above, p. 113), while the very name *Teutoburgiensis*, encountered only here in the whole of Latin literature, recalls that of the dreaded Teutoni, which for the Romans 'remained for centuries a name of terror'.[45] But the climax comes in the two final and evocative words.

In his recent account of the Great War in European cultural history, Jay Winter has described the feelings which swept across France when the war was over.[46] A minority of bereaved parents wished their sons to remain buried where they had fought and died, maintaining in death their comradeship with their fellows; but the majority wished the bodies of their sons to be returned home: 'Though they are dead, we want to remove them from those accursed places in the battlefields. They did their duty. Now we must do ours for them: to let them rest in peace in the cemetery of their ancestors. To abandon them there, is to condemn them to eternal torment.'[47] Each side in this argument could at least draw comfort from the proper burial of their sons, but Germanicus and his men enjoyed no such confidence. Lack of burial was a supreme misfortune in the ancient world, the constant source of inspiration to poets and prose-writers alike;[48] Cicero gives as one of the topoi of the lament (*conquestio*) the following example: 'inimicorum in manibus mortuus est, hostili in terra turpiter iacuit insepultus, . . . communi quoque honore in morte caruit' (*Inu.* 1. 108). Each of these misfortunes was applicable to the men of Varus' legions. As for *dicebantur*, poised between certainty and mere rumour,[49] its very imprecision, as Soubiran remarks, 'jette sur ce champ de bataille une sorte de brouillard,

---

[45] Anderson on G. 37. 1; cf. Vell. 120. 1 'Cimbricam Teutonicamque militiam Italiae minabantur' (of the Germans after the *Variana clades*).

[46] Winter (1995), 22–8.

[47] Quoted in Winter (1995), 25. The circumstances are not of course exactly parallel, since the young Frenchmen had died in their own country, defending it against attack.

[48] See Soubiran (1964), 56, who refers to the *Antigone* and *Aen.* 6. 305–30; cf. also Woodman on Vell. 53. 3, DuQuesnay (1992), 232 n. 79.

[49] For some of the varied usages of *dicuntur* and like expressions in Virgil see N. Horsfall, *PLLS* 6 (1990), 49–64.

il donne à ce coin perdu dans les marais et la forêt . . . une véritable atmosphère d'irréel.'[50]

After this introduction, the first of the two central episodes is described by Tacitus as follows (61–2):[51]

Igitur cupido Caesarem inuadit soluendi suprema militibus ducique, permoto ad miserationem omni qui aderat exercitu ob propinquos, amicos, denique ob casus bellorum et sortem hominum. praemisso Caecina ut occulta saltuum scrutaretur pontesque et aggeres umido paludum et fallacibus campis imponeret, incedunt maestos locos uisuque ac memoria deformis. primo Vari castra lato ambitu et dimensis princi- 2
piis trium legionum manus ostentabant; dein semiruto uallo, humili fossa accisae iam reliquiae consedisse intellegebantur: medio campi albentia ossa, ut fugerant, ut restiterant, disiecta uel aggerata. adiacebant 3
fragmina telorum equorumque artus, simul truncis arborum antefixa ora. lucis propinquis barbarae arae, apud quas tribunos ac primorum ordinum centuriones mactauerant. et cladis eius superstites, pugnam aut 4
uincula elapsi, referebant hic cecidisse legatos, illic raptas aquilas; pri-mum ubi uulnus Varo adactum, ubi infelici dextera et suo ictu mortem inuenerit; quo tribunali contionatus Arminius, quot patibula captiuis, quae scrobes, utque signis et aquilis per superbiam inluserit.

Igitur Romanus qui aderat exercitus sextum post cladis annum trium 62
legionum ossa, nullo noscente alienas reliquias an suorum humo tegeret, omnis ut coniunctos, ut consanguineos, aucta in hostem ira, maesti simul et infensi condebant. primum extruendo tumulo caespitem Caesar posuit, gratissimo munere in defunctos et praesentibus doloris socius. quod Tiberio haud probatum, seu cuncta Germanici in deterius tra- 2
henti, siue exercitum imagine caesorum insepultorumque tardatum ad proelia et formidolosiorem hostium credebat; neque imperatorem auguratu et uetustissimis caerimoniis praeditum adtrectare feralia debuisse.

Tacitus begins with Germanicus' desire to bury the dead soldiers ('cupido . . . inuadit soluendi suprema', cf. Sall. *J.* 89. 6 'cupido inuaserat') and the reaction of the present army ('omni qui aderat exercitu'), the two themes which will be resumed chiastically at the end of the episode (62: see below, p. 120). The enclosure of the narrative within this frame, which itself is enclosed within an outer frame (above, p. 115), mirrors the enclosed nature of the site which it describes. Tacitus next leads his readers step by step (*praemisso, incedunt, primo, dein*) to the very centre of site and

---

[50] Soubiran (1964), 56.   [51] For a translation see above, pp. 71–2.

narrative alike (61. 3 *medio*), after which we are gradually led outwards again (*adiacebant, propinquis*) to various points on the periphery (61. 4 *hic, illic, ubi, ubi, quo tribunali, quae scrobes*).

The site itself is first approached by Germanicus' lieutenant Caecina, who was sent ahead to reconnoitre the *occulta saltuum* and to make passable the *umido paludum* and *fallacibus campis* (61. 1): swamps, like *saltus*, are a defining feature of Germany's impenetrability (above, p. 113), while *fallacibus* merges the horror of present and past, evoking as it does both the physical treacherousness of the terrain and the ambush set for Varus six years before.[52] The soldiers then enter the site itself, its description an uncanny pre-echo of the title of Jay Winter's recent book: the *Teutoburgiensis saltus* is a 'site of memory' and a 'site of mourning' ('maestos locos uisuque ac memoria deformis').[53] As the narrative continues, we learn something of the battle which took place there: note the pathetic contrasts between the width of the camp and the shallow ditch (cf. Virg. *Aen.* 7. 157 'humili . . . fossa'),[54] between the precision of the headquarters and the half-destroyed rampart, between the legions when at full strength and their mortally wounded remains. The scattering of the bones (2) calls poignantly to mind the sepulchral formula *inuenies ossa sepulta*,[55] their whitening in the middle of the plain is Virgilian in inspiration (*Aen.* 9. 230 'castrorum et campi medio',[56] 12. 36 'campique . . . ossibus albent'), while the skulls fixed to the trunks of trees (3) are a sign of barbarism employed both

---

[52] Cf. Ov. *Tr.* 4. 2. 33 'perfidus hic nostros inclusit fraude locorum' (of Arminius); for swamps see e.g. Flor. 2. 30. 36, 38.

[53] In his book Winter (1995) expresses (e.g. p. 10) his debt to, and difference from, the work of P. Nora (ed.), *Les Lieux de mémoire* (1984–92), whose seven volumes are now in the process of being abridged into a three-volume English translation (*Realms of Memory* (1996–)). See also e.g. P. den Boer and W. Frijhoff (eds.), *Lieux de mémoire et identités nationales* (1993); on the relationship with historiography, see J. Le Goff, *History and Memory* (Eng. trans. 1992), and P. H. Hutton, *History as an Art of Memory* (1993); and, for the classical world, G. S. Shrimpton, *History and Memory in Ancient Greece* (1997).

[54] This parallel with Virgil, like almost all the others I quote, may be found in Baxter (1972), although often he is not the first to have spotted them. I have quoted only those passages which Tacitus may reasonably be thought to have had in mind (see e.g. n. 56 below). I am not suggesting that Tacitus was conscious of all of them, but their very presence seems to me to contribute to the Virgilian *color* of the whole. Goodyear (1981) seems to me excessively sceptical on this matter (see also below, Ch. 12, Sect. II).

[55] See DuQuesnay (1992), 73 and n. 80, where he quotes also the converse at *CE* 1126. 1 'cum disiecta ossa [the same phrase as in Tacitus] iacerent'.

[56] At first sight an unpromising parallel, and not mentioned by Baxter (1972), but Tacitus does seem to have the passage on his mind (see *Aen.* 9. 239, quoted on p. 123).

by Virgil (the victims of the monster Cacus at 8. 196–7 'foribusque
adfixa superbis | ora', Nisus and Euryalus after being killed by the
Latins at 9. 471 'ora uirum praefixa mouebant') and other authors
(e.g. victims of the Scythians at Amm. 22. 8. 34 'caesorum capita
fani parietibus praefigebant').[57] The barbarism of the Germans is
further underlined by the paronomasia of *barbărae ārae*, which in
Soubiran's words suggests 'la barbarie des rites d'immolation et la
répulsion du narrateur romain'.[58] Next (4) are introduced survivors
of the disaster, who point out where Varus committed suicide, for
which Virgilian phraseology is again deployed (10. 850 'uulnus
adactum', 2. 645 'manu mortem inueniam'), and where Arminius
gloated in victory, which also has a Virgilian tone (9. 634 'uerbis
uirtutem inlude superbis').

Anyone who has ever visited a battle-site will empathize with
Tacitus' account:[59]

A historian's eye interprets the evidence the headstones represent: at Last
Stand Hill a dense concentration of men fighting for their lives; here and
there along the road signs of an effort to form a firing line; down the
forward slopes small clumps where troopers tried to take battle to the
enemy; off in the hinterland individual stones marking the death place
of fugitives or stragglers; in half a dozen scattered spots small concen-
trations where isolated groups made last stands of their own. Beaver
Dam Creek remains a sinister place, but time has removed from it the
physical signs of who died where and when. The Custer battlefield
retains its chilling poignancy because each stone tells a story. It is a story
of a battle going desperately wrong for the man who initiated it and for
the soldiers who followed him into confrontation with savagery.

Custer's famous last stand in 1876 was indeed compared by Simon
Schama with the *Variana clades*,[60] but of course in the latter case
'the physical signs' of the dead were still all too painfully visible to
Germanicus and his men as they interpreted the evidence before
them. Tacitus therefore (62. 1 *igitur*) returns chiastically to the two
themes with which he began this central episode: the reaction to
the scene of the present Roman army ('Romanus[61] qui aderat

---

[57] Used also of the Gauls by Strabo. In one of the scenes on Trajan's Column, 'skulls set
on tall poles give a chilly welcome to the invaders' (F. Lepper and S. Frere, *Trajan's Column*
(1988), 72 [and plate xx] with further references).   [58] Soubiran (1964), 60.
[59] J. Keegan, *Warpaths* (1995), 300.   [60] Schama (1995), 88.
[61] The MS at this point reads *romanis*, emended to *Romanus* by Beroaldus and to *omnis*
by Andresen. Goodyear's note in support of the latter has been said to demonstrate 'his

exercitus') and Germanicus' laying of the first turf for the burial mound.[62]

The construction of the mound denotes burial and commemoration alike, and it is an essential element of both activities that the names of the dead be precisely known. There are 11,285 Canadian soldiers named on the monument which surmounts Vimy Ridge in the Vimy Memorial Park, while the Thiepval Memorial on the Somme commemorates the names of 73,077 British soldiers. Ancient society was no different: names are 'extraordinarily prominent on all categories of Roman inscription',[63] while *hic sunt ossa sita*, accompanied by the name of the deceased, is formulaic in sepulchral inscriptions.[64] Yet the soldiers in AD 15 knew not whose remains they were burying ('nullo noscente'); rather as families in France were encouraged to 'adopt' a dead soldier of the Great War,[65] the Romans treated all the relics as if they were kith and kin ('ut coniunctos, ut consanguineos'), their anger against the enemy increasing all the while ('aucta in hostem ira').[66]

The opening words of the second centrally placed episode (63. 1 'Sed Germanicus cedentem in auia Arminium secutus') bring

sureness of discrimination' in textual matters: 'The virtues of such a note can escape the perception of minds less finely tuned' (J. Diggle, *PBA* 74 (1988), 366–7). Perhaps. But Goodyear admits that the echo of 61. 1 is equally striking 'whether we adopt *omnis* or *Romanus*', and his remarks on *igitur* likewise apply in either case. He says that 'the point that all participate, from Germanicus downwards, is aptly stressed' (a point developed by S. Borzsák in his recent Teubner edition); but this is to disregard the explicit phrase *praesentibus doloris socius* in the next sentence. He argues that '*Romanus* seems vacuous, since the Roman army is not contrasted with any other', adding: 'Some, noting *qui aderat*, oddly fancy it is contrasted with the dead army. That army was Roman too.' Yet *Romanus* not only contrasts with Arminius, the subject of the previous clause, but interacts with *legionum* to point the pathos that Roman was burying Roman—and not in the immediate aftermath of battle, as might be expected, but 'sextum post cladis annum', as Tacitus pointedly says. Moreover, Goodyear seems oblivious of the fact that *omnis* is repeated later in the same sentence; and, though Latin poets were fond of repeating forms of *omnis* in close proximity, this particular repetition clearly falls outside the examples of such polyptoton discussed by Wills (1997), 224–5, and any potential effectiveness is gravely weakened by the intervening *ossa*.

[62] Since Germanicus was thought to be a second Alexander (see e.g. Goodyear on 2. 73. 1–3; Pelling (1993), 78 with further references), note esp. Curt. 7. 9. 21 'horum ossa tumulo contegi iussit et inferias more patrio dedit'.

[63] G. Woolf, 'Monumental Writing and the Expansion of Roman Society in the Early Empire', *JRS* 86 (1996), 28.

[64] e.g. *CIL* 1. 2. 1209: see DuQuesnay (1992), 74.   [65] See Winter (1995), 53.

[66] The sequel to this episode comes at 2. 7. 3, where Germanicus decides not to rebuild the *tumulus*, which had been destroyed by the Germans in the interim. Perhaps he had taken to heart Tiberius' objections at 62. 2.

home to the reader forcibly that the Roman general is confronting the same man whose total and barbaric victory over Varus has
just been so vividly described. Arminius gains an initial advantage
with troops whom he has hidden in the *saltus* ('quos per saltus
occultauerat'), a development which induces in the reader the
kind of suspense and fear which Cicero associated with historiography.[67] For had not Caecina at 61. 1 been sent ahead precisely
to reconnoitre the *occulta saltuum*? Has he not done his job
properly? Will the present leadership turn out to be as incompe-
tent as that of Varus? Is Germanicus in fact likely to go the same
way as Varus? Soon Arminius has trapped the Romans in a
treacherous marsh (63. 2 'paludem . . . iniquam'), but at the
very last moment Germanicus avoids defeat: with the appearance
of the legions, the enemy is overcome with terror, the Romans
boosted by confidence ('inde hostibus terror, fiducia militi', cf.
Sall. *H.* 2. 104 'terror hostibus et fiducia suis incessit').

At this point Germanicus withdraws his army, leaving Caecina
alone with his own troops to face Arminius (63. 3). Uncertain (63.
5 *dubitanti*) how to repair the marsh causeway and fight off the
Germans at the same time, Caecina decides to make camp. The
Germans attack all the same (64. 1–3), yet Caecina is undismayed
(64. 4): with his forty years' experience as a fighting soldier he has
seen it all before, 'secundarum ambiguarumque rerum sciens
eoque interritus'. These words bear some similarity to those
used of Lollius by Horace (*C.* 4. 9. 34–6 'est animus tibi |
*rerum*que prudens et *secundis* | temporibus dubiisque rectus'):[68]
since this was the Lollius whose notorious defeat in 17/16 BC at
the hands of the Germans is coupled with that of Varus earlier in
the *Annals* (1. 10. 4), it would be pointed of Tacitus thus to
underline the dissimilarity between the two men. However that
may be, Caecina thinks his men stand a chance if only they can
reach the level ground (*planities*) which lies between the mountain
and the marsh. Our estimate of Caecina begins to be revised: he
seems not to be a second Varus.

But the night is still not over (65. 1):

nox per diuersa inquies, cum barbari festis epulis, laeto cantu aut truci
sonore subiecta uallium ac resultantis saltus complerent, apud Romanos

---

[67] For which see *RICH* 73, 85, 90–1, 97.
[68] The similarity is noted by Keller–Holder ad loc. but not by Baldwin (1979).

inualidi ignes interruptae uoces, atque ipsi passim adiacerent uallo, oberrarent tentoriis, insomnes magis quam peruigiles.

To add to the despondency of the Romans, with their fitful fires and hesitant voices (cf. *Aen.* 9. 239 *interrupti ignes*), Caecina has a nightmare. He sees emerging from the marsh the figure of Varus himself (65. 2), foul with blood (for combinations of the words 'sanguine . . . cernere' cf. *Aen.* 2. 667, 5. 413, 6. 87) and beckoning to him (cf. *Aen.* 4. 460–1 'hinc exaudiri uoces et uerba uocantis | uisa uiri'). The reader's fear returns (see above, p. 122), and not without reason: when the battle is resumed at dawn (65. 3), Arminius encourages his men with the shout 'Here's Varus and more doomed legions!' With this identification of Caecina with Varus, the present and past merge into one, as they do so often in the *Aeneid*, and the battle seems to be going the way of its predecessor: the horses of the Romans keep slipping in their own blood (cf. *Aen.* 2. 551 'in multo lapsantem sanguine'), and Caecina's own horse is wounded and the man himself on the point of being taken (65. 5–6). Yet the Romans are assisted by the greed of the enemy ('hostium auiditas'), who are keener on looting than killing ('omissa caede praedam sectantium'). By nightfall, as Tacitus quietly informs us, the Romans have managed to reach open ground (*aperta et solida*). Caecina's plan of the previous night (see p. 122) has worked.

In front of them, however, there stretches another night of sheer hell (65. 7 *miseriarum*). They must dig fortifications but have lost their equipment; they are wounded but have no first aid; they are hungry but running out of food (as *cibos diuidentes* suggests). They might just as well be dead ('funestas tenebras'); the next day will surely be their last ('unum iam reliquum diem'). Suddenly a horse breaks loose, causing panic (66. 1); and though Caecina immediately establishes that his men's fear is groundless (66. 2 'uanam esse formidinem'), he can only prevent hysteria by a desperate act of personal courage. Thereupon his subordinates reassure the men that their fear is mistaken ('falsum pauorem esse'), a detail which underlines Caecina's experience: *he* had summed up the situation long before. He next makes a speech (67. 1), saying that their only hope is to fight (cf. *Aen.* 2. 354 *una salus* and 317 *in armis*): if the enemy can be lured close next day by the hope of an assault ('expugnandi . . . spe'), the Romans must break out and, with that break-out, they can reach the Rhine ('erumpendum; illa eruptione ad Rhenum perueniri').

Meanwhile the Germans are as restless as on the previous night (68. 1 *inquies*, cf. 65. 1: p. 122), their only problem being how to deliver the *coup de grâce*. Arminius, true to form, and using almost the same rhetorical device as Caecina had used just before (*egredi egressosque*),[69] urges luring the Romans out of their encampment, but Inguiomerus has a bolder plan which meets with the men's enthusiastic approval: a swift assault (*promptam expugnationem*) followed by looting (*praedam*). These words from the German chieftain mark the turning-point of the episode and guarantee the reader's suspense in exactly the way that Cicero had recommended (see p. 122 n. 67): for an assault was just what Caecina had been banking on, while the German greed for looting had let the Romans off the hook the day before (see p. 123).[70]

The Germans attack at dawn (68. 2) by rushing the Roman ditches and grasping the top of the outer mound (cf. *Aen.* 2. 444 'prensant fastigia dextris'). The Romans at first hang back invitingly but then take full advantage of the reliable and level ground (68. 3 *aequis locis*) which, in contrast to the treacherous marsh of two days before (63. 2 'paludem . . . iniquam': p. 122), Caecina had struggled so hard to gain the previous day: they sweep down on the German rear. Surprised and confused by the sound of the Romans' trumpets and the flash of their weapons (cf. Hor. *C.* 2. 1. 17–19 'minaci murmure cornuum | . . . fulgor armorum'),[71] and more accustomed to greedy looting than to caution under fire ('ut rebus secundis auidi, ita aduersis incauti'), the Germans fall back (68. 4). Arminius and the badly wounded Inguiomerus escape (5), but their troops are slaughtered for as long as daylight and Roman

[69] See Wills (1997), 327–8 and 311 ff. (esp. 312–13) for the devices of Caecina and Arminius respectively. For Arminius as 'Roman' see Pelling (1993), 80–1, and Woodman, *LH* 95.

[70] 'During May and June the Germans advanced to great effect near the rivers Lys and Marne. But unwittingly they were engaged in demonstrating the most ironic point of all, namely, that successful attack ruins troops. In this way it is just like a defeat . . . The spectacular German advance finally stopped largely for this reason: the attackers, deprived of the sight of "consumer goods" by years of efficient Allied blockade, slowed down and finally halted to loot, get drunk, sleep it off, and peer about' (P. Fussell, *The Great War and Modern Memory* (1979 edn.), 17–18, of the great German attack of 1918).

[71] I mention this parallel because, in this ode to Pollio, Horace is rightly thought to be singling out the details of dramatic historiography which Pollio's *Histories* typified: see B. L. Ullman, 'History and Tragedy', *TAPA* 73 (1942), 50–1 and Nisbet–Hubbard ad loc.

anger last ('donec ira et dies permansit'). This is the day which at 65. 7 the Romans thought would be their last (p. 123); this is the anger which has been waiting for release since 62. 1, when they saw what Arminius had done to their predecessors six years before (p. 120). Another night falls. The Romans have more wounded than on the previous night, the same scarcity of food, and Arminius has lived to fight again. But for the moment there is strength and health in victory ('uim sanitatem . . . in uictoria').

This alliterative sentence brings to a close the second and longer of the two central episodes of Tacitus' narrative of foreign affairs; he next describes the activities of Agrippina and the reaction to them of Tiberius (69), a vignette of in-laws which corresponds to the lengthier section on Segestes and Arminius earlier (57–60: above, p. 115). Agrippina is depicted as performing the standard tasks of an ideal general (69. 1–2),[72] a paradox underlined and corroborated by a rare Tacitean appeal to a source (69. 2: the elder Pliny). Yet the paradox is not restricted to a reversal of roles. The location of her actions in Germany combines with the repeated references to her sex (1 *femina*, 4 *femina*, *muliere*) to remind readers of what Tacitus had said towards the end of his *Germania*: amongst certain German tribes it is the woman who is chief (45. 6 'femina dominatur: in tantum non modo a libertate sed etiam a seruitute degenerant', cf. 8. 1, 18. 3).[73] Thus the reversal has the further implication that national boundaries too are being transgressed and that Roman society is acquiring the depravity of the barbarian.[74]

The penultimate section of the narrative deals with the withdrawal (70) and is a reprise of the approach (56). There the conditions were dry and the streams only moderate (56. 2 'siccitate et amnibus modicis inoffensum iter'), circumstances initially encountered now by P. Vitellius, to whom Germanicus had entrusted two legions (70. 2 'primum iter sicca humo aut modice adlabente aestu quietum'). But it had been recognized that these circumstances were unusual for Germany, and earlier fears for the way back are about to be justified (see above, pp. 115f.). The troops are devastated by the onset of a sudden storm (70. 2–4), which

[72] For these tasks see Woodman on Vell., indices s.v. 'ideal general'; Kraus on Liv. 6, index s.v. 'topoi: ideal general or leader'.

[73] See also F. Santoro L'Hoir, *The Rhetoric of Gender Terms* (1992), 132.

[74] See also above, n. 69.

sweeps away the boundaries between water, land, and shore (70. 2): 'eadem freto, litori, campis facies'. Just as the men cannot distinguish between what is safe and what is dangerous ('neque discerni poterant'), so all distinctions between the men themselves break down (70. 3 'permiscentur inter se', 'nihil . . . differre', 'cuncta pari uiolentia'). Only the arrival of daylight restored the boundaries of nature (70. 5 'lux reddidit terram'), allowing the troops to make their way to the appointed rendezvous with Germanicus.

Now, in the concluding paragraph, it is Germanicus, not his wife, who performs the standard tasks of an ideal general (71. 3). Though this restoration of social normality parallels that of nature in the storm episode, Tacitus has made the point that in an unstable world such breakdowns can and will occur: hence, though the double restoration here forms a satisfying closure to the foreign affairs of AD 15, the storm heralds the much more destructive storm with which Germanicus will be obliged to contend in the following year (2. 23–4), while such 'manly women' as Agrippina's daughter will play a prominent part in the unfolding *Annals*. According to Tacitus, Germanicus acted as an ideal general 'in order to soften the memory of disaster' (71. 3 'ut . . . cladis memoriam . . . leniret'). It is not clear what *clades* is meant;[75] but, if the reference is to the *Variana clades*, Tacitus has summed up the whole narrative of the German campaign in a most striking phrase. Normally *memoria cladis* is something to be obliterated by defeating those who inflicted the *clades*; but, despite their recent victory (68. 5), the precise memory of what the soldiers beheld in the *Teutoburgiensis saltus* is beyond obliteration and can be no more than softened by the general's compassion. The past, which Tacitus in his narrative has recreated so brilliantly, lives on.

Tacitus' narrative of the German campaign of AD 15 shows Roman historical writing at its dramatic best. Enclosed by an outer frame are two central episodes, the first rooted deep in memories of the past (61–2), the second a series of present

---

[75] The commentators are unhelpful. The storm evidently lasted only a single night (71. 4 *pernoctauere*) and, though Tacitus in part compares it to warfare in terms which would explain *saucios* and *uulnera* here (cf. 71. 4 'mulcato corpore, haud minus miserabiles quam quos hostis circumsidet'), it seems scarcely to justify the term *clades* (though this is, admittedly, the term used at 2. 24. 1 for the much worse storm of AD 16).

engagements from which the past is never far away and is at times indistinguishable (63–8). During the course of these engagements, which are carefully divided into three days and nights,[76] the Romans are in desperate straits during the first forty-eight hours (63–5) and even suffer from mass hysteria on the night before their victory (66). That the victory is achieved at all is due in no small measure to Caecina, who is at first portrayed in ambiguous terms and regarded by Arminius as a reincarnation of Varus (p. 123); but he nevertheless realizes his intermediate objectives (65. 6) and then has the experience to anticipate the Germans' weakness and capitalize on it (67. 1). Thus the contrast between the increasingly desperate Roman troops and their increasingly astute commander forms a sub-plot which increases the suspense of the major engagements. The various ironies and reversals of the narrative are underlined by the significant repetition of words or phrases, as I have indicated, and the epic quality of the encounter is brought out by the constant allusions to Virgil's *Aeneid*, which I have quoted.[77] Tacitus' account of the German campaign has all the qualities of which Cicero would have approved.

Now a considerable portion of Tacitus' account is derived from episodes in his own earlier *Histories* (see above, Ch. 5), a fact

---

[76] This principle of division is rightly adopted by Goodyear on 1. 63–8 (pp. 105–6).

[77] For ironies and reversals compare further Thucydides' narrative of the funeral speech and plague (*RICH* 33–5), and note the novelistic technique mentioned at *RICH* 64 n. 199.

It is to be noted that almost any of the literary allusions which Tacitus makes can be used to build up even the most meagre hard-core elements of genuine information (*exaedificatio* and *monumenta* in Cicero's terminology: see *RICH* 78 and 83 ff.) into a full-scale narrative. (This is quite apart from any emotive resonances which such allusions may convey.) Thus for the incident in which the horse breaks loose (66. 1) Goodyear follows Andresen in quoting Liv. 37. 20. 11 'equi . . . territi, cum uincula abrupissent, trepidationem et tumultum inter suos fecerunt'; and for Caecina's speech which immediately follows (67) he quotes Liv. 7. 35 (and note how Tacitus' *expugnandi . . . spe . . . succederent* echoes also Liv. 7. 7. 2 'ad castra Romana cum haud dubia expugnandi spe succedentes'). Other potentially useful parallels with Livy are cited by Goodyear on 61. 3–4, 64. 2, and 66. 2; and with Sallust on 61. 2, 64. 3, and 65. 1. We should also remember the conventional nature of much of what Tacitus says, e.g. the characterization of the Germans at 61. 3 (above, pp. 119f., with parallels cited there) and 64. 2 (see Woodman on Vell. 106. 1), and nightfall bringing the end of battle at 68. 5 (cf. e.g. Hdt. 1. 76. 4, 82; Plaut. *Amph.* 255; Virg. *Aen.* 11. 912–15; Liv. 4. 39. 6, 6. 32. 6 [and Oakley's commentary, p. 84], 9. 23. 4, 21. 59. 8; Plin. *Ep.* 4. 9. 9 etc.; D. P. Fowler, *MD* 22 (1989), 89 n. 56). Nor should we discount the possibility of further imitation by Tacitus of other sections of his own narrative in addition to that discussed above in Ch. 5: indeed it was the thesis of Bacha (1906) that much of the *Annals* is composed on precisely this principle. It is therefore easy to appreciate how quickly and successfully an episode can be constructed by resorting to these various techniques: see also below, Ch. 12, Sect. II.

which will have had the effect of encouraging readers to believe
that in the *Annals*, despite the lack of any such promise in the
preface (above, pp. 112–13), they were being given the same kind
of content which, as we know from his contemporary the
younger Pliny, had proved so successful in the earlier work (*Ep.*
7. 33. 1). As the *Annals* progresses, however, it becomes gradually
clear to the reader that any such belief is entirely mistaken. The
reworking of earlier material serves only to emphasize the extent
to which the reader's expectation is eventually thwarted.[78] Tacitus' repeated dwelling on and recreation of the past become
themselves symbolic of the obsolescence of conventional historiography in the face of Tiberius' later principate.

BOOK 4 OF THE *ANNALS*

Programmatic Elements

With *Annals* 4 Tacitus begins the second part of his account of
Tiberius' reign,[79] and at the very start he reaffirms the relationship
with Sallust which he had already established in the opening to
Book 1 (see p. 112). His statement that in AD 23 'fate suddenly
turned disruptive and the emperor himself savage' (4. 1. 1 'repente
turbare *fortuna coepit, saeuire* ipse') is borrowed from Sallust's
description of an earlier occasion on which Roman history had
taken a decisive turn for the worse (*C.* 10. 1 '*saeuire fortuna* ac
miscere omnia *coepit*'). Tacitus attributes the change in Tiberius to
his henchman Sejanus, who is duly described as if he were the
reincarnation of the republican traitor Catiline (4. 1. 2–3, cf. Sall.
C. 5).[80] Yet references to fate and to the malign influence of
Sejanus are not the only means by which Tacitus underlines the
change which now took place in Tiberius' reign.

Several chapters later in Book 4 Tacitus concludes his account
of the year AD 24 by interposing a digression in which he explains
the nature of the history which he is now writing (32–3):

---

[78] See further p. 134 and n. 101.

[79] Since the first hexad of books is devoted to Tiberius' reign, the break between Books
3 and 4 is the half-way point.

[80] This character sketch early in Book 4 balances that of Tiberius himself early in Book
1 (4. 3–5), thus further emphasizing the division of the hexad into two. (The sketch of
Sejanus also contains an echo of Sall. *J.* 48. 1.)

Pleraque eorum quae rettuli quaeque referam parua forsitan et leuia memoratu uideri non nescius sum; sed nemo annalis nostros cum scriptura eorum contenderit qui ueteres populi Romani res composuere. ingentia illi bella, expugnationes urbium, fusos captosque reges, aut si quando ad interna praeuerterent, discordias consulum aduersum tribunos, agrarias frumentariasque leges, plebis et optimatium certamina libero egressu memorabant; nobis in arto et inglorius labor: immota   2
quippe aut modice lacessita pax, maestae urbis res et princeps proferendi imperi incuriosus erat.

non tamen sine usu fuerit introspicere illa primo aspectu leuia ex quis magnarum saepe rerum motus oriuntur. nam cunctas nationes et urbes   33
populus aut primores aut singuli regunt. (delecta ex iis et conflata rei publicae forma laudari facilius quam euenire, uel si euenit, haud diuturna esse potest.) igitur ut olim plebe ualida, uel cum patres pollerent,   2
noscenda uulgi natura et quibus modis temperanter haberetur, senatusque et optimatium ingenia qui maxime perdidicerant, callidi temporum et sapientes credebantur, sic conuerso statu neque alia rerum <salute> quam si unus imperitet, haec conquiri tradique in rem fuerit, quia pauci prudentia honesta ab deterioribus, utilia ab noxiis discernunt, plures aliorum euentis docentur.

ceterum ut profutura, ita minimum oblectationis adferunt. nam situs   3
gentium, uarietates proeliorum, clari ducum exitus retinent ac redintegrant legentium animum; nos saeua iussa, continuas accusationes, fallaces amicitias, perniciem innocentium et easdem exitii causas coniungimus, obuia rerum similitudine et satietate.

tum quod antiquis scriptoribus rarus obtrectator, neque refert cuius   4
quam Punicas Romanasne acies laetius extuleris; at multorum qui Tiberio regente poenam uel infamias subiere posteri manent. utque familiae ipsae iam extinctae sint, reperies qui ob similitudinem morum aliena malefacta sibi obiectari putent. etiam gloria ac uirtus infensos habet, ut nimis ex propinquo diuersa arguens. sed ad inceptum redeo.

[a¹] I am well aware that many of the events which I have been describing, and will proceed to describe, perhaps seem insignificant and too trivial to mention. [b¹] But no one should try to compare my *Annals* with the work of republican historians. Their uninhibited narratives dealt with great wars, sieges of cities, the routing and capture of kings, or (on the domestic front) disputes between consuls and tribunes, agrarian and supply legislation, and power struggles between aristocracy and people. [a²] My work, on the contrary, is limited and mundane,   2
since peace reigned almost completely undisturbed, life in Rome was grim, and the emperor uninterested in imperialist expansion.

[a³] Yet there is some point in focusing on what at first sight are trivialities, since great events often originate from them. [c] Let me   33 explain what I mean. All governments, whether national or civic, are either democracies, oligarchies or monarchies. (A mixed constitution is more of an ideal than a reality, and if it becomes a reality cannot last very long.) Now when the government of Rome was democratic, as was once the case, it was essential to understand the character of the people and the appropriate methods of controlling it. Again, in the days of oligarchy, men achieved reputations as politicians and statesmen if they had acquired a thorough knowledge of the character of the senate and aristocracy. [*a*⁴] Similarly, with the change in constitution and the salvation of affairs depending on monarchy, it is useful to investigate and record topics such as mine. Few people have the capability of making moral or practical judgements in the abstract, but many of them can learn from reading about the experiences of others.

[*a*⁵] Yet for all their usefulness these topics provide hardly any pleasure. [*b*²] Geographical descriptions, fluctuating battles, and generals' glorious deaths are what hold the attention of readers and stimulate their imagination. [*a*⁶] My narrative, on the other hand, is a series of savage edicts, repeated accusations, treacherous friendships, and innocent people slaughtered, always for the same reasons—an obstacle course of monotony and saturation.

[*b*³] Then there is the fact that hardly anyone objects to ancient historians, and no one now cares if your treatment of the Carthaginians or Romans is too encomiastic. [*a*⁷] But many who suffered punishment or disgrace during Tiberius' reign have descendants alive today; and in cases where the families themselves have died out, you will find people whose own analogous behaviour leads them to assume that another's crimes are being imputed to themselves. Even distinction and excellence invite hostility since they constitute too harsh an indictment of their opposites merely by coexisting with them. But I return to my main theme.

This digression is of immense importance because in it Tacitus explains that his own work, which I have denoted by [*a*] in the above translation, is now significantly different from earlier historiography, which I have denoted by [*b*].⁸¹ Let us consider his various statements in turn.

Tacitus begins at [*a*¹] by stating that much of his material may seem insignificant and too trivial to mention, an exact reversal of Cicero's assumption in the *De Oratore* (2. 63) that the material of

---

⁸¹ [*c*] at 33. 1–2 is different in that there Tacitus points to political circumstances in earlier Roman history with which his present narrative might have some affinity; but he still does not suggest an affinity with the historiography of those earlier periods. (Note that our digression is not mentioned in E. Hahn, *Die Exkurse in den Annalen des Tacitus* (1933).)

history would be significant and worthy of being recorded ('in rebus *magnis memoriaque dignis*'). Indeed the importance of one's material was a commonplace of historiography, to be found particularly in prefaces,[82] and the full force of Tacitus' statement of the opposite can be appreciated if it is compared with the remarks with which Dionysius began his *Roman Antiquities* (1. 1. 2–3, 2. 1, 3–6). Some authors actually claimed that their material increased in significance as their work progressed. Thus Virgil, to quote a classic example, begins the second half of the *Aeneid* by announcing that the more weighty part of his epic is under way (7. 44–5 '*maior* rerum mihi nascitur ordo, | *maius* opus moueo').[83] Here Tacitus, at the equivalent point in *Annals* 1–6, does precisely the opposite: henceforward his material will apparently be less, not more, important than hitherto.[84]

Tacitus next at [*b¹*] discourages his readers from comparing his *Annals* with republican historiography. This in itself constitutes a reversal, since historians in their prefaces often claimed that their work was superior to those of their predecessors.[85] Tacitus sees his own inferiority in terms of content, which for earlier historiography consisted of precisely the topics which Tacitus himself had been so glad to advertise in the preface to his *Histories*: great wars, city sieges, and the tragedies of famous men (see above, pp. 109–11).[86] Since the topics which now offer themselves are the opposite of these [*a²*], his present work is correspondingly mundane: the Latin word *inglorius* perhaps suggests an inability on Tacitus' part to achieve the *gloria* which Sallust sought (*C.* 1. 1–4, 2. 9)[87] and

---

[82] See Avenarius (1956), 128–9, Herkommer (1968), 164 ff.

[83] Cf. also *Ecl.* 4. 1 'paulo maiora canamus'; Herkommer (1968), 169 n. 4 [p. 170].

[84] It is of course true that Tacitus twice says that the insignificance of his material is only apparent (32. 1 *uideri*, 2 *primo aspectu*), thus strictly preserving his historiographical self-respect. But no one, on reading the digression, could fail to derive the *impression* that his material is *actually* insignificant. He does the same at [*a³⁻⁴*] below (see p. 132), and creating such impressions is one of his most characteristic techniques (see p. 141).

[85] See *RICH* 6–7, 49 n. 24, 131; in general, Herkommer (1968), 102 ff., especially 109.

[86] Tacitus also mentions domestic issues, which, though they perhaps seem uninteresting to us, were presumably not so to his readers. We should remember that Livy regularly dressed up archaic Roman history in an exciting, late-republican guise (Ogilvie (1965), 10–16, 19). Since Tacitus refers to the *liber egressus* of earlier historians, it is possible that he is alluding to the topic of free speech, to which he devotes the last paragraph of the digression; but most scholars simply see a contrast with *in arto*, immediately following.

[87] That is, there is perhaps a suggestion that, because the author cannot describe exploits which win *gloria*, he will not achieve *gloria* himself. Such a connection between

hence also the readership amongst posterity for which Tacitus himself expressed concern in the *Histories* (1. 1. 1).[88]

Although the second paragraph of the digression contains a defence of his work based on the grounds of utility [a^{3-4}], which is also one of the standard topics in historical prefaces,[89] this defence is effectively undermined by the paragraph which follows and in which Tacitus denies the pleasurableness of his work [a^5]. Pleasure was regarded not only as an essential ingredient if literature in general was to be useful,[90] but also as a vital requirement for historiography in particular: Cicero refers to it no fewer than seven times in a single paragraph of his letter to Lucceius (*Fam.* 5. 12. 4–5), while whole sections of the prefaces of Thucydides and of Tacitus' own *Histories* are devoted to it.[91] Tacitus illustrates his point, as in the first paragraph, by comparing the pleasurable topics of conventional historiography [b^2]. Geographical descriptions were singled out as essential by Cicero in the *De Oratore* and *Orator* and by Tacitus himself in the preface to the *Histories* (p. 109);[92] and

the author and his material lies behind the notion of a hierarchy of genres (on which see D'Alton (1931), 413–14). Since Tacitus couples *inglorius labor* with *in arto*, commentators naturally quote Virg. *G.* 4. 6 'in tenui labor', which is immediately followed by 'at tenuis non gloria'. But Virgil is manipulating generic conventions in just the same way as Tacitus, and in any case he makes it clear in lines 4–5 that the bees can be treated like epic heroes. On Sallust see further *LH* 13–17.

[88] Concern for posterity is the touchstone by which Lucian judges the ideal historian: see e.g. *Hist. Conscr.* 61 'do not write with your eye only on the present . . . ; aim at eternity and prefer to write for posterity', 63 'history should be written . . . with truthfulness and an eye to future expectations . . . ; there is your rule and standard for impartial history'.   [89] See Herkommer (1968), 128 ff.

[90] The classic expression of this view is Hor. *AP* 343 'omne tulit punctum qui miscuit utile dulci': see D'Alton (1931), 483–8. Admittedly some theorists maintained that pleasure and usefulness were mutually exclusive, but such a stance is inapplicable in the case of historiography (see my next remarks).

[91] See *RICH* 25–30 and above, pp. 109–11. Cf. also Duris fr. 1 Jacoby, Cic. *De Or.* 2. 59, *Or.* 37, *Fin.* 5. 51; Vitr. 5 *praef.* 1; Plin. *Ep.* 5. 8. 4; also *RICH* 113 n. 125 and reference there to Fornara (1983), 120–34. Though it is often stated that Thucydides denied any pleasurable aspect to his work, I have argued that this is not the case (*RICH* 28–31). Polybius thought that some of his writing might appear austere and have a restricted appeal since he had excluded from it mythical, genealogical, and foundation history; but since he also professes to deal with the activities of nations, cities, and monarchs, topics which are 'novel in themselves and demand novel treatment', it seems clear that his apologia is greatly qualified (9. 1–2). Livy (*praef.* 4) suggests that readers might derive less pleasure from his account of early Roman history than from that of more recent times; but since it was precisely the earlier, mythical material to which readers were conventionally attracted, Livy's diffidence is somewhat disingenuous (cf. 5).

[92] See *RICH* 79, 83–5, 88–9, 91, 95 for Cicero. The absence of these descriptions here is underlined by Tacitus' use of the technical term *situs* (see Woodman on Vell. 96. 3).

the same two authors also emphasize the importance of suspenseful battles and the glorious deaths of famous men (see pp. 109–10 above). Indeed Tacitus' description of the effect of these topics here ('retinent . . . legentium') perhaps recalls Cicero's account of their importance in the letter to Lucceius (5 'in legendo . . . retinetur'):[93] if so, Tacitus' argument is all the more telling. Finally, the third paragraph of the digression ends, as again did the first, with a depreciatory account of Tacitus' present work [a^6]. The number of words suggesting monotony emphasizes that his work lacks the variety at which authors conventionally aimed and to which the word *uarietates*, just above, perhaps alludes.[94] Lacking as it does so many of the elements of which pleasurable historiography normally consists, his narrative at this point in the *Annals* presents an obstacle course to those readers who might otherwise have derived at least some profit from it.

In the fourth and last paragraph Tacitus engages in a final contrast between the indifference with which ancient historians are read and the hostility which he himself risks as he writes the *Annals*. He then concludes the digression with a standard 'signing-off' formula which itself is significant, as we shall see below.

It is therefore clear that in this digression Tacitus has comprehensively reversed a representative sample of the statements which we would expect to find in a historical preface and which are in fact found in the preface to his own *Histories*. In consequence it may reasonably be asked why he did not place his statements at the very beginning of Book 4, forming a kind of 'second preface' such as is found in some other historians,[95] but instead chose to reserve them for a digression in the body of the narrative. One answer to this question is that he would then have been deprived of his dramatic opening, with its Sallustian references to fate and Sejanus (above, p. 128); but there is also another consideration.[96] Rhetorical convention dictated that when a writer's material was

---

[93] Cf. also *H.* 2. 50. 2 'fictis oblectare legentium animos'.

[94] For variety see *RICH* 106 n. 51.

[95] e.g. Dion. *Ant. Rom.* 11. 1; Liv. 21. 1. 1. Hdt. 7. 20. 2–21. 1 and Thuc. 5. 26 are early examples of the same phenomenon. See Herkommer (1968), 10, and note also G. B. Conte, 'Proems in the Middle', *YCS* 29 (1992), 147–59; on *Aen.* 7. 44–5 in particular (above, p. 131) see D. P. Nelis, *The Aeneid and the Argonautica of Apollonius Rhodius* (1998), ch. 7 § 1, with further refs.

[96] Note also that, by ending on the topic of free speech, he leads neatly into the episode of Cremutius Cordus at 4. 34–5.

unattractive, as Tacitus now claims his to be, he should not use a direct opening but instead should adopt the technique of *insinuatio*, or the 'disguised opening'.[97] By adhering to rhetorical convention Tacitus has successfully underlined the unpleasantness of the material with which he is now dealing.

That his disguised opening takes the form of a digression, which is clearly identified as such by its signing-off formula ('sed ad inceptum redeo'),[98] is also of significance. We know from Cicero that digressions were regarded as a traditional means of entertaining one's readers;[99] and we know from Quintilian and Pliny that by Tacitus' time digressions were particularly associated with the genre of historiography.[100] Thus, by using a digression specifically to *deny* that his work contains any of the pleasurable elements of which conventional historiography was thought to consist, Tacitus could hardly have chosen a more ironically appropriate medium in which to emphasize the changed nature of his work.

That change will have seemed particularly striking to those readers of the *Annals* who were already acquainted with the *Histories*. The latter work, as we have seen (above, pp. 104–11), was equipped with an elaborate preface in which Tacitus explained fully the conventional nature of the narrative on which he was embarking. The preface to the *Annals*, on the other hand, is enigmatic in its brevity (above, pp. 112–13) and designedly, as it now appears, left readers guessing what line its author was going to take. From the narrative of Book 1, with its concentration on foreign fighting and some of its episodes actually borrowed from the *Histories* (above, Ch. 5), readers might reasonably have expected that the *Annals* would be a similar work to its predecessor. But it now transpires that Tacitus has capitalized on his *inuentio* there in order to frustrate those expectations in Book 4 and so emphasize the completely different kind of historiography which is appropriate for the second half of Tiberius' reign.[101]

Tacitus could hardly have written the digression in Book 4 if he and his readers had not regarded historiography as primarily a

---

[97] See Lausberg (1966), 1. 255–6 §§ 280–1.
[98] For which see Woodman on Vell. 68. 5.   [99] See *RICH* 106 n. 51.
[100] Quint. 10. 1. 33 'licet tamen nobis in digressionibus uti uel historico nonnumquam nitore'; Plin. *Ep.* 2. 5. 5 'descriptiones locorum . . . non historice tantum sed prope poetice prosequi fas est'.
[101] For this technique of surprise elsewhere see Cairns (1979), ch. 7.

literary activity. It is because classical historiography functions as a genre like poetry,[102] having its own conventions and generating its own expectations, that Tacitus is able to capitalize on his alleged reversal of them. In just the same way his contemporary, the poet Juvenal, begins his very first satire with an introductory paragraph in which he promises to drive like a charioteer across the open plain (1. 19–21); and he concludes the same satire by saying that he is opening up his sails to their full extent in the wind (149–50). These metaphors of the charioteer, the plain and the open sea, are conventional ways of describing the elevated style of epic poetry, whereas satire was traditionally a self-consciously humble genre. But Juvenal's claim now to be writing satire in the hitherto unacceptable style of epic is explained by his statement (149) that vice is now at its peak. Faced with such unprecedented material, the satirist is compelled to adopt an unprecedented style.[103] A similar position is adopted in the second volume, which consists entirely of the long sixth satire and which Juvenal concludes by suggesting that only the elevated style of tragedy can tackle appropriately the theme of modern women (634–7).[104]

These programmatic allusions to breaking the conventions of the genre resemble those of Tacitus, who, after signifying his unfashionable following of Sallust at the start of Book 1, claims in Book 4 to be unable to write conventional historiography at all. It is true that Juvenal's movement is from the basic to the elevated, whereas that of Tacitus is in the opposite direction;[105] but each writer is adopting the same technique of claiming to pervert generic convention in order to reflect and do justice to abnormal events.[106]

---

[102] See *RICH* 98–100.

[103] See J. Bramble, *Persius and the Programmatic Satire* (1974), 164 ff.; Rudd (1986), 108.

[104] Rudd (1986), 106–8.

[105] Juvenal does, however, adopt a technique analogous to Tacitus' at 4. 11 'sed nunc de factis leuioribus'.

[106] Though their relative chronologies are problematical (see Syme (1984), 1142–57), there are numerous other striking similarities between Tacitus and Juvenal. Some involve matters of technique (e.g. Martin–Woodman on *A*. 4. 57. 2), some involve linguistic parallels (e.g. Tac. *G*. 19. 1 *nemo . . . illic . . . ridet* ~ Juv. 13. 171–3 *illic | . . . ridet | nemo*, both ethnographical contexts). But others seem more basic. For example, the well-known 'credibility gap' between the obsolescence of Juvenal's material and his *persona* of the savage satirist (Rudd (1986), 70–81, 187–90) is paralleled by Tacitus' savage treatment of a still earlier

Metahistory

It is a commonplace that events are at their most abnormal during civil war,[107] and Tacitus in the *Annals* resorts to various devices to suggest that the Julio-Claudian era already displayed many of the symptoms of internecine strife long before the civil war actually broke out on Nero's death in AD 68 (the point at which the *Annals* closes).[108] One such device is the suggestion that first-century AD society was peopled by characters who, like Sejanus at the start of Book 4 (above, p. 128), have republican counterparts.[109] In this way Tacitus implies that the period is nothing other than a rerun of the late republic, an implication which serves as a constant reminder that, like its predecessor, it too will end in disaster.

Another device is the suggestion, which emerges in the second half of Book 4, that after his self-imposed withdrawal from Rome the emperor Tiberius made war on his own people. This intensi-fied version of the civil war motif, most appropriate to the second half of Tiberius' reign, is first used during Tacitus' account of the year AD 26, when astrologers predicted that the emperor, having left the city, would never return (58. 2–3):

> unde exitii causa multis fuit properum finem uitae coniectantibus uulgantibusque; neque enim tam incredibilem casum prouidebant ut undecim per annos libens patria careret. mox patuit breue confinium artis et falsi ueraque quam obscuris tegerentur. nam in urbem non regressurum haud forte dictum: ceterorum nescii egere, cum propin-quo rure aut litore et saepe moenia urbis adsidens extremam senectam compleuerit.

This resulted in the downfall of many who made no secret of their assumption that his death was imminent. They did not foresee the incredible development that he would willingly abandon his native land for eleven full years. But soon the narrow dividing-line between

---

period in the *Annals* (see also *LH* 92–3). The technique of attacking contemporary society indirectly was as well known in ancient times (see e.g. S. F. Bonner, *Roman Declamation* (1949), 43) as it is in modern (see e.g. M. Balfour, *Propaganda in War 1939–45* (1979), 112).

[107] See P. Jal, *La Guerre civile à Rome* (1963), *passim*.

[108] See Keitel (1984), 312–17. As she notes (p. 316), following Koestermann, a key passage for this interpretation is 3. 28. 1–3.

[109] Keitel (1984), 322–3. It follows from the observations in n. 106 above that Tacitus' characters can also prefigure those of his own lifetime: this two- or three-dimensional aspect of character is another area in which Tacitus resembles Virgil (see 'The Creation of Characters in the *Aeneid*', in J. Griffin, *Latin Poets and Roman Life* (1985), 183–97).

that science and falsehood was revealed, and with what obscurities the
truth is disguised. Although theirs had been no idle statement that he
would never re-enter Rome, they were unaware of its ramifications:
he lived out the last years of his life in the neighbouring countryside
or littoral, and on frequent occasions took up a position by the city
walls.

Here Tacitus depicts Tiberius as a voluntary exile (*libens patria
careret*)[110] who, since the verb *adsidere* can mean 'besiege',[111]
regularly returned to assault the very city from which he was
supposed to govern. And the same image is used later, as a
dramatic opening to Book 6 (1. 1–2):

He entered the gardens on the Tiber bank, but again returned to his
lonely cliffs by the sea, ashamed of the criminal lusts with which he
burned unchecked to such an extent that like an oriental monarch he
assaulted the virginity of free-born youngsters . . . Slaves were detailed
to search out suitable victims and produce them for the emperor; the
willing were rewarded, the unwilling threatened; and if relatives or
parents clung on to their charges, the slaves simply kidnapped them
and themselves had their way with them as though they were prisoners
of war [*uelut in captos*].

Not only is the scene here very like that of a sacked city, but the
final phrase *uelut in captos* shows that this is what Tacitus was
thinking of. It is as if Tiberius were the commanding officer of
the siege, directing it from a distance, while his subordinates exact
from their victims the traditional penalties of the victors. Later in
Book 6 there is a similar scene (39. 2): 'Tiberius heard this news
from just outside the city . . . as if able to see the blood flowing
through the houses and the executioners at work'.[112] In the light
of this evidence from Books 4 and 6 of the *Annals* it is likely, but
not of course provable, that Tacitus also exploited the same image
at strategic points in Book 5, which is now lost.

The alienation of Tiberius, which we have hitherto seen
expressed on a metaphorical level, is further emphasized in
Book 4 when, during the account of AD 27, Tacitus describes
the island of Capri to which Tiberius then retired (67. 1–3):

---

[110] For *patria carere* = 'live in exile' cf. e.g. Cic. *Att.* 3. 26, Val. Max. 3. 8. 4.
[111] See Koestermann ad loc., followed by Woodman (1972), 155 (below, p. 150) and
Keitel (1984), 307 n. 2. See *OLD* s.v. 2.   [112] See Keitel (1984), 307.

The island is separated from the tip of the promontory at Surrentum by a strait which is three miles wide. I am inclined to think that its isolation held a particular attraction for him since its entire coastline lacks any proper harbour and its few anchorages are scarcely adequate even for small sailing-craft. In any case no one could land there without alerting the guard. In winter the climate is mild, since a mountain protects it from the worst of the prevailing winds; but it catches the west wind during the summer, when the surrounding sea is seen to its best advantage. There also used to be a fine view across the bay towards the mainland, until the eruption of Mount Vesuvius altered the landscape. Tradition has it that the Greeks took possession of the island and that the Teleboae colonized it; but now it was Tiberius who had settled there in twelve individual and substantial villas, secretly dissipating his energies in depravity and idleness in sharp contrast to the conscientiousness with which he had previously carried out his public duties.

Now it has recently been pointed out that when ancient writers were describing a foreign country, there were five standard elements to which reference was conventionally made: (i) the physical geography of the area; (ii) climate; (iii) agricultural produce and mineral resources; (iv) the origins and features of the inhabitants; (v) the political, social, and military organiza-tion.[113] And it will be seen that four of these five elements are present in Tacitus' description of Capri: its geography, its climate, its original inhabitants, and the social and military organization of its present incumbent. In other words, Tacitus has here employed a kind of metonymy, by applying to Capri the form of geogra-phical description which was normally reserved for foreign coun-tries. The effect is to suggest that the island really was a foreign country, thus emphasizing further the alienation of the emperor who inhabited it.[114]

A similar tactic is used by Tacitus earlier in his account of the same year in order to increase the horror even of those events for which Tiberius was not directly responsible (chapters 62–3):

In the consulships of M. Licinius and L. Calpurnius an unexpected disaster took place. Though over almost as soon as it began, its effects rivalled those of a major military defeat [*ingentium bellorum cladem aequauit*]. An ex-slave called Atilius had started to build an amphitheatre

---

[113] See Thomas (1982), 1 ff.   [114] Thomas (1982), 128.

near Fidenae for gladiatoral displays, but he failed to sink the founda-
tions in solid ground and failed also to lock the wooden superstructure
together with reliable brackets. His behaviour was just what one would
expect of someone who was intent on making an unacceptable profit
without the proper capital or any sense of civic pride.

Deprived of their sport during Tiberius' reign, fans flocked in, men
and women of all ages, their numbers swollen because it was so close to
the town. That increased the scale of the disaster. The building was
packed, and when it gave way it collapsed both internally and exter-
nally: a large crowd of people, spectators and bystanders alike, were
hurled through the air and buried by the falling structure. Those who
were killed outright in the initial collapse (which is what happens when
fate strikes like this) escaped further suffering; more to be pitied were
those who clung on to life despite terrible mutilation and whose only
contact with husband, wife, or children were glimpses during the day
and wailing at night. Soon others, alerted by the news, came to mourn a
brother, a relative, or parents; even those whose friends or relatives were
only away on business became apprehensive: since it had not been
established exactly who had perished in the catastrophe, uncertainty
magnified the panic.

As people began to move away the rubble, there was a general rush to
embrace and kiss the dead; and often quarrels arose when disfigured
corpses, but of the right stature and age, led to cases of mistaken identity.
Forty thousand people were maimed or killed in that disaster . . . but
. . . the aristocracy opened up their houses to provide first aid and
doctors. Throughout the period, although the city was in mourning,
one was reminded of the customs of our ancestors, who in the aftermath
of every great battle [*magna post proelia*] tended the wounded with selfless
devotion.

Now this account can be compared, almost point by point, with
the advice given by Quintilian on how to describe the fall of a
besieged city (8. 3. 67–70).[115] According to Quintilian you should
mention the crash of falling roofs, the confusion, people clinging
to relatives, the wailing of women and children, and the cruelty of
fate. It is as if Tacitus has described the collapse of the amphitheatre in terms which are appropriate to the fall of a besieged
city. Indeed he actually invites the comparison himself since he
begins and ends his account by likening the disaster to a military
catastrophe of major proportions—and the type of military

---

[115] See Woodman (1972), 155–6 (below, Ch. 8, Sect. III). For Quint. see also *RICH* 89.

disaster most likely to involve the collapse of a building is of course the fall of a besieged city. On this occasion the disaster cannot strictly be laid at the emperor's door; but since the amphitheatre would not have been overcrowded if Tiberius had encouraged public spectacles, as Tacitus notes, he is portrayed as indirectly responsible for its collapse: indeed, suggestions of his responsibility are encouraged by the very use of a metaphor which, as we have seen, is elsewhere associated with Tiberius himself.[116]

Thus numerous episodes in the second half of *Annals* 4 can be interpreted metonymically or metaphorically. But although these interpretations have the effect of heightening Tacitus' critical treatment of Tiberius, they also cause the digression earlier in Book 4 to be seen in a different light. In the digression Tacitus claimed that he could do justice to the changed nature of Tiberius' reign only by adopting an alternative form of historiography from which such conventional elements as the besieging of cities and the description of foreign countries were excluded (see above, pp. 131–3). Yet in the subsequent narrative Tacitus comes to terms with the change in Tiberius' reign by providing, through the further alternative of 'metahistory',[117] precisely the elements which he earlier professed to exclude. This latter procedure, while not strictly at variance with the former,[118] is nevertheless intended to elicit an opposite reaction from his readers, whose attention is expected to be engaged by the metonymic or metaphorical presentation of elements whose absence they had been asked previously to deplore. Yet such ambivalence is entirely characteristic of a narrative in which we are warned repeatedly about the deceptiveness of first impressions by a writer whom we are often required to read 'very closely indeed to perceive that he has in fact denied what one thought he had said'.[119]

---

[116] Such continuity of metaphor is a regular Tacitean technique: see e.g. Walker (1952), 159; also below, Ch. 11, and, for further metonymy, pp. 183–5.

[117] This term is borrowed from the title of Hayden White's well known book on the 'historical imagination in nineteenth-century Europe': *Metahistory* (1973).

[118] That is, the narrative remains metonymic or metaphorical. It cannot be denied, however, that the fighting in Thrace in AD 26, which Tacitus describes in 4. 46–51, does indeed contradict the programmatic statements made in the digression only a dozen or so chapters earlier. I have no other explanation for this than that it is a large-scale example of the technique mentioned in the following note.

[119] Irving Kristol (*Encounter*, 6 (May 1956), 86). Tacitus, as is well known, regularly uses

such words as *species* or *imago* to suggest that in political life things are rarely what they seem to be (see e.g. Walker (1952), 240–1). This suggestion is so characteristic of his narrative that it almost constitutes a warning to view the narrative itself in that light. Certainly Tacitus, as I have tried to illustrate with reference to Book 4, likes to manipulate his readers in contrary directions. For example, at 1. 73. 1–3 the impressively sinister introduction to the trials of Falanius and Rubrius would lead one to think that they were found guilty and punished; but they are in fact acquitted. At 1. 74. 3 Granius Marcellus is arraigned on a charge of treason 'from which there was no escape' (*ineuitabile crimen*); yet he too is acquitted. At 1. 74. 4, when the emperor speaks, Tacitus comments bitterly about the state of freedom; but at 1. 77. 3, when the emperor remains silent, he comments equally bitterly about the state of freedom. (These two passages form a neat inversion of the scene described at Sen. *Contr.* 6. 8 *fin.*) Finally, the account of foreign affairs at 6. 31–7 is used to suggest at 38. 1 both that domestic events are frightful and that there are no foreign affairs worth the name to be described. This is, of course, only a selection from a much greater number of cases and types. See also above, n. 84.

The Structure and Content of
Annals 4. 57–67

I. The Evidence

Book 4 of the *Annals*, covering the years AD 23–8, traces the turning-point in the story of Tiberius' reign. Tacitus prepares us for disaster from the start. After a reference to *fortuna* in suitably Sallustian language (1. 1 *repente turbare fortuna coepit, saeuire ipse*, cf. Sall. *C.* 10. 1) and the *deum ira in rem Romanam* (1. 2), we are told that the year AD 23 'initiated the deterioration in Tiberius' principate' (6. 1).[1] Modern historians are agreed that a decisive factor in this deterioration was the emperor's determination to leave Rome in AD 26, a move which Tacitus gloomily portends in chapter 41 (AD 25) and eventually records, in due chronological sequence, at 57. 1. Suetonius is our other main source for this momentous event, and it is instructive to compare his treatment of it with that of Tacitus.[2]

Suetonius		*Tacitus*
secessum Campaniae petit; [39]	(*a*)	tandem Caesar in Campaniam [57. 1, cf. abscessus below]
constanti et opinione et sermone paene omnium quasi neque rediturus umquam et cito mortem etiam obiturus. [39]	(*b*)	ferebant periti caelestium . . . ut reditus illi negaretur, unde exitii causa multis fuit, properum finem uitae coniectantibus uulgantibusque; [58. 2]

---

[1] References to Tacitus' *Annals* are to Book 4 unless otherwise stated.

[2] Suet. *Tib.* 39–41. I have italicized those correspondences which seem of particular significance.

quod paulo minus utrumque
euenit: [39]

nam neque Romam amplius
rediit, [39]

et *paucos post dies* iuxta
Tarracinam (here follows the
cave disaster at Spelunca). [39]

peragrata Campania cum
Capuae Capitolium, Nolae
templum Augusti, quam
causam profectionis *praetenderat*,
dedicasset, [40]

Capreas se contulit, [40]

praecipue delectatus insula, quod
. . . (here follows a description
of the island). [40]

statimque reuocante assidua
obtestatione populo propter
cladem qua apud Fidenas . . .
(here follows the amphitheatre
disaster), [40]
transiit in continentem
potestatemque omnibus
adeundi sui fecit; [40]

(*c*)   mox patuit breue
confinium artis et falsi,
ueraque quam obscuris
tegerentur: [58. 3]

(*d*)   *nam* in urbem non
regressurum haud forte
dictum. [58. 3]

(*e*)   ac forte *illis diebus*
oblatum Caesari anceps
periculum (here follows
the cave disaster at
Spelunca). [59. 1–2]

(*f*)   at Caesar dedicatis per
Campaniam templis, [67.
1, cf. 57. 1 tandem Caesar
in Campaniam, *specie*
dedicandi templa apud
Capuam Ioui, apud
Nolam Augusto.]

(*g*)   Capreas se in insulam
abdidit; [67. 1]

(*h*)   solitudinem eius *placuisse*
maxime[3] crediderim,
quoniam . . . (here
follows a description of
the island). [67. 2] ||

(*i*)   nam coepto apud
Fidenam amphitheatro
(here follows the
amphitheatre disaster).
[62–3]

(*j*)

---

[3] *maxime* qualifies *placuisse*: cf. Gerber–Greef, 792b.

tanto magis quod urbe   (k)   quamquam *edicto*
egrediens *ne quis* se interpellaret   monuisset *ne quis* quitem
edixerat ac toto itinere adeuntis   eius inrumperet, [67. 1]
submouerat. [40]
regressus in insulam, *rei publicae* (l)   quanto intentus olim
quidem *curam* usque adeo   *publicas ad curas* . . .
abiecit ut . . . [41]   [67. 3]

Suetonius gives us what is surely the most natural account of the journey. Starting from Rome the imperial retinue took the Via Appia south as far as Spelunca, where the cave collapsed during a banquet (cf. (*e*) above); thence along the Appian Way inland to Capua and Nola for the dedication of temples (cf. (*f*) above), and finally to Capri (cf. (*g*) above). Tacitus' account is strikingly similar,[4] even in its circumstantial detail,[5] so much so that both authors would appear to be using the same source. Yet there is one glaring difference between the two accounts. Whereas Suetonius gives a continuous narrative of the emperor's departure, running through from chapter 39, Tacitus does not: having presented us from 57. 1 to 59. 2 with various initial aspects of the journey in AD 26 (57 reasons and motives, 58. 1 the retinue, 58. 2–3 rumours, 59. 1–2 the Spelunca incident), he then breaks off quite suddenly and does not return to the narrative of the journey until several chapters later at 67. 1–3 (cf. (*f*) above),[6] a point which is only two sentences away from the end of the *following* year, AD 27 (67.4). It is highly unlikely that the journey from Rome to Capri took this length of time,[7] quite apart from

---

[4] Tacitus does not make it clear that the episode at Spelunca (in (*e*) above) actually took place on the journey, but his introductory phraseology (*illis diebus*) closely resembles that of Suetonius, who *does* assign the incident to the journey (*paucos post dies*)—naturally, since Spelunca is in fact *en route* from Rome to Capua and Nola. The reason for Tacitus' obscurity on this point is doubtless to be attributed to his summary of the *reasons* for Tiberius' departure, an 'insertion' which somewhat disrupts the narrative (see Syme (1958), 695).

[5] Suetonius' slick comment at (*c*) above contrasts strongly with Tacitus' typically heavy philosophizing here, but the subjectivism of both authors would seem to have a common origin in some earlier source (see how their next statements both commence with *nam* (*d*)).

[6] Koestermann's note on 67. 1 is the only helpful observation on the problem. On this point he says: 'Tacitus begleitet nunmehr den Kaiser auf seiner Reise nach Capri und nimmt damit den cap. 58, 2 abgerissenen Faden wieder auf' (he ought to have said 59. 2, cf. my n. 4 above).

[7] Although Tiberius had spent a whole year in Campania before, AD 21–2 (cf. Tac. *A.* 3. 31. 1–64. 1). Koestermann (loc. cit.) opts for an intermediate view: 'Da sich die Erzählung

the evidence to the contrary of Suetonius, who definitely states that the collapse of the amphitheatre at Fidenae in AD 27 took place *after* Tiberius had settled on Capri (chapter 40, cf. especially (*j*) above); Tacitus, because he has interrupted the narrative of the journey so extensively, seems to imply || that the collapse of the amphitheatre (62–3, cf. (*i*) above) took place *before* Tiberius settled on Capri (67. 1).[8]

This presents us with a question. Why should Tacitus, a writer who on occasion can conjoin even the most protracted sequences of events,[9] here choose to interrupt a single and relatively short episode, one of the most decisive of the reign, by interposing an account of an amphitheatre disaster at Fidenae and various other apparently irrelevant topics?

The latest commentator on the *Annals*, E. Koestermann, has rightly suggested that Tacitus did so 'aus kompositionellen Gründen',[10] and it is my purpose to demonstrate what this means.

II. The Structure

We saw that the two points where Tacitus treats the journey to Capri are 57. 1–59.2 and 67. 1–3. It is important to note that when Tacitus resumes his narrative of the journey in the latter section, he picks up several aspects of it which he had already mentioned in the earlier section. Thus the actual retirement at 67. 1 'se in insulam abdidit' recalls 57. 1 'procul urbe' and 'abscessus'; the emperor's desire for solitude at 67. 2 'solitudinem eius placuisse maxime' recalls 57. 2 'secreto uitare coetus';[11] the emperor's dereliction of duty and voluptuous living at 67. 3 'quanto intentus

---

in dem Zwischenstück über zwei Jahre erstreckt, muß sich der Aufenthalt in Kampanien über längere Zeit am Ende des Jahres 26 ausgedehnt haben', a comment which, if I understand it correctly, would seem to be at variance with his next statement (quoted below, n. 10).

[8] Koestermann again: 'Das cap. 67 Erzählte geht also zeitlich dem Einsturzunglück in Fidenae und dem Brand in Rom (cap. 62 ff.) voraus, wie denn auch mit *dedicatis per Campaniam templis* auf cap. 57, 1 zurückgegriffen wird.'

[9] e.g. at *A.* 12. 31–40, on which see (most conveniently) Goodyear (1970), 24, who refers to Kroll (1924), 371 ff.

[10] 'Daß aber der Historiker den zeitlichen Zusammenhang aus kompositionellen Gründen unterbrochen hat, geht aus Suet. Tib. 40 hervor, wo es heißt, Tiberius sei auf die Kunde von der Katastrophe in Fidenae noch einmal auf das Festland zurückgekehrt.'

[11] This particular phrase strictly refers to Tiberius' previous sojourn in Rhodes, but we are clearly meant to understand it as referring to Capri also. Cf. n. 12.

olim publicas ad curas, tanto occultior<es> in luxus et malum otium resolutus' recalls 57. 1 'saeuitiam ac libidinem . . . locis occultantem', 57. 2 'recondere uoluptates',[12] and much of the section 58. 3–59. 2 (on which see below, pp. 150 and 152f.). Moreover, the actual wording with which Tacitus returns to the theme of the journey at 67. 1 ('at Caesar dedicatis per Campaniam templis') picks up almost identically the wording with which he introduced the journey at 57. 1 ('tandem Caesar in Campaniam, specie dedicandi templa'). Tacitus' treatment of the journey has thus come round in a circular movement, assisted by the repetition of ideas and even of phraseology. This method of writing, familiar from archaic Greek onwards, has been called 'ring-composition',[13] and though commonest perhaps in poetry,[14] is found also in historical prose. A classic example is the first twenty-three chapters of Thucydides,[15] but there is an excellent illustration in Tacitus' *Histories*, Book 3. Having described the burning of the temple || on the Capitol, Tacitus writes (71. 4), 'sic Capitolium clausis foribus indefensum et indireptum conflagrauit'; there then follows what E. Fraenkel has called 'a funeral speech to the temple',[16] which lasts until the end of the next chapter, where Tacitus concludes (72. 3), 'ea tunc aedes cremabatur'. Here it is two polar sentences which mark the limits of the ring-composition, whereas in our example from the *Annals* the device is extended beyond this to include repetitions of ideas as well as of phraseology;[17] but in both cases the end result is the same—the intervening narrative appears to be 'framed' by such repetition.[18]

---

[12] This phrase, together with the one that immediately precedes it in our texts (cf. n. 11), perhaps ought to follow on straight after 57. 1 'saeuitiam ac libidinem . . . locis occultantem'; cf. J. P. V. D. Balsdon, *CR* 61 (1947), 44 f., on the possibility of textual displacement. [But see now Martin–Woodman on 57. 2.]

[13] See A. Lesky, *History of Greek Literature* (1966), index, s.v. 'Ring composition'.

[14] For Latin instances see Williams (1968), index, s.v. 'Ring composition'.

[15] See F. E. Adcock, *Thucydides and his History* (1963), 91 f., who refers to R. Katičič, 'Die Ringkomposition im ersten Buche des Thukydideischen Geschichtswerkes', *WS* 70 (1957), 179–96. Cf. also N. G. L. Hammond, 'The Arrangement of Thought in the Proem and in other parts of Thucydides I', *CQ* 2 (1952), 127 ff.

[16] *Kleine Beiträge* (1964), ii. 594.

[17] On this extended type of ring composition compare the remarks of C. O. Brink, *Horace on Poetry* (1971), ii. 453–4.

[18] Cf. W. A. A. van Otterlo, *Untersuchungen über Begriff . . . der griech. Ringkomposition* (1944), 3, 'Der ganze Abschnitt . . . umrahmt . . . wird', although the rest of his definition

Being a primarily artistic device, ring-composition lends itself to various elaborations. Its essence, as we have seen, consists of certain repetitions at the beginning and end of a section of narrative, and similar structural correspondences, often of a quite complicated nature, are regularly found *within* a section of narrative framed by ring-composition.[19] I believe this to be true of the section which interrupts Tacitus' account of the emperor's journey to Capri, 59. 3–66. 2. It will be most easily explained if I start with chapters 62–3, the amphitheatre disaster at Fidenae.

The actual *disaster* at Fidenae (which I shall call A^1) lasts from 62. 1 to 63. 2, where Tacitus concludes the episode by referring to the *generosity* of some leading men (B^1), adding that their relief work recalled the practice of the *old days* (C^1): 'patuere *procerum* domus, . . . ueterum institutis similis, qui . . . *largitione* et cura sustentabant.' In these two chapters there are, as indicated, three main ideas. There is next a link-sentence at 64. 1 ('nondum ea clades exoleuerat *cum* ignis uiolentia urbem ultra solitum adfecit, deusto monte Caelio'), introducing a second set of topics, a fire on the Caelian Hill at Rome and its sequel (64–5). The actual *disaster* (A^2) is quickly dismissed in a few words by Tacitus, who proceeds (64. 2) to record the *generosity* of the emperor (B^2); the part Tiberius played in the relief work was, says Tacitus, epitomized by the discovery of a statue of him unharmed among the ruins (64. 3), an incident which leads Tacitus into recalling a similar incident in the *old days* (C^2), which in turn develops into information on the appellation of the Caelian Hill in the *old days* (chapter 65; again C^2): 'munificèntia iuuerat . . . euenisse

maio⋯itus'.

We⋯sented with two parallel episodes, each constituting two chapters, and their parallelism is confirmed by another link-sentence at 66. 1 where the two incidents are deliberately grouped together to contrast with the account of delation

is more narrow than the type under discussion here. For sentence-framing in Latin prose (Livy), cf. H. Klingelhöfer, *Philol. Quart.* 4 (1925), 321 ff.; in Latin poetry (Lucretius), P. H. Schrijvers, *Horror ac Divina Voluptas* (1970), 154. Reference may also be made to J. J. Keaney, 'Ring Composition in Aristotle's *Athenaion Politeia*', *AJP* 90 (1969), 406–23, which I came across only after my paper had been accepted for publication and which has some useful introductory remarks for those who cannot get hold of van Otterlo's monograph.

[19] See the complicated internal chiastic structure explained by Fraenkel on Aesch. *Ag.* 205, and compare the structure of some of Catullus' longer poems (esp. in Williams (1968)).

which follows: 'sed *ut* studia *procerum* [B¹] et *largitio* principis [B²]
aduersum casus solacium tulerant, *ita* accusatorum maior in dies et
infestior uis sine leuamento grassabatur.'[20] Within each of the two
|| episodes we have been given parallel treatments of three main
ideas (disaster, generosity, the old days); but whereas in the first
episode the disaster is magnified and the leading men's generosity
and the recollection of the past are only briefly mentioned, in the
second episode the disaster and the emperor's generosity are only
briefly mentioned, and the recollection of the past is extended by
means of the antiquarian addition. The scale of treatment is
therefore chiastic, in contrast to the parallel run of thought.

The link-sentence at 66. 1 firmly joins chapter 66 to the two
preceding episodes, although its subject-matter (the *delatores*) has,
of course, no correspondence in 62–5. But now that we have
observed the highly artificial arrangement of 62–5, we are entitled
to ask whether chapter 66 corresponds to anything earlier than
62, thus confirming the interrelated structure which seems to be
emerging. (It naturally cannot refer to anything later than 67,
since at section 1 of that chapter Tacitus returns to his narrative of
the journey.)

The chapter which immediately precedes 62 can, I think, be
omitted with justice from structural consideration. It is the final
chapter of the year AD 26; it consists entirely of an obituary notice
and is simply a conventional method used by the annalistic historian to conclude his account of a year's activities.[21] It is an
insertion into the narrative which has no bearing on the surrounding structure one way or the other.[22]

We are therefore thrown ▓▓▓▓▓▓▓▓▓▓▓▓▓▓▓▓▓▓▓▓▓▓
narrative, which most certa▓▓ ▓▓▓▓▓▓▓▓▓▓▓▓▓▓▓▓▓▓▓▓
(59. 3–60. 3; cf. *accusatorum* at the very beginning of 59. 3 and
accusatorum also in the link-sentence at 66. 1). Thus, in the same
way as we saw that 57. 1–59. 2 corresponded to 67. 1–3, so now

---

[20] *procerum* here picks up *procerum* at 63. 2; *largitio* used of Tiberius here picks up verbally
largitione at 63. 2, showing that the emperor's *munificentia*, like the activities of the *proceres* at
63.2, is to be applauded as *ueterum institutis similis*.

[21] See Syme (1958), 312 f., 'Obituaries in Tacitus', *AJP* 79 (1958), 18 f., 30 f. (= *Ten
Studies in Tacitus* (1970), 79 f., 89).

[22] Nevertheless there is a sort of correspondence between chs. 61 and 66: each contrasts
a pair of men, one of whom is *claris maioribus*, and in each case there is a distinguished
nobilis who fails to live up to his family tradition. This surely confirms the care which
Tacitus has put into the writing of this whole section.

59. 3–60. 3 corresponds to 66. 1–2. These correspondences, together with those between the disaster at Fidenae and the disaster on the Caelian Hill, are most clearly brought out with the help of a diagram.[23]

Tiberius' Journey to Capri

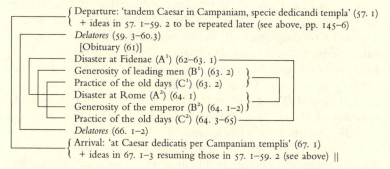

From what I have said in this part of my discussion it should be clear that in this section of the narrative of Book 4 Tacitus has arranged his material with great care. Whether this arrangement is successful, however, is a question we must leave until we have considered in more detail the content of the narrative at this point.

III. THE CONTENT

My remarks on the content of these chapters will be restricted to two main sections, the first part of the journey (57. 1–59. 2) and the disaster at Fidenae (62–3).

First, the journey. Why did Tacitus not discuss the dedication of temples in Campania, only mentioning them briefly at 57. 1 and 67. 1? There would seem to be two reasons. The subject of temples (this time in Asia) had already occupied the two chapters preceding 57; since it would have been monotonous to proceed directly and in detail to temples in Campania, Tacitus simply reports the emperor's intention and the eventual *fait accompli* without intervening comment. This is in the interests of *variatio*. We should also note that all of chapter 57 consists in various

---

[23] The correspondences indicated on the left-hand side of the list denote thematic links; those on the right denote scale of treatment.

motives for the emperor's departure for Campania, the dedication of the temples being only one of them. Tacitus is in reality much more concerned with the alternative and less pleasing motives, such as Tiberius' tendency to vice. This is the historian's characteristic *insinuatio*, and it is continued into chapter 58 by means of a brilliant double paradox which emphasizes the emperor's dereliction of duty. At 58. 2–3 Tacitus employs two phrases which can be taken to mean that he visualizes Tiberius as an exile ('patria careret') returning to assault the city which has evidently rejected him ('saepe moenia urbis adsidens').[24] Tiberius is made to look like a reincarnation of Marius. Yet Tacitus also describes Tiberius as *libens*: he is a *willing* exile, *not* rejected by his citizens, and, since his real duty is that of *princeps* (cf. Tiberius' speech in the senate as reported at 38. 1), he is reprehensible on this count too. This is a typically Tacitean use of language.

Secondly, the collapse of the amphitheatre at Fidenae (62–3). Tacitus begins the episode by likening it to a military disaster (62. 1): 'ingentium bellorum cladem aequauit malum improuisum'. He is preparing to treat the whole catastrophe in metaphorical terms derived from the sphere of warfare; more particularly, since it was a *building* that suffered the disaster (an amphitheatre), the most appropriate comparison within the general military sphere was that of a city under siege, where the collapse of buildings was to be expected. It is hardly surprising that Tacitus wanted to treat the episode at Fidenae in these terms. The besieging and capture of cities was an extremely popular *topos* with ancient historians,[25] so much so that references to beleaguered cities become proverbial for cruelty[26] and theorists like Quintilian issued detailed instructions || on how the topic should be treated.[27] Quintilian

---

[24] For *patria carere* in this sense cf. e.g. Cic. *Att.* 3. 26, Val. Max. 3. 8. 4. For *adsidere* see the remark of Koestermann here, 'An unsere Stelle klingt also die Bedeutung "feindlich belagern" mit unter', and to his examples of the verb in this sense now add R. O. A. M. Lyne, *Latomus*, 28 (1969), 694 ff.

[25] See P. G. Walsh, *Livy* (1961), 191 ff., and cf. Virg. *Aen.* 2. 746 'quid in euersa uidi crudelius urbe?' See also n. 26.

[26] e.g. Cic. *Dom.* 37. 98 'ea quae capta urbe accidunt uictis', Sall. *C.* 52. 4 'capta urbe nihil fit reliqui uictis', *H.* 1. 30 '*speciem* captae urbis efficere', Catull. 62. 24 'quid faciunt hostes capta crudelius urbe?', Ov. *Met.* 12. 225 'captaeque erat urbis *imago*'. [Add [Sall.] *Ep. Caes.* 2. 3. 4 with Vretska's n., Liv. 24. 39. 6, *per.* 80; G. M. Paul, '*Urbs Capta*', *Phoenix*, 36 (1982), 144–55.]

[27] Quint. 8. 3. 67–70, cf. Hermogenes in *Rhet. Graec.* ed. Spengel, ii. 16, *Rhet. Herenn.* 4. 39. 51 (and the parallels there cited by H. Caplan in the Loeb edn., p. 358 n.).

envisages two main parts to the description. First, the actual collapse of the city—and here most of the details which he mentions are also used by Tacitus in his own description.[28] Secondly, the plundering of the vanquished and the taking of spoils, activities not so apposite for a disaster-area such as there was at Fidenae, so Tacitus omits them. But this is not to say that Tacitus' writing becomes any the less rhetorical or dramatic: the commentators observe how his elaboration of the confusion (63. 1 'et saepe certamen, si confusior facies, sed par forma aut aetas errorem adgnoscentibus fecerat') finds its parallels in those two most rhetorical of writers, Curtius Rufus and the younger Seneca.[29]

Tacitus himself admitted the popularity of the 'captured-city *topos*',[30] and in view of the evidence there can be little doubt that he described the amphitheatre disaster in such terms simply because the *topos* was so popular with authors and readers alike. Indeed his treatment is so rhetorical, as we have seen, that I am inclined to think he had no more source-material for this episode than is provided by Suetonius, our only other authority for the event (*Tib*. 40): 'cladem qua apud Fidenas supra XX hominum milia gladiatorio munere amphitheatri ruina perierant'.[31] Having

---

[28] Quintilian mentions: the crash of falling roofs ('ruentium tectorum fragor'), the confusion ('ex diuersis clamoribus unus quidam sonus, aliorum fuga incerta'), the clinging to relatives ('alii extremo complexu suorum cohaerentes'), the wailing of women and children ('infantium feminarumque ploratus'), the cruelty of fate ('male usque in illum diem seruati fato senes'). Tacitus mentions: the falling structure ('conferta mole, dein conuulsa, dum ruit intus aut in exteriora effunditur, . . . praeceps trahit atque operit'), the confusion ('nequedum comperto quos illa uis perculisset, latior ex incerto metus'), the presence of women and children ('uirile ac muliebre secus' (an impressive phrase, cf. H. Tränkle, *WS* 81 (1968), 128), 'omnis aetas, . . . immensamque uim mortalium'), their wailing ('per diem uisu, per noctem ululatibus et gemitu coniuges aut liberos noscebant'), the loss of relatives ('iam ceteri fama exciti, hic fratrem, propinquum ille, alius parentes lamentari'), the cruelty of fate ('quos principium stragis in mortem adflixerat, ut tali sorte, cruciatum effugere: miserandi magis quos abrupta parte corporis nondum uita deseruerat').

[29] Curt. 8. 3. 13 'confuderat oris exsanguis notas pallor nec quis esset nosci satis poterat', Sen. *Tro*. 1112 ff. 'signa clari corporis | et ora et illas nobiles patris notas | confudit imam pondus ad terram datum'.

[30] In the famous digression in this book, 32. 1 (*expugnationes urbium*).

[31] This is a somewhat different appraisal from that of Koestermann, who says: 'Mit wenigen Strichen hat Tacitus so ein aussergewöhnlich lebendiges Bild der turbulenten Szenen entworfen. Die Erzählung, obwohl nicht frei von rhetorischen Elementen . . .'. Koestermann also invites us to compare Plin. *Ep*. 6. 20, on the eruption of Vesuvius. This letter was actually written to Tacitus, providing first-hand source-material for a part of his *Histories*, now lost. It would perhaps be attractive to imagine that when Tacitus came to write about Fidenae he reutilized the account of Vesuvius which Pliny had sent on request

thus displayed his prowess at vivid description, || Tacitus next proceeds to demonstrate his adroitness of *variatio* since, by coincidence, there was a second calamity in the same year, the fire on the Caelian Hill at Rome (64–5). Here Tacitus does not describe the disaster itself at all, for the same reason as he did not describe the temple dedications at 57. 1 (see above, p. 149), but concentrates instead on parallels with the past (64. 3–65), thus succumbing to another contemporary fancy, the love of antiquarianism.[32] It would appear that in these four chapters Tacitus is prepared to interrupt his account of the important journey to Capri for the sake of the rhetorical gratification of his readers.

But is Tacitus so frivolous a writer as this conclusion would imply? We agreed earlier that in this section of the narrative of Book 4 Tacitus has arranged his material with great care; we also agreed to leave in abeyance the question of whether his arrangement is successful (above, p. 149). We are now in a position to try to answer this question, and at the same time decide whether his method of composition at this point has been frivolous. The answer to these problems must lie with Tacitus' ability to link chapters 62–5—and, indeed, those other apparently irrelevant sections (59. 3–60. 3 and 66. 1–2)—to the narrative of the journey. In other words, we must determine fully what the above diagrammatic analysis of the narrative implies.

The incident in the cave at Spelunca, after which Tacitus actually interrupts his treatment of the journey (59. 1–2), plays an important part in answering these problems. When the cave collapsed, it was Sejanus who saved the emperor's life, and as a result of this action (says Tacitus) his influence with Tiberius

---

a few years earlier. But this romantic view cannot be contemplated because Pliny, like his hero Cicero (*Att.* 2. 1. 1–2), elaborates even the factual fundamentals to make it look like 'real' (i.e. rhetorical) history (cf. H. W. Traub, 'Pliny's Treatment of History', *TAPA* 86 (1955), 213 ff., esp. 229–31). Both Pliny and Tacitus, despite their different genres, are working within a common tradition. (An analogous case, also involving Pliny and Tacitus, can be found elsewhere in this book of the *Annals*. At *Ep.* 1. 20 Pliny writes to Tacitus on the question of style, saying (12): 'plerumque paruae res maximas trahunt'. At chs. 32–3 Tacitus has a famous digression on Tiberian historiography, saying (32. 2) that: 'non tamen sine usu fuerit introspicere illa primo aspectu leuia, ex quis magnarum saepe rerum motus oriuntur'. The sentiments are identical; but they constitute a commonplace [see e.g. Martin–Woodman ad loc., Woodman–Martin on 3. 31. 2].)

[32] On which cf. H. Peter, *Die geschichtliche Litteratur über die röm. Kaiserzeit* (Leipzig, 1897), i. 108 ff. For further cliché in this section (64. 1 *fortuita ad culpam trahentes*), cf. Cic. *Verr.* 5. 131, *Leg. Man.* 10, *Pis.* 43, *Rab. Post.* 29; Vell. 118. 4; Sen. *Clem.* 1. 2. 1.

increased and he could now intensify the delation against Nero
Caesar (59. 2–3 'maior ex eo et, quamquam exitiosa suaderet, ut
non sui anxius, cum fide audiebatur. adsimulabatque iudicis partes
aduersum Germanici stirpem . . . '). The first *delatores* episode is
thus made to arise out of the cave incident. From a different
angle, the same (it will be seen) may be said about the disaster at
Fidenae.

We have noted (above, p. 150) how in chapters 57. 1–58. 3
Tacitus portrayed the emperor in an odious light as a lonely
debauchee who has deserted his duty of *princeps*. The incident
at Spelunca, which follows immediately, is simply a concrete
example of this portrait. While he ought to have been engaged
in the government at Rome, Tiberius instead was celebrating a
banquet in the country (59. 2 'conuiuium celebrabant'); the
banquet, however, was suddenly (*repente*) and violently (*obruit*)
interrupted by a fall of rock, which killed some of the *ministri*,
but not Tiberius, whose life was saved by Sejanus: the emperor, in
other words, had his quite unjustifiable enjoyment cut short by
disaster, but he nevertheless (undeservedly, many would have
said)[33] escaped. We must now contrast this episode with the
disaster at Fidenae. During Tiberius' reign, Tacitus claimed, there
were but few public amusements (the word-order of 62. 2,
'imperitante Tiberio procul uoluptatibus habiti', almost implies
that Tiberius forbade them by law), with the result that when an
event did take place (62. 1 *spectaculum celebraret*), it was overcrowded (cf. *auidi*, 62. 2); such overcrowding was asking for
trouble, and when trouble came it was sudden (*improuisum*),
violent (*conferta, conuulsa, ruit, abrupta*), and all || the worse for
the excess of spectators (62. 2 'unde grauior pestis fuit'): many
thousands, in fact, had their highly justifiable enjoyment cut short
by disaster and a death which was as inescapable as it was unde-
served. In these chapters, therefore, we are given a sickening
contrast between what happens to the emperor and what happens
to his people.[34] The disaster at Fidenae is thus linked to the fore-
going narrative of the cave incident in a highly dramatic fashion.

The second disaster, the fire on the Caelian Hill (64–5), has a

---

[33] *praeter spem euasit*, as Suetonius remarks (*Tib.* 39).
[34] The pathos is driven home at 63. 1 where Tacitus tells us that the consequence of the
collapse of the amphitheatre was even fewer games. This is no less ironical than pathetic: it
almost vindicates the emperor's distaste for such spectacles.

more obvious *raison d'être*. This catastrophe too was an important event in the year AD 27, requiring the attention of the annalistic historian. What better than to make it parallel to the amphitheatre disaster (which had to be included at some length, for reasons we have just seen), yet treat it in such a way that the narrative of two successive disasters did not bore the reader? This Tacitus has done quite brilliantly, joining the two episodes by a link-sentence at 64. 1, and then varying the scale of treatment chiastically to achieve *variatio* (see above, pp. 147 f. and 152).

Another link-sentence joins the second *delatores* episode to both the disaster at Fidenae and the fire on the Caelian Hill (66. 1): here it is Tacitus' own characteristic *insinuatio* that enables him to bridge the gap between chapter 66 and the preceding narrative: 'sed *ut* studia procerum et largitio principis . . . solacium tulerant, *ita* accusatorum . . . uis sine leuamento grassabatur'.[35] Finally, with repetitions of phraseology and ideas from the beginning of the narrative of the journey at 57, we are brought back at 67. 1–3 to our starting-point.

We saw that the obituary notice of chapter 61 was the only section which did not play an active part in this sequence of narrative from Book 4. It nevertheless contains an important statement which R. Syme has called 'Tacitus' testimony to his own quality':[36] 'meditatio et labor in posterum ualescit'. It seems fitting that the narrative I have just discussed provides such ample evidence of *meditatio* and *labor*.[37]

---

[35] See above, pp. 147–8, and cf. e.g. *A.* 1. 72. 2 'non tamen ideo faciebat fidem ciuilis animi; nam legem maiestatis reduxerat', another typically Tacitean link-sentence.

[36] Syme (1958), 624 n. 3.

[37] I am extremely grateful to R. H. Martin and T. J. Saunders for their helpful comments on an earlier draft of this paper.

9

Tacitus' Obituary of Tiberius

To the memory of Frank Goodyear

casus prima ab infantia ancipites: nam proscriptum patrem exsul secutus,
ubi domum Augusti priuignus introiit, multis aemulis conflictatus est
dum Marcellus et Agrippa, mox Gaius Luciusque Caesares uiguere;
etiam frater eius Drusus prosperiore ciuium amore erat. sed maxime
in lubrico egit accepta in matrimonium Iulia, impudicitiam uxoris
tolerans aut declinans. dein Rhodo regressus uacuos principis penates
duodecim annis, mox rei Romanae arbitrium tribus ferme et uiginti
obtinuit.

morum quoque tempora illi diuersa: egregium uita famaque quoad
priuatus uel in imperiis sub Augusto fuit; occultum ac subdolum fingendis uirtutibus donec Germanicus ac Drusus superfuere; idem inter
bona malaque mixtus incolumi matre; intestabilis saeuitia sed obtectis
libidinibus dum Seianum dilexit timuitue; postremo in scelera simul ac
dedecora prorupit postquam remoto pudore et metu suo tantum ingenio utebatur. (6. 51. 1–3)

I

The standard interpretation of the obituary's final paragraph,
where Tacitus divides the emperor's life into five *tempora
diuersa*,[1] is that provided by F. R. D. Goodyear,[2] which may be
summarized as follows. During the last period of his life Tiberius,
now free from anyone who might act as a restraining influence,
revealed his own true, real, or innate character (*ingenium*) of
unmitigated evil. During the earlier periods, when he was

For their comments on earlier drafts of this paper I am most grateful to Profs. H. M. Hine,
R. H. Martin, T. P. Wiseman, and the *CQ* referee, not all of whom have been persuaded
by its theses. References are to Tacitus' *Annals* unless otherwise stated.

[1] The *tempora* are: (1) up to AD 14, (2) to early 23, (3) to early 29, (4) to late 31, (5) to
Mar. 37.   [2] (1972), 37–40.

restrained by one individual or another, he had appeared to be less evil than this; but the difference is not to be explained by the emperor's character having changed for the worse, since Tacitus, like other ancient writers, believed that a man's character was fixed at birth and incapable of change thereafter. Hence the difference between the earlier and the last periods of Tiberius' life can only be explained by the hypocrisy which Tacitus constantly attributes to him: during his earlier life Tiberius was hiding his vices (*dissimulatio*) and feigning virtues.

Naturally Professor Goodyear knew the two occasions when Tacitus shows himself explicitly aware of the changeability of character. On the first Tacitus not only claims that the emperor Vespasian changed for the better, but expresses his claim in such a way as might well imply that all previous emperors (including, therefore, Tiberius) changed for the worse: *H.* 1. 50. 4 'solusque omnium ante se principum in melius mutatus est.' On the second occasion Tacitus makes L. Arruntius state that Tiberius did indeed change for the worse: 6. 48. 2 'post tantam rerum experientiam ui dominationis conuulsus et mutatus.' Given the proximity of this statement to the obituary at 6. 51. 3, E. Koestermann suggested that Tacitus intended to provide readers with alternative scenarios from which they could choose.[3] Such a technique would not only be typical of Tacitus, especially if he were to leave readers in no doubt that his own opinion was different from that of Arruntius, but would also increase the || intrinsic significance of Arruntius' statement. Yet Goodyear dismissed both this and the former passage as 'intermittent insights', 'isolated', and 'of slight importance';[4] and the attractiveness of the traditional interpretation is shown by the fact that it has been endorsed more recently, either in whole or in part, by Ronald Martin and T. J. Luce.[5]

Two other scholars, however, have modified this traditional interpretation in two important respects. First, A. R. Hands pointed out that Tacitus' alleged belief in fixed characters does not explain why he continues to attribute *dissimulatio* to Tiberius during the last period of his life, when *ex hypothesi* all restraint had been removed and his truly evil nature had long since been revealed. See especially 6. 50. 1, when the emperor is on his

---

[3] (1963), 38.   [4] Goodyear (1972), 38, 40.
[5] Martin (1981), 105, 139–43, Luce (1986), 152–7.

deathbed: 'iam Tiberium corpus, iam uires, nondum dissimulatio deserebat.'[6] Second, C. Gill provided a great deal of evidence to show that the ancients were very familiar indeed with the concept of a changing character and hence that Tacitus' statements at *H.* 1. 50. 4 and 6. 48. 2 are by no means as 'intermittent' or 'isolated' as Goodyear believed but rather are illustrations of a common belief.[7] Yet despite the weight of his own evidence, Gill nevertheless maintained the traditional view of the Tacitean Tiberius: Tacitus' account 'is based firmly on the idea that Tiberius' character did not change, degenerate or "collapse" but was simply concealed until all external restraints were removed and he felt he could reveal it'.[8]

Nevertheless, the effect of Gill's evidence, when coupled with that of Hands, has been to modify our picture of Tacitus' Tiberius in such a way that it seems worth considering whether or not the modification can be carried further. The crux of the issue of course lies in the last four words of the obituary: *suo tantum ingenio utebatur.* 'The obituary', Luce has said, 'is based upon the premise that Tiberius' character, his *ingenium*, did not change: that seems inescapable.'[9] Yet the escape can be effected.

II

In the traditional interpretation of Tacitus' obituary it is axiomatic that *suo ingenio* means Tiberius' 'true' (Koestermann, Martin), 'real' (Martin, Gill), or 'innate' (Goodyear) character.[10] But if

---

[6] 'Postremo suo tantum ingenio utebatur', *CQ* 24 (1974), 312 ff., esp. 316–17. He explains *dissimulatio* as one of Tacitus' rhetorical devices for blackening Tiberius' character. It should be added that since Tacitus has chosen to present Tiberius in tyrannical terms, his characteristics will be the exact opposites of those of the good man or ideal ruler (Cic. *Off.* 2.44 'nullum obscurum potest nec dictum eius esse nec factum'; Plin. *Pan.* 83. 1 'nihil tectum, nihil occultum patitur').

[7] Gill (1983), 469 ff., esp. 481–7. Further bibliography on the whole question will be found in most of the works mentioned.

[8] Gill (1983), 482, cf. 484 'It seems clear that Tacitus' account is intended to show Tiberius' character did not change during his rule but was only more clearly revealed'.

[9] Luce (1986), 155, cf. 156 'I do not doubt, let me reaffirm, that he viewed the emperor's *ingenium* as perverse and unchanging'.

[10] Koestermann ad loc. ('indem er seiner wahren Natur freien Lauf liess'), Martin (1981), 105, Gill (1983), 485 ('The emphasis in *suo ingenio* is on *real* character', his italics), Goodyear (1972), 39. In the commentary of Draeger–Heraeus we read 'seitdem er . . . nur den Eingebungen seines Naturells folgte', and in that of Nipperdey–Andresen: 'sich aller Selbstbeherrschung entledigte, sich vollständig gehen liess'. The Loeb editor, J. Jackson,

ingenium is exclusive to Tiberius in this way, why does || Tacitus qualify *suo* by the word *tantum* ('only')? On this view the adverb seems redundant and without point.[11] In my view, the clear implication of the *whole* phrase *suo tantum ingenio utebatur* is that during earlier periods of his life Tiberius had used the *ingenium* of *other people as well as* his own. That his words are capable of such a meaning seems clear from what he says about Otho at *H.* 1. 90. 2: 'ut in consiliis militiae Suetonio Paulino et Mario Celso, ita in rebus urbanis *Galeri Trachali ingenio Othonem uti* credebatur'. Obviously this passage has nothing to do with 'true' or 'real' character: Otho is relying on Trachalus for help. But since its wording is so similar to that of Tiberius' obituary, it is worth considering whether the implications of the phrase *ingenio uti* are the same in both places.

A key feature of Tiberius' principate, as it is presented by Tacitus and other writers, is the emperor's desire to associate others in the running of the empire. At the beginning of the *Annals* Tacitus depicts the new emperor as reluctant to assume the full burden of office by himself (1. 11. 1 'non ad *unum* omnia deferrent'): while Augustus had had the capability to tackle the empire single-handed ('*solam* diui Augusti *mentem* tantae molis capacem'),[12] Tiberius himself would prefer the involvement of a plurality of people ('plures facilius munia rei publicae *sociatis laboribus* exsecuturos'). But the bewildered senators respond with a mixture of adulation and protestation (1. 12. 1–3), leaving Tiberius to rely on others for help. His two sons Germanicus and Drusus were given political honours *pari passu* during the early years of the reign and are both described by Strabo around AD 18 as 'assistants to their father' in the government (6. 4. 2).[13]

renders 'follow his own bent'; the Penguin translator, M. Grant (rev. repr. 1974) has 'he expressed only his own personality'; in the Budé editions we have 'il se laissa aller au penchant de sa nature' (H. Goelzer, 1938) and 'il ne suivait plus que le penchant de sa nature' (P. Wuilleumier). Knoche (1963), 213 says 'gibt sich der Kaiser, wie der Historiker es darstellt, seiner wahren Natur . . . hin' (cf. 216); R. Häussler, *Tacitus und das historische Bewusstsein* (1965), 322 collects various examples of (*suo*) *ingenio uti/uiuere* and τῇ φύσει χρῆσθαι.

[11] Its omission by Gill (1983), 485 (above, n. 10) is particularly striking.

[12] This interpretation of Tacitus' words allows *solam* a role in articulating the argument of the passage; the usual interpretation is 'only Augustus had a/the mind capable of such a great burden', although words for 'only' are regularly omitted in Latin (see e.g. Kenney on Lucr. 3. 144). My general thesis receives better support from the former rendering (see *OLD solus* 4) but is in no way embarrassed by the latter.

[13] See e.g. Levick (1976), 148.

Though Germanicus died in 19, Drusus' role as *adiutor imperii* is implied early in 21 (3. 31. 2 'ut amoto patre Drusus munia consulatus solus impleret') and forms the background to an episode early in Book 4 (7. 1–2). By 23 Drusus too was dead; but we know that at some point between 20 and 22 Sejanus began to be described as Tiberius' *adiutor* or *socius laborum*, a role which he fulfilled until his death in 31 (4. 2. 3, 7. 1; Vell. 127. 3, 128. 4; Dio 57. 19. 7, 58. 4. 3).[14] Now Germanicus, Drusus, and Sejanus are three of the individuals whom Tacitus uses in the obituary to designate the periods of Tiberius' principate; but he also mentions Livia, who might be thought disqualified from any such formal role on account of her sex. Yet Dio presents a graphic picture of Livia as Tiberius' partner (57. 12. 2–6), and Tacitus himself acknowledges it in his narrative of 26 (4. 57. 3): 'dominationis *sociam* aspernabatur neque depellere poterat, cum dominationem ipsam donum eius || accepisset.'[15] In other words Tiberius was compelled to use Livia as his *socia* despite himself, a situation which continued until a further watershed in the reign was marked by her death in 29 (5. 3. 1).

Thus from the very start Tiberius was a lonely and unwilling ruler whose various partnerships, successively described by Tacitus in the second paragraph of the obituary, were repeatedly thwarted by death and treachery until, during his seclusion on Capri, Sejanus too was dead and Tiberius 'had only himself to rely on' (*suo tantum ingenio utebatur*). The picture is that of a man who was increasingly isolated until he became, as he described himself when at last denouncing Sejanus by letter to the senate, 'senex et *solus*' (Suet. *Tib.* 65. 1).[16]

This interpretation of the obituary, and particularly of its last four words, explains the selection of each of the individuals mentioned there (including the pairing of Germanicus and

---

[14] These partnerships have been fully discussed by E. Kornemann, *Doppelprinzipat und Reichsteilung im Imperium Romanum* (1930) and P. Grenade, *Essai sur les origines du principat* (1961).   [15] See further Purcell (1986), 78–105.

[16] Tiberius' *solitudo*, hinted at in AD 21 (3. 31. 2 'longam et continuam absentiam paulatim meditans'), is a motif of Book 4, being urged on him by Sejanus at 41. 3 and twice emphasized at 67. 1–2 when he withdraws to Capri. Apart from some Greek intellectuals, Tacitus names only Cocceius Nerva and Curtius Atticus as the emperor's companions on his departure from Rome in 26 (4. 58. 1): the former starved himself to death in 33 (6. 26. 1–2), the latter had already been eliminated by Sejanus at some earlier point (6. 10. 2). For Sejanus himself see below, pp. 166–7 and n. 40.

Drusus, which scholars have often found strange),[17] accounts for the presence of the word *tantum*, and is supported by the parallel phraseology at *H.* 1. 90. 2. But it means, of course, that *ingenium* not only has nothing to do with 'true', 'real', or 'innate' character but has nothing to do with character at all. In the final paragraph of the obituary Tacitus is simply talking about Tiberius' *behaviour*,[18] which was unexceptionable before AD 14 and deplorable between 29 and 37.

It follows that we cannot adopt Koestermann's otherwise attractive proposal (above, p. 156) that at 6. 48. 2 and 51. 3 Tacitus is presenting readers with alternative scenarios in terms of change: on this new interpretation of 6. 51. 3 there is no immutability with which the change at 6. 48. 2 can be compared. Yet this does not mean that there are no grounds at all for comparing the two passages. At 6. 48. 2 Arruntius' opening words *post tantam rerum experientiam* must be given a concessive force: '*despite* his vast experience of affairs before AD 14, Tiberius was *nevertheless* overwhelmed by power and changed'. In other words Arruntius has addressed the puzzle which in Martin's view Tacitus himself was seeking to solve in his final paragraph: namely, 'How was it that a man who till his mid-fifties had been "excellent in both achievement and reputation" became at the end a cruel tyrant and licentious recluse?'[19] Yet this is not the case. In Tacitus' view there was no puzzle at all; but this emerges from the first paragraph of the obituary rather than the second.

The two paragraphs of the obituary are consciously juxtaposed and structurally complementary. There are five *casus ancipites* in the first, parallel to the five *tempora diuersa* in the second;[20] and just as the fifth *casus* comprises all but the initial *tempora*, || so the initial *tempus* comprises all but the final *casus*. Clearly Tacitus is inviting readers to see one paragraph in terms of the other, and the picture presented in the first is crucial for our understanding of the second. In the first we are reminded that Tiberius was exiled as a child, was sidelined by Augustus on several separate

---

[17] e.g. Luce (1986), 153 'a peculiar conflation: three years and a whole book intervene between these two [deaths]'. Knoche (1963), 214–15 seems to me not to come to terms with the problem at all. See further below, p. 161 and n. 24.

[18] So too Luce (1986), 156, but he sticks to the traditional view of Tiberius' *ingenium* (above, n. 9). Tacitus regularly uses *mores* = 'behaviour' rather than 'character', e.g. 1. 54. 2, 4. 13. 2, 13. 2. 1, *H.* 4. 44. 2.   [19] Martin (1981), 142.

[20] The five *casus* are: (1) *proscriptum . . . secutus*, (2) *ubi domum . . . amore erat*, (3) *sed maxime . . . declinans*, (4) *dein . . . annis*, (5) *mox . . . obtinuit*. For the five *tempora* see above, n. 1.

occasions in favour of others, was deserted by a notoriously unfaithful wife, and was recalled from Rhodes only when all other potential successors were dead. Thus what Arruntius saw in *active* terms as *tanta rerum experientia* is seen by Tacitus himself in *passive* terms as a series of *casus* consisting of isolations and rejections.[21] None of them would have mattered (except, of course, to the man himself), if Tiberius had remained out of public life (*priuatus*) or responsible to a superior ('uel in imperiis *sub* Augusto fuit');[22] but once he found himself in the position to *exercise* sole power, as Tacitus saw it ('rei Romanae arbitrium . . . obtinuit'), or of being *subjected to* the responsibility of power, as Arruntius put it ('ui dominationis'),[23] the *casus* of Tiberius' earlier life explained the diffidence with which he succeeded Augustus and which led him quite naturally to seek partnerships with the individuals mentioned in the second paragraph of the obituary. Yet here too (and these were the final ironies) he was in turn let down by Germanicus, Drusus, and Sejanus, either through death or treachery or both; and the one partner whom he did not seek was his mother Livia, whom 'aspernabatur neque depellere poterat' (4. 57. 3).

III

By accounting for each of the individuals mentioned in the second paragraph of the obituary, the above interpretation explains both Tacitus' dating of the five *tempora diuersa* and why some *tempora* discount other potential turning-points in Tiberius' life (such as his departure from Rome in 26). One difficulty which earlier scholars appear to have encountered is that they have (so to speak) read the paragraph backwards, and inferred from its last two sections, where Sejanus seems described as a restraining influence ('dum Seianum . . . remoto . . . metu'), that the earlier sections too are 'signalised by the removal of one more person's restraining influence'.[24] Yet this is not the case.

---

[21] That is, Tacitus has (as often) employed two different *colores*; for their relevance to historiography see Wiseman (1979), 7–8, 26.

[22] For this use of *sub* with a person see C. O. Brink, *Horace on Poetry: Epistles Book II* (1982), 426–7.   [23] These two are of course the converse of the *colores* just mentioned.

[24] Martin (1981), 105, cf. Goodyear (1972), 39, Gill (1983), 482. Martin's later statement (141 'There is no indication in Tacitus or anywhere else that Tiberius' behaviour was motivated by regard or fear of either Germanicus or Drusus') is a good illustration of this

Germanicus, Drusus, and Livia are presented in exclusively temporal terms (*donec . . . superfuere, incolumi matre*), and their roles, as we have seen, must be viewed logically in the light of the *preceding* paragraph, with which the statement about Augustus ('quoad . . . sub Augusto fuit') forms the link.

It will perhaps be said, however, that this interpretation is itself open to the converse objection, namely, that while there may be nothing to prevent our understanding Germanicus, Drusus, and Livia in the way proposed, Sejanus is presented in words which suggest that the reference to him at least should be understood differently. Yet not only is it arguable that scholars have misinterpreted those words (see Section IV below) but this objection is forestalled by the place which Sejanus occupies in the obituary.

Scholars have been greatly troubled by the relationship between the years 23–9 as || described in the obituary, where Sejanus does not figure at all, and as heralded at the start of the narrative of 23 itself, where Sejanus is described as the principal influence upon Tiberius: 'saeuire ipse aut saeuientibus uires praebere. initium et causa penes Aelium Seianum' (4. 1. 1). Martin, for example, sees 'a real difficulty' in the obituary at this point: 'the implication that Sejanus only began to exercise decisive influence upon Tiberius after Livia's death [in 29] is contrary to the assertions of 4. 1.'[25] But that difficulty immediately disappears once it is realized that in the obituary Tacitus' purpose is not to list individuals who influenced Tiberius but rather to date the progressive deterioration of the increasingly isolated emperor by the successive deaths of his various partners. Since it was the death of Livia as *dominationis socia* which marked the end of the period 23–9, Tacitus had no need to mention Sejanus' name at all in connection with those years. Thus the absence of Sejanus from the obituary's account of 23–9 actually confirms that the primary explanation of his presence there in 29–31 is that he is the last of Tiberius' *socii* to die.

IV

The apparent difficulty over the presentation of Sejanus arises from Tacitus' characteristic habit of projecting different aspects

retrospective inference: Tiberius' alleged regard or fear of the two men is nowhere mentioned in the obituary.

[25] Martin (1981), 141, cf. Luce (1986), 154 (below, n. 36).

of the same individual at different places in his narrative. Sometimes these aspects appear so different that Goodyear questioned
whether 'we are entitled to find a self-consistent picture', suggesting that we should perhaps be prepared to tolerate 'plain
inconsistency' in Tacitus' portrayal of certain individuals.[26] It
seems to me, however, that, especially in the case of Tiberius,
we must at least start from the assumption that Tacitus has not
presented an inconsistent portrait. This does not mean that we
should attempt to harmonize at all costs; rather, when considering passages which scholars have thought discrepant, we
should take into account Tacitus' extraordinary facility at
manipulating language and his well-known ability to create
impressions which are often misleading. On this basis, therefore,
we may consider the question of whether Tiberius' deterioration, as described in the three central periods of the obituary,
agrees with what Tacitus says at certain key points in the
narrative of the reign.[27]

During the years 14–23 Tiberius is said to have been 'occultum
ac subdolum fingendis uirtutibus', a negative appraisal which
seems at odds with the positive summary of the same years at 4.
6. 2–4, where Tacitus presents a creditable account of the first half
of the reign, apart from the issue of *maiestas*. Yet since the obituary
evidently charts a *progressive* deterioration, and since Tiberius is
described in the *following* period (23–9) as 'idem inter bona
malaque mixtus', the clear inference is that during 14–23 *bona*
must at least have counterbalanced *mala* and (in the light of the
extra evidence provided by 4. 6. 2–4, where *maiestas* alone was
criticized) significantly outweighed them.[28] It is true that this is
inferential and that Tacitus does || not actually say as much; but

---

[26] Goodyear (1972), 240–1.

[27] For the problem see e.g. Martin (1981), 140–2. Knoche (1963) expressed the view (*a*)
that the breaks between Books 3/4, 4/5, and 5/6 correspond to the three central turning-
points of the obituary at AD 23, 29, and 31; and (*b*) that these breaks represent the 'Fortfall
bestimmter Hemmungen' (216). While (*a*) is not in dispute, as will be seen, (*b*) founders
both on Tacitus' reference to Germanicus and Drusus (above, p. 161 and n. 24), which
Knoche has been compelled to fudge (above, pp. 159–60 and n. 17), and on the absence of
Sejanus from Tacitus' summary of 23–9 (see Section III above).

[28] This interpretation, if accepted, meets the complaint of Luce (1986), 153 that there is
no difference between the two periods: 'concealment and artful simulation of virtue
remained the same . . . The obituary says, in effect, that Tiberius was essentially the
same under Germanicus, Drusus, *and* Livia: that is, from the start of the *Annals* to the
beginning of the fifth book.'

neither does he not say it. Both the *suppressio ueri* and the following adjustment are typical of him.[29]

Conversely the appraisal of Tiberius during 23–9 as 'idem inter
bona malaque mixtus' seems relatively mild when compared with
the dramatic introduction to those same years at 4. 1. 1: ' . . . cum
repente turbare fortuna coepit, saeuire ipse aut saeuientibus uires
praebere. initium et causa penes Aelium Seianum'. Yet at first
sight this latter statement itself seems to square ill with the narrative of those years, which occupies the whole of Book 4. In that
narrative *saeuitia* is not attributed to Tiberius personally until
midway through the period, at the moment of his departure
from Rome in 26: 'saeuitiam ac libidinem, cum factis promeret,
locis occultantem' (57. 1). Previously to this, Tiberius' interventions in trials, which presumably constitute a reasonable guide to
his behaviour, resulted in *clementia* (4. 30. 1, 31. 4) or even outright acquittal (4. 31. 1, 36. 1) more often than the reverse (4. 31.
3, 42. 3)—and the first of the last two cases is admitted by Tacitus
himself to have been justified.[30] It is in fact other people than the
emperor who display *saeuitia* in the years 23–6 (e.g. the younger
Vibius Serenus, 'saeuitiae exemplum atrox' at 4. 28. 1).

On the evidence of the narrative of the years 23–6, therefore,
Tacitus' statement at 4. 1. 1 is misleading if it is interpreted to
mean that Tiberius himself began to turn savage 'suddenly'
(*repente*) in 23. It seems rather to be the case that *aut* in that
same statement has a corrective function ('or rather', 'or at least'),
whereby Tacitus, after the typically damning impression created
by the initial *repente . . . saeuire ipse*, adjusts his generalization to
make it harmonize with the evidence of the subsequent narrative.[31] The effect of this is that *aut* distinguishes two separate
periods of time:[32] namely, the years 23–6, during which any

---

[29] For Tacitus' use of 'self-correction' (*reprehensio*) see Luce (1986), 154–5.

[30] Any assessment of the remaining cases during this period must take into account the
fact that on five other occasions there were acquittals or the charges were dismissed (4. 13.
2, 29. 1, 36. 3) and that four of the convictions involved adulterous couples (4. 42. 3, 52. 3).
Even the savaging of a suicide's property is obliquely expressed (20. 1 'saeuitum tamen in
bona'), although it admittedly evokes from Tacitus the comment 'ea prima Tiberio erga
pecuniam alienam diligentia fuit'.

[31] For this use of *aut* see *OLD* s.v. 6b; the corrective function of the word at 4. 1. 1 is in
my view supported by the paronomasia *saeuire . . . saeuientibus*. The technique would be
typical of Tacitus (above, n. 29).

[32] In his note on Tacitus' use of *aut* Goodyear rightly comments that 'the shade of
meaning varies from passage to passage' (1. 8. 2 n.).

savagery was the property of the *saeuientes*,[33] and 26 onwards, during which Tiberius too was *saeuus*.[34] Hence the obituary's appraisal of the emperor in 23–9 as 'idem inter bona malaque mixtus' is not unreasonable for a man who, on the evidence of the main narrative, lacked personal *saeuitia* during the first half of the period and who, on the above interpretation of the opening of Book 4, only 'began' to reveal it in the second half (cf. 4. 1. 1 *coepit*).[35] ||

In the years 29–31 Tiberius is described in the obituary as 'intestabilis saeuitia sed obtectis libidinibus dum Seianum dilexit timuitue', which is interpreted by scholars to mean that Sejanus acted as 'a restraining influence on the emperor'.[36] If that interpretation is correct, there is a striking conflict with the main narrative. On the one hand it is to be inferred from 4. 1. 1 and 57. 1, as we have just seen, that Sejanus stimulated (rather than restrained) Tiberius' incipient *saeuitia* from 26 onwards. On the other hand we are told at 5. 3. 1 that after Livia's death in 29 there began 'praerupta iam et urgens dominatio' and that both Tiberius and Sejanus 'uelut frenis exsoluti proruperunt' and launched an attack on Agrippina and Nero; and since the latter had been Sejanus' (rather than Tiberius') intended victims since early in Book 4 (cf. 12.1–4, 15. 3), it follows that at the start of Book 5 Sejanus' stimulation of Tiberius' *saeuitia* has now become even more effective.[37] Yet so striking a conflict with the obituary's

---

[33] The *saeuientes* are primarily the *delatores* and/or Sejanus' henchmen. Whether they include Sejanus himself depends upon whether one thinks he is able simultaneously to be, as Tacitus says he is, their *initium et causa*.

[34] There is nothing unusual in the fact that these two periods correspond to the programmatic statement at 4. 1. 1 in reverse order. The Odyssean and Iliadic halves of the *Aeneid* similarly correspond to the first two words of the epic in reverse order (see e.g. A. Bloch, 'Arma virumque als heroisches Leitmotiv', *MH* 27 (1970), 207); and analogous devices are employed by Thucydides at more than one point in his first book.

[35] It is worth noting that although Tacitus has often *implied* Tiberius' *saeuitia* before now (e.g. 1. 4. 3–5, quoted on p. 167), his authorial imputations are restricted to very rare and specific occasions (e.g. 1. 53. 3).

[36] Martin (1981), 139, cf. Luce (1986), 154 'The role that Sejanus plays in the fourth stage of the obituary is also odd . . . This is the only place in the obituary in which Sejanus appears, and . . . his presence somehow prevented Tiberius' loathsome character from its full emergence.'

[37] The context at 5. 3. 1 is as follows: 'nam incolumi Augusta erat adhuc perfugium, quia Tiberio inueteratum erga matrem obsequium neque Seianus audebat auctoritati parentis antire; tunc uelut frenis exsoluti proruperunt, missaeque in Agrippinam ac Neronem litterae quas pridem allatas et cohibitas ab Augusta credidit uulgus.' It is important

account of these years should perhaps make us question whether the traditional interpretation of Sejanus as a restraining influence is correct after all.

The interrelationship between the last two periods of Tiberius' life, as described in the obituary (29–31 and 31–7), has long been recognized by scholars. In the penultimate period Tiberius was 'intestabilis *saeuitia* sed obtectis *libidinibus*', while in the final period he 'in *scelera simul ac dedecora* prorupit'. In other words, although his criminal cruelty remained constant throughout both periods, the difference between them is that in the former period Tiberius concealed the sexual excesses which he revealed in the latter.[38] But Sejanus' influence is not limited to his being responsible for this concealment. What Tacitus says is that in 29–31 Tiberius 'Seianum dilexit timuitue', from which I infer that *dilexit* and *timuit* correspond to *saeuitia* and *libidinibus* in exactly the same way as do *scelera* and *dedecora*. In other words, Tiberius' *affection* for Sejanus fostered his *saeuitia*, while his *fear* of him forced a cover-up of his *libidines*.[39] Hence in the obituary Sejanus, while a restraining || influence on Tiberius' sexual habits during 29–31, is also a stimulating influence on his criminal cruelty during the same period.[40] On this interpretation there is no conflict with the main narrative at all.

to be clear (*a*) that this is the only certain passage in Tacitus' main narrative where the idea of a restraining influence is expressed, (*b*) that the restraint is not exclusive to Tiberius (as scholars often seem to assume) but is applicable to Sejanus as well. In my view the second of these points detracts from the value of 5. 3. 1 as a support for the traditional view of the obituary. But, however that may be, it should be noted that the passage does not contradict my own earlier argument that the persons mentioned in the obituary, including Livia (cf. 4. 57. 3), had been collaborators of Tiberius and are presented as such in the obituary: 5. 3. 1 is typical of Tacitus (see above, pp. 162–3) in that it simply reveals a different aspect of Livia from that portrayed in the obituary. The passage therefore resembles 4. 1. 1 on Sejanus as *initium et causa* and 4. 6. 2–4 on the general excellence of the years 14–23 (above, pp. 163–5): all three passages provide information which supplements but does not contradict statements made in the obituary.

[38] See e.g. Koestermann ad loc. Similarly *obtectis* and *timuit* in the penultimate sentence are picked up by *pudore* and *metu* respectively in the final one.

[39] In the same way at 1. 59. 1 ('ut quibusque bellum inuitis aut cupientibus erat, spe uel dolore accipitur') *inuitis* and *cupientibus* correspond to *dolore* and *spe* respectively; or at H. 2. 40. 3 ('ut cuique audacia uel formido, in primam postremamue aciem prorumpebant aut relabebantur') *audacia* and *formido* correspond to *primam* and *postremam* etc. Martin (1981), 141 takes *dilexit* and *timuit* chronologically: 'At what point Tiberius ceased to love Sejanus and began to fear him is not clear.'

[40] It is clear that Sejanus could not have exercised such influence if he had not been

It may be objected that all this is simply playing with words; but such an objection is hardly telling in the study of Tacitus' *Annals*, in which 'there are many occasions when we have to read him very closely indeed to perceive that he has in fact denied what one thought he had said'.[41] It will not be forgotten that in the obituary he also describes Tiberius' life before AD 14 as *egregium*, which is not at all the impression given of the same period at 1. 4. 3–5: 'multaque indicia saeuitiae, quamquam premantur, erumpere.'[42]

Tiberius' *socius laborum*. This is particularly true of the period after Tiberius had settled on Capri in 26, since it was by virtue of his position that Sejanus then realized his ambition of controlling the access of others to the emperor while at the same time maintaining regular access himself (4. 41. 2, 67. 3, 71. 3; Dio, 58. 4. 9). But the same is also true of the earlier years, during which he is described by Tacitus as a man who capitalized on his role as *socius laborum*, pretending to help the emperor while all the time furthering his own aims through a cruel series of trials and assassinations. This indeed is one of the principal themes of Book 4 as a whole, and the statement at 4. 59. 2 is as good a summary of the position as any: 'quamquam exitiosa suaderet, ut non sui anxius cum fide audiebatur.' Sejanus' manipulation of Tiberius was an intrinsic element of his role as *socius laborum*, a role which he had indeed manipulated Tiberius into bestowing in the first place. Thus it cannot be objected that Sejanus' presentation in the obituary conflicts with the explanation of his presence there as Tiberius' *socius* or *adiutor* (above, p. 162).

[41] Irving Kristol, *Encounter* 6 (May 1956), 86.

[42] Despite Goodyear on 1. 4. 1 there is no actual conflict between these two passages since 1. 4. 3–5 is in *oratio obliqua* (nor, perhaps surprisingly, is this one of those places in Tacitus where it is not immediately obvious whether he is speaking *in propria persona* or not). [On 1. 4. 4–5 see also below, Ch. 12, Sect. III.]

10

Nero's Alien Capital: Tacitus as Paradoxographer (*Annals* 15. 36–7)

THE CONTEXT

According to Tacitus' narrative of AD 64, the centrepiece of which will be the Great Fire of Rome (38–41), Nero began the year with a keen desire to go on a concert tour of Greece (33. 2).[1] Feeling that he needed some preliminary experience, however, the emperor decided to give a practice performance in Naples, because of its resemblance to a genuinely Greek city. The Neapolitan theatre was packed (33. 3), and Suetonius tells us that Nero was captivated by the rhythmic applause of some visitors from Alexandria, whose techniques were subsequently taught to *equites* and others on the emperor's insistence (*Nero* 20. 3).

When Nero had completed his performance (of which Tacitus pointedly omits all mention), and the crowds had dispersed, the theatre promptly fell to the ground (34. 1). Most people interpreted the collapse as a sinister omen (*triste*), but the emperor himself looked on the bright side and interpreted his escape as providential (*prouidum*). Then, having duly composed his own *Te Deum* in thanksgiving, he proceeded on his way to Beneventum for the gladiatorial games of one Vatinius, during which a distinguished ex-consul, Silanus Torquatus, was forced to commit

An oral version of this paper was delivered at Case Western Reserve University, Cornell, Hunter College (where I had the honour of giving the Josephine Earle Memorial Lecture for 1990), Madison, Toronto, the University of California at Berkeley, Los Angeles and Santa Barbara, the University of Pennsylvania, and Yale. I am extremely grateful for these invitations to speak and for the comments I received at each place; I am also glad to acknowledge help of various kinds from D. M. Bain, I. M. Le M. DuQuesnay, D. C. Feeney, J. R. Harris, T. J. Luce, R. H. Martin, and B. D. Shaw. All references to Tacitus are to the *Annals* unless stated otherwise; references to Book 15 omit the book-number.

[1] It cannot be taken for granted that Tacitus' narrative in the *Annals* reflects the historical order of events: see Ginsburg (1981), 18–30.

suicide for being a descendant of Augustus like Nero himself (35.
1). A charge had been trumped up that he was set on revolution
(35. 2); and although Nero maintained that the man was indeed
guilty, he also said that he as emperor would have shown *clementia*
if Silanus had given him the chance (35. 3). On this cynical note
Tacitus then passes on to the episode which leads up to the Fire
and which is the subject of this discussion (36–7).

THE TEXT

Nec multo post omissa in praesens Achaia (causae in incerto fuere)
urbem reuisit, prouincias Orientis, maxime || Aegyptum, secretis imagi-
nationibus agitans. dehinc edicto testificatus non longam sui absentiam
et cuncta in re publica perinde immota ac prospera fore, super ea
profectione adiit Capitolium. illic ueneratus deos, cum Vestae quoque	2
templum inisset, repente cunctos per artus tremens (seu numine exter-
rente seu facinorum recordatione numquam timore uacuus) deseruit
inceptum, cunctas sibi curas amore patriae leuiores dictitans: uidisse	3
maestos ciuium uultus, audire secretas querimonias, quod tantum itin-
eris aditurus esset, cuius ne modicos quidem egressus tolerarent, sueti
aduersum fortuita aspectu principis refoueri: ergo, ut in priuatis neces-
situdinibus proxima pignora praeualerent, ita populum Romanum uim
plurimam habere parendumque retinenti.
   Haec atque talia plebi uolentia fuere, uoluptatum cupidine et (quae	4
praecipua cura est) rei frumentariae angustias, si abesset, metuenti.
senatus et primores in incerto erant procul an coram atrocior haberetur.—dehinc (quae natura magnis timoribus) deterius credebant quod
euenerat.—ipse, quo fidem adquireret nihil usquam perinde laetum sibi,	37
publicis locis struere conuiuia totaque urbe quasi domo uti; et celeberrimae luxu famaque epulae fuere quas a Tigellino paratas ut exemplum
referam, ne saepius eadem prodigentia narranda sit.
   Igitur in stagno Agrippae fabricatus est ratem, cui superpositum	2
conuiuium nauium aliarum tractu moueretur. naues auro et ebore distinctae, remigesque exoleti per aetates et scientiam libidinum compo-
nebantur. uolucris et feras diuersis e terris et animalia maris Oceano
abusque petiuerat. crepidinibus stagni lupanaria adstabant inlustribus	3
feminis completa, et contra scorta uisebantur nudis corporibus. iam
gestus motusque obsceni; et, postquam tenebrae incedebant, quantum
iuxta nemoris et circumiecta tecta consonare cantu et luminibus clar-
escere. ipse per licita atque inlicita foedatus nihil flagitii reliquerat quo	4
corruptior ageret, nisi paucos post dies uni ex illo contaminatorum
grege (nomen Pythagorae fuit) in modum sollemnium coniugiorum

denupsisset: inditum imperatori flammeum, <ad>missi[2] auspices, dos et
genialis torus et faces nuptiales. cuncta denique spectata quae etiam in
femina nox operit. ||

Not long afterwards, neglecting Greece for the present (his reasons were
unclear), he revisited the City, with the provinces of the East, particularly Egypt, stirring in his private fantasizings. Subsequently, having
testified by edict that his would be no long absence and that everything
in the state would be as stable as it was prosperous, he approached the
Capitol to consult about his departing thither. There he venerated the   2
gods; but, after he had entered the temple of Vesta too, suddenly
trembling in all his limbs (whether with the godhead terrifying him
or, through the recollection of his actions, being never free from fear),
he abandoned the project, insisting that his collective concerns were less
weighty than his love for his country: he had seen the sad looks of his   3
citizens, he could hear their private complaints that he was to approach
so great a journey, given that they found even his limited excursions
intolerable, accustomed as they were to being kept warm by the sight of
the *princeps* as an antidote to accidents: therefore, just as in personal
relationships one's closest connections counted most, so it was the
Roman people who had the most control and, as they held him back,
he must comply.

Words such as these were welcome to the plebs, with their desire for   4
entertainments and dreading straitened corn-supplies (which are their
primary concern) if he were absent. The senate and leaders were unclear
whether to consider him more hideous at a distance or in their midst.—
Subsequently (such is the nature of great terrors) they came to believe
that what had happened was worse.—As for the man himself, to obtain   37
additional credit that nothing anywhere was as delightful for him, he set
up parties in public places and used the whole city as if it were his own
house; and especially celebrated for its luxury and notoriety was the
banquet organized by Tigellinus, which I shall recount as an example, to
avoid too frequent a narrative of the same prodigality.

It was on Agrippa's lake, then, that he constructed a pontoon, on   2
which a party was mounted and moved along by traction from other
ships. The ships were picked out in gold and ivory, and their rowers,
pathics, were arranged by age and expertise in sexual pleasures. He had
tracked down birds and wild beasts from foreign lands, and marine

---

[2] The paradosis reads *misit*, which is conventionally emended to *missi*; yet the simple
verb usually suggests 'send away', which would be mistaken here (cf. 11. 27, quoted on p.
186), and exceptions are rare and apparently unambiguous (e.g. followed by *in* + accus., as
Cic. *Planc.* 47, *Rab. Post.* 4; cf. *TLL* 8. 2. 1174. 55–72). <in>missi would be a simpler
correction, but this verb usually (and especially in Tacitus) has a hostile connotation.
Another possibility is perhaps *iussi*; Rhenanus' *uisi* is adopted in *TLL* 2. 1541. 47–9.

animals all the way from the Ocean. On the embankments of the   3
lake stood love-lairs filled with female luminaries, and, opposite,
whores were visible, their bodies naked. Already obscene gestures
and movements were in evidence, and, after darkness came on, every
adjacent grove and the surrounding || housing echoed to a symphony
of song and shone with lights. As for the man himself, defiled by acts   4
both permitted and proscribed, there was no outrage which he had
forsaken in his search for increasingly deviant behaviour—except that
after a few days he took one of that herd of perverts (his name was
Pythagoras) in a mock-solemn wedding to be his husband: there was
placed on the Commander a bridal veil, the officials were admitted,
there was a dowry, marriage-bed, and nuptial torches. Everything,
finally, was witnessed which even in the case of a woman is covered
by night.

In the first paragraph Tacitus describes how Nero postponed his
tour of Greece and decided instead on a visit to the East; but, after
the shock he receives in the temple of Vesta, the emperor changes
his mind about that too.[3] In the following paragraph Tacitus
presents three reactions to Nero's change of plan, arranged in
descending order of satisfaction.[4] The people were extremely
satisfied, since all they wanted was the bread and circuses which
Nero's presence guaranteed (36. 4).[5] Leading politicians did not
know whether to be satisfied or not,[6] although after the Fire,
which is foreshadowed,[7] they realized that Nero's presence was a
good deal more dangerous than his absence. Finally the emperor
himself (37. 1 *ipse*) was extremely dissatisfied, although his dis-
satisfaction has to be inferred from his efforts to convince people
of the opposite: *laetum*.

Nero's feigned *laetitia* takes the form of organizing public
parties and treating the whole city as if it were his own house,
behaviour which Tacitus illustrates with an extended description
of Tigellinus' *epulae*: 'quas . . . ut exemplum referam' (37. 1). This
statement, with its combination of the noun *exemplum* and a

---

[3] Nero's public explanation of his change of mind, in which he refers to 'personal
relationships' (36. 3), is of course ironical in view of his elimination of Silanus Torquatus, a
distant relative, just previously (35. 1). See also below, n. 7.

[4] This point is obscured by the conventional paragraphing of the passage.

[5] *uoluptatum cupidine* is Sallustian (*J*. 95. 3, of Sulla).

[6] This sentence too is Sallustian (*J*. 46. 8): see further Syme (1958), 732.

[7] I assume that *quod euenerat* (36. 4) refers to the Fire, which has already been foreshadowed ironically at 36. 3 also ('sueti aduersum fortuita aspectu principis refoueri').

first-person verb, is unique in the *Annals* and signals that the
following description is digressive. The start of the digression
is marked by *Igitur* (37. 2), which picks up *ut exemplum referam*,
and its closure is marked by *denique* (37. 4). But since so
extended a description of revelling is itself unusual for Tacitus,
he defends his practice on the grounds that he will thereby
avoid the necessity of repeating similar material in the future
(37. 1 'ne saepius eadem prodigentia narranda sit'). The claim to
be seeking variety is of course standard, but Tacitus' authorial
statements should rarely be taken simply at face value,[8] and here
the almost tautologous expression *celeberrimae . . . fama*[9] suggests
that the present paragraph is motivated at least as much by the
intrinsic unusualness of the material as by the desire to avoid
monotony. Tacitus' implicit position at this point is in fact not
unlike that adopted by Herodotus: 'I propose to lengthen my
account when speaking about Egypt because it contains more
remarkable features || than any other country . . . That is why
more will be said about it' (2. 35. 1).[10]

The *stagnum*, on which Tigellinus' banquet takes place (37. 2),
is assumed to be a man-made reservoir serving the Thermae
Agrippae. Whether it too, like the baths, was actually dignified
with the name of its founder (as Tacitus implies) seems
unknown,[11] but Tacitus no doubt relished pointing the contrast
between the engineering of Agrippa, Nero's own great-grand-
father, and that of Tigellinus, Nero's henchman: the one was
intended for use and regular enjoyment, the other exclusively
for irregular pleasures. Now pleasure-boats or *cumbae* had already
been mentioned by Cicero and Seneca in connection with the
infamous resort of Baiae;[12] but *cumbae* are small, lightweight craft,
and those of Baiae in particular are mentioned by Juvenal pre-

---

[8] See Martin–Woodman, 95–6, 123–5, and 223.

[9] There are parallels for this kind of expression (e.g. Ov. *Met.* 3. 339 'fama celeberri-
mus'; Virg. *Aen.* 2. 21–2 'notissima fama | insula'; cf. also Tac. *H.* 1. 52. 3 'ipsum celebri
ubique fama' and Heubner ad loc.; Cic. *Arch.* 5 'hac tanta celebritate famae . . . notus'),
but Tacitus' phrase has been variously interpreted: see Koestermann ad loc., where the
explanation of Nipperdey seems preferable.

[10] See Hartog (1988), 234, 344.

[11] See S. B. Platner and T. Ashby, *A Topographical Dictionary of Ancient Rome* (1929), 496;
F. Coarelli, 'Il Campo Marzio occidentale. Storia e topografia', *MEFRA* 89 (1977), 816 ff.,
esp. 826–30. Cf. Ov. *Ex P.* 1. 8. 37–8, Strabo 13. 1. 19.

[12] Cic. *Cael.* 35 'nauigia'; Sen. *Ep.* 51. 4 'comisationes nauigantium', 12 'praenauigantes
adulteras . . . et tot genera cumbarum'.

cisely because of their fragility.[13] Tigellinus' construction, by contrast, was evidently massive; and whereas one might expect the construction of gigantic pontoons to meet a military emergency, as Livy describes (21. 27. 5 'ratesque fabricatae in quibus equi uirique et alia onera traicerentur'), no such justification was provided by the large-scale *conuiuium* which Tacitus goes out of his way to report, emphasizing by his language the paradoxical nature of Tigellinus' feat: *superponere*, when used of building, would more normally suggest dry land.[14]

There are two aspects to Tigellinus' construction. By holding on water a party which more naturally would be held on land, he reveals that he and his emperor are victims of the same syndrome as those rich Romans of the late republic and early empire whose passion for building houses over the sea was attacked by moralizing authors as tyrannical, hybristic, and an affront to nature. 'In their sickness they need unnatural fakes of sea or land out of their proper places to delight them', says a speaker whose words are reported by the elder Seneca.[15] Such men are the Roman counterparts of the Persian kings, who in Herodotus' narrative build bridges over rivers or over the sea and eventually pay the penalty for their hybris by an untimely death.[16] Yet not every case of building over water is a symptom of hybris in Herodotus' narrative: he tells his readers about the Paeonians, who lived in the area of Thrace and Macedonia and 'actually (καί) dwelt on the lake [of Prasias] as follows: platforms are supported on tall piles and stand right in the middle of the lake' (5. 16. 1). Such behaviour naturally has remarkable consequences ('to prevent their babies from tumbling out, they tie a string to their feet'), and Herodotus mentions the Paeonians' customs because they are the reverse of normal behaviour and hence typical of foreign peoples. So

[13] Juv. 12. 80 'interiora petit, Baianae peruia cumbae'; see further Tarrant on Sen. *Thy.* 592.

[14] As Suet. *Galba* 4. 1 'uilla colli superposita'; contrast 12. 57. 2 'conuiuium effluuio lacus appositum'. Tigellinus' craft resembles Gaius' pleasure-ships, which Suetonius describes (*Gai.* 37. 2) and the like of which were discovered at the bottom of Lake Nemi (see A. A. Barrett, *Caligula* (1989), 201–2, 304 nn. 38–9); but Suetonius associates paradox rather with Gaius' subsequent activities (2–3 'nihil tam efficere concupiscebat quam quod posse effici negaretur. et iactae itaque moles . . . mari' etc.): see further below, n. 16.

[15] Sen. *Contr.* 2. 1. 13; for the topos see further Nisbet–Hubbard on Hor. *C.* 2. 18. 21.

[16] See Hartog (1988), 331. Again cf. Suet. *Gai.* 19. 1–3, where the parallel with Xerxes is made explicitly.

too the Egyptians are remarkable because 'they have reversed all the || customs and habits of other men' (2. 35. 2), and the Scythians 'are completely opposed to adopting the customs of other peoples, but especially those of the Greeks' (4. 76. 1).[17] Hence Tacitus' account of Tigellinus' water-borne *conuiuium* not only suggests that such behaviour is morally defective but also that it is unnatural and foreign. And indeed, since the effect of the pontoon is to produce an island in the middle of Agrippa's lake, we should remember that islands attracted the particular attention of writers like Herodotus;[18] and, since Tigellinus' construction was also capable of floating along (*moueretur*), it is tempting to recall in particular the floating island about which Herodotus was told in Egypt (2. 156. 2–6) and which was later ridiculed by Lucian in his parody *True History* (1. 40).[19]

Tacitus tells us nothing about the aesthetic appeal of the pontoon, which we are obliged to infer from his description of the *aliae naues* as 'auro et ebore distinctae'. If mere tugs, whose function was utilitarian, were decorated with ivory, 'a conventional symbol of regal magnificence' and 'often combined with gold',[20] then the *ratis* itself must surely have been even more exotic.[21] The ships' crews are also paradoxical: they are male pathics (*exoleti*)[22] as much as rowers (*remiges*); they are evidently chosen for their *scientia libidinum* rather than their *scientia naualis*;

---

[17] Hartog (1988), 62–3 and *passim*; Wiedemann (1986), 189–92.

[18] See Wiedemann (1986), 191; Gabba (1981), 55–60.

[19] For this work and its genre see J. R. Morgan, 'Lucian's *True Histories* and the *Wonders Beyond Thule* of Antonius Diogenes', *CQ* 35 (1985), 475–90. Floating islands are mentioned frequently in scientific, pseudo-scientific, and paradoxographical contexts: see e.g. Hecataeus, *FGrH* 1 F 305, Plin. *NH* 2. 209 with Beaujeu ad loc.; C. Fensterbusch, 'Schwimmende Ziegel, schwimmende Inseln', *RhM* 103 (1960), 373–7. I owe this information to Prof. H. M. Hine.   [20] Nisbet–Hubbard on Hor. *C.* 2. 18. 1.

[21] Dio refers to purple rugs and soft cushions (62. 15. 3).

[22] It is maintained by J. Boswell, *Christianity, Social Tolerance, and Homosexuality* (1980), 79 that '*catamiti* were passive, *exoleti* active', adding (n. 87): 'On the function of *exoleti*, see Lampridius 13. 4, 26. 4, 31. 6; cf. Martial 12. 91 etc.; Suetonius, *Galba* 21'. But there are objections. (*a*) By 'Lampridius' Boswell means *Historia Augusta* 17 (*Vita Heliog.*), to which only the third of his references is fully correct: the first contains no mention of *exoleti* at all, while the second should be 26. 4–5. The reference to Suetonius should be *Galba* 22. (*b*) None of Boswell's references clearly supports his statement. (*c*) Boswell seems to contradict himself by saying '"catamitus" is supposedly derived from "Γανυμήδης"', the name of the Greek youth raped by Zeus', since Ganymede was himself described as *exoletus* (cf. *TLL* 5. 2. 1543. 30–1).

and the plural *per aetates* suggests that the criterion for inclusion was age at least as much as it was fitness.[23]

When Virgil in the *Aeneid* wished to emphasize that the Trojans have at last reached home, he contrasted the wild animals (*ferae, monstra*) of Circe's promontory, which Aeneas and his men successfully avoid (7. 10–24), with the birds which enjoy their natural habitat at the mouth of the Tiber (7. 32–3): 'uariae circumque supraque | adsuetae ripis uolucres et fluminis alueo.' Tacitus, on the other hand, here adopts an opposite technique in order to emphasize that the world created by Tigellinus in Rome was alien and unnatural (37. 2). There was an abundance of birds and wild animals from a variety of other lands ('diuersis e terris'); and, since *stagnum* usually implies fresh water,[24] even the aquatic creatures are out of place, since they come all the way from the salt sea: 'Oceano abusque'. This last is a most unusual phrase. The distance from which the creatures have been brought is underlined by the uncommon preposition *abusque*, which itself is further emphasized by being placed after its noun.[25] And when Tacitus elsewhere refers to *Oceanus* in his own person (as opposed to in reported speech), he means a specific sea such as the English || Channel or the North Sea;[26] only here does he use *Oceanus* without qualification, evidently referring to the sea or great river which, according to ancient legend, encircled the world but about which even Herodotus expressed some scepticism on several occasions.[27]

Facing each other on the banks of Agrippa's lake were upper-class women and low-class prostitutes (37. 3). Normally the former would be parading themselves, behaviour to which *inlustribus* perhaps partly alludes; but *scorta uisebantur* suggests that the *feminae* are indoors, as the reference to their housing implies ('lupanaria adstabant . . . completa'). Conversely, the nakedness of the *scorta* would normally mean that they were out of sight; yet it is they who

---

[23] Tacitus' passage looks like a parody of a normal slave household, in which one would find 'beautiful slaves of varied ages', who 'may be subdivided into various specialist activities' (Horsfall on Nepos, *Att.* 13. 3, with further bibliography).

[24] As Cat. 31. 2–3 'in liquentibus stagnis | marique uasto'; see further *OLD* 1 and (of the sea) 2a.

[25] 'The effect is to make the "sea-beasts" very rare and exotic indeed' (Miller (1973), 87). For *abusque* see *OLD* 1 (in this sense only at Virg. *Aen.* 7. 289 before Tacitus); for anastrophe of prepositions in Tacitus see Martin–Woodman on 4. 5. 1.

[26] See Gerber–Greef, 1009.

[27] Hdt. 2. 23, 4. 8. 2, 4. 36. 2; Hartog (1988), 295–6.

are on display (*uisebantur*). These paradoxes and reversals lead to another. Since the *scorta* are naked ('nudis corporibus'), the suggestion is that the *feminae* are clothed;[28] and, since the *feminae* are also *inlustres*, there is a contrast between their presumed *haute couture* and their incongruous surroundings (*lupanaria*).[29] Indeed Tacitus' choice of the term *lupanaria*, rather than (say) *fornices* or Suetonius' *deuersoriae tabernae* (*Nero* 27. 3), is itself revealing: it suggests that the aristocratic women were playing the role of *lupae*,[30] which, being a slang word, is therefore indicative of low-class behaviour[31] rather than the sophisticated dalliance associated with the more socially acceptable *meretrices*. As the original meaning of *lupa* is of course 'she-wolf', there is a further implication of the adoption of animal behaviour. In particular, lycanthropy (if that is the right term) is 'the ultimate symbol' of barbarian as opposed to civilized man, and Suetonius makes a similar point about Nero himself, when, 'covered in the skin of a wild animal, he was released from a cave and attacked the sexual organs of men and women who had been bound to stakes' (*Nero* 29).[32]

If the women are seen in terms of animals, it is only natural that they should be surrounded by groves ('quantum iuxta nemoris'), which more normally would be associated with life outside the boundaries of a city.[33] And whereas Suetonius says conventionally that Nero's banquets lasted from midday till midnight (*Nero* 27. 2), Tacitus says that, when darkness fell, the area echoed with song and blazed with lights, as if the revellers turned night into day. The reversal of day and night is a well-known symptom of decadent and luxurious living:[34] it was a characteristic of the

---

[28] Nakedness 'indicates the lowest class of whore' (Courtney on Juv. 6. 121 ff.); for clothed prostitutes see Hor. *Epist.* 1. 18. 3–4 (by implication), Sen. *Contr.* 1. 2. 7, Juv. 3. 135.

[29] There is a similar contrast earlier at 32: 'feminarum inlustrium senatorumque plures per arenam foedati sunt'.

[30] For the sequence *scorta . . . exoletos . . . lupas* see Cic. *Mil.* 55.

[31] See *TLL* 7. 2. 1859. 23–4 '(uox) ad mulieres abiectissimas pertinere uidetur'.

[32] See Wiedemann (1986), 192 for lycanthropy and 190–1 for caves. The term 'lycanthropy' is not being used in its technical sense, which is evidently reserved for those who really imagine themselves to be wolves (R. Buxton, 'Wolves and Werewolves in Greek Thought', in J. Bremmer (ed.), *Interpretations of Greek Mythology* (1987), 67–8).

[33] Hartog (1988), 65. For groves in the city see further 42. 1–2, where their unnaturalness is made explicit.

[34] See Mayor on Juv. 8. 11. Night is again turned into day, but for different purposes, at 44. 4 below.

hedonist author Petronius (16. 8. 1 'illi dies per somnum, nox officiis et oblectamentis uitae transigebatur') and a point of pride with the later emperor Elagabalus (*Historia Augusta* 17. 28. 6 'transegit et dierum actus noctibus et nocturnos diebus, aestimans hoc inter instrumenta luxuriae'). A whole letter was devoted to the subject by the younger Seneca, who regarded the habit as an inversion of nature: the phrase *contra naturam* || runs as a refrain through significant portions of his letter (122. 5–9). And since such behaviour was unnatural, it was therefore also suitable for attribution to foreign peoples, for whom luxury was itself regarded as a defining characteristic.[35] Herodotus tells the story of King Mycerinus, who, by turning night into day, hoped to turn six years into twelve in order to frustrate an oracle: 'He had many lamps made, and would light them in the evening and drink and make merry; by day or night he never ceased from revelling, roaming in the marsh country and the groves and wherever he had heard of the likeliest places of pleasure' (2. 133. 4).[36] Phylarchus, a historian of the third century BC, alleged that the reversal of day and night was practised by some of the people of Colophon in Asia,[37] and as a motif it is perhaps taken to its paradoxical extreme once again by Lucian, who describes a land which enjoys neither day nor night but a kind of continuous twilight (*True History* 2. 12).[38]

As the climax of his description, as of the preceding paragraph (above, p. 171), Tacitus introduces the emperor himself (37. 4 *ipse*), using a polar expression ('per licita atque inlicita foedatus') to embrace every possible vice except that which is described in the final episode of all (*nisi . . .*).[39] This *nisi*-clause is a calculated exercise in paradox and suspense. *uni* is separated from its governing verb by three word-groups: *ex illo contaminatorum grege*, where *grege* keeps alive the animalism of *lupanaria* above and this time

---

[35] See e.g. E. Hall, *Inventing the Barbarian* (1989), 80–3, 127–9, 209–10.

[36] The king is associated with other reversals in Herodotus' text: he was said to have committed incest with his daughter, for example, while his sister had been forced by their father Cheops to work in a brothel (2. 131. 1 and 126. 1 respectively).

[37] *FGrH* 81 F 66 (= Athen. 12. 526A–C).

[38] Cf. also Hom. *Od.* 10. 86. For some different examples of temporal inversion see Hartog (1988), 213 n. 4.

[39] For polar expressions in Tacitus see B.-R. Voss, *Der pointierte Stil des Tacitus* (1963), 124–6.

associates it with men;[40] *nomen Pythagorae fuit*, which is perhaps intended to be ironical in view of the famous philosopher's recommendation that one should abstain from sexual intercourse altogether;[41] and *in modum sollemnium coniugiorum*, which looks forward to the details of the following sentence. Up to this point there is no indication that Tacitus is not about to complete the sentence with an expression such as *puellam conciliasset*, perhaps describing an episode like the bizarre under-age marriage portrayed in an early scene of Petronius' novel (25–6). Tacitus' actual verb *denupsisset* therefore comes as a shock: unlike his 'marriage' on another occasion, when Nero adopted the male role and his boyfriend Sporus the female,[42] on the present occasion the emperor is playing the role of the woman—a role which is worked out in all its paradoxical detail in Tacitus' penultimate sentence.

In keeping with his desire for a military reputation, Nero had accumulated nine salutations as *imperator* by AD 64, and it is by this title that he is described here; but since 'the most tangible indication of the way the Emperor and his subjects regarded his role was his dress',[43] Tacitus' juxtaposition of the title with the bridal veil (*flammeum*) could scarcely be more pointed or paradoxical. Any such reversal of roles was || regarded as an affront to nature, as Seneca makes clear (*Ep.* 122. 7 'non uidentur tibi contra naturam uiuere qui commutant cum feminis uestem?'), and a precisely analogous point to Tacitus' is made by Juvenal when describing the homosexual marriage of one Gracchus, who as a priest once carried the sacred shields of Mars but who now wears the bridal veil (2. 124–6).[44] Gracchus too, like Nero, bestows a dowry (2. 117–18); and Juvenal makes much of his inability to bear children

---

[40] For *grex* of wild animals see e.g. Tac. *H.* 5. 3. 2 'grex asinorum agrestium'; Curt. 9. 4. 18 'immanium beluarum gregibus'; *OLD* 1a. Cf. also e.g. Sen. *Contr.* 10. 4. 17 'castratorum greges'.

[41] Cf. Diog. Laer. 8. 9. Pythagoras himself was of unblemished sexual reputation (id. 8. 19).

[42] See Suet. *Nero* 28. 1–2; Dio 62. 28. 3.

[43] Griffin (1984), 222 (and 231–2 for imperial salutations). [We might also remember that the name 'Nero' denoted *fortis ac strenuus* in Sabine: see Suet. *Tib.* 1. 2; Maltby (1991), 409.]

[44] For the polarity in Greek thought between war and wedlock see Hartog (1988), 216–17. See also Mart. 12. 42, and below, p. 184.

(2. 137–8), something to which, in the case of Nero, Tacitus makes only a brief, though telling, allusion ('genialis torus').[45]

These and other details of Tacitus' penultimate sentence are all in keeping with a Roman bride and hence with Nero's unnatural adoption of that role; but Roman brides were not expected to have sexual intercourse in public, something which Ovid associates with animals (*Ars Amatoria* 2. 615–16). This final atrocity (*denique*) was, however, nevertheless accomplished by Nero, who therefore went even beyond the exchange of male and female roles (hence '*etiam* in femina') and practised sex in a manner more normally associated with foreigners and barbarians.[46] Herodotus tells us that in the Caucasus men and women have intercourse openly 'like animals' (1. 203. 2), and the same practice is attributed to the Mossynoeci on the shores of the Black Sea by both Xenophon and Apollonius, and to the Irish by Strabo (who adds incest for good measure).[47] Predictably the motif recurs in Lucian's parody (*True History* 2. 19), and it is combined with its animal aspect by Herodotus when he says that in a certain part of Egypt a woman was seen mating with a goat 'openly' (2. 46. 4). Hence Nero's behaviour, as described by Tacitus, is not only foreign but also serves to keep alive the suggestions of animalism in *lupanaria* and *grege* earlier.

THE SUB-TEXT: AUTHOR AND AUDIENCE

Although Tigellinus' revels are described also by Dio (62. 15. 1–6), he concentrates on the construction of the pontoon and on the heterosexual couplings which took place by the lakeside. Only Tacitus describes the revels in terms of a series of reversals, the sheer number of which suggests that he intends to describe Rome as if it were an alien place. Reversals, as we have seen, are the standard method by which ancient authors described foreign countries and peoples. And, since Tacitus also presents the revels as the sequel to the incident in the temple of Vesta, his precise suggestion would seem to be that Nero himself turned Rome

---

[45] 'The *genius* (a word derived from the root indicating procreation) is concerned with propagation of the family and therefore with the marriage-bed' (Courtney on Juv. 6. 21).

[46] See also Hartog (1988), 221, 226.

[47] Xen. *Anab.* 5. 4. 33; Ap. Rhod. 2. 1023–5 (1015–22 are also full of reversals); Strabo 4. 5. 4.

into a foreign city to compensate for the eastern tour which he had been || obliged to call off. But can we go further, and identify any particular foreign city at which Tacitus may be hinting?

Later in his narrative of AD 64 Tacitus sarcastically implies that Nero's new house, under construction after the Great Fire, was almost co-extensive with the city of Rome itself: Tacitus refers to 'the parts of the city which were superfluous to the house' (43. 1 'urbis quae domui supererant').[48] Now this statement is a fruitful source of irony. Nero in a speech at the start of his reign had promised that he would keep his *domus* separate from the *res publica* (13. 4. 2 'discretam domum et rem publicam') and had implied that he would follow in Augustus' footsteps (13. 4. 1), an implication which, in Suetonius' version, is made explicit: 'He declared that he would rule according to the principles of Augustus' (*Nero* 10. 1). Yet Nero's house after the Fire, so far from being separate from the *res publica*, not only takes over practically the whole city but also represents a reversal of Augustus' behaviour, who had opened up his own house to the public (Velleius, 81. 3 'publicis se usibus destinare professus est'). Yet these ironies become directly relevant only after the Fire: what is curious, therefore, is that Tacitus should make a very similar point here at 37. 1 *before* the Fire: 'totaque urbe quasi domo uti'.

It is however interesting to recall that, according to the geographer Strabo (17. 1. 8), successive Ptolemies had so extended the royal residence at Alexandria that it came to occupy a large area of the city, which was actually called 'the Palaces' (τὰ βασίλεια). This area was connected to the headland of Lochias by 'the Inner Palaces', in which, says Strabo, there were 'groves and numerous lodges of various types' (17. 1. 9).[49] According to the *Memoirs* of Ptolemy Euergetes, this same area also contained a zoo, established by Ptolemy Philadelphus, which exhibited exotic

---

[48] This point was made much of at the time: see Suet. *Nero* 39. 2; Griffin (1984), 138; cf. also, for the motif, Sall. *C.* 12. 3 'domos atque uillas . . . in urbium modum exaedificatas'; Ov. *F.* 6. 641 'urbis opus domus una fuit'. For recent studies of the Roman *domus*, and its significance for public and private life, see R. P. Saller, '*Familia, Domus*, and the Roman Conception of the Family', *Phoenix*, 38 (1984), 349 ff.; T. P. Wiseman, '*Conspicui postes tectaque digna deo*: The Public Image of Aristocratic and Imperial Houses in the Late Republic and Early Empire', *L'Urbs: Éspace urbain et histoire* (1987), 393–413; A. Wallace-Hadrill, 'The Social Structure of the Roman House', *PBSR* 56 (1988), 43–97.

[49] For the topography of Alexandria see Fraser (1972), i.14–15, 22–3.

birds and animals.[50] Alexandria had an artificial harbour called
Cibotus, which, though placed by Strabo in the west of the city, is
located in the eastern Palaces area by a papyrus of 13 BC.[51] And
though I can find no evidence that parties were held actually in
this harbour, we are told by Callixenus, a historian of the second
century BC, that Ptolemy Philopator constructed a massive royal
barge, with an assortment of cabins, the largest of which could
hold twenty couches and was decorated with gold and ivory, and
saloons for holding dinner parties.[52] This accumulation of details
suggests that, if Tacitus is not describing Alexandria here, he is at
least describing a city very like it.

At this point in the argument it is necessary to recall the
observation (which has often been made) that Tacitus' description
of Nero's entourage as *illo contaminatorum grege* (37. 4) is an allusion
to Horace, *Odes* 1. 37. 6-10: ||

> Capitolio
> regina dementis ruinas
> funus et imperio parabat
>
> *contaminato* cum *grege* turpium,[53]
> morbo uirorum.

Horace was referring to the eunuchs who were conventionally
associated with Egypt in the ancient world;[54] and in his ode their
leader, being a woman (*regina*), is an appropriate analogue to
Nero, who in his wedding to Pythagoras adopts the female
role. Yet Cleopatra was not only a woman but queen of, precisely,
Alexandria. Similarly Tacitus' account of Nero's wedding ends
with the words *nox operit*, which are borrowed from the fourth
book of Virgil's *Aeneid*.[55] There Aeneas says that, as often as night
covers the earth (351-2 'quotiens . . . | nox operit terras'), he
dreams he must seek a foreign kingdom (350 'et nos fas extera
quaerere regna'). Aeneas' words may well seem significant enough
in themselves, but we must also remember that this is his last

---

[50] *FGrH* 234 F 2 (= Athen. 14. 654C).

[51] *BGU* 1151, verso, ii. 40; Strabo 17. 1. 10. See Fraser (1972), i. 26, 144, and ii. 78–9.

[52] *FGrH* 627 F 1 (= Athen. 5. 204 F, 205 BC). See E. E. Rice, *The Grand Procession of Ptolemy Philadelphus* (1983), 144–8.

[53] D. R. Shackleton Bailey's punctuation, now enshrined in his Teubner text (1985): see C. O. Brink, 'Horatian Notes II', *PCPS* 17 (1971), 17.

[54] Balsdon (1979), 277–8.   [55] The words also recur at e.g. Stat. *Theb.* 1. 455.

speech to Dido—another queen 'reigning on the African continent' and regarded by many scholars as an allegory of Cleopatra.[56] And it was Cleopatra, we recall, who famously used a Ptolemaic barge for her meeting with Mark Antony. According to Plutarch's account (*Antony* 26. 1–2, 4), it had a gilded poop and purple sails; Cleopatra herself reclined beneath a canopy spangled with gold; and, when Antony arrived on board for dinner, what most astonished him was 'the multitude of lights, . . . [which] were let down and displayed on all sides at once'. And though the meeting between the two took place at Tarsus in Cilicia, it seems safe to assume that the barge itself had voyaged there from its base at Alexandria.[57]

Tacitus' allusions to Virgil and especially Horace strongly support the suggestion that the author is providing a 'metonymical' description of Alexandria;[58] and that we as his audience are intended to recognize the description seems confirmed by what we are told at the very beginning of the episode. At 36. 1 Tacitus said that, of all the eastern provinces which Nero had proposed to visit, it was *particularly Egypt* ('maxime Aegyptum') which he had in mind. Now we know from other authors that Alexandria was rumoured to be Nero's planned destination during the final days of his life;[59] but Suetonius also tells us that it was Alexandria which the emperor proposed to visit in the present year, AD 64, until he was deterred by the frightening incident in the temple of Vesta (*Nero* 19. 1, cf. 35. 5). Clearly it is this Alexandrian trip to which Tacitus refers with his mention of Egypt; but what is interesting is the way he presents the proposal as part of Nero's *private* fantasizings' || ('secretis imaginationibus'). If it was a private fantasy of the emperor's, there was no onus upon Tacitus to refer to it;[60] but, by doing so, he has activated the coded sub-text which the audience is meant to elicit from the description which follows at 37. 2–4.

[56] See Pease on *Aen.* 4, pp. 24–8 for discussion (quotation from p. 24).

[57] So Pelling (1988), 188.

[58] For metonymy of this type elsewhere in Tacitus see *RICH* 188 [above, p. 138] and Martin–Woodman, 242–4. Note that Augustus and his successors seem actually to have used Alexandria as a model for Rome when redeveloping their capital city: F. Castagnoli, 'Influenze alessandrine nell' urbanistica della Roma Augustea', *RFIC* 109 (1981), 414–23.

[59] Plut. *Galba* 2. 1; Dio 63. 27. 2; cf. Suet. *Nero* 47. 2; Griffin (1984), 229.

[60] I am not here concerned with the question of why Tacitus has chosen to represent as private something which in Suetonius is public, but with the fact that Tacitus so represents it.

Such a procedure is very much in Tacitus' manner.[61] Earlier in this same book he has encouraged his readers to see the foreign campaigns of AD 62–3 in terms of the famous disaster which the Romans suffered at the hands of the Samnites several centuries previously at the Caudine Forks and which had been described in Book 9 of Livy. Tacitus records a rumour that, as a result of the leadership of the commander (Paetus), 'sub iugum missas legiones' (15. 2), just as had famously happened in 321 BC, when, according to Livy, 'primi consules . . . sub iugum missi . . . tum deinceps singulae legiones' (9. 6. 1). Tacitus says that when the troops of the commander-in-chief (Corbulo) met those of Paetus, 'uix prae fletu usurpata consalutatio' (15. 4), which recalls the Capuans' report to their senate about the Romans after the Caudine disaster: in Livy's words 'non reddere salutem salutantibus . . . prae metu potuisse' (9. 6. 12). And when Tacitus makes the Parthian envoys boast to Nero that their possession of Armenia was gained 'non sine ignominia Romana' (24. 1), that recalls Livy's authorial description of the Caudine episode as one of 'Romanae ignominiae' (9. 15. 10). All these allusions to Livy and his account of the Caudine tragedy have been activated earlier at 13. 2, where Tacitus had depicted Paetus' troops as actually calling to mind that very same event (*Caudinae*)—a depiction which itself constitutes an allusion to Livy (35. 11. 3 'Caudinaeque cladis memoria non animis modo sed prope oculis obuersabatur').[62]

If Tacitus here at 36–7 has used similar techniques to prompt his audience to believe that Nero transformed Rome into Alexandria, the transformation is not simply a literary *jeu d'esprit* but plays a significant part in the author's presentation of the emperor. Alexandria was an essentially ambiguous city, half Greek and half Egyptian.[63] Its Greekness not only provided a potential target for the prejudice of Tacitus' audience but also meant that the city could be represented as the object of Nero's personal enthusiasm and devotion, since his love of all things Greek was notorious.[64] On the other hand, the city's Egyptian character meant that it was at the same time genuinely alien in a sense that Greece itself was

---

[61] [See now Woodman–Martin on *A*. 3. 33. 4.]

[62] I owe this reference to Miss Jane Chaplin. [63] Balsdon (1979), 68.

[64] For Nero's philhellenism see Griffin (1984), 208 ff.; Juvenal is perhaps an indication of contemporary attitudes to Greeks (Rudd (1986), 184–92); for Tacitus' own attitude see Syme (1958), 515–17.

not. In this respect too it was target for popular prejudice, since 'Egyptians generally were regarded by the Romans with hatred and contempt'.[65] Indeed Tacitus' allusion to Horace's Cleopatra ode may be intended to awaken thoughts of the propaganda of the late republic, in which it was alleged that Mark Antony proposed to stay with Cleopatra || in Alexandria and transfer the capital thither from Rome.[66] This propaganda in its turn continued the taunts directed against Antony in 44 BC by Cicero, who in his second *Philippic*, for example, had accused him of a homosexual marriage in very similar terms to those used by Tacitus about Nero (44): [67]

sumpsisti uirilem, quam statim muliebrem togam reddidisti. primo uulgare scortum, certa flagitii merces (nec ea parua); sed cito Curio interuenit, qui te . . ., tamquam stolam dedisset, in matrimonio stabili et certo collocauit.

It was of course the Battle of Actium in 31 BC between Antony and the future Augustus which ensured that Alexandria, where Antony committed suicide a year later, would not become the capital of the empire. There is thus considerable irony in the notion that Nero, descended equally from both men, should proclaim himself a follower of Augustus (above, p. 180) but at the same time, having killed his relative Torquatus for enjoying Augustan ancestry too (p. 169), should be depicted at the end of the Julian dynasty as adopting an overtly 'Antonian' lifestyle and as transforming Rome into Antony's hated Egyptian city.

Yet the popular Roman hatred for Alexandria does not mean that Nero himself did not share the same attitude to its Egyptian character. One of the features which distinguishes Tacitus' portrayal of the emperor is a complex of metaphors by which he is presented as an aggressor attacking his own city.[68] These metaphors start right at the beginning of Tacitus' narrative of the reign (13. 25. 1–2) but are particularly prominent in Book 15. For

---

[65] Balsdon (1979), 68. Cf. e.g. Juv. 6. 82 ff.

[66] See Dio 50. 4. 1. Gaius, Nero's uncle, was thought to have harboured similar ambitions (Suet. *Gai.* 49. 2), and Germanicus, his grandfather, had paid a famous visit to Egypt and Alexandria in AD 19 (cf. 2. 59–61). 'Alexandrianism' evidently ran in the family.   [67] Cf. I. Opelt, *Die lateinischen Schimpfwörter* (1965), 155.

[68] Keitel (1984), 307–9. It is relevant to note that Egypt was an imperial province of a special kind, which 'emperors treated as a sort of personal domain' (P. A. Brunt, *JRS* 73 (1983), 61). See also Tacitus' remarks at 2. 59. 3, where Goodyear observes that Philo called Egypt the greatest of the emperor's possessions (*Flacc.* 158).

example, after hinting strongly that the Fire at Rome was started by Nero himself (38. 7),[69] Tacitus says that he 'laid Italy waste' and 'looted the temples in the City' (45. 1 'peruastata Italia . . . spoliatis in urbe templis'). From the standpoint of a Roman audience these metaphors identify Nero as a foreign aggressor, as is made clear by a passage of indirect speech in which Calpurnius Piso says that Nero 'built his house from the spoils of the citizens' (52. 1 'spoliis ciuium exstructa domo'); but the metaphors inevitably carry the further implication that Nero himself viewed Rome as a foreign city, which nothing prevented him from sacking. In terms of the analogy which I have been pursuing, Alexandria was the only foreign city in the whole empire which had this dual capacity of attracting Nero's favouritism and hatred in equal measure, a city to be decorated or destroyed according to his changing whim. Thus, when Tacitus depicts Nero as transforming Rome into Alexandria, he is not merely illustrating || the emperor's exorbitant compensation for his frustrated wanderlust[70] but is also underlining still further the schizophrenic element in the emperor's personality which we observed at the end of the preceding paragraph.

Since Rome's transformation into an alien capital has depended upon numerous reversals of situation and behaviour, as we have seen, it is at least arguable that Tacitus' authorial role has also changed: from that of historian in chapter 36 to that of paradoxographer in chapter 37.[71] Earlier in the *Annals*, for example, Tacitus had gone out of his way to scorn the technicalities of engineering as unworthy of inclusion in historiography proper (13. 31. 1); but feats of construction form a staple ingredient of paradoxographical narratives such as that of Herodotus, and Tacitus here provides an account, albeit brief, of the construction

---

[69] Unlike Rome before the Great Fire (cf. 43. 1–5), Alexandria had been supposed to be 'incendio fere tuta' ([Caes.] *Bell. Alex.* 1. 3); yet it too suffered severe fire damage in 48 BC (Fraser (1972), i. 334–5, ii. 493–4).

[70] As Nero had wanted to visit Greece as well as Egypt (cf. 33. 2, 36. 1), his transformation of Rome into the ambiguous city of Alexandria is peculiarly apposite.

[71] I am here using 'paradoxographer' in a broad sense, which might also include e.g. Herodotus, rather than in its technical sense, which would refer to an author such as Phlegon of Tralles (*FGrH* 257 F 35 ff.), a contemporary of the emperor Hadrian: see *OCD* s.v. 'paradoxographer', Gabba (1981), 53–5, Rutherford (1989), 182, and below, p. 189 and n. 84. For the notion that Tacitus manipulates his authorial role elsewhere too see my discussions in *RICH* 180–90 [above, pp. 128–41] and in Luce–Woodman (1993) [below, Ch. 11].

of Tigellinus' remarkable party pontoon. The exceptional nature of the account is reflected in Tacitus' use of language, for in this single sentence we meet *superponere*, which he does not employ elsewhere, *tractus*, which he does not employ elsewhere in the sense of 'traction' or 'towing', and *moueri*, which in its simple form and primary sense he again seems not to employ elsewhere.[72] Yet at the same time none of these words is unusual in itself. Tacitus has evidently adopted one of the main techniques of producing an impression of 'otherness', which is 'to describe practices which are abominable (to us) in an altogether neutral fashion, even using technical vocabulary, as if they were the simplest and most common practices in the world'.[73]

Another example resides in the parenthetical reference to Pythagoras' name. The primary function of the reference is to guarantee the genuineness of an incident which otherwise seems beyond belief; but this in its turn implies the privileged stance of the paradoxographer, who has specialized knowledge and for whom naming is an activity which characterizes his role.[74] This explains why ancient historians, including Tacitus, tend to mention names in ethnographical or foreign contexts.[75] Yet it is the actual wedding of Pythagoras to Nero which provides the most notable example of all.

Earlier in the *Annals* (11. 27) Tacitus had described a solemn wedding ceremony (termed *nuptiarum sollemnia*: 11. 26. 3) involving Messalina, wife of the emperor Claudius, and C. Silius, consul designate:

Haud sum ignarus fabulosum uisum iri tantum ullis mortalium securitatis fuisse in ciuitate omnium gnara et nihil reticente, nedum consulem designatum cum uxore principis praedicta die, adhibitis qui obsignarent, uelut suscipiendorum liberorum || causa conuenisse, atque illam audisse auspicum uerba, subisse <flammeum>, sacrificasse apud deos; discubitum inter conuiuas, oscula, complexus; noctem denique actam licentia coniugali. sed nihil compositum miraculi causa, uerum audita scriptaque senioribus trado.

---

[72] Gerber–Greef 1657a and 870; though Tacitus of course likes using simple for compound verbs, their statement in the latter place that *moueo* here = *amoueo* seems mistaken: if so, it is also mistaken to say that *moueo* is never literal in Tacitus.
[73] Hartog (1988), 256.   [74] Hartog (1988), 247–8.
[75] e.g. Sall. *J*. 18. 1 'quae mapalia illi uocat'; Liv. 23. 24. 7 'Litanam Galli uocabant', 33. 17. 2 'ad Heraeum, quod uocant'; Vell. 102. 3 'Limyra nominant'; Martin–Woodman on 4. 73. 4.

I am not unaware it will seem mythical that, in a community aware of
everything and silent about nothing, there were any members of
humanity at all who felt such unconcern, still less that a consul designate
and the wife of a *princeps*, on a pre-announced day and with signatories
summoned, came together for the purpose of begetting children; that
she for her part listened to the officials' words, put on the <bridal veil>,
and sacrificed in front of the gods; that they reclined amongst guests,
with kisses and embraces; and, finally, that their night was spent in
wedded licence. Yet none of this has been composed for the purpose
of producing a marvel; in reality I am recounting what was heard and
written by an older generation.

This wedding is conventional in the sense that it was heterosexual
but unconventional in the sense that the woman was already
married—and to the emperor at that. Inasmuch as it has a conventional aspect, the wedding falls squarely within the boundaries
of *historia*, which was defined by the ancients as the narrative of an
event which occurred.[76] But, in order to highlight just how
extraordinary it was for someone to marry the emperor's wife,
Tacitus in his role as historical author invites his audience to
indulge in the momentary speculation that the wedding was
actually the product of *fabula*, which was defined by the ancients
as the narrative which 'contains things neither true nor plausible'.[77] In fact, however, *fabula* was normally restricted to the
narrative of things which were physically impossible or contrary
to nature, such as the metamorphoses of mythology or the mar-
vels of paradoxography proper (*miracula*, τὰ θαυμαστά);[78] and,
since Messalina's wedding clearly did not fall into such a category,
there was no real question that the event should *actually* be
classified as *fabulosum*.[79] Hence Tacitus, while affirming that the
event belongs to *historia* ('nihil compositum miraculi causa'), is
nevertheless able to make literary capital out of the explicit
suggestion that it belongs to *fabula*.[80]

---

[76] *Rhet. Herenn.* 1. 13, Cic. *Inv.* 1. 27.   [77] *Rhet. Herenn.* 1. 13, Cic. *Inv.* 1. 27.

[78] See F. W. Walbank, 'History and Tragedy', *Historia*, 9 (1960), 226 = *Selected Papers:
Studies in Greek and Roman History and Historiography* (1985), 234.

[79] 'The event was implausible but demonstrably true—a paradox with which the
historians of the ancient world were ill-equipped to deal' (T. P. Wiseman, 'Practice and
Theory in Roman Historiography', *History*, 66 (1981), 390 = *Roman Studies: Literary and
Historical* (1987), 259). Cf. esp. *Rhet. Herenn.* 1. 16, Quint. 4. 2. 34, 56.

[80] Cf. how at 4. 10–11, but for a different purpose, Tacitus makes similar capital out of
his alternative account of Drusus' murder (Martin–Woodman, 130–1).

If readers of the account of Nero's wedding to Pythagoras remember the earlier marriage of Messalina to Silius (as they are surely intended to do, from the similarity of detail provided by Tacitus in each case), they will perhaps conclude that such a genuinely unnatural marriage does || indeed belong to *fabula*; and, since many of the other descriptions in 37. 2–4 are also contrary to nature, as we have seen, the audience may draw the further conclusion that the author is now writing *fabula* of the paradoxographical variety rather than *historia*. On this occasion Tacitus does not of course make any explicit reference to *fabula*, and he certainly makes no attempt to define his narrative in 'fabulous' terms. For otherwise he might have invited the fate of Herodotus, from whose work, and especially the Egyptian narrative, so many of my paradoxographical illustrations have been taken. As Cicero said, 'in *historia* most things have their basis in *ueritas*, . . . although in Herodotus, the father of *historia*, . . . there are countless *fabulae*';[81] and it was for this reason that Herodotus became famous as 'the liar' quite as much as 'the father of history'.[82] Yet, from the accumulation of evidence in chapter 37,[83] it seems undeniable that Tacitus has produced the *implication* of *fabula*, without which he could not fully impress upon his audience that Nero's behaviour, though true, was beyond belief, and hence beyond the normal boundaries of *historia* also. These are the most telling paradoxes of all.[84]

[81] *Leg.* 1. 5. On this passage see *RICH* 98–100 and 114–15 n. 141.

[82] O. Murray, 'Herodotus and Hellenistic Culture', *CQ* 22 (1972), 205; Hartog (1988), 297–309.

[83] Miller on 37. 1 remarks that *prodigentia* is 'a vigorous and allusive word ("monstrous behaviour")', evidently thinking that it is connected with *prodigium*. Unfortunately, though her instincts were clearly correct, there seems to be no evidence that this was or is the case. (I am not of course suggesting that the mythical and foreign are not attributed to Nero elsewhere in Tacitus or by other authors: cf. e.g. 11. 11. 3 'fabulosa et externis miracula adsimilata', 16. 6. 2 'non . . . , ut Romanus mos'; Suet. *Nero* 6. 4. It is merely the accumulation at 15. 37. 1–4 which I wish to emphasize.)

[84] i.e. Tacitus not only resorts to the devices of *fabula*, which is the conventional antithesis of *historia*, but comes to adopt a position which is the mirror-image of that

adopted by paradoxographers proper (above, n. 71), namely that their subject-matter, though beyond belief, is true. See e.g. Gabba (1981), 53–4: '[Paradoxography's] unifying characteristic was its acceptance without question of any available information; the problem of truth or credibility of the phenomena or facts, which were presented, was simply not raised, since the question of truth was not present in the minds of readers . . . Its concern was not to distinguish the true from the false . . . but to provide lively and highly-coloured pictures of milieus and situations, whose historicity was already accepted. Pseudo-historical or paradoxographical narrative was enriched with learned trivia, intended to ensure greater verisimilitude and hence win greater acceptance' (cf. the 'strange, therefore true' topos in the English novel: M. McKeon, *The Origins of the English Novel 1600–1740* (1987), 528). Since the *ueritas* claimed by *fabula* in general and by paradoxography in particular is not that claimed by historiography, it is clear that Tacitus is here, as elsewhere (see n. 71), merely pretending to adopt a certain authorial role. If the role is not appreciated, its full effect in the narrative is lost; if the pretence is not recognized, mistaken conclusions might be drawn.

11

Amateur Dramatics at the Court of Nero
(*Annals* 15. 48–74)

I

The Pisonian conspiracy against Nero in AD 65 is described as 'a dismal failure' in the emperor's most recent English biography, where the subject is assigned a mere two and a half pages.[1] Similarly Suetonius and Dio provide only brief accounts.[2] Yet Tacitus devotes to the conspiracy and its aftermath the last twenty-seven chapters of *Annals* 15: it is thus the longest single episode in the whole of the extant *Annals*[3] and the longest by far in the later books.[4] This is a striking discrepancy. Moreover, by making the start of his account coincide with the start of the narrative of the year 65, and by making the end of it coincide with the end of Book 15, Tacitus has given to the conspiracy a coherence and unity it did not possess in real life. This is clear from his

---

I am most grateful to D. M. Bain, D. C. Feeney, E. Henry, T. J. Luce, R. H. Martin, and J. L. Moles for commenting on earlier drafts of this chapter, an oral version of which was delivered not only at Princeton at the 1990 Colloquium 'Tacitus and the Tacitean Tradition' but also at Columbia, Harvard (where I had the honour of delivering a Loeb Lecture), University of California at Riverside, and at the Triennial Meeting of the Hellenic and Roman Societies in 1991 at Cambridge. I greatly appreciate these invitations to speak and the stimulating discussions that took place afterwards. A particular debt of gratitude is owed to Elizabeth Keitel, who with great generosity gave me the benefit of her own unpublished analysis of *A*. 15. 48–74.

All references to Tacitus are to the *Annals* unless stated otherwise; references to Book 15 omit the book number.

[1] Griffin (1984), 166–8.

[2] Suet. *Nero* 36. 1–2; Dio 62. 24. 1–27. 4 (but not a homogeneous account).

[3] The account of the mutinies at 1. 16–52 is longer but comprises two distinct episodes (cf. 1. 31. 1).

[4] It is more than twice as long as the downfall of Messalina (11. 26–38) and the murder of Agrippina (14. 1–13). In fact the conspiracy is given more than twice as much space as all the other events of AD 65 put together (16. 1–13) and is significantly longer than the *complete* narrative of any other exclusively domestic year. (AD 62 at 14. 48–15. 22 is longer but contains a substantial section on foreign affairs at 15. 1–17.)

very first sentence at 48. 1 ('Ineunt deinde consulatum Silius Nerua et Atticus Vestinus, coepta simul et aucta coniuratione in quam certatim nomina dederant senatores, eques, miles, feminae etiam, cum odio Neronis tum fauore in C. Pisonem'), where the pluperfect tense of *dederant* indicates that the beginning of the || conspiracy—and hence also a certain portion of Tacitus' subsequent narrative—preceded the entry of the consuls into office and thus does not belong strictly to the narrative of AD 65 at all.[5]

Tacitus' evident determination to present the Pisonian conspiracy as a single, unified episode will perhaps remind us of Cicero's famous letter to Lucceius, in which he advised that his friend's writing would be all the more effective if it concentrated on the single episode of the Catilinarian conspiracy (*Ad Familiares* 5. 12. 2). Cicero pressed home his argument by adding that, on the basis of its episodes and reversals (6 'habet enim uarios actus mutationesque et consiliorum et temporum'), the whole affair could be seen in terms of a play (*quasi fabulam*). And since Cicero could suggest so clearly that the Catilinarian conspiracy was suitable material for dramatic treatment, it would not be surprising if Tacitus, as F. Graf proposed long ago, has presented his account of the Pisonian conspiracy according to a dramatic structure.[6] What I hope to demonstrate here, however, is that Tacitus has brought out the implications of that presentation by the introduction of metaphors from acting and the suggestion of role-playing,

---

[5] This is contradicted by Koestermann on 48. 1 and implicitly denied by both Griffin (1984: 167 'Tacitus states firmly that the whole conspiracy was both conceived and hatched in 65') and Martin (1981), 183. The last sentence of Book 14 (65. 2) evidently contains a reference to the Pisonian conspiracy but is controversial: see Syme (1958), 745 and Griffin (1984), 85. On the basis thereof Nipperdey (1908), 267, nevertheless suggested, and Graf (1931), 102, agreed, that the conspiracy stretched back at least as far as AD 63; but we do not need such precision to assent to Graf's general view that 'Bewusst wird hier das chronologische Zurückgreifen verschleiert, um auch die Einheit der Zeit im Ablaufe des Dramas zu wahren'. Cf. also Tresch (1965), 172.

[6] Graf (1931), 101–5, consistently analyses Tacitus' account in terms of 'das Drama der pisonischen Verschwörung' and offers a 'schematische Ueberblick' of its 'dramatischen Aufbau': chs. 48–53, 'Vorgeschichte'; 54–8, 'Entdeckung'; 59–71, 'Unterdrückung der Verschworung. Katastrophe ihrer Häupter'; 72–4, 'Ausklang, Dank an die Götter'. Chs. 48–50 in particular have been described as 'the cast of conspirators' by Morris (1969), 221, and as 'the cast of characters' by Griffin (1984), 166; and indeed the sketch of Piso (48. 2–3) and the list of names (49. 2–50. 3) do recall the expository nature of dramatic prologues. On the aptitude of a conspiracy narrative for drama, see e.g. T. F. Scanlon, 'Historia Quasi Fabula: The Catiline Theme in Sallust and Jonson', J. Redmond (ed.), *Themes in Drama 8: Historical Drama* (1986), 17–29; also below, n. 58.

and that these in their turn shed light on why the conspiracy was
the 'dismal failure' to which Nero's biographer referred.

II

The conspirators' plan for killing Nero is described by Tacitus at
53. 1–2:

Tandem statuere circensium ludorum die, qui Cereri celebratur, exsequi
destinata, quia Caesar rarus egressu domoque aut hortis clausus ad ludicra
|| circi uentitabat promptioresque aditus erant laetitia spectaculi. ordinem   2
insidiis composuerant, ut Lateranus, quasi subsidium rei familiari oraret,
deprecabundus et genibus principis accidens prosterneret incautum pre-
meretque, animi ualidus et corpore ingens; tum iacentem et impeditum
tribuni et centuriones et ceterorum ut quisque audentiae habuisset,
adcurrerent trucidarentque, primas sibi partes expostulante Scaeuino,
qui pugionem templo Salutis . . . siue (ut alii tradidere) Fortunae Fer-
entino in oppido detraxerat gestabatque uelut magno operi sacrum.

At last they decided to follow through their proposals on the day of the
circus games celebrated for Ceres, because Caesar, rare to emerge and
shut in his house or gardens, habitually came to the entertainments of
the circus and there was readier access in his enjoyment of the show.
They had agreed the procedure for the ambush: as if begging support for   2
his patrimony, Lateranus, entreating and falling at the *princeps'* knees,
would floor him when off guard and pin him down (being strong of
nerve and mighty in physique); then the tribunes, centurions, and
others in order of daring would rush up and butcher him as he lay
trapped—with the leading role being demanded for himself by Scaevinus, who had removed a dagger from a temple of Salus . . . or (as others
have recounted) of Fortuna in the town of Ferentinum and carried it
about as if consecrated for some great task.

First, Plautius Lateranus, the consul designate (cf. 49. 3), is to
impede Nero; then Flavius Scaevinus, a senator (cf. 49. 4),
demands the leading role in actually killing him. The phrase
primas . . . partes at 53. 2 is of course a technical theatrical expression, which indicates that Scaevinus sees himself and (by implication) his collaborators too as acting in a drama.[7] Now normally it

---

[7] *OLD pars* 9b. Since *primas . . . partes* is the object of a verb of saying (*expostulante*), it is
not possible to maintain that the words are not imagined as being Scaevinus' own (see
further discussion in the text). Neither Koestermann nor Miller (1973) comments on the
metaphor, presumably regarding it as dead (see further, n. 11).

was regarded as disgraceful if senators actually performed on the stage;[8] but Nero, characteristically, had done everything in his power to encourage such people to perform. Juvenal devotes a scathing paragraph of his eighth satire to the topic (183–210), and Tacitus himself has already described how in AD 59 the emperor had compelled impoverished members of noble families to perform on stage (14. 14. 3). For the Youth Games that same year, says Tacitus, 'names were submitted on all sides: neither nobility nor age nor political offices were an impediment to performing the routine of a Greek or Latin actor, even down to effeminate gestures and songs' (14. 15. 1). At the climax of the performance, Tacitus adds, 'the man himself took the stage last' ('postremus ipse scaenam incedit', || 14. 15. 4).[9] It is therefore not without irony that Tacitus here in Book 15 depicts Scaevinus as seeing himself and his colleagues as actors. Evidently they too are responding to the emperor's pressure, except that on this occasion there were to be no effeminate gestures and their hope was that Nero would once again join in the performance himself—but this time as victim.

Because the conspirators perceive themselves to be acting out roles, we may ask what roles it is that they are playing. As the commentators point out, the details of Nero's ambush are modelled on those of the ambush of Julius Caesar.[10] Lateranus plays the part of Tillius Cimber, who had approached Caesar as if to present a petition and then clung on to his toga, while Scaevinus plays the part of Casca, who had struck the first blow.[11] Nero, the last of the Julian line, is to play the part of Julius Caesar himself, his own ancestor. Even the venue chosen for the ambush perhaps supports the notion of a play. We know that the Festival of Ceres, which was celebrated between 12 and 19 April, was the occasion of *ludi scaenici* or theatrical shows on all except its last day, when,

---

[8] Cf. especially the *senatus consultum* of AD 19 from Larinum: B. Levick, *JRS* 73 (1983), 75–115.

[9] Trimalchio's entrance at his own dinner party is similarly staged: see Petr. 32. 1 with Sandy (1974), 331.

[10] See e.g. Koestermann or Miller (1973) on 53. 2. There are also similarities with Caligula's assassination: see e.g. Jos. *AJ* 19. 70–95; also see nn. 11, 47.

[11] See e.g. Suet. *Diu. Iul.* 82. 1–2, who himself uses the phrase *primas partes susceperat* to describe Cimber's role. My point about Tacitus' phrase, however, is that his context activates and sustains the metaphor—which he may of course have borrowed from some earlier version: cf. App. *BC* 2. 146 ὁ δῆμος οἷα χορός ('the crowd like a chorus', again of Caesar's murder); Suet. *Gai.* 56. 2 'cum placuisset Palatinis ludis spectaculo egressum meridie adgredi, primas sibi partes Cassius Chaerea [see n. 34] . . . depoposcit'.

as is clear from our text, circus games were held instead.[12] It is as though the conspirators intended that spectators should not after all be deprived of a *ludus scaenicus* on the final day: namely, the re-enactment of the murder of Julius Caesar, which itself had been staged in a place with theatrical connections.[13]

Plays at Rome were traditionally occasions for both actors and audience to make political points. Cicero mentioned the theatre as one of the key locations where 'the judgement and wishes of the Roman people about public affairs can be most clearly expressed'.[14] His letters to Atticus reveal that in April of 44 BC, shortly after the murder of Julius Caesar, actors were alluding to the event in their performances and eliciting a favourable || reaction from their audiences.[15] Out of many subsequent examples[16] we may recall Suetonius' story about an actor in the reign of Nero who recited the line 'Goodbye, father; goodbye, mother', with accompanying gestures of drinking and swimming, as if to remind his audience of the popular belief that Nero had poisoned Claudius and attempted to drown Agrippina (*Nero* 39. 3). Similarly we are told by Dio (61. 20. 3–4) and Tacitus himself (16. 5. 1) that Nero packed audiences with soldiers to make sure that the crowd's supposedly spontaneous reaction to him would be suitably enthusiastic. What the conspirators in AD 65 are planning is that on 19 April a section of the spectators, consisting of themselves, should become actors in a drama which itself constitutes its own political point: its climax is not to act a scene of murder but actually to carry it out.

Such a proposed blending of the real and the dramatic would have struck a chord with Tacitus' readers in the early second century AD. His older contemporary Plutarch, for example, described in his *Life of Crassus* how the Parthians celebrated their

---

[12] See Tac. *H.* 2. 55. 1 with Chilver, Courtney on Juv. 14. 262; also J. G. Frazer on Ov. *F.* 4. 393.

[13] Namely, the *curia Pompeii* adjoining Pompey's theatre, where a spectacle was taking place to celebrate a festival (cf. e.g. App. *BC* 2. 115). For the potential of the circus for various forms of staged display, see Coleman (1990), 52; for *ludi scaenici* in general, see J.-M. André, 'Les "ludi scaenici" et la politique des spectacles au début de l'ère antonine', *Association G. Budé: Actes du IXe Congrès* (1975), 1. 468–79. Cf. Jos. *AJ* 19. 92 τυραννοκτονίας ἀγὼν πρόκειται.   [14] *Sest.* 106; cf. 115 and 118.

[15] Cic. *Att.* 14. 2 (356). 1, 14. 3 (357). 2.

[16] For which see MacMullen (1966), 171–2 and 339–41, Cameron (1976), 157–92, and K. Hopkins, *Death and Renewal* (1983), 14–20; also Nisbet–Hubbard on Hor. *C.* 1. 20. 3.

victory at the Battle of Carrhae. An actor was reciting scenes from Euripides' *Bacchae* when suddenly someone produced the head of the Roman general, Crassus himself, which then became a stage prop for a performance in which the dismemberment of Pentheus had unexpectedly acquired a real-life dimension (33. 2–4).[17] Indeed it has been suggested that Nero himself re-enacted a scene from the *Bacchae* when, as Suetonius and Dio allege, he inspected his mother's corpse;[18] but, whether or not this was the case, less heroic blendings of the real and the dramatic were a feature of Nero's reign. Dio tells us that the elaborate plan for murdering Agrippina was a restaging of a scene with a collapsible boat that had been put on in the theatre (62. 12. 2);[19] and we know that it is Nero's reign that provides the earliest and some of the most significant evidence for those 'fatal charades' in which criminals and other social outcasts were punished by being condemned to die in a manner that re-enacted a scene from mythology or, more rarely, history.[20] We also know that during || Nero's reign there were actualizations of the mythological stories that were performed in pantomime. 'In one', says Suetonius (*Nero* 12. 2), 'a bull mounted Pasiphae, who was concealed in a wooden model of a heifer'; in another, Icarus' wings fail him and he crashes to the ground, 'spattering the emperor with his blood'. In such performances, as has been remarked, the principle 'lay in the search for an ambiguity between the imaginary and the real. This is shown in startling fashion by the trait which consists in making the actor whose very essence is to *represent* perish in flesh and blood. What

[17] On the whole subject of drama and its varying interaction with 'life', see the superb pages of Garton (1972), 23–40; also Goffman (1974), N. Rudd, *Lines of Enquiry* (1976), 168 ff., and O. Taplin, 'Fifth-Century Tragedy and Comedy', *JHS* 106 (1986), 164, and my discussion later in the text with nn. 60 and 74.

[18] Suet. *Nero* 34. 4; Dio, 61. 14. 2: see B. Baldwin, 'Nero and his Mother's Corpse', *Mnem.* 32 (1979), 380–1. See J. G. F. Hind, 'The Death of Agrippina and the Finale of the "Oedipus" of Seneca', *AUMLA* 38 (1972), 204–11, esp. 208 for the further suggestion that Agrippina dramatized her own murder, as does Gaius' wife at Jos. *AJ* 19. 199 (ἐπὶ τελειώσει τοῦ δράματος οὗ ἐπ' αὐτοῖς συνέθεσαν).

[19] Tacitus' account of this episode is interestingly analysed in dramatic terms by A. Dawson, 'Whatever Happened to Lady Agrippina?', *CJ* 64 (1968), esp. 261–3, 266–7; it has also been suggested that Nero dramatized the murder of his stepson Rufrius Crispinus (Suet. *Nero* 35. 5): see R. M. Frazer, 'Nero the Artist-Criminal', *CJ* 62 (1966), 17–20. On the theatricality of Nero's reign in general, see e.g. Dupont (1985), 430 ff.

[20] See Coleman (1990), 60–73, esp. 70. One of the Pisonian conspirators sees Nero's projected death as a punishment for his treasonable government (51. 3 'prouisum quonam modo poenas euersae rei publicae daret').

is found here [is] not represented but "reified." '[21] Thus the
conspirators' proposal to restage the murder of Caesar, with
Nero as the real victim, is an archetypal product of the reign of
Nero and not unlike what the emperor himself had planned for
his own mother.

III

Yet the conspirators' proposal is never realized because the details
of the plot are betrayed by the same Scaevinus who had
demanded the leading role in the murder. Tacitus describes the
scene at 54. 1–4:

Sed mirum quam inter diuersi generis, ordinis, aetatis, sexus, dites,
pauperes taciturnitate omnia cohibita sint, donec proditio coepit e
domo Scaeuini. qui pridie insidiarum multo sermone cum Antonio
Natale, dein regressus domum testamentum obsignauit, promptum
uagina pugionem (de quo supra rettuli) uetustate obtusum increpans,
asperari saxo et in mucronem ardescere iussit eamque curam liberto
Milicho mandauit. simul adfluentius solito conuiuium initum, ser-   2
uorum carissimi libertate et alii pecunia donati; atque ipse maestus
et magnae cogitationis manifestus erat, quamuis laetitiam uagis sermonibus insimularet. postremo uolneribus ligamenta quibusque sistitur   3
sanguis parare eundem Milichum monet, siue gnarum coniurationis
et illuc usque fidum seu nescium et tunc primum arreptis suspicionibus
(ut plerique tradidere). nam cum secum seruilis animus praemia perfi-   4
diae reputauit simulque immensa pecunia et potentia obuersabantur,
cessit fas et salus patroni et acceptae libertatis memoria. etenim uxoris
quoque consilium adsumpserat, muliebre ac deterius: quippe ultro
metum intentabat, multosque astitisse libertos ac seruos, qui eadem
uiderint; nihil profuturum unius silentium, at praemia penes unum
fore qui indicio praeuenisset.

But it is amazing how among people of different background, rank, age,
and sex, rich and poor, everything was contained in silence until
treachery started || from the house of Scaevinus. On the day before the
ambush, after a long conversation with Antonius Natalis, he then
returned home and sealed his will; getting his dagger (about which I
spoke above) ready from its sheath, and complaining that it was blunt
with age, he ordered it to be whetted on a stone and sparking to a point,
and that he entrusted to the concern of Milichus, a freedman. At the   2

---

[21] Auguet (1972), 103.

same time an unusually sumptuous banquet was embarked upon, and
the dearest of his slaves were presented with their freedom and others
with money; as for the man himself, he was despondent and caught in
the act of great contemplation, although he feigned happiness in ran-
dom conversations. Last of all he warned the same Milichus to prepare   3 ·
ligatures for wounds and the things by which bleeding is stopped, the
man being either aware of the conspiracy and trustworthy up to that
point or else ignorant and only then seizing on suspicions for the first
time (as many have recounted). For when his slave's mind reflected on   4
the prizes of perfidy, and at the same time untold money and power
were confronting him, obligation and his patron's well-being and the
memory of his gift of freedom all receded. In fact from his wife too he
had accepted advice, womanly and baser: for voluntarily she brandished
terror, saying that many freedmen and slaves had stood by, witnessing
the same events; no advantage would come from one man's silence, but
the prizes would go to the one man whose information achieved
priority.

This version of the discovery and betrayal of the conspiracy is
found only in Tacitus. Our only other source is Plutarch (*Moralia*
505 C–D), who says that one of the conspirators spoke cryptically
to a passing prisoner who unfortunately was able to interpret the
message correctly and communicated his interpretation to Nero.
Of these two versions scholars prefer that of Tacitus as being more
detailed and plausible;[22] but precision and the accumulation of
detail are not in themselves guarantees of veracity, as we know,
and to my mind Tacitus' version is even less plausible than Plutarch's. What serious conspirator ever behaved like Scaevinus? In
his dramatic gestures he seems almost to wish death upon himself
rather than upon Nero.[23] Yet the very implausibility of his behaviour reveals that he is less concerned with the reality of his task
than with playing a role.[24]

Consider, for example, how Scaevinus produces the dagger
from its sheath, complains of its bluntness, and demands that

---

[22] See e.g. Miller (1973), 107 or W. C. Helmbold, *Plutarch's Moralia* (Loeb edn., 1957)
vi. 414 n. *a*.

[23] Scaevinus' dinner-scene resembles the theatricality of Stoics who are already set on
killing themselves (see e.g. my comments in the text with n. 53), and he is aptly described
by MacMullen (1966), 71 as 'the martyr of an exaggerated sense of theater'; for death
wishes in general, see Rutherford (1989), 216 and n. 108. Whether Scaevinus' tourniquets
etc. are seen as a wise precaution or a subconscious anticipation of failure will no doubt
depend on one's point of view.

[24] Walker (1952), 135 rightly refers in passing to Scaevinus' 'theatrical preparations'.

Milichus sharpen it. Tacitus appears to be inviting his readers to visualize Scaevinus' actions, || and especially his testing of the blade;[25] we are invited to hear Scaevinus' complaints and commands: it is as if the whole performance were being staged. Indeed the dagger itself plays a role in the text analogous to that played by similarly dangerous or fatal stage properties in actual dramas. One of the most famous examples is the sword in Sophocles' *Ajax*, to the sharpening of which Ajax at one point actually alludes (819–20).[26] And just as the sword recurs significantly throughout the play, so does Scaevinus' dagger in Tacitus' account: it is removed from the temple at 53. 2, it is taken and shown to Nero by the treacherous freedman at 55. 1, Scaevinus himself is confronted with it by Nero at 55. 2, and it reappears for the last time in the final scene of the book (74. 2).[27]

Tacitus' text suggests drama on another level too. In his first sentence at 54. 1, he alludes to the diversity of the conspirators in very similar terms to those he had used when introducing his account of the conspiracy at 48. 1 (see the previous quotation). The repetition has an articulating function, as often in classical texts, and here serves to separate one part or 'act' from another at precisely the moment when the conspiracy is about to be betrayed: that is, at the moment of reversal or *peripeteia*.[28] Thus Tacitus' manner of writing at this point suggests the composition of a dramatic text, such as that which Cicero urged upon his friend Lucceius. And indeed it may be relevant to note that it is in the drama of Seneca that we find the only parallels for Tacitus' phrases *cessit fas* and *metum intentabat*.[29]

---

[25] The testing foreshadows that of Nero himself moments before his own death (Suet. *Nero* 49. 2).

[26] See e.g. Taplin (1978), 85–8. A blunt knife featured in Encolpius' pretended suicide at Petr. 94. 12–95. 1, which is described as both a *mimica mors* and a *fabula*: see Sandy (1974), 344. Cf. also Ach. Tat. 3. 15. 1 ff. and 5. 7. 4 ff.

[27] Quoted in Section VIII. Compare how Cassius commits suicide with the same dagger he had used on Caesar (Plut. *Caes.* 69. 3), and Chaerea dies by the same sword he had used on Gaius (Jos. *AJ* 19. 270–1, where also another assassin makes 'a poor exit').

[28] A break is seen here also by Graf (1931), 103. See my n. 6.

[29] Sen. *Medea* 900, 'fas omne cedat' (spoken by Medea), and *Phaedra* 727, 'mortis intentat metum' (spoken by the nurse about Hippolytus), respectively, though for the latter cf. also *A*. 3. 28. 4 'terror omnibus intentabatur'. It is perhaps possible to infer from the phrases *seruilis animus* (which, as subject of a transitive verb, seems unique in Latin) and *consilium . . . muliebre* that the man and wife are seen in terms of stock characters: Milichus' behaviour is in fact the opposite of that which his name ('kind' in Greek) suggests, a

Tacitus is encouraging the notion of a play, and in particular is depicting Scaevinus in acting terms, because he is capitalizing on one of the essentials of drama: that it is not real life but pretence. Having perceived the assassination as a realistic drama, Scaevinus has now become the victim of his own perception and, as Tacitus' text clearly demonstrates, experiences the || greatest difficulty in coming to terms with actually killing Nero.[30] Unlike the soldier who, when Nero was playing the role of *Hercules furens*, tried to rescue the emperor from his bonds and thereby mistook drama for real life,[31] Scaevinus' own dramatics have led him to mistake real life for drama. Yet this mistake—or should one say *hamartia?*—is not restricted to Scaevinus but afflicts the conspiracy in general from the very start.

IV

At 48. 1 Tacitus says that the conspirators 'certatim nomina dederant'. Now *nomen dare* is a technical expression for signing up as a soldier and therefore suggests that the conspirators are to be seen, or see themselves, in appropriately military terms.[32] Yet the expression is qualified by *certatim*. What sort of *certamen* is this? One possible explanation is that Tacitus is alluding to the *certamen uirtutum*, associated with the idealized past by Sallust and now returning to replace the *certamen uitiorum* that Tacitus has hitherto attributed to the principate.[33] Yet this explanation seems precluded by the motives of the conspirators as given at the end of the same sentence: 'cum odio Neronis tum fauore in C. Pisonem'. For it soon becomes clear that *odium Neronis* constitutes inadequate grounds for participation in the enterprise: at 49. 3

---

regular device in comedy. [That the meaning of his name is active is confirmed later (71. 1), when he takes on a new name—but also in Greek.] For such types in Tacitus' narrative of Claudius, see S. K. Dickison, 'Claudius: Saturnalicius Princeps', *Latomus*, 36 (1977), 634–47; in Livy, see A. Scafuro, 'Livy's Comic Narrative of the Bacchanalia', *Helios*, 16 (1989), 119–42 [to which now add P. G. Walsh, 'Making a Drama out of a Crisis: Livy on the Bacchanalia', *GR* 43 (1996), 188–203]; see also below, Section IV, with n. 41.

[30] See esp. 54. 2 'ipse maestus et magnae cogitationis manifestus erat, quamuis laetitiam uagis sermonibus simularet': Scaevinus now must actively pretend that which he previously took to be real.   [31] Suet. *Nero* 21. 3; Dio, 62. 10. 2.

[32] *OLD nomen* 21b.

[33] Sall. *C.* 9. 2 'ciues cum ciuibus de uirtute certabant'; Walker (1952), 241. Cf. also Vell. 26. 2 'in qua ciuitate semper uirtutibus certatum erat, certabatur sceleribus'.

both Lucan and Lateranus contributed *uiuida odia*, but Lucan's was
a personal vendetta ('Lucanum propriae causae accendebant'), like
that of the affronted Quintianus at 49. 4 ('contumeliam ultum
ibat');[34] only of Lateranus could it be said that 'nulla iniuria sed
amor rei publicae sociauit' (see further discussion). Similarly *fauor*
towards Piso is an unworthy motive, because in the following
sketch he is revealed to be mere show (48. 2–3, *species*, explained
by *namque . . . sed . . .*) and to have attracted support only
because he was seen, in Syme's words, as 'an inoffensive Nero'
(cf. 48. 3, 'idque pluribus probabatur qui in tanta uitiorum dul-
cedine summum imperium non restrictum nec perseuerum
uolunt').[35] By the end of the sketch, therefore, *fauor in Pisonem*
is shown to be not only unworthy as a motive but almost || illogical
as the counterpart of *odium Neronis*, something that the brave and
independently minded Subrius Flavus alone realized: he wished
to kill Piso as well as Nero, on the grounds that the former was as
much a *tragoedus* as the latter was a *citharoedus* (65). Hence the
conspirators' *certamen* seems scarcely connected with *uirtus* and
requires another explanation.

Now *certamen* is of course the regular word for a competition of
actors, whose rivalry was notorious in Roman times and often
spilled over into society at large.[36] Tacitus in *Annals* 1 refers to
'discordia ex certamine histrionum' (54. 2), and in Nero's reign
these fracas became so serious that they resembled pitched battles
('uelut in proelia') and the emperor was compelled to expel actors
from Italy for four years (13. 25. 4; cf. 14. 21. 4).[37] But Tacitus'
language suggests that, in the guise of the Pisonian conspirators,
actors have now returned with a vengeance; and the credibility gap
between their military pretensions, signalled by *nomina dederant*,
and their actors' behaviour, signalled by *certatim*, is a basic motif,
which, as we shall see, lies at the heart of Tacitus' account.[38]

---

[34] The reasons for Quintianus' affront ('mollitia corporis infamis et a Nerone probroso
carmine diffamatus') resemble those of Cassius Chaerea (see. n. 11) at Suet. *Gai*. 56. 2
'quem Gaius seniorem iam et mollem et effeminatum denotare omni probro consuerat'.

[35] Syme (1958), 575. For the man in general, see E. Champlin, 'The Life and Times of
Calpurnius Piso', *MH* 46 (1989), 101–24.   [36] See e.g. Cameron (1976), 223–4.

[37] Cf. also Philo, *Agr.* 35 τὸν ἐπὶ σκηνῆς ἀεὶ πόλεμον συγκροτοῦσι, which is likely to
mean 'they [actors] wage perpetual on-stage war'.

[38] It must be admitted that Livy has the same phraseology at 27. 46. 3 ('certatim nomina
dantes') without any suggestion of actors, but in my view Tacitus' context is once again
decisive (see n. 11). See further discussion towards the end of this chapter.

As for individual conspirators, we have just noted that Lucan was blazing 'quod famam carminum eius premebat Nero prohibueratque ostentare' (49. 3). The poet linked up with his other colleagues and, as Tacitus tells us, 'scelera principis et finem adesse imperio deligendumque qui fessis rebus succurreret inter se aut inter amicos iaciunt' (50. 1). Yet these words are a complex condemnation of the conspirators. The phrase *inter amicos* not only constitutes an ominous foreshadowing of the conspiracy's eventual betrayal in Scaevinus' house but also suggests that a disproportionate amount of energy was spent on words rather than on deeds, a suggestion that *iaciunt*, with its implications of boasting or carelessness or both, reinforces. Moreover, the content of these conversations was also flawed: the plotters talk blithely about *finis imperio* without ever mentioning the murder of the emperor, which was its essential precondition.[39] In thus putting the cart before the horse the conspirators reveal a lack of realism, which is underlined finally by the language in which they express themselves. Commentators point out that *fessis rebus succurreret* is an echo of *Aeneid* 11. 335 ('consulite in medium et rebus succurrite fessis') but not || that Virgil's line was also echoed by Lucan himself in his own poem on the civil war ('quemnam Romanis deceat succurrere rebus', 8. 278).[40] The plotters are all show and bravado, so intent on quoting the outlawed poetry of one of them, complete with its Virgilian allusion, that they entirely omit to mention the reason why the conspiracy itself exists.

A little later we are told that *militares manus* were enlisted in the plot and that 'summum robur in Faenio Rufo praefecto uidebatur' (50. 3). Yet ominous signs are detectable here too. Rufus only 'seemed' (*uidebatur*) to be the *summum robur*, and his allegiance rested only on 'his own frequent assurances' ('crebro ipsius sermone'). We must remember that the *miles gloriosus* was one of the standard characters in Roman comedy, as Cicero said: 'it is also disfiguring to pontificate about oneself, especially falsely, and to

---

[39] It is not until 50. 4 that *caedes* is first mentioned. Even the conspirators' phrase *scelera principis* is undercut, since in the context it seems to refer only to the personal affronts suffered at Nero's hands by Lucan and Quintianus. Contrast the realistic Epicharis at 51. 3 'omnia scelera principis orditur'.

[40] The former line is spoken by King Latinus when urging an end to the fighting; the latter by Pompey.

play the *miles gloriosus* to the derision of one's audience' (*De Officiis* 1. 137). The appearance of such an incongruous figure in this tragedy marks trouble,[41] and Rufus, unfortunately for his fellow conspirators, will in due course play his part only too well (to be discussed shortly); but for the moment his joining the plot was decisive, as Tacitus explains at 50. 4: 'igitur . . . promptius iam de tempore ac loco caedis agitabant'. Yet the comparative expression *promptius iam*, when seen in the light of the conversation at 50. 1, quoted previously, suggests that there has been a lack of real activity hitherto. And indeed little seems to have changed two sentences later, where, despite the addition of Rufus, the conspirators are again hesitating and delaying ('cunctantibus prolatantibusque spem ac metum', 51. 1).[42]

Weary of this delay (*lentitudinis*, 51. 1), a woman called Epicharis decided to intervene with an initiative of her own. She is described by Tacitus here as without any previous concern for *res honestae*, and later as a *libertina mulier* (57. 2); we are told by Polyaenus (8. 62) that she was the mistress of Annaeus Mela, Seneca's brother and the father of Lucan, and a prostitute. Whether she was in fact a real-life actress, as this evidence and her name perhaps suggest,[43] is unknown; but, however that may be, she becomes a genuine conspirator and thus distinguishes herself from the || others, who are merely acting out roles. She teams up with a sea captain called Volusius Proculus in an effort at putting the conspiracy on the kind of military basis that hitherto it has conspicuously lacked: 'accingeretur modo nauare operam et militum acerrimos ducere in partes, ac digna praemia exspectaret' (51. 3). Thus Epicharis' intervention indicates that she is the exact counterpart of Milichus' wife (see 54. 4, quoted earlier);[44] but Proculus shares the characteristics of Milichus himself. Just as the latter is typified by ingratitude and motivated by greed, so Proculus thinks himself the victim of Nero's ingratitude and is also motivated by greed (51. 2). Hence the interaction of each

---

[41] For the combination of comic and tragic in the same narrative, see Pelling (1988), 21; for characters, see my n. 29.

[42] Hesitation and delay are motifs of the Catilinarian conspiracy too: see Sall. *C.* 43. 3; Plut. *Cic.* 14. 1, 16. 1, and 17. 5 with Moles. Also of that against Gaius (Jos. *AJ* 19. 70–83).

[43] An actress with the stage name Eucharis is recorded on an inscription: see Garton (1972), 162 and 251 no. 83. For Epicharis in general see Corsi Zoli (1972), esp. 334.

[44] So too Graf (1931), 102. Koestermann on 51. 3 remarks on the 'dramatischer Kraft' of Epicharis' appeal.

couple produces one of the 'mirroring effects' so typical of ancient drama.[45]

Overcome by his greed, Proculus denounces Epicharis to Nero, who holds her on suspicion (51. 4). Her arrest terrifies the other conspirators and appears to goad them into action ('placitum maturare caedem', 52. 1); but once again there is delay, caused this time by the excuses of Piso himself: 'melius apud urbem . . . in publico patraturos quod pro re publica suscepissent'. But of course the man's elegant alliteration and polyptoton cannot disguise the hollowness of his protestation: in reality, as we have seen, the conspirators are largely motivated by private vendettas, and it was Lateranus, not Piso, who alone had any concern for the *res publica*. As Tacitus proceeds to tell us, Piso's true motive for procrastinating was a secret fear that his rival L. Silanus, nobler and more distinguished than himself,[46] would become emperor (52. 2). Besides, in the opinion of many, Piso was also afraid that the consul Vestinus, who was not a conspirator, might restore *libertas* or choose someone else to head the *res publica* (52. 3). Hence Piso's own supporters will later urge him in vain to individual action when, in a passage heavy with dramatic irony, they base their appeals on his embrace of the *res publica* and his support for *libertas* ('quanto laudabilius periturum, dum amplectitur rem publicam, dum auxilia libertati inuocat!', 59. 3). Not without reason was Piso dismissed as a role-player by the brave tribune Subrius Flavus.[47] ||

V

Scaevinus for his part was deprived of the leading role he coveted, as we have seen, but it is nevertheless clear that, when confronted by Nero, he slips into another role with surprisingly accomplished ease (55. 2–4).

---

[45] On which see Taplin (1978), 122–39. Corsi Zoli (1972), 333 remarks of Epicharis that 'La sua figura non sembra reale, ma inventata . . . da un drammaturgo . . . Epicharis s'identifica con la tragedia.'

[46] With 52. 2 '*eximia* nobilitate . . . ad *omnem claritudinem* sublatus' (of Silanus), cf. 48. 2 '*paterna* nobilitate . . . *claro apud uulgum rumore* erat' (of Piso).

[47] It is worth recalling at this point that *libertas* was the watchword of the Caesarian tyrannicides (Weinstock (1971), 142), as David West has reminded me. Cf. also Jos. *AJ* 19. 54 and 186 (of Gaius' assassination).

is raptus per milites et defensionem orsus, ferrum, cuius argueretur, olim religione patria cultum et in cubiculo habitum ac fraude liberti subreptum respondit; tabulas testamenti saepius a se et incustodita dierum obseruatione signatas; pecunias et libertates seruis et ante dono datas, se ideo tunc largius quia tenui iam re familiari et instantibus creditoribus testamento diffideret; enimuero liberales semper epulas struxisse: egisse   3
enim uitam amoenam et duris iudicibus parum probatam. fomenta uolneribus nulla iussu suo sed, quia cetera palam uana obiecisset, adiungere crimen cuius se pariter indicem et testem faceret. adicit dictis   4
constantiam: incusat ultro intestabilem et consceleratum, tanta uocis ac uultus securitate ut labaret indicium, nisi Milichum uxor admonuisset Antonium Natalem multa cum Scaeuino ac secreta conlocutum et esse utrosque C. Pisonis intimos.

Seized by soldiers, he began his defence by responding that the allegedly incriminating weapon had been venerated for a long time as a pious heirloom and kept in his bedroom and seized secretly by the deception of his freedman; the pages of his will he had sealed often enough and without any vigilant observation of the days in question; money and freedom had been given to slaves as presents previously too, but more generously now for the simple reason that, with his patrimony already reduced and creditors on his heels, he distrusted his will; in fact he had   3
always set up lavish banquets: for he led an idyllic life, scarcely approved of by hard judges; there had been no compresses for wounds by any order of his, but, because the other accusations had been plainly groundless, the man was appending a charge of which he could make himself both informer and witness. Adding resolution to his words, he in his   4
turn accused the man of being an infamous criminal, doing so with such nonchalance of delivery and demeanour that Milichus' information was on the point of collapsing, had not his wife reminded him that Antonius Natalis had held a long and private conversation with Scaevinus and that they were both intimates of C. Piso.

This is superb acting on Scaevinus' part,[48] as is underlined by the signposting references to his *uox* and *uultus*, words that Cicero combines to de||scribe a convincing imitative performance.[49] And Scaevinus' performance almost pays off, except that Milichus' wife once more intervenes.

    The fact that Scaevinus continues to act after his arrest

---

[48] *duris iudicibus* in particular is cleverly designed to appeal to the dissolute side of Nero's character.

[49] *De Or.* 2. 242, though the words are also combined elsewhere: see Heubner on Tac. *H.* 3. 58. 3.

produces in the reader a different response from his previous behaviour. The man whose injudicious role-playing had led to the detection of the conspiracy is now, when confronted by Nero, able to capitalize on that same histrionic proclivity and so compel our admiration. What before was a culpable failing is transformed into heroism by the reversal of circumstance. The tragedy is that the heroism has come too late and that Scaevinus' eventual death, despite its bravery (70. 2), was both avoidable and futile. This is a familiar Tacitean theme.[50]

Another death is that of Lucan, by suicide. Though he has earlier betrayed his own mother as well as others (56. 4, 58. 1), his blood is now pouring forth and his limbs are chilling (70. 1); nevertheless, says Tacitus, 'recordatus carmen a se compositum, quo uolneratum militem per eiusmodi mortis imaginem obisse tradiderat, uersus ipsos rettulit, eaque illi suprema uox fuit'. Lucan's final appearance thus resembles his first, noted already: seeing himself in the role of a soldier, he recited his own poetry—with the Virgilian allusion this time supplied by Tacitus himself (cf. *Aeneid* 2. 369 'plurima mortis imago').[51] At the other end of the scale is Rufus, the *miles gloriosus*. Before being found out himself, Rufus 'behaved hideously toward his partners to convince people of his own ignorance' (58. 2); and when he is finally detected, he is portrayed as able neither to speak nor to remain silent: with a marvellous irony, this former boaster can only stammer (66. 2), and he dies a cowardly death (68. 1).

Yet none of these deaths can compare with that of Seneca, Lucan's uncle, which Tacitus describes at great length (60. 2–65). Although Seneca had evidently had no part in the plot, Nero's private hatred of him (cf. 64. 1 'proprio odio') reflects that which many of the genuine conspirators felt for Nero. Taking advantage of the conspiracy's aftermath to pressure the man into suicide, Nero learns with dismay that the great philosopher is showing no signs of fear or sadness at all (61. 2). He therefore issues an explicit order, and Seneca at length poisons himself. Tacitus' typically periphrastic description of the hemlock ('uenenum quo damnati

---

[50] Esp. with reference to the Stoics: see Walker (1952), 229–32.

[51] Whether Tacitus' Virgilian supplement is malicious is perhaps a matter of judgement; certainly there seems to be grim humour at the end of the following sentence: 'mox reliqui coniuratorum periere, nullo facto *dictoue* memorando' (70. 2). There is an analogy to Virgil's phrase also at Thuc. 3. 81. 5, as e.g. Koestermann points out.

publico || Atheniensium iudicio exstinguerentur', 64. 3) prompts
us to think of the account of Socrates' death in Plato's *Phaedo*
(116A, 117A–C, 118A),[52] the parallels with which, perhaps more
numerous and detailed than Tacitean commentaries suggest,
clearly indicate the extent to which Seneca's suicide is to be
seen as a role-playing performance.[53] 'The Murder of Julius
Caesar' is replaced by 'The Execution of Socrates', and the
guilty but ineffectual conspirators are entirely upstaged by the
innocent but successful Seneca. With his final gesture a libation
to Iuppiter Liberator (64. 4), Seneca, though the victim of Nero,
has chosen a manner of dying that might have been envied by
the emperor himself, whose own reputed last words were:
'Qualis artifex pereo!'[54] It was the only form of revenge to
which Seneca, like Petronius in his later parody (16. 19. 2–3),
could resort.[55]

Seneca's elaborate imitation of Socrates is only the most flam-
boyant of the series of public deaths that punctuate the latter
sections of Tacitus' account. It is therefore at the opposite extreme
from the death of Epicharis, which is described earlier at 57. 1–2.
Nero, anxious to acquire more information about the plot,
remembers that he has detained Epicharis in custody and orders
her to be tortured. But on the first day neither beatings nor
burnings can move her; the next day's events are described by
Tacitus as follows:

cum ad eosdem cruciatus retraheretur gestamine sellae (nam dissolutis
membris insistere nequibat), uinclo fasciae, quam pectori detraxerat, in

---

[52] For similar prompting elsewhere by Tacitus see [now Woodman–Martin on *A*. 3. 33. 4].

[53] Most scholars accept this, using such words as 'histrionic' or 'theatrical' to describe Seneca's performance: see e.g. W. H. Alexander, 'The Tacitean "non liquet" on Seneca', *Univ. Calif. Publ. Class. Philol.* 14 (1952), 348; Koestermann on 64. 3; Morris (1969), 236, 240, 242; Martin (1981), 184. The suicide of Cato Uticensis had already provided a model for Seneca's imitation of Socrates: see e.g. K. Döring, *Exemplum Socratis* (1979), 39. And Socrates' own trial and its consequences had been portrayed in theatrical terms by Plato in their turn (*Crito* 45E), as E. E. Pender has pointed out to me.

[54] Suet. *Nero* 49. 1 (cf. *OLD artifex* 5), Dio, 63. 29. 2. The latter has already (63. 28. 4–5) prepared for Nero's death scene with elaborately dramatic language: 'That was the drama [δρᾶμα] that Fate now prepared for him, in order that he should no longer play the roles [ὑποκρίνηται] of other matricides and beggars but only his own [ἑαυτόν] at last, and he now repented of his past deeds of outrage, as if he could undo any of them. Such was the tragic part that Nero now played [τοιαῦτα ἐτραγῴδει]' (Loeb translation, slightly adapted).

[55] For Petronius, see e.g. Syme (1958), 538.

modum laquei ad arcum sellae restricto indidit ceruicem et corporis pondere conisa tenuem iam spiritum expressit, clariore exemplo libertina mulier in tanta necessitate alienos ac prope ignotos protegendo, cum ingenui et uiri et equites Romani senatoresque intacti tormentis carissima suorum quisque pignorum proderent. ||

When she was being dragged back to the same tortures in a portable chair (for she was unable to stand on her wracked limbs), having attached the fastener of her brassiere, which she had dragged from her bosom, to the roof of the chair to form a noose, she inserted her neck and, relying on the weight of her body, expelled her now faint breath, a more brilliant example being provided by a woman at such an extremity—and a freedwoman too—in her defence of others who were neither relatives nor scarcely acquaintances, when freeborn men untouched by torture—Roman knights and senators—were each denouncing the dearest ones of their own relations.

This scene combines eroticism with the partiality for torture and suicide that is associated with Seneca's own drama.[56] Yet Epicharis' actual suicide takes place within the confines of the portable chair. Although Tacitus' readers are offered, by means of the accumulated detail, a privileged glimpse of the scene,[57] the woman herself is observed by no spectator and makes no dramatic speech. She dies without histrionics and without betraying anyone else—to the very end providing a contrast with the role playing of her fellow conspirators.[58]

VI

Nero perhaps took the cue for his famous last words from Augustus himself, who on his deathbed is said to have asked his friends whether he had given a good performance in 'the farce of

---

[56] For torture, see e.g. Sen. *Phaedra* 882–5 'uerbere ac uinclis anus | altrixque prodet quidquid haec fari abnuit. | uincite ferro. uerberum uis extrahat | secreta mentis.' For suicide, especially as 'the ultimate guarantor of human liberty', see *CHCL* ii. 523. Interestingly, Tacitus' description of Epicharis' death ('tenuem iam spiritum expressit') is paralleled at Sen. *Oed.* 344 'animamque fessus uix reluctantem exprimit' (though the subject there is a bull). For the hanging motif in novels, see Petr. 94. 8–11, Apul. *Met.* 1. 16. Eroticism featured in 'fatal charades' (Auguet (1972), 102; Coleman (1990), 63–4) but was common in mime: see e.g. Sandy (1974), 339–40.

[57] Interior scenes are a feature of Senecan drama: see *Phaedra* 384 ff., 863 ff., *Thy.* 901 ff., *Herc. Fur.* 999 ff.

[58] The theatrical possibilities of Epicharis' story (also see nn. 44–5) were realized in 1902 by Giovanni di Simone in a verse tragedy: see Corsi Zoli (1972), 339.

life' (*mimum uitae*).[59] Yet describing individuals in terms of
actors, and their actions in terms of acting, is a common motif
in Greek and Latin literature:[60] Marcus Aurelius maintained
that 'the whole court of Hadrian and the whole court of ||
Antoninus and the whole court of Philip, Alexander, Croesus
. . . were all just the same, except that different actors played
the parts' (10. 27).[61] It is also the case that historical writing is
often said to have affinities with drama through so-called tragic
history:[62] scholars have suggested various dramatic elements in
Tacitus' *Annals*,[63] while studies of Plutarchean biography have
done much to draw attention to the influence of tragedy on his
Lives.[64]

We have seen that Tacitus' consistently dramatic writing of the
Pisonian conspiracy, with its vivid scenes and reversals, is combined at the appropriate moments with the acting motif.
Plutarch's technique is evidently sometimes similar;[65] but whereas
Plutarch provides such authorial directions as 'like a tragedy' or
'the drama is complete',[66] explicit references of this type are
absent from Tacitus' account, encouraging the reader's belief
that the dramatic perception is the conspirators' own rather
than the author's.

[59] Suet. *Aug*. 99. 1.

[60] See e.g. Curtius (1953), 138; L. G. Christian, *Theatrum Mundi: The History of an Idea*
(1987), 9–29; D. Bain, *Actors and Audience* (2nd edn., 1987), 208–22, 'Some Reflections on
the Illusion in Greek Tragedy', *BICS* 34 (1988), 1–14; Powell on Cic. *Senec*. 5, 64, 70. The
motif seems especially common in Petronius and other novelists: see e.g. Sandy (1974),
Bartsch (1989), 127–34.   [61] Quoted by Rutherford (1989), 166.

[62] There is a vast bibliography on this subject, though I myself doubt whether 'tragic
history' existed as a distinct form of historiography: see *RICH* 116 n. 151. Rather different
are cases where a historian is thought to have written with an actual drama in mind, as Livy
in the case of Lucretia: see Ogilvie (1965), 219. Since tragedies were not only staged but
also merely recited from the 1st c. BC onward (cf. *CHCL* ii. 519–20), they were thus
brought closer to historical narratives, which might also be recited.

[63] e.g. Everts (1926); Mendell (1935), 3–53; A. Betensky, 'Neronian Style, Tacitean
Content: The Use of Ambiguous Confrontations in the *Annals*', *Latomus*, 37 (1978), 419–
35; A. D. Leeman, *Form und Sinn: Studien zur römischen Literatur* (1985), 305–15.

[64] See De Lacy (1952); Mossman (1988); and Pelling (1988), 21 and (1989), 272–4.

[65] See De Lacy (1952), 168 and esp. Mossman (1988), 88, 91–2. So too Heliodorus, for
example, 'not only makes liberal use of theatrical vocabulary but also presents each large-
scale spectacle with a view to the crises and climaxes of such [i.e. staged] plays' (Bartsch
(1989), 129, in a chapter entitled 'Descriptions of spectacles: The reader as audience, the
author as playwright'; see also her p. 140).

[66] Plut. *Ages*. 23. 6 and *Demet*. 53. 10, with Pelling (1989), 273 and (1988), 21, 117
respectively.

Certain types of assassin have perhaps always been inclined to dramatize their activities,[67] but it is presumably no accident that in Tacitus' text it is the assassins of Nero whose dramatics are portrayed.[68] For Nero not only presided over productions whose essence was 'an ambiguity between the imaginary and the real' (as already discussed), but of course also performed on stage himself. Ironically, in a society where the emperor was expected to provide examples of behaviour for his citizens,[69] the conspira||tors' behaviour reflects that of Nero only too accurately. This is precisely the point of Juvenal's *sententia* in his eighth satire (198–9): 'res haut mira tamen citharoedo principe mimus | nobilis.' Yet when Juvenal soon proceeds to a catalogue of Nero's crimes, which has as its climax the emperor's performances on stage (211–30, esp. 220–1), we can see that the perception of Nero as an actor could eclipse all other aspects of the emperor.[70] So too Dio gives to the insurgent Julius Vindex a speech in which he quickly passes over Nero's murders and instead spends an apparently disproportionate amount of time on his dramatic performances (63. 22. 3–6); even the innocent Seneca, as we have seen, chose actually to die in a manner calculated to infuriate the theatrical Nero; and after Nero's own death it was an impostor's ability to sing that persuaded people that he was genuine.[71]

This, then, was a perception of Nero that it was natural to entertain—and it is entertained, inevitably and fatefully, by the Pisonian conspirators. When they urge decisiveness upon their nominal leader, they use these words (59. 2):

---

[67] See e.g. H. H. A. Cooper, *On Assassination* (1984), 7 'The *spectacular* aspects of assassination, . . . the symbolic toppling of a crowned head are of immense importance to the perpetrator. He needs a *platform* . . . Without an adequate *audience* his *act* is robbed of its power. . . . Where the killing takes place in public, it may be assumed that a major component of the operation is the involvement of the largest possible *audience*' (my italics). See also MacMullen (1966), 70.

[68] I am not of course suggesting that Tacitus' use of dramatic metaphors is restricted to the conspiracy narrative: see e.g. R. Boesche, 'The Politics of Pretence: Tacitus and the Political Theory of Despotism', *History of Political Thought*, 8 (1987), 207–9; and my n. 75.

[69] See Woodman on Vell. 126. 5.

[70] Juvenal's climax worries Courtney (p. 383) in his introduction to the satire; S. H. Braund (*Beyond Anger* (1988), 119), regards it as humorous. Both scholars think that Juvenal's point is the same as Flavus' at 15. 67. 2, on which see my subsequent discussion. Cf. also Plin. *Pan.* 46. 4 'scaenici imperatoris'.

[71] Cf. Tac. *H.* 2. 8. 1 'citharae et cantus peritus, unde illi super similitudinem oris propior ad fallendum fides.'

nihil aduersum haec Neroni prouisum. etiam fortes uiros subitis terreri, nedum ille scaenicus, Tigellino scilicet cum paelicibus suis comitante, arma contra cieret.

No contrary provisions had been made by Nero. Even brave men were terrified by sudden events; still less would that role player, accompanied naturally by Tigellinus and his concubines, stir up arms against them.

Encouraged no doubt by the conventional antithesis between acting and soldiering that existed in the ancient world,[72] and mesmerized by the role-playing that Nero both practised himself and pressured others into accepting, the conspirators cannot see him in any other light and imagine themselves as engaging with him in a great dramatic enterprise on the occasion of a public spectacle.[73] Ironically, however, it is their own circumstances, rather than Nero's, to which the antithesis between acting and soldiering applies. They have been led by their own dramatics to the tragic confusion || of drama with reality, and hence with the military action that a conspiracy demands. For they, after all, are only amateur actors, their unwonted status determined by the perception of themselves as the Caesarian tyrannicides; Nero, on the other hand, is a veteran performer, able at will to slip in and out of the many roles that his repertoire contained but which, for the moment at least, excluded that of murder victim.[74]

[72] Cf. Plut. *Eum.* 2. 1, *Otho* 5. 5. Actors were traditionally prevented from serving in the Roman army (Liv. 7. 2. 12 (cf. 3 'ludi quoque scaenici, noua res bellicoso populo'), Val. Max. 2. 4. 4).

[73] It is clear from 65, where Subrius Flavus' point about Piso depends upon the conspirators' view of Nero as *citharoedus*, that this was their consistent view and was not adopted simply for persuasive purposes at 59. 2 only.

[74] This is perhaps the appropriate moment to acknowledge that any discussion of roles, especially when an actual actor is involved, is extremely complicated, since it concerns different categories of role and the question of what constitutes a role: see Goffman (1974), e.g. 128 ff. For example, the evidence suggests that Nero, unlike all the conspirators except perhaps Piso himself, took acting seriously; yet not even he was professional in the same sense as competitors in a dramatic contest. This means that Nero, despite his seriousness, was merely playing the role of an actor: this indeed is vividly illustrated by the fact that when, as an actor, he played a role, his mask bore his own likeness (Suet. *Nero* 21. 2). To this extent he is as amateur as the conspirators in Tacitus' text; the difference is one of degree rather than of kind. For Nero's 'true profession' was, after all, that of *princeps*. Yet this in its turn is difficult to define except in terms of a variety of subordinate roles (*iudex, imperator*, etc.); and the difficulty is especially acute in the case of Nero, who, according to our sources, not only reversed many of these roles with acting (as in his 'actor's triumph' at Suet. *Nero* 25. 1–2), but so loved all forms of disguise (e.g. as a beggar; cf. Suet. *Nero* 26. 1)

VII

Nero hated the consul Vestinus ('Neroni odium aduersus Vesti-
num', 68. 3), a hatred about which we have already been warned
(52. 3) and which, as in the case of Seneca, reflects the conspirators' personalized hatred of the emperor. Unfortunately, however,
Vestinus was not a conspirator, and Nero was therefore deprived
of his preferred role as judge ('non crimine, non accusatore
existente . . . speciem iudicis induere non poterat', 69. 1);[75]
nevertheless the emperor, pretending that Vestinus was || playing
the military role expected of a conspirator (but which the real
conspirators had conspicuously failed to play), himself assumes the
role of commander in chief and directs a pre-emptive attack
against the innocent consul (69. 1):

ad uim dominationis conuersus Gerellanum tribunum cum cohorte
militum inmittit iubetque praeuenire 'conatus consulis', occupare 'uelut
arcem eius', opprimere 'delectam iuuentutem'.

Resorting to his violence as a master, he sent in the tribune Gerellanus
with a cohort of soldiers and ordered them to forestall 'the attempts of the
consul', to seize 'his so-called citadel', and to suppress his 'élite youth'.

Similarly, when the real conspirators had begun to reveal the
names of their collaborators, Nero, whose cowardice and fear
match theirs, plays the typical tyrant. Like the vengeful Atreus
in Seneca's *Thyestes* (180–9), he places the whole city and its
environs under extravagant military arrest (58. 2):

---

that Dio can describe his death scene, when Nero was in disguise, by saying that the
emperor 'played the role of himself' (see n. 54). No wonder that the conspirators can be
represented implicitly as mesmerized by Nero.

   These complications are intensified when the discussion also involves the medium of a
text. Had Tacitus' account of the Pisonian conspiracy been an actual drama, rather than a
narrative, one might usefully have invoked the idea of a 'play within a play' (see e.g.
Goffman (1974), 474–5 or Slater (1985), 189 (index); also my nn. 17 and 60) or the concept
of 'metatheatre' in each of its meanings (for which see Slater (1985), 14): the conspirators'
lives are 'already theatricalized' and are derived from a 'previously existing' play. As it is, of
course, Tacitus' text is not technically dramatic but narrative; yet this distinction (on which
see Goffman (1974), 151–4 simply makes the whole issue more, rather than less, difficult
to expound. I hope readers will make allowances for these considerations and bear in mind
that the subject is probably even more complicated than my analysis suggests. On role-
playing in general, see further N. W. Slater, *Reading Petronius* (1990).

[75] For this use of *species*, see Koestermann ad loc. For the idea of playing the role of a
judge, see the interesting passage at Philo, *Leg. Gai.* 359, where there is a reference to
mime; also Martin–Woodman on *A.* 4. 59. 3.

quin et urbem per manipulos occupatis moenibus, insesso etiam mari et amne, uelut in custodiam dedit. uolitabantque per fora, per domos, rura quoque et proxima municipiorum pedites equitesque, permixti Germanis, quibus fidebat princeps quasi externis.

In fact the city too, with its walls taken over by maniples and even the sea and river under occupation, he put into custody, as it were. Through the markets, through the houses, the countryside also, and neighbouring townships, there flew infantry and cavalry, interspersed with Germans, whom the *princeps* trusted as being foreign.

It is therefore only logical that, at the end of Book 15, Nero should celebrate the results of his military efforts by playing the triumphant commander ('tum quasi gesta bello expositurus uocat senatum et triumphale decus . . . tribuit', 72. 1).

In each of these passages Nero's description in military terms emphasizes the chasm that exists between the conspirators' professions and their actions and which has been present since Tacitus' very first sentence.[76] The tragedy of the Pisonian conspiracy is that the conspirators' acting, being amateur, prevents their realizing the military action that circumstances required; whereas Nero, the true actor, is able to play the precise military role that a conspiracy demands. This tragedy is strikingly encapsulated in Tacitus' treatment of the brave tribune Subrius Flavus.

Flavus is the counterpart of the *miles gloriosus* Rufus, in the same way as the equally brave Epicharis was that of Milichus' wife, and from the very || start he emerges as an independent figure. The first conspirator to be named after Piso himself (49. 2, where he and Sulpicius Asper are described as *promptissimi*), he is said at 50. 4 already to have contemplated a freelance attack on Nero[77] and at 58. 4 his attempt on Nero's life is stopped almost in mid-course by the treacherous Rufus.[78] We meet him for the last time after he has been betrayed and is about to die: unlike his opposite number, the *miles*

---

[76] Tacitus' general stance throughout the *Annals* is of course to display 'an acute sensitivity for the disparity between men's professions and their actions' (Martin (1981), 215).

[77] As Flavus is stated to have had alternative venues for his attack (while Nero was 'in scaena canentem' or 'cum ardente domo per noctem huc illuc cursaret incustoditus'), we are perhaps to infer that he did not have his partners' one-dimensional view of Nero as an actor. See further n. 83.

[78] According to Plut. *Brut.* 16. 3 there was a comparable moment in the murder of Caesar.

gloriosus, Flavus reserves his own claim to *gloria* till the very end (67. 1–3):

Mox eorundem indicio Subrius Flauus tribunus peruertitur, primo dissimilitudinem morum ad defensionem trahens, neque se armatum cum inermibus et effeminatis tantum facinus consociaturum; dein, postquam 2 urgebatur, confessionis gloriam amplexus interrogatusque a Nerone quibus causis ad obliuionem sacramenti processisset, 'oderam te', inquit, 'nec quisquam tibi fidelior militum fuit, dum amari meruisti. odisse coepi postquam parricida matris et uxoris, auriga et histrio et incendiarius exstitisti.' (ipsa rettuli uerba, quia non, ut Senecae, uulgata erant, nec 3 minus nosci decebat militaris uiri sensus incomptos et ualidos.)

Subsequently on the same men's information the tribune Subrius Flavus was overthrown, who at first brought his dissimilar behaviour to his defence; nor would he co-operate, under arms as he was, with unarmed effeminates in such a great action. Then, after he was pressed, he 2 embraced the glory of confessing and, asked by Nero what motives had led him to forget his oath, said: 'I hated you, and yet none of your soldiers was more true to you as long as you deserved affection. I only started to hate you after you turned out to be the parricide of your mother and wife, a charioteer, an actor, and an arsonist.' (I have repeated 3 his actual words because, unlike those of Seneca, they were not publicized and the feelings of the military man deserved equal recognition for being spontaneous yet telling.)

In this little scene, which again is highly dramatic,[79] Flavus first contrasts himself, an armed soldier (*armatum*), with his fellow conspirators, who are unarmed effeminates (*inermibus et effeminatis*). Now *effeminatus* is one of the standard words used to slander actors,[80] and it seems that Flavus || is attempting to defend himself by convicting his ineffectual partners of the very distinction between acting and soldiering that has been at the heart of Tacitus' account from the very start.[81]

---

[79] As direct speech is one of the defining features of drama, Tacitus' drawing attention to Flavus' words itself helps to dramatize the scene. The subsequent execution (67. 4) is equally dramatic.

[80] e.g. Plin. *Pan.* 46. 4, 54. 1; Apul. *Apol.* 78, the point of course being that 'actors were often reproached for effeminacy' (Courtney on Juv. 3. 98–100, who refers to *RAC effeminatus* 627, where other passages are listed). It is true that Scaevinus and Quintianus have been associated with actual effeminacy at 49. 4, but at 70. 2 *mollitia* is used not only of these two but also of Senecio, whose effeminacy has not otherwise been hinted at. It therefore seems not unreasonable to interpret Flavus' words in these terms.

[81] *inermibus* even constitutes a denial of the famous dagger.

Finally, however, Flavus goes on the attack and accuses Nero of having been a parricide, a charioteer, an actor, and an arsonist, accusations that Tacitus, in an authorial comment, describes as telling (*ualidos*). Yet the reason they are telling is that Tacitus himself has made them so, as a comparison with Dio's version of the same episode reveals. In Dio (62. 24. 2) Flavus makes only two accusations, those of charioteer and lyre player, as if to suggest that his perception of Nero is no different from those found in Juvenal or Vindex' speech, noted previously; and there is no authorial comment. It therefore seems that Tacitus has added the accusations of parricide and arsonist to the traditional account,[82] changed lyre player to *histrio*, and arranged the four charges chiastically as if to suggest that they were each of comparable significance. In this refashioned statement Flavus is made to proclaim, only when moments from death, that Nero the charioteer and actor could not be divorced, as the other conspirators had imagined, from Nero the parricide and arsonist.[83] Such late recognition of true identity is itself reminiscent of tragedy,[84] and its importance is underlined by Tacitus' own comment. ||

[82] It could of course be argued that all four charges were present in the common source of Tacitus and Dio and that the latter omitted the two gravest: so e.g. Furneaux ad loc., though describing Dio's hypothesized omission as 'remarkable'.

[83] It cannot be inferred from 65, where Flavus says that Nero and Piso are both role-players, that his view of Nero was in fact the same as the others': his target there is not Nero but Piso, whom he describes in terms his partners will understand (see also my n. 73). The only others in the Pisonian narrative who recognize Nero's violence are also exceptional: Epicharis (see n. 39) and Seneca (cf. 62. 2 'cui enim ignaram fuisse saeuitiam Neronis?'—a question not without its own irony). Contrast [Sen.] *Oct.* 648–9, where 'Seneca still considers Nero a headstrong boy given to tantrums' (Whitman ad loc.), i.e. making a similar mistake to that of the conspirators in Tacitus. For some apposite remarks on Nero's character, see Tresch (1965), 128, 168.

[84] Evidently for dramatic reasons Tacitus has deferred till now the expression of Flavus' recognition, which must in fact have taken place a little earlier. Flavus' four accusations are arranged chronologically as well as chiastically, and five years separate the first (AD 59) from the last (AD 64, the previous year); yet, despite *coepi*, the perfect tense *exstitisti* cannot refer to a gradual realization lasting the length of this period but must rather indicate that the truth dawned on Flavus only after the fire of Rome, after which the other three aspects of Nero slotted into place. For late recognitions in tragedy, see R. Rutherford, 'Tragic Form and Feeling in the *Iliad*', *JHS* 102 (1982), 145–60, esp. 145–50; for comparable scenes in the Greek novel, see Bartsch (1989), 132.

VIII

The closing stages of Tacitus' drama are marked at 73. 2 by phraseology that recalls the beginning at 48. 1:[85]

ceterum coeptam adultamque et reuictam coniurationem neque tunc dubitauere quibus uerum noscendi cura erat, et fatentur qui post interitum Neronis in urbem regressi sunt.

Yet that the conspiracy started and grew and was overthrown was not doubted at the time by those whose concern was for realistic knowledge, and is asserted by those who returned to the city after Nero's demise.

Curiously, however, this sentence seems to suggest that some people had questioned, or perhaps even denied, the very existence of an episode to which Tacitus has devoted more space than to any other in the *Annals*.[86] Yet if the grounds of these unnamed objectors were the 'dismal failure' of the conspiracy, to which Nero's modern biographer referred (see p. 190), a detailed exposition of its nature would be entirely characteristic of Tacitus, for whom contrariety and failure held an equal attraction.[87]

The final scene is set in the senate, where an attack on Seneca's brother by the unsuitably named Clemens is interrupted 'ne publicis malis abuti ad occasionem priuati odii uideretur' (73. 3). The irony of the fathers' reasoning will not be lost on those who recall the private hatreds that have gripped conspirators and Nero alike throughout the conspiracy. As for the emperor himself, he dedicated Scaeuinus' dagger to Iuppiter Vindex, a reversal

---

[85] The recall would be clearer if Tacitus, as R. H. Martin suggests, had written *adulta* rather than *aucta* at 48. 1. The hypothesized corruption is of course simple, but would in turn preclude the 'framing' of Piso's digressive character sketch (48. 2–3) by the echo of *aucta* in 'primus *auctor*' at 49. 1.

[86] There are other curiosities about this sentence. *ceterum* suggests a correction of the immediately preceding statement that Nero 'crebro uulgi rumore lacerabatur, tamquam uiros claros et insontes ob inuidiam aut metum exstinxisset'; yet Tacitus himself, with his vivid accounts of the dying Seneca and Vestinus (68. 2–69. 3), has characteristically done nothing to allay the rumour that innocent notables were killed. Again, the correction of the earlier sentence by the later remains no more than a suggestion, since the validity of the second sentence does not depend upon the invalidity of the first: each sentence is in fact equally valid, as Tacitus' own narrative has once again demonstrated.

[87] Morris, maintaining that Tacitus' account of the conspiracy 'is not always completely successful' and that 'as a literary set piece [it] is always less than the sum of its parts', mistakenly argued that his manner of describing the conspiracy was designed deliberately to reflect its failure (1969: 218, 225).

of Seneca's dying libation to Iuppiter Liberator. But after the revolt of Julius Vindex in Gaul three years later, this reversal was itself reversed, as Tacitus || observes: 'ad auspicium et praesagium futurae ultionis trahebatur' (74. 2). And this note of future disaster is maintained to the very end.[88] The consul designate proposed that a temple should be erected to Nero as a god, on the grounds that he now exceeded every mortal peak and deserved the veneration of mankind. But, though references to the establishment of cult occur at the end of Euripidean tragedies,[89] Nero was evidently reading a different script: no doubt conscious that Julius Caesar's apotheosis had preceded his murder, Nero rejected the honour, lest 'ad omen malum sui exitus uerteretur' (74. 3).[90] Yet such foreshadowing of tragic events, while characteristic of Tacitus at the end of a book, is itself dramatic, being 'a familiar device with Seneca for closing a scene or act'.[91]

But anticipation of the future is not only dramatic; it is also apposite. Tacitus in the last twenty-seven chapters of Book 15 has portrayed a world of unreality from which almost no one is immune. The conspirators are so mesmerized that they mistake life for drama, while Seneca chooses to die a theatrical death. The few realists, such as Epicharis and Subrius Flavus, are betrayed and overwhelmed, and Nero emerges unscathed from the confusion

---

[88] A slightly earlier example of the same phenomenon is Tacitus' Sallustian introduction of Nymphidius Sabinus at 72. 2: 'quia nunc primum oblatus est, pauca repetam: nam et ipse pars Romanarum cladium erit.' Since pars (singular) can be used for 'part/role [in a play etc.]', et ipse appears to confirm that the characters in the Pisonian conspiracy have been seen as playing roles in an unfolding tragedy of Rome.

[89] See Barrett on Eur. Hipp. 1423–30. I owe this point to Richard Seaford.

[90] The point about Caesar was made to me by Stephen Harrison. It is nevertheless tempting to speculate which divine identity would have been appropriate for Nero. Wearing his hair long in tiers of curls (Suet. Nero 51), the emperor has appeared in our text as a patron of the theatre, possessed of mesmerizing power, and capable of wreaking terrible violence, while earlier in Book 15 the female side of his personality has been vividly described (cf. 37. 4). This evidence seems to suggest Dionysus, and E. Cizek, Néron (1982), 89 and 116, states that Nero was in fact regarded as a New Dionysus. Although A. Henrichs, 'Changing Dionysiac Identities', in B. F. Meyer and E. P. Sanders (eds.), Self-Definition in the Greco-Roman World (1982), 158, 233 n. 190, does not mention Nero in his list of emperors who were identified with the god, nevertheless Nero was described as ἀγαθὸς δαίμων τῆς οἰκουμένης ('good spirit of the world': CIG 3. 4699, P. Oxy. 1021), a title that has connections with, or actually suggests, Dionysus: cf. J. E. Harrison, Themis (2nd edn., 1927), 277 and 315, and G. Schumann, Hellenistische und griechische Elemente in der Regierung Neros (1930), 8–9.

[91] Mendell (1935), 28 n. 11. Cf. how, at the end of Plut. Cic., the tragedy of the triumphant Antony unfolds after the tragedy of Cicero himself: see Moles on 49. 6.

that he has himself created. But his life was catching up with him. After juggling his various roles for more than a decade, he is about to lose the ability to sustain the boundaries between them. It was in this very year AD 65, according to his biographer, that he finally 'escaped more and more into a world of fantasy'.[92] The first symptom is his comprehensive decep||tion by the story of Dido's gold, which Tacitus describes at the start of the very next book (16. 1–3). That book, as a modern scholar has remarked, 'begins like a satyr-play'.[93] What more fitting sequel could there be to the tragedy of the Pisonian conspiracy?[94]

---

[92] Griffin (1984), 164; so too Dupont (1985), 431 'La fin du règne voit se réaliser ce théâtre généralisé où spectacle et réalité s'échangent et se confondent'. Nero thus becomes the opposite of Marcus Aurelius later on, who ideally 'would be playing the part *on the real stage of the world*, and would *actually be* the tyrant' (Rutherford (1989), 176 (my italics)).

[93] Tresch (1965), 173.

[94] 'In classical dramatic traditions there seems to be a recurrent tendency to present serious drama and broad farce in immediate juxtaposition. Much as, for instance, Roman tragedy was followed by *exodia* (usually consisting of Atellan farces), . . . so for most at least of the fifth century BC the three tragedies of a trilogy were followed by a satyr play, composed by the same author' (*CHCL* i. 346).

12

Epilogue: *Lectorum Incuria*?

I

In AD 14 Germanicus, weeping for a second time during Tacitus' narrative of that year (1. 49. 2, cf. 40. 3), contemplates the disastrous effects of a second letter of his that has gone wrong (1. 48. 1–49. 1, cf. 36. 3–37. 1): in a scene worse than any civil war, his own troops have turned on one another, wreaking a terrible slaughter. For the commander it is a tragic moment of truth; but, even after such carnage, the hearts of his men are still hardened and their desire is to attack the enemy as an atonement for their madness (1. 49. 3).

This is perhaps the lowest and most solemn point in the whole of Tacitus' long narrative of the mutinies in Pannonia and Germany (1. 16–51), and he conveys the troops' desire in the following terms: 'truces etiam tum animos cupido inuolat eundi in hostem, piaculum furoris'. Koestermann remarks that the main verb is highly unusual and is used instead of *inuadit*; Goodyear manages to imply that the verb's unusualness, which he admits, is considerably qualified by the personification of *cupido*, for which he compares 1. 61. 1 'cupido Caesarem inua-dit'.[1] In fact the truth is exactly the opposite. The personifica-tion of *cupido*, when combined with a verb of 'flying', invites at least a fleeting image of the winged god, Cupid himself. Thus Apuleius writes 'deus amator . . . inuolauit proximam cupres-sum' (*Met.* 5. 24) and 'diceres tu Cupidines ueros de caelo uel mari commodum inuolasse' (10. 32). What is going on in Tacitus' text? What is the significance of his language? Not

---

For their comments on earlier drafts of this Epilogue I am most grateful to C. S. Kraus, D. S. Levene, R. Maltby, and R. H. Martin.

[1] Part of Goodyear's agenda seems to have been to minimize Tacitus' novelty: see (1972), 22–3.

only do the commentators offer no help, as we have observed, but they appear not to have seen the image at all.[2]

Within a page Tacitus has Germanicus 'cutting' through a wood whose name suggests 'cutting' (1. 50. 1 'siluam Caesiam . . . scindit'),[3] his troops are 'greedy' (1. 51. 1 'auidas legiones') when encountering an enemy satiated by food and drink (1. 50. 4 'propterque mensas . . . temulentos'),[4] and, amongst the things 'both profane and sacred' which the men devastate, there is a precinct dedicated to the deity Tanfana (1. 51. 1 'pro*fan*a simul et sacra et templum . . ., quod Tan*fan*ae uocabant, solo aequantur'). Two years later, after Germanicus' fleet has been wrecked by a storm, Tacitus sums up as follows (2. 24. 1):

quanto uiolentior cetero mari Oceanus et truculentia caeli praestat Germania, tantum illa clades *nouitate* et magnitudine excessit, hostilibus circum litoribus aut ita uasto [et] profundo ut credatur *nouissimum* ac sine terris mare.

This is another desperate and tragic moment in the career of Germanicus, who can scarcely be restrained from throwing himself into the sea in remorse; yet Tacitus has chosen to mark the moment by a play on words (*nouitate* = 'novelty', *nouissimum* = 'ultimate' or 'furthest'). On none of these passages also do the commentators offer comment; yet Goodyear is not alone in his belief that Tacitus is 'the most exacting of Latin stylists' and that he displays an 'obsessive concern to find words which are, for his purposes, exactly right in quality and tone'.[5] Such evidence suggests that there is a cognitive gap between what is said about Tacitus' use of language and the language he actually uses.

In one of Tacitus' earlier works, the *Agricola*, there is a well-known textual crux (10. 3):

---

[2] It is of course true that the image 'disappears' once we realize that *cupido* governs *eundi*; but one might counter this objection by arguing that the separation of the two words was itself deliberate and designed to suggest the image. For other discussions of this effect elsewhere see J. T. Dyson, 'Birds, Grandfathers, and Neoteric Sorcery in *Aeneid* 4. 254 and 7. 412', *CQ* 47 (1997), 314–15, with bibliography in n. 2 (I owe this reference to Dr D. P. Nelis).

[3] As if from *caedo*, although the adj. *caesius* of course = 'grey-blue'.

[4] Commentators realize that *auidas* requires comment but go no further than illustrating the sense 'eager (for battle)' by parallels from Sallust, Horace, Silius, and Statius.

[5] Goodyear (1972), 233 and 22 respectively.

formam totius Britanniae Liuius ueterum, Fabius Rusticus recentium eloquentissimi auctores oblongae scutulae uel bipenni adsimulauere.

scutulae *A* (oblongo scutulo *Lacey*): scupulae *B*: scapulae *Ogilvie–Richmond*

The arguments for and against the various alternative readings are set out in the commentary of Ogilvie and Richmond (1967), who conclude by supporting their own conjecture *scapulae*; but subsequently, though Ogilvie retained this reading in his revision of the Loeb edition (1970), in his Oxford text (1975) he reverted to *scutulae*, which is also preferred by Delz (1983) and Heubner (1984). Yet we should perhaps consider a passage which occurs a few pages later (14. 1):

consularium primus Aulus Plautius praepositus ac subinde Ostorius *Scapula*, uterque bello egregius; redactaque paulatim in *formam* prouinciae proxima pars *Britanniae*.

Earlier Tacitus had proceeded to modify the comparison made by Livy and Rusticus for the whole of Britain, saying that Agricola's circumnavigation of the island had demonstrated that the comparison was applicable only to the area south of Caledonia (10. 3–4); here at 14. 1 he is surely making a further (and pointed) modification, saying that it was a man named Scapula who had concluded the process of reducing to a different 'shape' the nearest part of the *scapula*-like area. The verbal repetitions seem almost to serve as cross-references to the earlier passage, as if to underline the relationship between them. Tacitus' procedure may seem to us bizarre, but it is no more bizarre than the suggestions that Volusius Proculus should '*nauare* operam' if he is to fulfil his responsibilities as a *nauarchus* (15. 51. 2–3) or that Silia should be exiled by Nero for not living up to her name (16. 20. 1 'tamquam non *siluisset* quae uiderat pertuleratque').[6]

At the very end of Book 15 of the *Annals* is found Tacitus' only certain reference to his consultation of the *acta senatus*: 'reperio in commentariis senatus Cerialem Anicium consulem designatum pro sententia dixisse . . .' (74. 3). Scholars have pounced on this reference as belated but welcome evidence that Tacitus has been

---

[6] *tamquam* almost suggests a parody of the regular use of *quod* or *quia* in etymologies 'per antiphrasin' (as in *lucus eo quod non luceat*: see e.g. Maltby (1991), 349). Cf. also Woodman–Martin on *cohortem . . . cohortatus* at 3. 20. 1–2 and on *Florus . . . florentes* at 3. 40. 2–3, where add the case of the moneyer Aquillius Florus, whose name is accompanied by a six-petal flower on the reverse of his coins (see K. Galinsky, *Augustan Culture* (1996), 31–2).

consulting a primary source throughout the whole of the *Annals* and hence that his information is essentially reliable. Yet Tacitus' original intention may be rather different in its implications. Since the name of the consul designate happened to coincide with a subject raised earlier in the same senatorial debate (74. 1 'circensium *Cerialium*[7] ludicrum') this looks like one of those rare occasions when Tacitus refers to a source in order to underline some special point.[8] If that is the case, it would be at best unwise to draw far-reaching conclusions from the evidence.

It cannot be simply coincidence that Dillius *Vocula* first wins a war of words (*H*. 4. 25. 4 'conscendit tribunal Vocula . . . prensumque militem ac *uociferantem* duci ad supplicium iussit') and then is attacked so suddenly that he has no time to speak (*H*. 4. 33. 1 'adeoque improuisi castra inuolauere ut *non adloqui*, non pandere aciem Vocula potuerit').[9] When Cossutianus Capito attacks Thrasea Paetus on the grounds that, if many others were equally bold, there would be war (16. 22. 2 'si idem multi *audeant*, bellum esse'), we are surely intended to be aware that *Thrasea*, when transliterated into Greek, means 'bold things' or 'boldness': Capito is saying, 'if there were many more Thraseas'. Likewise, when Tacitus writes 'erat medicus arte insignis, nomine Charicles' (6. 50. 2), it helps to know that in Greek the term *charientes* is almost a technical description of 'distinguished physicians':[10] Tacitus is evidently playing on and glossing Charicles' name. Elsewhere Tacitus describes the celebrated occasion when, after Nero had finished singing at Naples, the theatre in which he had been performing collapsed—an event which was interpreted by many as a gloomy omen but by Nero as the opposite (15. 34. 1 'illic, plerique ut arbitrabantur, triste, ut ipse, *prouidum* potius *et secundis numinibus euenit*'). Was it Tacitus' idea or Nero's that the

---

[7] This is the spelling of the word in MS M and is evidently a recognized form (so *OLD*); editors tend to prefer 'Cerealium'.

[8] For another example see above, p. 125 (and note G. O. Hutchinson, *Latin Literature from Seneca to Juvenal* (1993), 52 ff.). I am assuming, at least for the sake of argument, that Tacitus' statement of his consultation of the *acta* is to be taken at face value. Tacitus could, of course, point such a coincidence without referring to a source: see e.g. the C. Bibulus who complains about luxurious drinking and dining at 3. 52. 2.

[9] I owe this example to Robert Maltby.

[10] See Ph. J. van der Eijk, 'Aristotle on "Distinguished Physicians" and on the Medical Significance of Dreams', in van der Eijk *et al.* (eds.), *Ancient Medicine in its Socio-cultural Context* (1995), ii. 448–9. I am grateful to Prof. van der Eijk for supplying this information.

princeps should next proceed at once to *Beneuentum*, a town whose name was said to have been changed from Malventum to avoid an inauspicious appellation?[11]

Cumulative evidence such as this leaves little doubt that Tacitus habitually plays on names and is in no way immune to the fascination which names and their significance have for other Greek and Latin authors, including historians.[12] When Capito uses the verb *audere* to attack Thrasea at 16. 22. 2, we have to remember that *audax* and θρασύς and their derivatives were virtually technical terms for 'revolutionary':[13] Thrasea's stance was revolutionary, and the man was dangerously living up to his name. Yet neither on this nor on any of the other passages cited above do the commentators offer comment. How is their silence to be explained?

Consider the following examples:

1. effusa . . . im*man*is u*is Germa*n*arum g*entium
2. dum . . . instituta *P*art*horum sumit*, patriis *mo*ribus im*p*ar *mo*r*b*o *absumptus* est
3. tum *Sen*t*ius, forte et solus et ab*sen*te Caesare consul
4. *pos*tera die . . . apud consules *pos*tulauit
5. D*ru*sus . . . meliore in omnia ingenio animoque quam fortuna *usus*
6. abst*rusum* . . . Tiberium pepulere ut D*rusum* mitteret

By whom were these written? By Velleius Paterculus early in the first century AD or by Tacitus early in the second? It is a virtual certainty that the informed reader—informed, that is, by reading the standard handbooks or commentaries—will answer these

---

[11] See Maltby (1991), 78. As it happens, the Pisonian conspiracy of AD 65 was followed in the next year by the Vinician, which originated at Beneventum—a reversal which Tacitus no doubt exploited in the missing part of Book 16. (The penultimate item in Book 15 deals with a similar reversal: see 74. 2.)

[12] For other plays on names in Tacitus see Woodman–Martin on 3. 75. 1, adding Sinclair (1995), 259 (index, 'names'). The general bibliography which we cite there is deliberately selective: to it one might now add R. Maltby, 'The Limits of Etymologising', *Aevum Antiquum*, 6 (1993), 257–75; R. L. Fowler, 'Herodotos and his Contemporaries', *JHS* 116 (1996), 72–3 and nn. 77–8; O'Hara (1996), esp. 16 (and n. 62) and 42–3, and also in *CJ* 91 (1996), 255–76; T. P. Wiseman, 'The Minucii and their Monument', in J. Linderski (ed.), *Imperium Sine Fine* (1996), 67–9; T. Harrison, 'Herodotus' Conception of Foreign Languages', *Histos* (forthcoming). Further bibliography will be found in C. S. Kraus, 'Dangerous Supplements: Etymology and Genealogy in Euripides' *Herakles*' (forthcoming).

[13] C. Wirszubski, '*Audaces*: A Study in Political Phraseology', *JRS* 51 (1961), 12–22.

questions with the name of Velleius. But, if the reader were to be informed that some of the above were written by Velleius and some by Tacitus, it would be considerably more difficult to identify which is which. In fact the odd-numbered examples are from Velleius and the others from the *Annals*,[14] but it will be clear that there is no intrinsic difference between them. Yet on none of the Tacitean examples do the commentators offer comment. Why should this be?

In his note on the words 'hon*ora ora*tione' at 1. 10. 7 Goodyear says: 'Hardly an intentional jingle', adding that, 'Of course intentional ones may be found in some writers, e.g. Nep. 5.1.2 *non magis amore quam more.*' The choice of Nepos is significant, since Goodyear later writes:[15]

As Norden, *Kunstprosa* 1.207–8, has illustrated, Nepos is much given to the use of sound-effects and word-play. Many instances in his writings are of so striking and extravagant a character that they must be deliberate. It follows that elsewhere in Nepos, where similar, but less striking, effects occur, intention is more likely than it would be in an author who had none of Nepos' extravagances.

Evidently lesser writers such as Nepos are acknowledged to practise word-play, especially if it has been stated by a scholar as authoritative as Norden, who compares Nepos and Velleius;[16] but Tacitus is above such things, and, if any instances present themselves to the commentator, they are to be regarded as unintentional. Yet here are some further examples of Tacitean word-play of various types, all taken from Book 15 of the *Annals*:

*usur*patas nomine ten*us ur*bium expugnationes *dicti*tans: se tributa ac leges et pro umbra regis Romanum ius u*ictis* impositurum (6. 4)

---

[14] The Velleian examples (2. 12. 2, 92. 2, 2. 13. 1) are taken from H. J. W. Verhaak, *Velleius Paterculus en de Rhetoriek van zijn Tijd* (1954), 105–6, in the course of a discussion of word-play; the Tacitean examples are 6. 32. 2, 3. 10. 1, 1. 24. 1.

[15] Goodyear (1972), 337 n. 3. Goodyear's remark occurs in the course of a substantial appendix (336–41) which he devotes to alliteration in Tacitus and in which he gives most prominence to arguments favouring his usual stance of 'extreme scepticism'; contrast Woodman–Martin, 499 (index, 'alliteration': forty-six entries). Goodyear nevertheless refers without complaint to G. B. A. Fletcher, 'Assonances or Plays on Words in Tacitus', *CR* 54 (1940), 184–7, where an attempt was made to distinguish between intentional and unintentional cases (p. 185).

[16] See Norden (1958), 204–9 and 302–3 on Nepos and Velleius respectively.

Parthi omisso *para*tu (9. 2)

uis si ingrueret, pro*uisis* exemplis (13. 2)

o*perire re*liquias malae pugnae im*per*auit (28. 2)

tuta et sal*uta*ria capessentem. ille . . . ce*tera t*emperan*ter a*diungit (29. 1)

ne quam imaginem seru*iti-i T*iridates per*ferr*et neu *ferr*um traderet (31)

scilicet externae *su-per*biae *su*eto non *in-*erat *notiti*a *n*ostri, apud quos *u*is im*per*ii *u*alet, *in*ania tram*it*tuntur (31)

*su*trinae tabernae al*um*nus, cor*pore* de*torto*, facetiis scurrilibus; pri*m*o in cont*um*elias ad*sum*ptus, dehinc op*tim*i cui*usque* criminatione eo *usque* ualuit ut . . . (34. 2)

n*isi si* c*u*pi*do d*omin*a*ndi c*u*nc*tis* adfec*tib*us flagra*n*tior est (53. 4)

pugionem, de quo supra ret*tu*li, ue*tu*state ob*tu*sum (54. 1)

consilium adsumpserat *mu*liebre ac deterius: quippe *ultro* metum intentabat, *multo*sque adstitisse libertos . . . (54. 4)

crimen cuius se pariter *in-dic*em et *test*em faceret. a*dicit dicti*s constantiam: *in*cusat ultro *in-test*abilem (55. 3–4)

nec ul*lum* sile*nti*i emo*lument*um (56. 3)

non uox ad*uer*sum ea Faenio, *non* silentium, sed *uer*ba sua praepediens et pauoris *m*anifestus, *c*eterisque ac *m*axime Ceruario Proculo equite Romano ad *con*uincendum eum *con*isis, iussu imperatoris a Cassio milite, qui *ob* insigne *corpor*is rob-*ur* adstabat, *corr*ipit*ur* uincit*urque* (66. 2)

No doubt readers may dispute individual cases, but, if the criteria are frequency, strikingness, and extravagance, as they are for Goodyear, this selection from a single book of the *Annals* makes it hard to understand why scholars such as Goodyear have not concluded that Tacitus is at least as concerned with word-play as are Nepos and Velleius.[17]

The scholarly perception of Tacitus is remarkably uniform. In his recent survey of Latin literature the influential Italian scholar G. B. Conte describes Tacitus as 'austere'; in his still more recent book on Tacitus the American historian R. Mellor refers to the 'unremitting bleakness of his vision'.[18] Goodyear wrote that

---

[17] Indeed the very example from Nepos which Goodyear has lifted from Norden reappears in Tacitus at 14. 43. 1 'nimio *amore* antiqui *moris*'.

[18] G. B. Conte, *Latin Literature: A History* (Eng. trans. 1994), 541 (1st pub. 1987); Mellor (1993), 3.

Tacitus 'is not given to stylistic frivolities' and that 'he shied away from affectation and preciosity'.[19] Nor is this uniformity a recent phenomenon. To support his first statement Goodyear appeals to the late nineteenth-century Tacitean A. Draeger; his second statement echoes that of Niebuhr even earlier, with which Norden, in agreement, closes his assessment of Tacitus' style: 'a disgust and an aversion to all exuberances of style. There is not a trace of affectation'.[20] It seems to be the case that scholars are so used to the perception of Tacitus as 'austere' that they are preconditioned not to see what they regard as 'stylistic frivolities' or 'affectation'.

If this conclusion seems hard to believe, it is sobering to recall that Goodyear, for all his intimacy with Tacitus' text, alleged that even so routine an adornment as chiasmus is 'not a device of style he uses very frequently'; yet there are over sixty entries under 'chiasmus, chiastic arrangement' in the index to the commentary of Woodman–Martin on *Annals* 3 alone.[21] If this is the reaction of a distinguished Tacitean commentator to chiasmus, it is *a fortiori* more likely that denial will also be the response to phenomena which are conventionally designated by the term 'play', such as 'plays on names' and 'word-play', and which conflict with the general perception of Tacitus as 'austere'. Yet we have already noted that names and naming were regarded as serious by the ancients (above, p. 222), and the same can be said about word-play.

Paronomasia or *adnominatio* was discussed by writers of Latin rhetorical theory,[22] and the point which emerges clearly from their discussions is that the appropriateness of the device will depend upon the frequency of its use: a less frequent use will be appropriate to judicial oratory, for example, and a more frequent use to epideictic. In one respect it is (fortunately) unnecessary to try to assess the relative frequency of Tacitus' word-play; the key consideration is that, in the ancient world, historiography was seen in terms of oratory, whether judicial or epideictic.[23] When

---

[19] Goodyear (1972), 89 n. 3 and in *CHCL* ii. 651.

[20] Norden (1958), 343 and n. 1.

[21] Goodyear on 1. 2. 1; contrast Woodman–Martin, 499. In his note on 1. 55. 3 Goodyear (1981) modified 'not very frequently' to 'quite often'; he does not refer to, and I have not seen, R. B. Steele, 'Chiasmus in Sallust, Caesar, Tacitus and Justinus', diss. (Johns Hopkins University, Baltimore, 1890).

[22] e.g. *Rhet. Herenn.* 4. 29–32; Quint. 9. 3. 66–72; see also O'Hara (1996), 60–2.

[23] *RICH* 70 ff., esp. 95–8. Also *LH* 1–6.

Atticus famously stated that historiography is 'a task singularly
well suited to the orator' (Cic. *Leg.* 1. 5, cf. *De Or.* 2. 62), it
would not have occurred to him that certain resources of the
orator, such as word-play, should be unavailable to the historian.
The persistent presence of paronomasia in Tacitus' text simply
provides further evidence of the rhetorical nature of Latin
historiography and hence of its fundamental difference from
the modern genre. Since this difference is a crucial issue in
the reading and understanding of Tacitus, it is worth pursuing
a little further.

The following lines come from a familiar passage of *Aeneid* 8
(342–4):

> hinc lucum ingentem, quem Romulus acer Asylum
> rettulit, et gelida monstrat sub rupe Lupercal,
> Parrhasio dictum Panos de more Lycaei.

Here we find a similar combination of elements to that discussed
in the reading of Tacitus. The learned reader understands the
etymological play of *Lupercal* and *Lycaei*,[24] but there is perhaps
also a further etymology in *Parrhasio* and *dictum Panos*: despite the
difference in vowel-quantity, the adjective suggests the Greek
parrhēsia, a compound of *pas* + *rhēsis* upon which *dictum Panos*
seems to be a chiastic play. We observe the threefold play '*luc*um',
'*Lu*percal', and (the final word echoing the start) '*Ly*caei', with its
threefold reversal in 'Rom*ulus*', 'Asy*lum*', and 'rettu*lit*'; we note
the assonance of '*ingentem*' and '*gelida*' and of '*rupe*' and '*Luper*-
cal', where there is the additional play of anagrammatism; and we
see the alliteration of '*monstrat*' and '*more*' and of '*Parrhasio*' and
'*Panos*'. Such features as these are accepted by readers as an
integral and enhancing part of Virgil's poetry, and the same
acceptance should apply, at least in principle, to Tacitus' prose.
It was Tacitus' contemporary, Quintilian, who famously stated
that 'historiography is very close to poetry and is rather like a
poem in prose' (10. 1. 31). The comparison between Tacitus and
Virgil indicates that such a statement, like those which describe
historiography in the alternative terms of oratory, is to be taken
seriously.[25]

If we take seriously the analogy between historiography and

---

[24] For which see O'Hara (1996), 209–10.   [25] See *RICH* 98–101.

poetry, we shall be less surprised at encountering in Tacitus' text the presence of an image such as *animos cupido inuolat eundi*, with which we began (1. 49. 3: above): Horace's *Odes* are, after all, full of such conceits.[26] But this does not mean that we are any the less surprised at the unusualness of the image itself;[27] on the contrary, the degree of its unusualness suggests at the very least that Tacitus is drawing our attention to some emphatic point. This suggestion may be elaborated by reference to the commentary of Goodyear, since he, like others, appears not to have seen the image at all (above, p. 218).

Tacitus in his very next sentence says of Germanicus: 'sequitur ardorem militum Caesar' (1. 49. 4). Goodyear, quoting only the first and last of these words as his lemma, comments as follows: 'Dio 57.6.1 attributes the initiative to Germanicus. . . . The discrepancy between Tacitus and Dio, though not easily reconcilable, is not serious.' In fact, however, the discrepancy is crucial, at least for Tacitus' presentation of Germanicus and his troops. By trying to normalize the phrase *cupido inuolat* (as we have seen), and by disregarding the phrase *ardorem militum* (evidently as a consequence), Goodyear misconceives both the soldiers' potential for impassioned action and the significance of Germanicus' reaction to them. Previously Tacitus has told us that, when the troops in Germany began their mutiny, they were ready and willing to use violence to set Germanicus on the throne (1. 31. 1 and 5):

Germanicae legiones turbatae, quanto plures, tanto uiolentius, et magna spe fore ut Germanicus Caesar imperium alterius pati nequiret daretque se legionibus ui sua cuncta tracturis. . . . sua in manu sitam rem Romanam, suis uictoriis augeri rem publicam, in suum cognomentum adscisci imperatores.

---

[26] See e.g. L. P. Wilkinson, 'The Language of Virgil and Horace', *CQ* 9 (1959), 188–9; Nisbet–Hubbard on *Odes* 2 *passim*; and, for other effects, note D. Armstrong, 'The Impossibility of Metathesis', in D. Obbink (ed.), *Philodemus and Poetry* (1995), 229–31.

[27] Is Tacitus drawing some comparison between sexual lust and bloodlust, reversing the common motif whereby 'love' is seen in terms of 'war'? Is he taking to its logical and (so to speak) literal conclusion the metaphor used by Thucydides for the launching of the Sicilian Expedition (6. 24. 3 ἔρως ἐνέπεσε τοῖς πᾶσιν ὁμοίως ἐκπλεῦσαι)? For the former cf. R. O. A. M. Lyne, *Words and the Poet* (1989), 36–7. Other examples of Thucydides' expression will be found at Aesch. *Ag.* 341 and Soph. *Ant.* 782, and note Sapph. 47 with M. S. Silk, *Interaction in Poetic Imagery* (1974), 105 and 107 n. 9 (Silk's book contains many helpful remarks on several of the matters which I have been discussing here).

Although Germanicus in fact remained steadfast in his support for Tiberius (1. 34. 1), his submission to the troops' extraordinary *cupido* at 1. 49. 3–4 throws into sharper relief both the nature of their pressure at the start of the mutiny and the firmness with which he resisted it. The later passage not only underlines his earlier loyalty but also emphasizes how, as a man of *cupido* himself,[28] he might so easily have 'followed the soldiers' ardour' on that previous and much more critical occasion. This is surely a point deserving of emphasis, yet it depends upon our recognizing and responding to a highly unusual and provocative image, and this recognition in turn depends upon our being receptive to the notion that Latin historiography was analogous to poetry and aimed at many of the same effects. It is perhaps paradoxical that those who have most to gain from such receptiveness are those who, reading the *Annals* simply as a source of information about the Julio-Claudian period, are least likely to be receptive.

Yet this may not be the whole story. Although we have been concentrating on verbal effects which come under the broad heading of 'play', it is perhaps misleading to view them in isolation. The standard commentaries and handbooks rightly list and discuss numerous other idiosyncrasies of Tacitus' technique, such as his fondness for periphrasis, his brevity, his strained syntax, his striking metaphors, his avoidance of technical and similar terms, his unusual sentence-structure, his relentless variation in all its various forms, and so on.[29] One has the impression of a writer who consistently challenges the conventions of language and pushes against the boundaries of literary expression. It is difficult not to place Tacitus' 'playfulness' in this context; on the basis of this unusual accumulation of other effects we might even infer that his 'playfulness' too exceeds the notional norm to which the theoretical writers appealed (above, p. 225). If that is so, we are perhaps entitled to speculate a little further.

Sir Ronald Syme in his inimitable way has remarked that 'Verbal disharmonies reflect the complexities of history and all that is ambiguous in the behaviour of men', a remark with which few would disagree.[30] Yet the ancients drew a distinction between

---

[28] See the evidence assembled in Goodyear's note on 1. 61. 1; and note also Pelling (1993), 68–9.   [29] See e.g. Syme (1958), 340–52.

[30] Syme (1958), 347; see e.g. *LH* 12, 111.

res and *uerba*, between matter and manner, and some readers
may well conclude from the energy and imagination which
Tacitus devoted to *uerba* that at least on some occasions he
was more interested in the manner than the matter and that
he deserves to be described as a 'mannerist'.[31] Historically
minded readers of Tacitus might be tempted to draw some
encouragement from this description, since it seems to suggest
that, once one has stripped his text of such externals as literary
adornments, one will be left with a residual content (*res*) which
can be used straightforwardly as historical evidence. Yet the
encouragement is only temporary. For, if Tacitus was indeed a
mannerist, that implies a preoccupation with style which in turn
calls into question his seriousness as a historian. Few would be
prepared to countenance such a conclusion; besides, most students of Tacitus are agreed that 'at his best', as Ronald Martin
has observed, 'there is no dichotomy between Tacitus the historian and Tacitus the writer'.[32]

II

Modern historians often find it convenient and practical to alter-
nate between the treatment of domestic and foreign affairs, and J.
Ginsburg has valuably demonstrated the varieties of such alterna-
tion in the case of Tacitus' Tiberian *Annals*. But the parallel
between ancient and modern goes little further. When Ginsburg
shows how Tacitus refers to and manipulates an inherited annalistic format which was made canonical by Livy, she confirms by
implication how different from each other the ancient and modern genres are. This difference becomes even more marked when
we consider such more complicated arrangements as ring-composition and triadic organization: these are as likely to be alien to
the compositional processes of modern historians as they are
absent from the works of those Tacitean commentators who do

---

[31] For this description see e.g. P. Burke, 'Tacitism', in T. A. Dorey (ed.), *Tacitus* (1969),
153. For mannerism see Curtius (1953), 273–301 (p. 299 for Tacitus), and *The New
Princeton Encyclopedia of Poetry and Poetics* (1993), 732–3. The latter quotes with approval
the former's listing of typical mannerist devices—hyperbaton, periphrasis, paronomasia and
affected metaphor. A related term to mannerism is 'baroque'.

[32] Martin (1981), 243. S. Borzsák concludes his discussion of mannerism ('Tacitus—ein
Manierist?', *ANRW* 2. 33. 4 (1991), 2581–96) by arguing that Tacitus was 'kein Manierist'.

not look out for them;[33] but they are regular in Tacitus and are fundamental elements in classical literature from Homer onwards. Tacitus belongs to a tradition which includes poets and orators as well as historians.[34]

Cicero regarded it as possible to see historiography in terms of drama and to conceive of narrative as being divided into 'acts' (*Fam.* 5. 12. 6), and several scholars have suggested that Nero as *princeps* lived out the life of an actor.[35] Tacitus married these two concepts in *Annals* 15, if I am right to have argued that the historian sees his narrative of the Pisonian conspiracy in terms of a drama and the conspirators as ineffectual actors mesmerized by the superior playing of their would-be victim.[36] In this respect it is interesting to compare Tacitus' method with that of Modris Eksteins in his account of the Great War and the birth of the modern age, which is introduced in the preface as follows:[37]

Our century is one in which life and art have blended, in which existence has become aestheticized. History, as one theme of this study will try to show, has surrendered much of its former authority to fiction. In our postmodernist age a compromise may, however, be possible and necessary. In search of this compromise our historical account proceeds in the form of a drama, with acts and scenes, in the full and diverse sense of those words.

The book as a whole, duly divided into three 'Acts' in which the scenes change from (to take Act One as an example) Paris to Berlin to Flanders, begins with early twentieth-century theatre and ends with the theatricality of the Third Reich:[38]

From first to last, the Third Reich was spectacular, gripping theater. That is what it was intended to be. . . . [Hitler] looked on himself as the

---

[33] There is virtually nothing on such arrangements in the commentaries of Koestermann and Goodyear; contrast Woodman–Martin on *A.* 3 (e.g. 275–7, 283–4, 327–8, 374–8, 413, 431–2, 450–1) and Martin–Woodman on *A.* 4 (15–19), and, on ring-composition, Woodman (1972), 152–4 (above, Ch. 8, Sect. II). This last scarcely receives wholehearted endorsement from Wille (1983), 442 n. 7, who has investigated in minute detail the structure of each of Tacitus' works and who mentions earlier bibliography.

[34] See e.g. the useful survey of ring-composition in Cairns (1979), 193 ff., who notes it as surprising that 'there is little sign of ancient recognition of the practice' (p. 195).

[35] Cf. e.g. J. Elsner and J. Masters (eds.), *Reflections of Nero* (1994).

[36] 'Amateur Dramatics at the Court of Nero', in Luce–Woodman (1993), 104–28 (above, Ch. 11). For later studies see S. Bartsch, *Actors in the Audience* (1994), esp. ch. 1, and A. M. Gowing, 'Cassius Dio on the Reign of Nero', *ANRW* 2.34.3 (1997), 2558–90.

[37] Eksteins (1990), p. xvi.   [38] Eksteins (1990), 313, 314–15.

incarnation of the artist–tyrant Nietzsche had called for, as the executor of the 'dictatorship of genius' Wagner had craved. In dealing with foreign policy, he boasted that he was 'the greatest actor in all Europe'.

Though the similarity between this and Nero is clear enough, the whole point of Eksteins's prefatory apologia is that his method is not that of a conventional historian. Moreover, even if we press the similarities between Eksteins's conceit and Tacitus' ambitiously sustained metaphor, we must remember that, just previously in *Annals* 15, Tacitus has adopted the method and techniques of a paradoxographer to underline the otherness of Nero's principate;[39] likewise in Book 4 he pretends that he is obliged to write 'alternative' history if he is to do justice to the introspective nature of Tiberius' later principate.[40] It is true that in this latter case Tacitus too presents a prefatory apologia (4. 32–3),[41] but his remarks are directed not so much at method as at subject-matter; and it is of course typical of him that, having presented his apologia, he proceeds to write—both literally (in the case of the war in Thrace: 4. 46–51) and metaphorically (in the case of Tiberius' withdrawal to Capri: 4. 57–60, 67)—precisely the kind of history which he had previously seemed to declare impossible.[42] Such manipulations of the narrative mode confirm the fundamentally literary nature of Tacitus' historical writing.

Defenders of a more traditional Tacitus might nevertheless maintain that such features as structure and metaphor are external adornments rather than intrinsic characteristics: that is, these features are somehow separable from what the 'real' Tacitus is 'really' saying—much as general accounts of the author will conventionally devote a separate chapter to 'Style'. Yet in Tacitus, as Goodyear himself remarked, 'the style is part of the interpretation'.[43] It is therefore worth considering a further aspect of Tacitus' essential literariness.

Fifty years ago R. Wellek and A. Warren in their well-known *Theory of Literature* remarked that 'Parallel-hunting has been widely discredited recently'.[44] But many classical scholars are

---

[39] See above, Ch. 10.   [40] *RICH* 180–6 (above, pp. 128–35).

[41] On which see further Martin–Woodman ad loc.

[42] See *RICH* 186–90 (above, pp. 136–41) and Martin–Woodman ad locc.

[43] Goodyear (1972), 46 (perhaps a veiled reference to the format of Koestermann's first two volumes, in which annotations on 'content' are separated from those on 'style').

[44] p. 258 of the 3rd (1963) edn.; the book was first published in 1949.

avid parallel-hunters, and post-war commentaries on Tacitus abound in parallels, capitalizing on the work of G. B. A. Fletcher above all and, more recently, on the resources of computerized searches.[45] Wellek and Warren were naturally not averse to parallels in themselves, since 'by a judicious study of sources it is possible to establish literary relationships'. Goodyear, though keen on parallels to illustrate syntactical and linguistic usage, was characteristically sceptical about other, especially 'literary', parallels. His scepticism extended even to Tacitus' principal model, Sallust, regarding it as 'perhaps coincidence' when the thought and language of *H.* 4. 76 are repeated in successive sentences of the *Annals* (1. 64. 3);[46] but he was particularly reluctant to entertain parallels with Virgil.

In his note on 'arma in Segestem, arma in Caesarem poscens' at 1. 59. 1, Goodyear admits a 'superficial similarity' to various passages of *Aeneid* 7 (340 'arma . . . poscat', 460 'arma . . . fremit, arma . . . requirit', 583–4) but concludes that Tacitus' text is not 'certainly reminiscent' of Virgil, as Baxter had alleged. Goodyear might have supported his case by noting that in the conventional call to arms (*ad arma*) 'the duplication of the expression is stereotyped',[47] but C. E. Murgia, in a review of Goodyear, argued that the resemblance to Virgil 'is not merely one of diction but also of circumstance': '*Aeneid* 7.340 describes Turnus' rage at the loss of Lavinia; and, as Arminius' hostility is directed against Segestes and Germanicus, Turnus' is directed at Latinus and Aeneas.'[48] In fact the matter is rather more complicated. Murgia sees Arminius in terms of Turnus, yet Tacitus describes Arminius and Segestes as respectively son-in-law and father-in-law (1. 55. 3 'gener inuisus inimici soceri'), which is precisely the relationship which Virgil famously uses to describe Aeneas and Latinus slightly earlier in the same book of the *Aeneid* (317 'gener atque socer').[49] The parallelism of these last two passages seems both to confirm Tacitus'

---

[45] See G. B. A. Fletcher, *Annotations on Tacitus* (1964); *Latomus*, 30 (1971), 146–50 and 383–5; *Studies in Latin Literature and Roman History* (1983), iii. 299–324; *LCM* 10 (1985), 27–8; *SIFC* 3 (1986), 68–75; and elsewhere. Unless it is indicated otherwise, the parallels I am about to discuss have not, so far as I know, been noted previously.

[46] Goodyear (1981), 110 and n. 4.

[47] Nisbet–Hubbard on Hor. *C.* 1. 35. 15; see now Wills (1997), 62–5.

[48] *CP* 79 (1984), 317.

[49] And, of course, behind Aeneas and Latinus are to be seen Caesar and Pompey.

allusion to *Aeneid* 7 and to question Murgia's otherwise attractive identification.

In the light of this example it may be wondered what Goodyear would have made of Tacitus' comment on those who, after Tiberius' departure from Rome, claimed to foretell the future: 'patuit . . . uera . . . quam obscuris tegerentur' (4. 58. 2). These words seem closely to resemble those used by Virgil of the Sibyl in *Aeneid* 6 (100 'obscuris uera inuoluens').[50] And, in the light of this example, would Goodyear have described it as 'perhaps coincidence' that the phrase *longo ordine* is used to describe both the procession at the end of the same book of the *Aeneid* (6. 754) and the funeral procession of Drusus in the same book of the *Annals* (4. 9. 2)?[51] Neither of these cases is noted in commentaries on *Annals* 4, but one naturally stands less chance of establishing the truth if a pre-existing scepticism inhibits one's alertness to the evidence.

A rather different issue is raised by two adjacent sentences in *Annals* 1. In his notes on 1. 70. 1 'quo . . . uadoso mari innaret uel reciproco sideret' and 1. 70. 2 'sidere aequinoctii' Goodyear parallels the language only from the elder Pliny's *Natural History* (respectively 5. 26 'uadoso ac reciproco mari' and 18. 311 'aequinocti sidus'). Since Tacitus has just previously referred to Pliny by name as the historian of the German wars (1. 69. 2 'tradit C. Plinius, Germanicorum bellorum scriptor'), it is perhaps worth asking whether Pliny in this latter work had described the background to Germanicus' imminent disaster in similar language to that which he had used in his *Natural History*, and hence whether Tacitus was still following Pliny at 1. 70. 1–2. As for Sallust (above, p. 232), there will obviously be a finite number of parallels between his work and that of Tacitus, but it is reasonable to assume that despite intensive scholarly investigation many still remain to be detected.[52] For

---

[50] *TLL* 9. 2. 173. 2–3 cites only these two examples from classical Latin.

[51] This is a more testing case, since the phrase is also used elsewhere in the *Aeneid* and in other authors: see D. Fowler, 'Even Better than the Real Thing: A Tale of Two Cities', in J. Elsner (ed.), *Art and Text in Roman Culture* (1996), 64–5 and n. 30. For a recent study of such issues see S. Hinds, *Allusion and Intertext* (1998), esp. 34–47, although he nowhere considers examples of allusion in prose authors.

[52] See e.g. Ch. 2 above. It is remarkable that no commentator before Martin–Woodman had noted Sall. *H.* 1. 55. 26 'potiorque uisa est periculosa libertas quieto seruitio' on 4. 24. 1 *quibus libertas seruitio potior*, or *H.* 1. 11 'stante Carthagine' on 4. 56. 1 *stante . . . Punica urbe*. We should perhaps have added Sall. *H.* 5. 27 'manum in os intendens' to the note on 4. 3. 2 *intenderat . . . manus et contra tendentis os uerberauerat*.

example, when Tacitus sums up Tiberius' ambivalent reaction to the news of the settlement of the German mutiny (1. 52. 1 'nuntiata ea Tiberium laetitia curaque adfecere: gaudebat . . . sed . . . angebatur'), he surely alludes to Cicero's ambivalent reaction when he heard *per nuntios* of events at the Mulvian Bridge (Sall. *C.* 46. 2 'at illum ingens *cura atque laetitia* simul occupauere: nam laetabatur . . . porro autem anxius erat').[53] And, when Tacitus describes a lull in the fighting between Romans and Germans (1. 63. 2 'inde hostibus terror, fiducia militi'), he has most likely abbreviated and rendered chiastically a sentence of Sallust's (*H.* 2. 104 'terror hostibus et fiducia suis incessit').

The juxtaposition of Sallust and the elder Pliny raises the question of the nature of these parallels. There can scarcely be anything more literary than one text referring to another text or to a plurality of other texts; but historiography is supposed to refer to, and be an account of, 'what really happened': modern historians read *Annals* 1–6 because they want to know what happened in Tiberius' reign. Tacitus was not of course a contemporary of Tiberius, and it is accepted that his text depends, at least in part, upon a series of other texts which stretches back through the first century AD until Tiberius' reign itself is reached. If to describe Germanicus' plight in AD 15 Tacitus was using Pliny's account of the same incident, his procedure illustrates one link in this chain of evidence and presumably bears some resemblance to the procedure of many a modern historian. But if to describe Tiberius' ambivalent reaction to Germanicus' settlement in the previous year Tacitus was relying exclusively on Sallust's account of an entirely different incident nearly eighty years earlier, Tacitus' reference is of quite a different order and has quite different implications: this is an example of what I have called 'substantive imitation',[54] which happens when an author, in the absence of a 'genuine' source such as the elder Pliny, imitates an altogether unconnected text in order to substantialize what he wishes to say.

It may be asked whether it matters if a passage such as 1. 52. 1

---

[53] In Tacitus' next sentence (1. 52. 2 'multaque . . . memorauit . . . uerbis adornata') there is perhaps an allusion to Thuc. 3. 67. 6 λόγοι ἔπεσι κοσμηθέντες. The same book of Thucydides perhaps discloses other parallels at 53. 2 (~ *A.* 1. 6. 3) and 82. 2 (~ 4. 60. 1).

[54] Woodman (1979), 143–55 (above, Ch. 5).

constitutes substantive imitation. One answer is that it matters if the imitation is not recognized and is presented as hard fact by a modern historian.[55] Another answer is that some cases will matter more than others. When during his account of the Pannonian mutiny Tacitus observes that 'minds once struck' are prone to superstition (1. 28. 2 'perculsae semel mentes'), he alludes to Horace's *Epodes* (7. 16 'mentesque perculsae'):[56] the allusion no doubt results from a similarity of context, since Tacitus' soldiers are engaged in a quasi-civil war and Horace's citizens are rushing into a real civil war; but the allusion, though interesting in itself, is of little historical moment because Tacitus' statement about the troops' mental state, while no doubt plausible in the circumstances, is part of a wider generalization. Tiberius' relationship with Germanicus, on the other hand, is recognized as being of considerable historical significance, so any item of evidence is potentially important.

A further consideration is that it is difficult to distinguish substantive imitation from other types. If we were to accept for the sake of argument that Tacitus had some genuine information for Tiberius' reaction to Germanicus in the senate in AD 14,[57] his allusion to Sallust at 1. 52. 1 could perhaps be dismissed as mere 'literary reminiscence' and of little consequence: hard fact is clothed in the language of a distinguished literary predecessor. But the problem is that on this occasion we do not actually know, and on very many other occasions cannot know, whether such information was available to Tacitus and, if it was, whether he made use of it. We are obliged to operate on the basis of a balance of probabilities, alive to the possibility that almost any identified case of imitation is as likely to be substantive as not.[58] Thus in his description of the war in Thrace in AD 26 (4. 46–51) Tacitus imitates not only Sallust's account of the war with the Isaurians in 76/75 BC (*H.* 2. 87) but also

---

[55] Thus e.g. Seager (1972), 73: 'When he heard the outcome of the German mutiny Tiberius' feelings were mixed. He was naturally glad . . . but he suspected . . .'.

[56] No other example of this expression is given in *TLL* 10. 1. 1198. 20–1. The parallel is not mentioned by Baldwin (1979).

[57] R. J. A. Talbert believes that Tacitus' references to the facial expressions of Tiberius and others in the senate are derived from literary accounts and/or contemporary reminiscences (*The Senate of Imperial Rome* (1984), 331–2). If one believes that, one is perhaps likely to believe that Tacitus will have had information for Tiberius' reaction to Germanicus.   [58] See also above, Ch. 7, n. 77.

Caesar's account of the Battle of Alesia in 52 BC (*G.* 7. 69–90); in addition there is imitation of Livy and other texts, and the deployment of conventional themes and motifs.[59] In this example the sheer extent of Tacitus' imitation suggests that the whole military campaign, rather than simply incidental details, may be a literary construct. And, if that is the case on this occasion, there is no reason why the same should not be true on other occasions. Goodyear, in response to the argument that significant portions of *Annals* 1 are imitated from Books 2 and 5 of Tacitus' own *Histories*, drew the following conclusion:[60] 'May not Tacitus have written history in this free and easy manner in places where his every word matters and we cannot test him against independent evidence?' Thus another reason why Tacitus' imitation of Sallust at 1. 52. 1 matters is that in its small way it provides further confirmation of Tacitus' general technique. Moreover, the fact that his imitation has hitherto remained unidentified alerts us to the realization that there must be many other passages which historians regard as factual but which are really examples of substantive imitation. The number of such passages is of course ultimately unknowable; all we can hope for is that a clearer picture will emerge from the discovery of further comparative material, whether in the form of still latent parallels or of primary sources such as the *Senatus Consultum de Cn. Pisone Patre*, recently found in Spain and now superbly edited and discussed by W. Eck and his colleagues.[61] In the meantime we should be prepared to acknowledge that Tacitus' extensive imitative practices are an intrinsic feature of his historical writing and denote a literariness which raises fundamental questions about the nature of the history which he writes.

---

[59] For Sallust see Syme (1958), 729 and n. 6, referring to W. Heraeus; for the rest see Martin–Woodman, 206–15.

[60] For the argument that Tacitus has imitated himself see Woodman (1979), 143–55 (above, Ch. 5); for the response by Goodyear (1981), see his notes on 1. 61. 3–4 and 1. 64–5 (the quotation from p. 108). Less impressed was M. G. Morgan, 'The Smell of Victory: Vitellius at Bedriacum (Tac. *Hist.* 2.70)', *CP* 87 (1992), 14–29 (p. 22, 'Woodman's approach is manifestly too cavalier', p. 23, 'his analysis of this narrative too is faulty').

[61] W. Eck, A. Caballos, and F. Fernández, *Das senatus consultum de Cn. Pisone patre* (1996). For an English trans. of the *senatus consultum*, and a thorough review-discussion of its publication by Eck and his colleagues, see now M. Griffin, 'The Senate's Story', *JRS* 87 (1997), 249–63.

III

The remarkable unearthing of the *Senatus Consultum de Cn. Pisone Patre* has given a new impetus to the study both of Tiberius' principate and of the way in which Augustus' successor is presented in the narrative of Rome's greatest historian. Whether or not we agree with Syme that the *Annals* in its original form was divided into three hexads,[62] the first six books are exclusively devoted to Tiberius. The summing-up of the emperor in his obituary notice at the end of Book 6 is matched by a formal character-sketch near the start of Book 1 (4. 3–5), the two passages together constituting an outer frame.[63] We might naturally expect these examples of so-called 'direct characterization' to guide and influence our reading of the intervening narrative, but, though scholars continue to discuss the obituary,[64] they seem to have paid little, if any, attention to the introductory sketch.[65] The reason for this neglect is perhaps that the sketch is less 'direct' than one might wish, since it is cast in the form of a rumour which is voiced by contemporaries of the failing Augustus (1. 4. 2 'pars multo maxima imminentis dominos uariis rumoribus differebant'); but we shall see that the sketch nevertheless repays detailed analysis.

The last section of the sketch reads as follows (1. 4. 5):

accedere matrem muliebri impotentia: seruiendum feminae duobusque insuper adulescentibus, qui rem publicam interim premant, quandoque distrahant.

A seemingly obvious question posed by these words concerns the implied subject of *seruiendum*; but this seems not to be a question which scholars have asked. The older commentators (such as Walther, Ruperti, Ritter, Furneaux, and Nipperdey–Andresen) say nothing at all. Koestermann, referring back to the phrase

---

[62] Syme (1958), 686–7. In a paper delivered in 1996 in Nashville, Michael Hendry has interestingly suggested that the *Annals* originally consisted of only sixteen books and was divided into two 'ogdoads'. I am most grateful to the author for the opportunity to read his paper.

[63] See *LH* 103. For some recent heterodox speculation on the end of Book 6 see C. Ando, 'Tacitus, *Annales* VI: Beginning and End', *AJP* 118 (1997), 285–303.

[64] The latest discussion is that of Vielberg (1996).

[65] It appears to be passed over by e.g. Martin (1981), 108–9, (1990), 1507–8, and Sage (1990), 970–3.

imminentis dominos at 1. 4. 2, implies that the subject is the people who were voicing the rumour; Goodyear, quoting the alien practices of a German tribe (*G.* 45. 6 'femina dominatur: in tantum non modo a libertate sed etiam a seruitute degenerant'), conveys the same implication.[66] Translators such as Church and Brodribb, Ramsay, and Jackson are explicit and unanimous that the subject is indeed the Roman people ('They'). Yet *seruiendum* is an ambiguously passive construction; might there not be an alternative interpretation?

If Tacitus is saying, as the scholarly consensus maintains, that under Tiberius the Roman people would be enslaved to a woman and two young men, what are the implications of such a statement? Although enslavement to Livia is a natural enough notion, since her love of dominance was proverbial, how could the people imagine themselves as enslaved to Germanicus and Drusus, about whom nothing detrimental in this respect is known? The two *adulescentes* seem to have nothing in common with the elderly matriarch which would justify their being co-ordinated in such a baseless and implausible slur. Again, although natural malice might predict that at some distant point the two brothers would fight each other for the succession ('quandoque distrahant'),[67] how are they conceived as oppressing the State in the meanwhile ('interim premant')?[68] And, finally, why is Tiberius entirely missing from this envisaged scenario? It seems very odd indeed that the future *princeps* has dropped out of the very sketch which is evidently designed to introduce him, however distortedly, to Tacitus' readers. An alternative interpretation seems positively desirable.

Since Tiberius is the subject of the character-sketch, it seems much more natural to regard him as the implied subject of *seruiendum*, especially as Livia is referred to as *matrem* in the immediately preceding sentence. Tacitus is making the paradoxical point that this particular *imminens dominus* would be obliged

---

[66] The best parallel is in fact 12. 7. 3 'cuncta feminae oboediebant' (Claudius).

[67] Under AD 17 Tacitus says that Tiberius' court was divided in its loyalties between Drusus and Germanicus but that the brothers themselves were strikingly harmonious and unaffected by the rivalries of their entourages (2. 43. 5–6).

[68] The conjunction of the verbs *premant* and *distrahant* recalls Herodotus' description of Pisistratus (1. 59. 1 τὸ μὲν Ἀττικὸν κατεχόμενόν τε καὶ διεσπασμένον . . . ὑπὸ Πεισιστράτου).

to be enslaved to a woman and to two young men. How can this be? What Livia and the two young men have in common is that all of them will be designated as 'helpers' or 'partners' of Tiberius (*adiutores, socii*).[69] Of course the rumourmongers in the years before Augustus' death cannot know this; but the author, writing with the benefit of hindsight, can allow them the natural inference that the *princeps'* mother and joint heirs will enjoy a privileged position in the new principate, a position which, on a malicious interpretation, they will use to manipulate Tiberius to their own advantage. Indeed the very first episode of the reign, if my analysis of it is correct, shows precisely this manipulation in the case of Livia.

Scholars have assumed that Tacitus uses the episode of Agrippa Postumus' murder (1. 6. 1–3) to blacken Tiberius from the very start and that he accuses Tiberius and Livia as being jointly responsible for a murder which is paradigmatic of the reign as a whole. But I have argued that these assumptions are based on a misreading of the text.[70] Tacitus presents Tiberius as ignorant of the murder and anxious for it to be discussed openly in the senate; he attributes the crime to Livia and Sallustius Crispus; and he shows Livia successfully persuading Tiberius not to raise the matter in the senate. On this interpretation the episode illustrates exactly the point which in my opinion Tacitus has just made at 1. 4. 5, namely that Tiberius would be obliged to be enslaved to a woman. Scholars have rightly drawn attention to parallels between the start of Tiberius' reign as described at the beginning of Book 1 and the start of Nero's reign as described at the beginning of Book 13. On the present analysis a further parallel emerges, since Nero too was allegedly dominated by the woman who was his mother (13. 6. 2 'quod subsidium in eo qui a femina regeretur').

A further example of Livia's influence is provided by the trial of Cn. Piso and his wife Plancina in AD 20. Since Livia's relationship with Plancina was well known, Tacitus cynically represents their contemporaries as reflecting, while the trial was in progress, how much scope she would allow the *princeps* for dealing with Plancina

[69] For the evidence see above, pp. 158–9, and also my remarks in *LH* 103–9, which are developed but not (I hope) repeated here. On Livia in particular see also Woodman–Martin, 14–17 and references there. I have not seen F. Hurlet, *Les Collègues du prince sous Auguste et Tibère* (1997).   [70] See above, Ch. 3.

(3. 15. 1 'quantum Caesari in eam liceret'). And, after Piso has
died and Tiberius has relayed to the senate his mother's pleas on
Plancina's behalf, Tacitus adds that feelings against Livia were
running high (3. 17. 1 'in quam optimi cuiusque secreti questus
magis ardescebant'): for Livia's intervention ensured Plancina's
acquittal (3. 17. 2). Livia's successful pleas are also highlighted in
the inscription which resulted from the trial (*SCPP* 111–20), but
in this official document they are given a positive and reverential
gloss which contrasts strongly with Tacitus' contempt (3. 17. 3
'hac imagine cognitionis') but is echoed in Velleius' enthusiastic
endorsement of Livia's power (130. 5 'cuius potentiam nemo
sensit nisi . . . leuatione periculi'). Which of these views more
accurately represents contemporary opinion it is perhaps impossible to say; but Tacitus' treatment of such episodes as Postumus'
murder and Plancina's trial suggests at least some correspondence
between himself and the rumourmongers who at 1. 4. 5 predict
Tiberius' subservience to Livia.

If there was ever any prospect that Germanicus and Drusus
would collaborate in the manipulation of their father, it was
removed by the former's premature death early in the reign.
But we should note that the appearance of their names alongside
Livia's in the introductory sketch is matched by the reappearance
of all three names in Tiberius' obituary notice at the end of Book
6 (51. 3), where the presence of Germanicus and Drusus has been
regarded by scholars as extremely problematic. On the usual
interpretation of the obituary, Tacitus is portraying Tiberius as a
man of fixedly evil character; that character was gradually revealed
during successive periods of the *princeps*' life (AD 14–23, 23–9, 29–
31, 31–7); and those periods are demarcated by Tacitus with
reference to the deaths of Germanicus and Drusus (in AD 19
and 23 respectively), Livia (AD 29), and Sejanus (AD 31), each of
whom is featured as a restraining influence upon the evil Tiberius.
There is so much wrong with this interpretation, a great deal of it
admitted by the very scholars who espouse it, that the details
cannot be repeated here;[71] but scholars are agreed that Tacitus'
identification of the period AD 14–23 by the deaths of *both*
brothers is exceedingly odd: four years and a whole book of the
Annals separate the two deaths, and nowhere in the narrative is

---

[71] See further above, Ch. 9.

either brother depicted as a restraining influence upon the *princeps*. Yet these problems disappear if, as I have argued,[72] one assumes that the four individuals mentioned in the obituary owe their presence there to the fact that each of them was a 'helper' or 'partner' of Tiberius: on this assumption Germanicus and Drusus are naturally linked, since, as brothers, they were joint partners—the two 'Dioscuri', as they are styled by Ovid (*Ex P.* 2. 2. 83–4).[73] If this argument is correct, the framing passages at 1. 4. 5 and 6. 51. 3 support each other. In the latter passage it is shown by the very individuals whom Tacitus chooses to name that Tiberius' dependence upon others provides the key to understanding his career; in the former passage it is the *princeps*' dependence on three of the same four individuals which is subjected to proleptic and malicious distortion with the word *seruiendum*. By failing to question the conventional view of that ambiguously passive construction, scholars have misread, even before the Tiberian narrative formally starts at 1. 6. 1, a passage which provides vital evidence for the interpretation of the *princeps*' reign.

It is Sejanus who is mentioned in the obituary notice but is missing from the introductory sketch, the reason for his omission being that in the years before AD 14 no one could possibly have foreseen that Germanicus and Drusus would die so young and that Tiberius would become increasingly dependent upon a partner who was not a member of the imperial family. Drusus' death in AD 23 was in fact engineered by Sejanus (4. 3. 1–2, 8. 1), who thereby procured for himself greater freedom to influence the *princeps*: two years later he attempted to persuade Tiberius to withdraw from Rome (4. 41), in the following year his persuasion was at last successful (4. 57. 1). When Livia finally died in AD 29, Tiberius and Sejanus together embarked on what Tacitus calls

[72] Above, Ch. 9. In disagreement are Vielberg (1996), 455 n. 2, and C. Pelling, 'Is Death the End? Closure in Plutarch's *Lives*', in D. H. Roberts *et al.* (eds.), *Classical Closure* (1997), 237 n. 32; but see also the latter's 'Biographical History? Cassius Dio on the Early Principate', in M. J. Edwards and S. Swain (eds.), *Portraits: Biographical Representation in the Greek and Latin Literature of the Roman Empire* (1997), 122 n. 25.

[73] See B. Poulsen, 'The Dioscuri and Ruler Ideology', *SO* 66 (1991), 127. (At *LH* 117 n. 91 I mistakenly said that *SEG* iv. 515 also refers to Germanicus and Drusus as the Dioscuri; the reference is in fact to the twin sons of Drusus and Livi(ll)a: see now C. B. Rose, *Dynastic Commemoration and Imperial Portraiture in the Julio-Claudian Period* (1997), 176.) Particularly telling evidence for the partnership of Germanicus and Drusus will be found at *SCPP* 126–30 (written, of course, after the former's death).

'praerupta . . . et urgens dominatio' (5. 3. 1). It was thus Sejanus who fulfilled the prophecies of enslavement (*seruiendum*) and oppression (*premant*) which were uttered of Germanicus and Drusus at 1. 4. 5; his is the absent presence whose shadow falls across the narrative as early as the introductory sketch of Tiberius.

If we allow our reading of the Tiberian narrative to be guided and influenced by the emperor's introductory sketch and closing obituary, as Tacitus surely intends, it will come as less of a surprise that the accession debate takes the form for which I have argued in this book.[74] Tiberius' highly developed sense of propriety, so well illustrated by the actions he took on Augustus' death (1. 7. 3–5), was severely compromised by the knowledge that he had been rejected so often by Augustus, who even at the last, until dissuaded by Livia, toyed with the idea of giving the young Germanicus precedence over him (4. 57. 3). During the time which elapsed between Augustus' death and the accession debate Tiberius had an opportunity to reflect, and we may speculate that his sense of propriety eventually gave way to his sense of inferiority: in cryptic terms he announced that he was withdrawing from a position to which only Augustus had been equal (1. 11. 1). But, as the fathers reacted with increasing strength to an announcement which at first they found difficult to comprehend, Tiberius proposed by chance (*forte*) the compromise that he should share his responsibilities with others (1. 11. 3–12. 1). 'Tacitus', observed Sir Ronald Syme, 'insists on chance and hazard in the affairs of men',[75] and it is ironical that Tacitus should attribute to chance a proposal which he took as the leitmotif of Tiberius' reign. It is also ironical that the proposal should be promptly rejected by the senators whose pressure had led Tiberius to make it (1. 12. 2–3), and that Tiberius' submission to that pressure anticipates the subservience to powerful individuals which Tacitus' rumour-mongers had maliciously predicted (1. 4. 5).

IV

Tacitus, it is said, was claimed as a relative by the third-century emperor who was his namesake. The latter, worried that his distinguished predecessor might perish through the unconcern

---

[74] Above, Ch. 4.   [75] Syme (1958), p. vi.

of readers ('lectorum incuria'), ordered that ten copies of his works should be produced officially each year and placed in public libraries.[76] Today the historian perhaps suffers from *lectorum incuria* of a different kind. Traditional views die hard, and, despite the range and eminence of the scholars who have studied Tacitus during the twentieth century, the standard interpretations of his text have been too little questioned. Readers, as a general rule, have read what they expected to read; familiarity has bred complacency; the *Annals* has become, ironically, a comfortable narrative.

In this book I have tried to raise questions about the nature and meaning of that narrative, often proposing radically different readings of famous passages on which there exists a scholarly consensus. Frequently I have focused upon details, of which the ambiguity of *seruiendum*, discussed above, is an example; yet it is upon such details—an individual word, an ellipse, a pair of commas, a metaphor, an image, a point of syntax—that an entire interpretative edifice may depend. As Tacitus himself expressed it (4. 32. 2): 'non tamen sine usu fuerit introspicere illa primo aspectu leuia, ex quis magnarum saepe rerum motus oriuntur.' The word-play will not escape notice.

[76] *HA Tac.* 10. 3.

BIBLIOGRAPHY

Articles and monographs, etc., if mentioned more than once, are referred to by author's name, date, and page-number; but references to commentaries, translations, and lexica are generally abbreviated still further, except where there is potential ambiguity or a need to be more specific. Full details of all such works may be found below.

Auguet, R. (1972), *Cruelty and Civilization: The Roman Games*, Eng. trans. (London).

Avenarius, G. (1956), *Lukians Schrift zur Geschichtsschreibung* (Meisenheim am Glan).

Bacha, E. (1906), *Le Génie de Tacite* (Brussels and Paris).

Baldwin, B. (1979), 'Possible Horatian Echoes in Tacitus', *WS* 13: 144–50.

Balsdon, J. P. V. D. (1979), *Romans and Aliens* (London).

Bartsch, S. (1989), *Decoding the Ancient Novel* (Princeton).

Baxter, R. T. S. (1972), 'Virgil's Influence on Tacitus in Books 1 and 2 of the *Annals*', *CP* 67: 246–69.

Cairns, F. (1979), *Tibullus: A Hellenistic Poet at Rome* (Cambridge).

Cameron, A. (1976), *Circus Factions: Blues and Greens at Rome and Byzantium* (Oxford).

Carmody, W. M. (1926), *The Subjunctive in Tacitus* (Chicago).

Charlesworth, M. P. (1927), 'Livia and Tanaquil', *CR* 41: 55–7.

Chilver, G. E. F. (1979), *A Historical Commentary on Tacitus' 'Histories' I and II* (Oxford).

Church, A. J., and Brodribb, W. J. (1884), *Annals of Tacitus* (London).

Coleman, K. M. (1990), 'Fatal Charades: Roman Executions Staged as Mythological Enactments', *JRS* 80: 44–73.

Corsi Zoli, D. (1972), 'Aspetti inavvertiti della congiura pisoniana', *Studi Romani*, 20: 329–39.

Curtius, E. R. (1953), *European Literature and the Latin Middle Ages*, Eng. trans. (London).

D'Alton, J. F. (1931), *Roman Literary Theory and Criticism* (New York).

De Lacy, P. (1952), 'Biography and Tragedy in Plutarch', *AJP* 73: 159–71.

De Ste Croix, G. E. M. (1972), *The Origins of the Peloponnesian War* (London).

Detweiler, R. (1970), 'Historical Perspectives on the Death of Agrippa Postumus', *CJ* 65: 289–95.

Draeger, A., and Heraeus, W. (1914), *Die Annalen des Tacitus*, i, 7th edn. (Leipzig and Berlin).

Dupont, F. (1985), *L'Acteur-roi ou le théâtre dans la Rome antique* (Paris).

DuQuesnay, I. M. Le M. (1992), '*In Memoriam Galli*: Propertius 1. 21', in Tony Woodman and Jonathan Powell (eds.), *Author and Audience in Latin Literature*, 52–83 and 225–36 (Cambridge).

Eksteins, M. (1990), *Rites of Spring: The Great War and the Birth of the Modern Age*, first pub. 1989 (New York).

Everts, P. S. (1926), *De Tacitea Historiae Conscribendae Ratione* (Kerkrade).

Fornara, C. W. (1983), *The Nature of History in Ancient Greece and Rome* (Berkeley, Los Angeles, and London).

Fraenkel, E. (1957), *Horace* (Oxford).

Fraser, P. M. (1972), *Ptolemaic Alexandria*, 3 vols. (Oxford).

Furneaux, H. (1896, 1907), *Annals of Tacitus*, 2 vols., 2nd edn. (Oxford).

Gabba, E. (1981), 'True History and False History in Classical Antiquity', *JRS* 71: 50–62.

Garton, C. (1972), *Personal Aspects of the Roman Theatre* (Toronto).

Gerber, A., and Greef, A. (1962), *Lexicon Taciteum*, repr. (Hildesheim).

Gill, C. (1983), 'The Question of Character-Development: Plutarch and Tacitus', *CQ* 33: 469–87.

Ginsburg, J. (1981), *Tradition and Theme in the Annals of Tacitus* (New York).

Goffman, E. (1974), *Frame Analysis: An Essay on the Organisation of Experience* (New York).

Goodyear, F. R. D. (1970), *Tacitus* (*Greece & Rome* New Surveys in the Classics, 4) (Oxford).

—— (1972, 1981), *The Annals of Tacitus*, 2 vols. [Books 1–2] (Cambridge).

Graf, F. (1931), *Untersuchungen über die Komposition der Annalen des Tacitus* (Thun).

Grant, M. (1970), *The Ancient Historians* (London).

Griffin, M. T. (1984), *Nero: The End of a Dynasty* (London).

—— (1995), 'Tacitus, Tiberius and the Principate', in I. Malkin and Z. W. Rubinsohn (eds.), *Leaders and Masses in the Roman World*, 33–57 (Leiden).

Gronovius, J. F. and J. (1685), *C. Cornelii Taciti Opera* (Amsterdam).

Hartog, F. (1988), *The Mirror of Herodotus*, Eng. trans. J. Lloyd (Berkeley, Los Angeles, and London).

Herkommer, E. (1968), *Die topoi in den Proömien der römischen Geschichtswerke*, diss. (University of Tübingen).

Heubner, H. (1963–82), *P. Cornelius Tacitus: Die Historien*, 5 vols. (Heidelberg).

Hohl, E. (1935), 'Primum Facinus Novi Principatus', *Hermes*, 70: 350–5.

Jackson, J. (1931–7), *Tacitus: The Annals*, Loeb edn., 3 vols. (London and New York).

Kampff, G. (1963), 'Three Senate Meetings in the Early Principate', *Phoenix*, 17: 25–58.

Kehoe, D. (1984/5), 'Tacitus and Sallustius Crispus', *CJ* 80: 247–54.

Keitel, E. (1984), 'Principate and Civil War in the *Annals* of Tacitus', *AJP* 105: 314–26.

Knightley, P. (1975), *The First Casualty: From the Crimea to Vietnam* (London).

Knoche, U. (1963), 'Zur Beurteilung des Kaisers Tiberius durch Tacitus', *Gymn.* 70: 211–26.

Koestermann, E. (1961), 'Der Eingang der Annalen des Tacitus', *Historia*, 10: 330–55.

—— (1963–8), *Cornelius Tacitus: Annalen*, 4 vols. (Heidelberg).

Kohl, A. (1959), *Der Satznachtrag bei Tacitus*, diss. (University of Würzburg).

Kroll, W. (1924), *Studien zum Verständnis der römischen Literatur* (Stuttgart).

Lausberg, H. (1966), *Manual de retórica literaria*, Spanish trans. (Madrid).

Leeman, A. D. (1973), 'Structure and Meaning in the Prologues of Tacitus', *YCS* 23: 169–208.

Levick, B. (1976), *Tiberius the Politician* (London).

Lipsius, J. (1627), *C. Cornelii Taciti Opera* (Antwerp).

Luce, T. J. (1986), 'Tacitus' Conception of Historical Change', in I. S. Moxon, J. D. Smart, and A. J. Woodman (eds.), *Past Perspectives: Studies in Greek and Roman Historical Writing*, 143–58 (Cambridge).

—— (1991), 'Tacitus on "History's Highest Function": *praecipuum munus annalium* (Ann. 3.65)', *ANRW* 2.33.4: 2904–27.

—— and Woodman, A. J. (1993), *Tacitus and the Tacitean Tradition* (Princeton).

MacMullen, R. (1966), *Enemies of the Roman Order* (Cambridge, Mass.).

Maltby, R. (1991), *A Lexicon of Latin Etymologies* (Leeds).

Martin, R. H. (1955), 'Tacitus and the Death of Augustus', *CQ* 5: 123–8.

—— (1981), *Tacitus* (repr. 1989, 1994) (London).

—— (1990), 'Structure and Interpretation in the "Annals" of Tacitus', *ANRW* 2.33.2: 1500–81.

—— and Woodman, A. J. (1989), *Tacitus Annals Book IV* (rev. repr. 1994, 1997) (Cambridge).

Mellor, R. (1993), *Tacitus* (New York and London).

Mendell, C. W. (1935), 'Dramatic Construction in Tacitus' Annals', *YCS* 5: 3–53.

Miller, N. P. (1959), *Tacitus: Annals Book I* (London).

—— (1973), *Cornelii Taciti Annalium Liber XV* (London).

Morris, J. M. (1969), 'Compositional Techniques in Annals XIII–XVI', diss. (Yale University).

Mossman, J. M. (1988), 'Tragedy and Epic in Plutarch's *Alexander*', *JHS* 108: 83–93.

Nipperdey, K., and Andresen, G. (1908), *P. Cornelius Tacitus*, ii. *Ab Excessu Divi Augusti XI–XVI*, 6th edn. (Berlin).

—— (1915), *P. Cornelius Tacitus*, i. *Ab Excessu Divi Augusti I–VI*, 11th edn. (Berlin).

Norden, E. (1958), *Die antike Kunstprosa*, i. 5th edn. repr. (Stuttgart).

Ogilvie, R. M. (1965), *A Commentary on Livy Books 1–5* (Oxford).

O'Hara, J. J. (1996), *True Names: Vergil and the Alexandrian Tradition of Etymological Wordplay* (Ann Arbor).

Orelli, J. C. (1859), *P. Cornelii Taciti Opera*, i. 2nd edn. (Zurich).

Pelling, C. B. R. (1988), *Plutarch: Life of Antony* (Cambridge).

—— (1989), 'Aspects of Plutarch's Characterisation', *ICS* 13: 257–74.

—— (1993), 'Tacitus and Germanicus', in Luce and Woodman (1993), 59–85.

Pfitzner, W. (1892), *Cornelii Taciti Annales*, 2nd edn. (Gotha).

Pippidi, D. M. (1944), *Autour de Tibère* (Bucharest).

Plass, P. (1988), *Wit and the Writing of History* (Madison and London).

Purcell, N. (1986), 'Livia and the Womanhood of Rome', *PCPS* 32: 78–105.

Ramsay, G. G. (1904), *The Annals of Tacitus Books I–VI* (London).

Ritter, F. (1848), *Cornelii Taciti Annales* (Cambridge and London).

Rudd, N. (1986), *Themes in Roman Satire* (London).

Ruperti, G. A. (1834), *C. Cornelii Taciti Opera*, i. (Hanover).

Rutherford, R. (1989), *The 'Meditations' of Marcus Aurelius: A Study* (Oxford).

Sage, M. M. (1982/3), 'Tacitus and the Accession of Tiberius', *Anc. Soc.* 13/14: 293–321.

—— (1990), 'Tacitus' Historical Works: A Survey and Appraisal', *ANRW* 2.33.2: 851–1030 and 1629–47.

Sandy, G. N. (1974), 'Scaenica Petroniana', *TAPA* 104: 329–46.

Schama, S. (1995), *Landscape and Memory* (London).

Seager, R. (1972), *Tiberius* (London).

Shotter, D. C. A. (1965), 'Three Problems in Tacitus' Annals I', *Mnem.* 18: 359–61.

Sinclair, P. (1995), *Tacitus the Sententious Historian* (University Park, Pa.).

Slater, N. W. (1985), *Plautus in Performance* (Princeton).

Soubiran, J. (1964), 'Thèmes et rhythmes d'épopée dans les *Annales* de Tacite', *Pallas*, 12: 55–79.

Syme, R. (1958), *Tacitus* (Oxford).

Syme, R. (1984), *Roman Papers*, iii (Oxford).

Taplin, O. (1978), *Greek Tragedy in Action* (London).

Thomas, R. F. (1982), *Lands and Peoples in Roman Poetry. The Ethnographical Tradition*, Camb. Philol. Soc. Suppl. 7 (Cambridge).

Tresch, J. (1965), *Die Nerobücher in den Annalen des Tacitus* (Heidelberg).

Vielberg, M. (1996), 'Ingenium und Mores: Beobachtungen zur historischen Begriffsbildung an Tac. *Ann.* 6.51.3', *Mnem.* 49: 452–6.

Walker, B. (1952), *The Annals of Tacitus: A Study in the Writing of History* (Manchester).

Walther, G. H. (1831), *C. Cornelii Taciti Annales* (Halle).

Weinstock, S. (1971), *Divus Julius* (Oxford).

Wiedemann, T. E. J. (1986), 'Between Men and Beasts: Barbarians in Ammianus Marcellinus', in I. S. Moxon, J. D. Smart, and A. J. Woodman (eds.), *Past Perspectives: Studies in Greek and Roman Historical Writing*, 189–202 (Cambridge).

Wille, G. (1983), *Der Aufbau der Werke des Tacitus* (Amsterdam).

Williams, G. (1968), *Tradition and Originality in Roman Poetry* (Oxford).

Wills, J. (1997), *Repetition in Latin Poetry* (Oxford).

Winter, J. (1995), *Sites of Memory, Sites of Mourning* (Cambridge).

Winterbottom, M. (1974), *The Elder Seneca*, Loeb edn. (Cambridge, Mass. and London).

Wiseman, T. P. (1979), *Clio's Cosmetics* (Leicester).

Woodman, A. J. (1972), 'Remarks on the Structure and Content of Tacitus, *Annals* 4.57–67', *CQ* 22: 150–8.

—— (1979), 'Self-Imitation and the Substance of History: Tacitus, *Annals* 1.61–5 and *Histories* 2.70, 5.14–15', in David West and Tony Woodman (eds.), *Creative Imitation and Latin Literature*, 143–55 and 231–5 (Cambridge).

—— (1989), 'Tacitus' Obituary of Tiberius', *CQ* 39: 197–205.

—— and Martin, R. H. (1996), *The Annals of Tacitus. Book 3* (Cambridge).

Wuilleumier, P. (1978), *Tacite: Annales Livres I–III*, 2nd edn. Budé. (Paris).

INDEX OF PASSAGES

GENERAL INDEX